CRESCENT IN A RED SKY
The Future of Islam in the Soviet Union

CRESCENT IN A RED SKY

The Future of Islam in the Soviet Union

by Amir Taheri

HUTCHINSON

London Melbourne Auckland Johannesburg

First published in 1989 by
Hutchinson & Co. (Publishers) Ltd,
an imprint of Century Hutchinson Ltd,
Brookmount House, 62–65 Chandos Place,
London WC2N 4NW

Century Hutchinson Publishing Group (Australia) Pty Ltd,
PO Box 496, 16–22 Church Street, Hawthorn,
Melbourne, Victoria 3122

Century Hutchinson Group (NZ) Ltd,
PO Box 40–086, 32–34 View Road, Glenfield, Auckland 10

Century Hutchinson Group (SA) Pty Ltd,
PO Box 337, Bergvlei 2012, South Africa

Set in Monotype Sabon and printed and bound in Great Britain by
Butler & Tanner Ltd, Frome and London

British Library Cataloguing in Publication Data

Taheri, Amir
Crescent in a red sky
1. Soviet Union. Political aspects
I. Title
297′.1977′0947

ISBN 0-09-173463-0

Contents

Islam in the USSR

Regions with Muslim majorities

KAZAKHSTAN   KARAKALPAKISTAN

UZBEKISTAN   TATARSTAN

TURKMENISTAN   BASHKIRIA

TAJIKESTAN   DAGHESTAN

KIRGHIZESTAN   AZARBAIJAN

NAKHICHEVAN

NORWAY

SWEDEN

FINLAND

POLAND

BALTIC
STATES

UKRAINE

Moscow

R S

Kazan

Ufa

Orenburg

Volga

ASTRAKHAN

Astrakhan

CRIMEA

BLACK SEA

Terek

TURKEY

Aras

GEORGIA

Derbent

ARMENIA

Nakhichevan

Sumgait

Baku

Lenkoran

CASPIAN SEA

Aral
Sea

Syr-Darya

Lake Balkash

Khiva

Amu-Darya

Turkestan

Chimkent

Alma-Ata

IRAQ

Ashk-
Abad

Atrak

Tashkent

Samarkand

Kokand

Frunze

Doshanbeh

IRAN

AFGHANISTAN

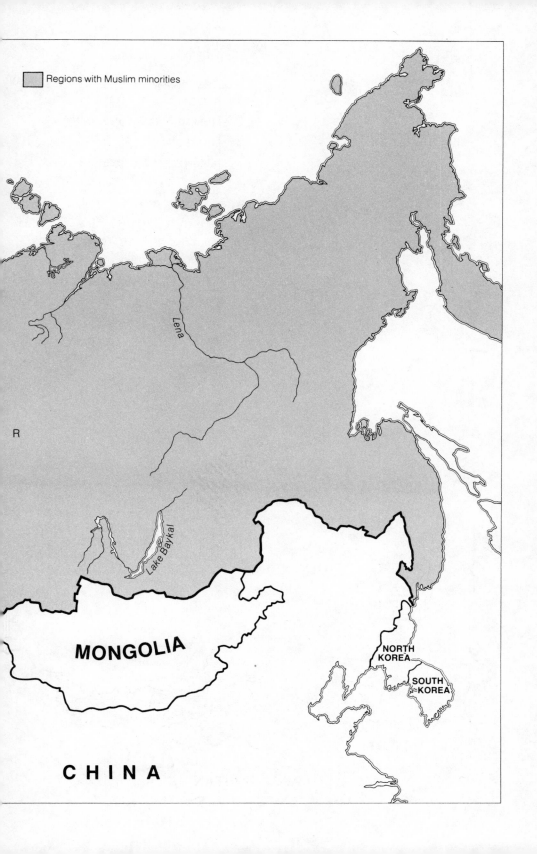

Regions with Muslim minorities

Lena

R

Lake Baykal

MONGOLIA

NORTH
KOREA

SOUTH
KOREA

C H I N A

Introduction

In the heart of Moscow on Red Square stands Saint Basil's cathedral, an almost surrealistic edifice built under Ivan the Terrible, the tsar who turned Russia into a rising imperial power. The cathedral's multicolour domes evoke oriental fairy-tale images of giant tulip bulbs. Few people remember that the monument was built to mark the destruction of a Muslim kingdom by Ivan's 'soldiers of Christ'. And history has all but forgotten that the onion-shaped domes were intended to symbolise the severed, turbaned heads of eight Muslim chiefs who fell in defence of the Crescent against the Cross. As an imperial power, Russia had its baptism with Muslim blood, when Kazan was captured and its population massacred in 1552.

More than four centuries later, on 15 February 1989, another Russian army returned home after another savage war against Muslims. As General Gramov led the last of the Soviet invading troops out of Afghanistan and across the Syr-Darya into Termez, the latest chapter in one of history's longest duels came to a close.

What happened between Kazan and Termez is the history of the emergence of Russia, and its successor state the Union of Soviet Socialist Republics (USSR), as a world power spreading from the heart of Europe to the Pacific. The Soviet retreat from Afghanistan, in fact, represented the only conclusive defeat suffered by the successors of Ivan the Terrible in more than four centuries of territorial expansion at the expense of Islam. From Kazan to Termez Islam passed through a long period of steady decline which many Muslims would agree has not yet fully ended.

Ivan the Terrible and his successors initially hoped to eliminate Islam from their empire through forced conversions, mass deportations and massacres. But Islam was able to mobilise its tremendous moral and cultural resources, and proved resilient enough to survive and – whenever given half a chance – to grow under conditions of exceptional adversity. The Russians became the first conquerors of Islam to refuse conversion to the faith of Muhammad. Later they even tried to impose their own religion on conquered Muslim peoples, but failed.

Eventually a *modus vivendi* was found and Muslims were allowed to live their own lives as part of a multinational empire. After the Bolshevik Revolution, a new conversion drive was directed against the Muslims; this time they were invited to reject God and adopt Marxism-Leninism as their faith. Once again they suffered mass deportations and massacres – and once again they refused to abandon their religion and culture. The Communists were eventually forced to abandon their anti-Islam campaign at least in its more brutal forms, but they seldom allowed Islam to operate outside the strict limits imposed on it within the framework of an ideological state. Yet Islam not only held its own against incredible odds but retained enough vitality to make it one of the potentially dynamic forces in a society plunged into uncertainty provoked by the ideological crisis symbolised by Mikhail Gorbachev's call for a 'second revolution'. As new – and mostly illegal – mosques mushroomed in many villages and towns, including Moscow itself, Islam began to recapture some of the ground it had lost during more than seventy years of Soviet rule. Even the more enthusiastic advocates of 'scientific atheism' agreed that, together with other religious faiths in the USSR, Islam was becoming popular again. Many people returned to their ancestral faith in search of a haven of peace and certainty that Marxism-Leninism no longer even pretended to offer.

'They are souls lost in a sea of doubt,' said a student at the Mir-Arab Islamic seminary in Bokhara, referring to members and leaders of the Communist Party. 'They have just discovered that man-made beliefs could also be destroyed by men.'

Rigestan, where the Mir-Arab seminary is situated, was formerly the heart of Bokhara when Bokhara was the heart of Islam. Today it is the abode of the poor, the city's Islamic ghetto, away from the Russian city of steel and concrete – a piece of the Third World in a remote part of the USSR. And yet its Seljuk mosques and madrassehs, restored with help from the Soviet government, stand beautiful and serene under the ultra-bright sun of Central Asia. What a contrast with the buildings of the Russian city which are already rusting and crumbling away!

In Samarkand, the Russian city is even more dramatically marked out from the old Islamic metropolis which served as the capital of the Teymurid Empire. The new city was constructed outside the old, so that Socialism and Islam could be kept apart and compared. The Russian city has wide boulevards named after Lenin, Maxim Gorki, Yuri Gagarin and other 'saints' of the Soviet state. The Muslim city has narrow alleys, a covered bazaar – the largest in Transoxiana – and numerous mosques and shrines. Giant portraits of Lenin hang from some walls, as a reminder that Samarkand is part of the USSR. But the Muslim city has its own life, and is self-confident enough to ignore the indecent intrusion of such icons. In the Russian city the shops and the boulevards are both empty; it is a ghost town built on the edge of an ancient capital which is still full of beauty and life.

The Muslim regions of the USSR have undergone profound change: from rural to urban life. They have become more literate, more industrial. The price paid has been the violent death of millions. Today as the USSR seeks a way out of the labyrinth created by Stalin and his successors, the Muslims of the union begin to think of rebuilding their own life on the basis of their own culture and civilisation. Will Gorbachev allow Islam to reconstitute its social, religious and cultural structures and offer an alternative to the 'Communist way of life'? Or will he, as he has done in the past four years, continue to consider Islam as a dangerous enemy of the Soviet state that ought to be kept under tight control?

These are just two of the many questions that I have tried to answer in this book. But before studying current developments in the USSR the history of Islam's encounter with Russia has been traced to its origins. We shall see how the first Slavs to adopt a monotheistic religion chose Islam and how the Russian people were converted to Christianity for largely political reasons. Russia first encountered Asia and Islam as a victim and suffered more than two centuries of Mongol domination. Later the victim became an oppressor of exceptional brutality.

Divided among themselves as to their true identity, the Russians were never quite able to choose between Asia and Europe. They fought many wars in Europe, but reserved most of their expansionist energy for Asia. In eastwards and southwards expansion Russia encountered many Muslim nations and defeated them all; it pushed the Iranians out of the Caucasus and Transoxiana, and the Turks out of Crimea and Daghestan. It fought a particularly bitter and lengthy duel against the Tatar nation and ended by reducing that once great and proud nation to the level of a subject people under colonial rule.

Under Russian rule Muslims retained their close ties with the rest of the Muslim world and played a crucial role as a link between Islam and Europe. The Islamic revivalist movement of the nineteenth century was, in part, inspired by intellectuals from Muslim regions of Russia who were convinced that only through educational reform and social progress would Islam be able to hold its own against the rising power of Western imperialism.

The fall of the tsarist empire offered Russia's Muslims a chance to gain control of their own destiny; but this was no more than a brief moment. Very soon they were engulfed in the Russian Civil War which was almost entirely fought on Muslim land. The victory of the Bolsheviks spelled the end of all hopes for the emergence of independent

Muslim states in the Caucasus and Central Asia. Stalin's brutal reign pushed Islam further on the defensive and the anti-religious campaign begun in the 1920s was resumed with fresh vigour under Khrushchev in the 1950s. Under Brezhnev the Muslim regions of the USSR were treated as resource-rich colonies, administered by a largely corrupt local elite in the service of the Soviet Nomenklatura.

What is remarkable is Islam's ability to continue its 'inner history' in the face of cataclysmic events during more than four centuries of struggle against Russian domination. Even when the history of Muslims under Russian rule seemed to have merged with that of the empire as a whole, that 'inner history' continued to take shape in accordance with its own dynamics.

The West discovered the Muslims of the Soviet Union in the 1950s and tried to use them as a weapon in the Cold War. In the late 1970s Soviet Muslims were, once again, included in global strategies as the Achilles' heel of the USSR. The Islamic Revolution in Iran and the war in Afghanistan shifted the epicentre of Islamic fundamentalism away from Egypt and the Levant to the borders of Soviet Caucasus and Central Asia. Predictions that the USSR would soon disintegrate partly as a result of a Muslim revolt were made at many gatherings of learned geostrategists.

Some of the questions originally raised in the first phases of the Cold War are still being asked, despite the new era of détente initiated by Mikhail Gorbachev. Will the USSR survive? Is it an empire on the verge of being fragmented? Is it an empire at all? And if yes, is it an evil empire? Whatever the answers to these questions – and we shall discuss some of them – the USSR today is a far more exciting place than at any time since the early days of its foundation. Its new leaders are genuinely convinced that problems will not go away simply by being ignored. They admit that change and transformation are inevitable. What is important is to make sure that this does not assume violent forms. Events in Kazakhstan, Azarbaijan, Armenia and Tajikestan between 1986 and 1989 showed that the danger of violent outbursts against the real or imagined injustices of the past and the frustrations of today cannot be underestimated.

The incorporation of many Muslim lands into the Tsarist empire and its successor state, the USSR, did not put an end to Russian prejudices against Islam – which, in one form or another, continue to this day. Even Russian thinkers and philosophers often failed to fully shed these prejudices. To them Muslims were either dangerous barbarians who had to be civilised or the heirs to an exotic civilisation which had to be protected against Westernisation. Both these contradictory, yet in a sense complementary attitudes were best reflected in Tolstoy's work.

The future pacifist participated in the war against Muslim rebels in Daghestan with exceptional enthusiasm. He saw this as a 'crusade for civilisation' and, in 1853, noted in his diary: 'I shall help with my guns in the destruction of the predatory Asiatics.' Three decades later, however, he wished to exclude the same 'Asiatics' from the benefits of Western civilisation. He wrote: 'Everything the West does can and ought to be an example for the peoples of the East not of what should be done but of what ought not to be done in any circumstances. To pursue the path of the western nations is to pursue the direct road to destruction.'

While Platon Obodovsky offered a romantic and thoroughly unrealistic vision of Islam in his *Orsan and Leyla*, Pushkin tried to distinguish the Muslims with whom Russia came into contact from the rest of the Islamic community. He wrote: 'The Tatars were different from the Moors. They conquered Russia but brought neither algebra nor Aristotle.'

Anti-Muslim sentiments provide a major theme in Russian literature, music, theatre and even cinema. *Prince Igor* is by no means the only Russian work in which Muslim Tatars and Kazakhs are shown in a less than flattering light. Most recently the film *Andre Roublev* by Alexander Tarkovsky had to be banned in the Muslim-inhabited regions of the USSR because of its strong anti-Tatar tone.

The advent of Communism in 1917 did not end anti-Muslim prejudices. On the contrary, in some respects it even intensified them. Lenin wrote: 'We must combat religion – that is the ABC of Marxism. The combating of religion must be linked up with the concrete practice of the class struggle, eliminating the social roots of religion.'

Lenin had the merit of being brutally frank. Stalin, who added lie to Leninism, sought a variety of ways to combat Islam. These ranged from trying to portray Marxism as the culmination of Islam's aspirations, to mass murder practised against restive Muslim populations. In 1917 he sent a message, written in Arabic, to congratulate Imam Ibrahim Gotso on his election as Shaykh al-Mashayekh (The Supreme Theologian) of Daghestani Muslims. A few years later he had the imam executed as a brigand. In 1920 Stalin inspired a pamphlet by Klevliev whose theme was 'the roots of Communism in the Holy Qur'an'. Yet in the 1920s and 1930s he ordered the execution of thousands of peoples whose sole crime had been the possession of copies of the Muslim Holy Book. He also put into effect the policy of dividing the Muslim peoples of the USSR into smaller and smaller units (*razmezhevanie*).

It was also Stalin who engineered the incorporation of Bokhara and Khiva into the 'empire' after the 1917 Russian revolution. The people of these emirates had for centuries been accustomed to government by murder. Under Stalin they learned about government by mass murder.

Under the emirs political murder usually took place at the palace. Under the Bolsheviks it came to city streets, bazaars and villages. The grander the ideals advocated, it seemed, the larger the scale of political murders organised. In Islam 'harmful individuals' could be removed by the dagger of the assassins; under Bolshevism the state arranged for the physical removal of whole peoples.

The Bolsheviks were the only conquerors of Central Asia to bomb the region's Muslim towns and villages from the air and to use heavy artillery and tanks to crush peasant armies often armed with no more than picks and shovels. The new conquerors showed even less respect for Islam than their tsarist predecessors. The Muslim nations of Kazakhstan, Central Asia and the Caucasus were described as 'backward peoples', an appellation that was dropped only in 1988. Muslim culture was routinely described as 'the death pangs of feudalism'. And Victor Kozlov, the leading Soviet ethnologist, had no qualms about the assertion that 'Muslim literature consisted mainly of religious tracts'. Mussa Mahmud, a Crimean Tatar who set fire to himself and died of burns during a nationalist demonstration in Moscow in 1978, described himself before he died as a 'human torch in the dark night of Russian prejudices against Islam'.

More than seventy years of life under Communism failed to create the promised 'new Soviet man' who would transcend the barriers of nationality and religious faith. The Azari–Armenian riots in 1988 and 1989 over Nagorno-Karabakh (Artakh in Armenian), the revolt of the Abkhaz Muslims of Georgia in 1989 and nationalist upheavals in Central Asia, Kazakhstan, the Ukraine, the Baltic states and Georgia showed that the so-called 'problem of nationalities' was likely to continue in the USSR well into the next century.

The Soviet invasion of Afghanistan – a Muslim country – in 1979 went a long way towards provoking an upsurge of anti-Russian feelings among the Islamic communities of the USSR. The first sign of this came in 1980 when riots broke out in Alma-Ata, the capital of Kazakhstan, over Soviet attempts to bury a Muslim officer (who had been killed in action in Afghanistan) in a cemetery reserved for Soviet war heroes. Muslim demonstrators seized the coffin and buried the officer in a Muslim graveyard. A Muslim buried next to atheist Communists would not enter paradise! The riots led to at least four deaths in the Kazakh city.

Between 1969 and 1989 the various Muslim republics of the USSR have been the scenes of frequent riots against Russian rule. The slogan 'Russians, go home', often heard in Central Asia in the late 1960s, has been replaced by a more sober demand for greater national autonomy in the 1980s. The Muslim republics have become increasingly aware of their economic and strategic importance for the USSR; more than 51 per cent of all arable land in the union belongs to the Muslim republics, which have the fastest demographic growth rate anywhere outside the Third World. It was, in fact, thanks to its domination of regions with vast resources and growing populations that Russia was able to emerge as a major power in the nineteenth century. And today the USSR's status as a superpower is partly sustained by the presence within the union of non-Russian republics, especially Muslim ones, which provide major sources of raw material and large reserves of population. Although the USSR under Gorbachev has increasingly looked towards Europe, the fact remains that its frontiers with Muslim countries (4,600 kilometres) are more extensive than those it has with the European states (3,200 kilometres).

Until Gorbachev came to power the official USSR line justifying the attachment of Muslim peoples to the union emphasised the economic progress achieved in Central Asia, Kazakhstan, Daghestan and Azarbaijan since the Russian revolution of 1917. However, by 1985 the economic boom of the Brezhnev era had become a distant memory in most Muslim regions of the Soviet Union. With Communism and the heritage of the Russian revolution seriously questioned under Gorbachev, attention was focused on the reality of the situation in the Muslim republics.

Soviet Muslims began to recognise their status as a semi-colonial people living under a peculiar type of alien hegemony. To be sure the USSR was no 'Russian' empire. Ethnic Russians enjoyed minimal special privileges. If empire there was, it was not administered in the name and in the interest of a dominating nation or ethnic group. The USSR was an ideological empire; but this was little or no consolation to Muslims who had never subscribed to an ideology which was now seriously questioned by its own original propagators.

The semi-colonial status of the Muslim republics was amply illustrated by a number of facts. The republics played only a minor role in decision-making, which remained heavily concentrated in Moscow despite Gorbachev's reforms. The right of self-determination, recognised by the Soviet constitution, remained purely theoretical. Russian and other European troops remained stationed in all the republics. Under the Soviet constitution, the right of the republics to raise armies of their own could not even be discussed. Large numbers of Russian and other European administrative, technical and political personnel filled key posts in all republics. In some republics, notably Kazakhstan and Daghestan, the effect of this was further compounded by the presence of large numbers of Russian and other European settlers. The terms of trade between the republics and the European 'metropole' remained heavily tipped in favour of the latter. The republics exported raw material and cheap labour and imported manufactured goods and technological services.

Under Gorbachev, nationalism emerged as a major political theme not only among the 'peripheral republics' but also in Russia itself. Russian nationalism – strong among army officers, followers of the Orthodox Church and sections of the Communist Party – had its own mouthpieces in the magazines *Veche* and *Molodaja Gvardia*. Some of its advocates, notably Vladimir Osipov the editor of *Veche*, strongly opposed Gorbachev's 'European illusions' and also warned of a revolt of 'the backward peoples that might lead to the destruction of the Russian nation'.

The Russian nationalist movement, reflected in the Derevenshiki literary school, plays on nostalgia for the Holy Russia of pre-revolutionary times in which 'the Asiatics' were seen but not heard. Afraid of being overwhelmed by Muslims who might emerge as the single largest group within the union during the next few decades, Russian nationalists are divided on the issue of future relations with the peripheral republics. Some Russian nationalists openly advocate independence for the Muslim republics, considering Muslims as largely responsible for the USSR's political and economic backwardness. Others, however, want Gorbachev to keep the 'empire' intact and strengthen Moscow's control over the peripheries.

Faced with nationalist explosions throughout the USSR, Gorbachev has dug deep into Marxist–Leninist literature for an answer to at least part of his problem. There is no evidence that he has found one.

Gorbachev has often spoken of a return to Leninism, especially with regard to the problem of nationalities; but Lenin, a pragmatic politician despite appearances to the contrary, lacked a clear position on the issue. He invented his policies as he went along. In 1922 Lenin strongly criticised Stalin for the forcible inclusion of Georgia into the Soviet state. But he did nothing to restore Georgia's independence. Lenin was a passionate advocate of independence for the nations which had fallen under Western colonial domination at the same time as the tsars conquered Central Asia and the Caucasus. However, even during his long years of struggle against the tsarist state, the founder of Bolshevism never went as far as calling for the independence of Russia's colonies.

Some of Gorbachev's closest advisers refuse to acknowledge the existence of a veritable nationalities problem. They refer to 'ethnic issues'. But even at this level, the Gorbachev administration does not appear to have a clear vision. Broadly speaking there are two theories of ethnicity. The primordialists emphasise the assumed relevance of shared values, common culture, common faith and historical background. Muslims, for example, believe that Islam is undoubtedly better than and superior to all other cultures. To most Americans, it is the 'American Way of Life' that provides the pinnacle of human achievement. Instrumentalists, on the other hand, consider ethnicity as a means of protecting and enhancing common social and economic advantages in a multi-ethnic society. Ethnicity is therefore basically political; it cannot exist outside politics, as a cultural or religious attribute. In the context of the USSR as a multi-ethnic state, an Azari is automatically in competition with a Russian. While this does not necessarily imply antagonistic relations, although such might well be the case in practice, it certainly underlines real or perceived contradictions between respective views of each ethnic group's interests and aspirations.

The Russians are surprised that at one stage their presence in the Muslim republics was generally appreciated by the 'natives', while they are now quite openly made to feel unwelcome. They were appreciated as doctors, engineers, teachers and technicians who helped to improve the lives of the people; but now the Muslims have trained personnel of their own who are in direct competition with Russians.

The harmonious point of balance in inter-ethnic relations, if it exists at all, represents but a brief moment in history. Inter-ethnic relations cannot remain static and are subject to constant change – and change implies the constant presence of dynamic tension.

Since Stalin's time, and especially under Brezhnev, the Soviet system was based on the instrumentalist theory of ethnicity. A person's ethnic identity was important in securing jobs, educational opportunities and social advantages. In the armed forces, for example, a Kazakh who wished to become an officer had much less chance of attaining his goal than an ethnic Russian in the same position. Under Brezhnev, positive discrimination in favour of 'formerly backward peoples' added to the value of belonging to some minority groups.

The 1977 Soviet constitution states that the USSR citizens 'of different races and nationalities have equal rights', and adds that 'any direct or indirect advantage for citizens on a racial or national basis' is punishable by law (article 36). The principle of equality for all citizens of the USSR, however, is not reconcilable with the concepts of nationality, race and ethnic background which is amply recognised in the USSR.

The western media have focused their attention on nationalist movements in the Baltic states and, to a lesser extent, in the Ukraine, but both the Balts and the Ukrainians belong to the 'common European home' depicted by Gorbachev. Even Armenia and Georgia might be admitted because of their Christian background and their long admiration for the western nations. The Muslim nations of the USSR, however, are fully aware that they can have no place in Gorbachev's 'common European home'. These nations live in Asia and look to the Muslim world as their natural cultural habitat.

The Turkic peoples of the Volga converted to Islam less than a century before their Russian neighbours chose Christianity. In March 922 the Turkic chief, Yabghu, was invited by an emissary of the Caliph of Baghdad to embrace Islam. In exchange he received 50 dinars (about £3,000 in present-day value), 15 grammes of musk, two pairs of leather boots and a veil for his favourite wife. At the time, even the caliph's emissary was not convinced that this rather strange conversion marked a permanent fact of Turkic life for over a thousand years. The Turkic peoples were eventually defeated and conquered by Christian Russians, but refused to abandon Islam.

The anniversary of Yabghu's conversion to Islam was marked on 14 March 1989 with numerous ceremonies throughout Kazakhstan, Central Asia, the Volga region, Daghestan and Azarbaijan. One such ceremony took the form of a congress of Islamic muftis, mullahs and Imam-Khatibs from Kazakhstan and Central Asia in Tashkent. The congress elected Haj Shaikh Muhammad-Sadeq Muhammad-Yussuf as the new Grand Mufti of Tashkent. A graduate of the al-Azhar Islamic University in Cairo, the new mufti, who was born in 1952, became the youngest scholar to attain the highest post in official Islam in the USSR.

The ceremony, clearly intended to rival the celebration in 1988 of the first millenium of Russia's conversion to Christianity, assumed a new dimension when the Uzbek Communist Party leader, Rafiq Neshanov, dropped in to pay his respects. Neshanov did not come empty-handed; he brought with him a solemn document under which the custody of the famous Qur'an of Caliph Osman was transferred to the muftiate of Tashkent. The precious relic, confiscated by the Russians in the nineteenth century and transferred to Petrograd, was returned to Uzbekistan and kept at Tashkent Museum after the Russian revolution of 1917. Now it was to be guarded by Muslim authorities after a lapse of more than a century. Neshanov also announced that scores of mosques and places of pilgrimage which had been closed since 1921 will be repaired and reopened.

The ceremonies led to marches throughout Kazakhstan and Central Asia and provided an occasion for 'the manifestation of a religious fervour rarely seen in the USSR', according to a Tass report.

At one public gathering in Bakhara copies of Ayatollah Ruhollah Khomeini's letter addressed to Gorbachev were distributed. In the letter, delivered in February 1989, the Iranian 'Supreme Guide' stated at some length his reasons for believing that Islam was superior to Communism. He concluded by inviting the Soviet leader to send his aides to study in the holy city of Qom and seek the solution of the USSR's problems in the teachings of the holy Qur'an. Soviet leaders in Moscow greeted the letter with sarcastic smiles. But many Muslims in the USSR seemed to support Khomeini's claims that Islam might have an answer to some of the questions which Communism can no longer even pose correctly. To be sure, in 1989 Khomeini's brand of fundamentalism did not appear to have much of an audience among Soviet Muslims. But his contention that Islam is a living force fully capable of confronting the current crisis of civilisation on a global scale appealed to some sections of the population in the Soviet Muslim regions.

Muslims today represent the fastest growing section of the USSR's population; by the end of the next decade, they will form the second largest group of peoples in the USSR after Russians. They would also account for more than forty per cent of all new entries in the Soviet labour market and nearly fifty per cent of the conscripts serving in the Soviet army. Under Gorbachev, however, the share of Muslims in decision-making within the party, the state and the armed forces has continued to decline. Will the benefits of *glasnost* (transparence) and *perestroika* (restructuring) be reserved only for the European peoples of the USSR? The answer to this question must come soon and, when it does, will determine future developments in Central Asia, the Volga region and the Caucasus.

The idea for writing a book on Muslims in the Soviet Union was first suggested to me in 1970 by Grand Ayatollah Kazem Shariatmadari, who had devoted part of his life to helping Islam stay alive in Soviet Azarbaijan under extremely difficult conditions. I took a personal interest in the subject as a result of frequent visits to the USSR during the 1970s, when I had the privilege of making many friends among Soviet Muslims. Shariatmadari's tragic death in Tehran in 1986 came as a dramatic reminder of a topic we had discussed together on a number of occasions both in Qom and Tehran. An advance from my British publishers, Hutchinson, and a great deal of encouragement from my editor Anthony Whittome and my literary agent Toby Eady – both highly esteemed friends – set me on the road to writing this book in 1987. I wish to thank them both, together with Anthony Cheetham of Hutchinson. Thanks are also due to the staff of the Alisher Nava'i library in Tashkent and the Kamaleddin Behzad Museum in Doshanbeh for helping me use some of the precious manuscripts and research papers they have accumulated over years of dedicated work.

I must also express my gratitude to a number of senior Soviet officials who offered extensive briefings and patiently responded to detailed and at times even provocative questions regarding a highly sensitive subject. In this context special mention must be made of V. Falin, V. Zagladin, N. Efimov, A. Vlassov and G. Shishkin among others. Needless to say, none of the personalities mentioned are in any way responsible for the views expressed in this book. Their contribution was strictly limited to putting the current Soviet official position on the subject, a position critically examined in the final chapter as well as in the conclusion.

Finally I must thank Marie-Therese Borra for her help in preparing the bibliography.

I

A Russian Nightmare

Visitors to the National Museum at Doshanbeh, the capital of the Soviet Republic of Tajikestan, are routinely treated to lectures on the darkness of the past and the brightness of the Socialist future.[1] Official guides, reciting their part without evident conviction, relate how the real history of Central Asia, of which Tajikestan is a part, really began only with the Bolshevik Revolution in 1917. Paraphrasing Marx, they describe the region's ancient civilisations as part of pre-history.[2]

The dark pre-history is represented in a small section of the museum by a collection of instruments of torture used under the emirs. Large canvases depict pot-bellied mullahs staring spitefully at unveiled, smiling schoolgirls marching towards the bright sun of Socialism. Islam is represented as a universe of whips and chains, of veils and recipes for deadly poisons administered in the dark corners of the harem.

Mikhail Gorbachev's policy of *glasnost* does not seem to have much affected a long tradition of representing Central Asia and the Caucasus – where Muslims form a majority of the native population – as orphans of history who ought to be grateful to their Russian 'elder brother' for having saved them from a barbarous way of life. Official propaganda more than implies that where Russia has a history others have nothing but old women's tales. Russian culture is presented as the focal point of the new Soviet civilisation. Others, however, are said to have not full-fledged cultures but folk traditions.

Geographically, the Muslim-inhabited regions of the USSR enjoy positions of major importance. As its name indicates, Central Asia is situated at the heart of the largest and most populated of the six continents. For centuries it served as a trade and cultural link between the Middle East, India and China. The Caucasus has several windows to the Mediterranean and is a bridge between Europe and Asia. Yet the image of all these regions today is one of remoteness and marginality.

I

The average non-Muslim Soviet citizen considers Central Asia and the Caucasus as mere backyards where time had come to a standstill before Russian conquest.

The Central Asians, the Azarbaijanis and the Daghestanis, however, are becoming increasingly aware of their long and chequered histories. Samarkand, the capital of ancient Sogdiana, celebrated the twenty-fifth centenary of its foundation in 1970.[3] But even that, many archaeologists argued, was an underestimation since Samarkand was almost certainly inhabited as early as the seventh century BC.

Central Asia contains at least a dozen other cities whose history dates back to the pre-Christian era. Marv, the capital of ancient Margiana on the river Morghab, Khiva near the Aral Sea, Bokhara in the heart of Transoxiana and Tashkent[4] all existed during the Achaemenid era (sixth to fourth century BC). Even Ashk-Abad, now the modern capital of Turkmenistan, dates its foundation to the era of the first Parthian kings over 2,000 years ago.[5] Under the Achaemenids, Central Asia, which naturally includes part of Afghanistan and northern Iran plus the southernmost districts of what is now the Soviet Republic of Kazakhstan, was one of the most prosperous regions of the Persian Empire. The birthplace of Zarathustra, this vast region was the cradle of the Mazdeen faith.

It was also a rebellious satrapy and a constantly threatened frontier. Cyrus the Great, the founder of the Achaemenid dynasty, was killed in a battle against the rebellious Massagetes in Central Asia. Cyrus's successors had to cope with constant raids by the nomadic tribes of the steppes, notably the Scythians.[6]

The collapse of the Persian Empire after its defeat at the hands of Alexander the Great (356–323 BC) opened Central Asia to European colonisation spearheaded by the Macedonians. Alexander founded a few cities, notably Herat (now in Afghanistan) and Eskhatia,[7] and gave his name to many others that already existed.[8] The settlement of Greek, Macedonian, Persian, Mesopotamian and even Egyptian 'colons' brought in by Alexander and his successors in Central Asian cities was in accordance with an already established tradition under which the urban population often consisted of non-natives of the region. The tradition continues to this day with some of Central Asia's most important cities dominated by Europeans.

Alexander's immense empire, from India to Egypt and from the confines of Mongolia to the Persian Gulf, was divided into three kingdoms after his death. Central Asia, as well as present-day Afghanistan and parts of north-eastern Iran, together formed the kingdom of Bactria (250 to 140 BC) which, gradually turning its back to the west, established closer contacts with China. The Bactrians, in turn, were succeeded by the Kushanites (first to fourth century AD) whose culture emerged as a synthesis of Hellenism, Buddhism and Mazdeen traditions. It was then the turn of the Sassanids, a Persian dynasty established by the grandson of a Zarathustran high priest, to dominate the region (third to seventh centuries).

Archaeological discoveries during the past eighty years have amply demonstrated the region's pivotal role in world trade as early as the Achaemenian era. The minting of Darric coins under Darius the Great in c. sixth century BC greatly facilitated trade relations which had already developed between China and the Middle East via Central Asia.

This earliest version of international trade was at first focused on luxury items – relatively light but highly priced goods such as silk, gold and silver, spices and precious stones. The main artery of this profitable exchange came to be known as the 'Silk Route' which, in its heyday, linked the Chinese city of Si-An to the Mediterranean via Iran and the Levant. The caravans that carried the coveted goods all had to pass the high mountains of the Pamir or the northern slopes of Tian-Chan (Celestial Mountains) to reach China, which meant that Central Asia was the crucial link in commercial exchanges between East and West. Cities such as Marv, Samarkand and Khojand – all caravan stations on the Silk Route – were truly golden prizes for would-be conquerors.

With only one exception, all these conquerors came from the west or the south-west. That exception was provided by Emperor Wu-di (156–87 BC) who, having conquered Korea and most of China, also annexed parts of Central Asia. This trend was to be reversed at the end of the fourth century when nomads of Altaic extraction began to infiltrate into Central Asia from the steppes of the north-west and the vast wastelands that stretch from present-day Kazakhstan to Siberia and Mongolia. The more warlike of these nomadic warriors, the Huns, extended their terror across a vast region from India to the heart of Europe.[9] The domination of the region by the Huns took place through successive invasions which did not come to an end until the end of the sixth century.

By that time the invaders had succeeded in altering the racial and ethnic composition of the entire region. To the earliest inhabitants, mostly Iranic, had already been added Hellenic and Anatolian elements brought in under Macedonian domination. The newcomers belonged to an altogether different ethnic stock. Although racial purity was more of a fiction than a scientific fact even then, the newcomers had sufficiently specific features to mark them out from the original inhabitants. In time, the newcomers were to be referred to first as the Turanians[10] and later as the Turks.[11] The task of containing these warrior shepherds became the central concern of rulers of Iran from the fifth century onwards.

At the time of Prophet Muhammad's death (632) and on the eve of the Arab invasion, Central Asia was truly a melting-pot of nations and tribes. In time many Iranic peoples had become 'Turkicised' while new Turkic settlers adopted Iranic languages and ways of life. With the initial shock of every invasion over, there is no evidence that the fusion of different nations and peoples provoked any violent clashes. The intermingling of widely different tribes and nations only reinforced the region's role as a vital link between Asia, the Middle East and Europe. Central Asia also became a mosaic of religious faiths and practices. Zoroastrianism, Bhuddism, the cult of Tengri,[12] Nestorian Christianity, Judaism and even Hinduism were all represented in the region at the time the Holy Qur'an was revealed to Muhammad in Mecca.

While Central Asia became a melting-pot of nations and tribes, the Caucasus emerged as a uniquely complex mosaic of ethnic and linguistic groups. Archaeological studies have shown that the mountainous region between the Caspian Sea and the Black Sea was inhabited as early as the third millenium before the Christian era. It became a major trade partner for the various Mesopotamian empires and was also in contact with the Phoenicians, Tripolytans and the Balkans. From the seventh century BC onwards Hellenic colonies established on the Black Sea came into contact with Caucasian states such as Iberia, Albania and Colshidia.

The Caucasus also became a scene of invasions. Scythians, Sarmatians, Huns, Avars and Khazars poured in from the north and dominated parts of the region for varying lengths of time. The nature of the terrain, centred on steep mountains with few easy passes, was largely responsible for the isolation imposed on the many tribes and ethnic groups which settled in the Caucasus. It was not unusual for two nations which lived back to back, as it were, on opposite slopes of the same mountain, to ignore each other almost completely and to develop their respective languages and cultures across divergent lines.

The region produced two major native kingdoms, Georgia and Armenia. Both were early converts to Christianity.[13] In time both came to be dominated either by Iran or by the Roman Empire. The Sassanids controlled most of the Caucasus from the seventh century onwards and established Persian colonies all along the western coasts of the Caspian. Thus, while eastern Caucasus firmly looked towards Asia, its western kingdoms increasingly considered themselves as outposts of Europe.

The rise of Islam in the Arabian Peninsula of the seventh century coincided almost exactly with the decline of both the Sassanid and Byzantine empires that dominated the entire region between eastern Mediterannean and the steppes of Kazakhstan. The Muslim armies began their invasion of the Sassanid empire in 635, less than three years after the death of the Prophet. Within fifteen years the green banner of the House of Hashem bearing the sign of the crescent had reached the southern frontiers of Central Asia.

The conquest of Central Asia proved a much more difficult task and took more than fifty years to complete. Marv fell to Muslim armies in 651, but Samarkand and Bokhara resisted until 710. Even then, however, the Muslim domination of Central Asia did not appear fully assured. Nomadic steppe tribes, at times backed by Chinese forces, continued to wage war against the invaders from the south-west. In 751, however, Muslim forces engaged a Chinese and nomad army east of the river Syr-Daria and won a decisive victory. Nevertheless, the battle of Talas marked the limits of Muslim expansion into the heart of Asia. The spread of Islam into Kazakhstan, Siberia and the Chinese Sinkiang had to be postponed for several centuries and was eventually achieved by preachers, teachers, traders and adventurers rather than soldiers.

Soviet historians, basing themselves on highly selective readings of Muslim chroniclers, have for more than half a century portrayed the Islamic conquest of Central Asia as a tragedy for the region. They relate how Arabs burned libraries, took slaves and forced the conquered people either to embrace Islam or to pay a poll tax (*jiziah*) that ruined many families.

There is little doubt that some atrocities were committed in the early phases of the conquest, but the Arabs were not present in sufficiently large numbers to be able to control so vast a region by the force of arms alone.[14] Islam, a simple religion that preaches the equality of all believers and promises divine justice both in this world and in the next, did not feel – in its early period of ascent at least – the need to force people into its own ranks. According to recent research completed by Muslim scholars, conversion to Islam was a very slow and gradual process in Central Asia and was mostly accomplished long after the Arabs had either returned home or been merged with the native populations. Islam's tolerant attitude towards other faiths was reflected in the persistence of major Jewish, Christian, Mazdeen and even Bhuddist minorities in various parts of the region right up to the Bolshevik Revolution. Marv and Samarkand remained important Christian archbishoprics up to the fifteenth century.

One direct result of the Muslim conquest was the emergence of Arabic as the lingua franca of a vast empire that stretched from China to the Pyrenees. Through Arabic translations of ancient texts, Central Asian scholars came into contact with Greek philosophy and political ideas. Arabic did not, however, develop into a popular language and remained confined to the administrative, intellectual and military elites as well as merchant classes. The mass of the people continued to speak Dari

5

Persian or one of the varieties of Turkic dialects brought in by settlers from the north and east.

The penetration of Islam into the Caucasus was undertaken at a much later date and continued right up to the Bolshevik Revolution. Some of the most zealous of Muslims in the Caucasus did not convert to the new faith until the nineteenth century. No Arab armies entered the Caucasus, and Islam created a constituency of its own almost solely through propaganda and the force of example. Only in rare cases, such as for small groups of Armenians and Georgians, was force used to secure conversion to the new faith.

Almost at the same time that Islam embarked on its Asian conquests the Khazars, a south European people who had converted to Judaism, were expanding their khaqanate into the forest inhabited by groups collectively referred to as the 'Rus'. The etymological origin of this name has been a subject of much controversy since 1749.[15] What is certain, however, is that a distinct people, referred to as the 'Rus' or Russians, were known to chroniclers and scholars as early as the ninth century.

No one has been able to establish with any certainty where the Russians originally came from, although their likeliest original home might have been to the north of the Carpathian mountains between the rivers Vistula and Oder to the west and present-day Belorussia to the east. For decades, Russian historians wished to believe that their nation descended from the ancient Scythians, but it is now established that the Russians entered their present area of settlement from the west and in the second half of the first millenium of the Christian era. As they moved in, they drove out the original inhabitants of the forest zone, who were of Finnish and Baltic stock.

The Russians constituted the principal branch of a wider ethnic group referred to by Pliny the Elder and Tacitus as the Venedii or the Venetii. These groups described themselves as Sloviana, which means 'those with the gift of words' as opposed to the Nemtsiy or the 'speechless barbarians', meaning Germans and, to a lesser extent, other Europeans.

By the ninth century the principal trend of Russian history had been established in the form of a constant push towards the south and the east. It was not until 1945 that Russian expansionism in these two directions came to a halt of which no one could know its eventual duration.[16] This expansion eastwards and southwards was bound to bring Russia into contact with both Central Asia and the Caucasus. The historical expansionism of Russia was not due to any acquired taste for empire-building and adventure; harsh climatic conditions which made agriculture a hazardous enterprise at best and rendered life difficult acted as a constant encouragement to the search for better farmland and a bit more sunshine.

To the north the Russians were stopped by the treeless tundra of the Arctic Circle, while the permafrost zone allowed only small scrub and moss to grow. It was by clearing part of the forest that lies to the south of the tundra that the Russians were able to secure some arable land. Further south lay the universe of the steppe, a vast semi-arid plain between Hungary and Mongolia which could be exploited for raising livestock.

For centuries the steppe was closed to the Russians by warlike nomadic tribes whose ranks continued to swell, thanks to seemingly endless supplies from the heartland of Asia. Sandwiched between the frozen ocean and the forbidden steppe, Russia was bound to try to break into new and larger breathing spaces.

The impact of such factors as climate, geographical landscape and, more importantly, access to dependable sources of food in shaping the history of different nations is often disregarded or minimised in an age when technological progress has promoted exaggerated – not to say illusory – confidence in man's ability to shape his own destiny. Precisely these factors have played a crucial role in moulding the Russian mindset and charting the path of Russia's history. A land where at least one out of three consecutive harvests was certain to be poor was bound to dictate frugality and a generally pessimistic view of existence. Russian peasants did not have to wait for the collectivisation era under Stalin to discover the necessity of communal enterprise. They helped each other through collective work while retaining an individual relationship with the soil.

Living with ever-recurring natural disasters such as drought, floods, epidemics and famine, the Russian came to see existence as the sum total of ordeals that could only be surmounted either through liberal doses of alcohol or through an ascetic mysticism reinforced by fatalism. Those with a stronger will could invest in the hereafter by devoting their lives to prayer punctuated by periods of self-imposed pain. Since there was to be no joy in this world, one could at least seek oblivion. The Russians' immense capacity for suffering has seen them through many a dire moment in their history – moments which might have broken other nations not so accustomed to expecting very little or nothing in exchange for great sacrifices. Some scholars have gone as far as detecting a masochistic streak in the Russian soul.[17]

Nature's oppressive immediacy prevented the Russians from venturing into the realm of metaphysics to the point of developing full-scale religious systems of their own. Often they came to worship what they feared most. Grozniy, the god of lightning, was put on top of the

7

national pantheon. Symbolising nature's immense powers of destruction, with a single stroke it could set the forest on fire and wipe out whole *dvorishche* (communes). The wolf was also worshipped as the true lord of the wild, a dreaded enemy which had to be pacified through prayer and sacrifice. Winter, frost, wind and thunder were also worshipped, as were a variety of ghosts who subsequently populated the *skazki* (children's tales).

Above all, however, the Russians worshipped their soil, which they saw as a loving though awe-inspiring mother. It has even been suggested that the very word Russia might have been derived from the Slav *rodina* (motherland). Serfdom, introduced from the end of the sixteenth century and retained until its abolition in the nineteenth, was at times presented as a mystical expression of the bond tying the peasants to their 'Mother Russia'. The black soil of Russia was both the womb which gave life to its children and the tomb which welcomed them to a world of eternal peace after a life-time of suffering.

Although the Russians, as already noted, did not develop religious systems of their own, nonetheless they did search for a larger framework of faith that could explain to them some of the more basic issues of existence. From the eighth century onwards, the Russians were in direct contact with the Khazars who had converted to Judaism, first as the tributaries of the khaqanate and, two hundred years later, as its conquerors. Through their association with the Khazars, the Russians discovered the basic outline of Middle Eastern monotheistic religion, which in its Christian and Islamic versions conquered one nation after another in Europe and Asia.

From the ninth century onwards the Russians also had some knowledge of Christianity, especially in its Byzantine variety. Some trade already existed between the Russian forest and Constantinople, the capital of Byzantium, and Russians provided the bulk of a Norman-led army which organised a raid on Constantinople and returned with much booty and news of an entirely different life-style.

Earliest contacts between Russia and Islam were established thanks to the Bolghars or Bulgars[18] who lived along the river Volga and considered themselves to be under the protection of the Caliph of Baghdad. A few of the Muslim theologians dispatched from Khorassan and Mesopotamia to instruct the Bolghars about the intricacies of Muhammadan doctrine became missionaries to the land of the 'Rus', with varying degrees of success.

By the end of the ninth century the two main Slav cities of the time, Novgorod and Kiev, had been united into a single Russian state under Prince Oleg. The next logical step to be taken was to break the power of the Khazars and secure domination over the neighbouring Bolghars.

Both these objectives were achieved within a century and marked just one more phase in the struggle between the Slavic peoples, led by Russia, and the many Turkic tribes and nations which constantly poured into the steppe.

Having shown its armed strength and confident in its future, the newly-established Kievan state was bound to look for an official religious faith capable of reinsuring its legitimacy. It fell to Prince Vladimir (c.987–1015) to pursue the project of acquiring a religion for the new state to a successful conclusion. Vladimir proceeded like a man on a shopping spree. According to accounts by both Muslim and European chroniclers, he invited Jewish, Christian and Muslim doctors of theology to debate the merits of their respective faiths at a series of conferences in Kiev. Orthodox delegates came from Byzantium, while supporters of the Church of Rome (Catholics) arrived from Germany. The Jewish claim was defended by the Khazars, while Bolghars presented the case for Islam. At the same time the prince dispatched special emissaries as far as Germany and Byzantium to attend church ceremonies and report back. Vladimir's men also attended special prayers at mosques among the Bolghars and ceremonies at Khazar synagogues.

Vladimir finally opted for the Byzantine version of Christianity, represented by the Greek Orthodox Church. Legend has explained reasons for his decision to reject other faiths. Islam, so the story goes, was deemed unacceptable because it forbade drink, an impossible proposition in a land where alcohol was universally considered to be 'the joy of life'. The prince also disliked the idea of submitting to circumcision, and found Islam's five daily prayers rather too much. Judaism, on the other hand, was pushed aside by him because of its alleged austerity and the fact that it was the religion of a people who had been driven out of their own land as a result of divine anger.

The true reasons for Vladimir's decision, however, must have been political and the choice he made appears the most perfectly logical at the time. Both Judaism and Islam were identified with Russia's traditional Turkic enemies, the Khazars and the Bolghars. A triumphant nation could not be expected to submit to the faith of its defeated enemies. Fear of being overwhelmed by the Turkic waves from the heart of Asia constituted an early Russian nightmare and proved one of the most long-lived. Conversion to Islam must have appeared to Vladimir and his advisers as a sure step towards 'Turkicisation'.

The rejection of Catholicism was equally understandable, for next to the Turkic peoples it was the Germanic family of nations that represented a source of permanent danger for the Slavs in general and Russia in particular. The Turkic and Germanic peoples were early established as the two arms of a pincer that might eventually crush

Russia. This double nightmare of the Russians in turn became a self-fulfilling prophecy when Vladimir decided to cut off his people from their immediate neighbours by rejecting both Catholicism and Islam. In other words, a new and potentially far more dangerous dimension was added to the potential conflicts between Russia on the one hand and its Turkic and Germanic neighbours on the other. Treated as eternal foes of Russia, the Turkic and Germanic peoples went on to play the role reserved for them throughout nearly a thousand years of conflict and war.

Vladimir's choice had other long-term consequences; it isolated Russia from the rest of Europe and propelled it into the position of an adversary for Asia. To most Europeans Russia came to appear as 'Asiatic', while to Asians she represented the advance guard of Christian Europe. The adoption of Orthodox Christianity linked Russia, a rising power at the time, to an empire already in decline. The Byzantine Church had for long assumed the role of an active partner for the established political order. It preached poverty and self-abnegation for the poor, but was more than prepared to condone – and share – the unjust privileges of the rich and the powerful few who dominated Byzantine society.

Russia found in its new faith ample confirmation for some of its own well-entrenched values and habits, such as dogmatic commitment to a set of beliefs and extremism in both submission to authority and its rejection. Some historians have portrayed the Russians as a rather sheepish people more than glad to bear the double yoke of domination by the church and the state. In reality, however, Russian history is filled with accounts of peasant uprisings which were always crushed with exceptional cruelty.

When he opted for Orthodox Christianity, Vladimir could not have known that by doing so he had paved the way for the emergence of Russia as the eventual successor of Byzantium in its pretended mission of protecting the 'True Faith' and expanding its frontiers. That Byzantium had for long been little more than a magnificent cadaver was demonstrated in 1204 when Crusaders from western Europe captured Constantinople. Russia, itself threatened by Polvotsy Turks, was hardly in a position to help.[19] The fiction that the Byzantine Empire was still alive was perpetuated until 1453, when Osmanli Turks finally captured Constantinople and included it in their own Islamic empire.[20] But long before that event, Russia itself had undergone an even more dramatic experience under Mongol domination.

The Mongol invasion might have been just another episode in Russia's long struggle against Turkic marauders from the east and the south. Various Turkic tribes had for centuries raided outlying Russian settlements and at times even forced Kiev and Novogrod to pay tribute. At no time, however, had they tried to penetrate into the forest – always considered as a safe haven for the Slavs – and to bring Russia under their direct rule. They had been raiders, not empire-builders. After the defeat of the Khazar and the Bolghars a truce was established between Russia and the Cumans, once considered as the most 'savage' of all Turkic enemies of the Slavs. That truce had been followed by a slow process of ethnic fusion through marriage, exchange of hostages and even joint raids against other neighbouring peoples. At the same time the Polvotsys, who had raided Russia almost every year between 1010 and 1068 and laid siege to Kiev, had long been contained. Meanwhile, the defeated Bolghars had all but abandoned their warlike traditions and now acted as a trading link between the Slavs to the north and west and the Muslim kingdoms of Central Asia. Their two principal cities on the Volga, Suvar and Bolghar, were prosperous centres of trade as well as of Islamic scholarship and art. On the eve of the Mongol invasion peace seemed to reign from Russia to Central Asia.

The gradual emergence of Russia as an organised power from the ninth century onwards had been paralleled by what was subsequently and justly described as 'The Golden Age' in Central Asia. It would be no exaggeration to suggest that Mavara al-Nahr (Transoxiana) – as Central Asia was then known – became the most dynamic centre of Islamic civilisation under the Samanids (874–999).

A Persian dynasty, the Samanids claimed to be the descendants of Bahram Chubin, a general in the Sassanid armies in the seventh century. Although they had converted to Islam long before they founded their kingdom, the Samanids revived many of the Zarathustran traditions of the past and also encouraged the revival of Persian as a language of literature and philosophy.

The Samanid state consisted of almost the whole of present-day Tajikestan and Uzbekistan, plus parts of Afghanistan and large chunks of Iranian territory from Rey, near present-day Tehran, to Khorassan and Sistan.[21] The Samanid capital of Bokhara was estimated to have a population of more than 300,000 in the middle of the tenth century and was thus one of the world's greatest cities. Fortified by an eleven-kilometre-long wall,[22] the Samanid capital contained 250 Islamic seminaries with thousands of pupils from all over the Muslim world as far as Andalusia and the Yemen.

In the heart of the city, on a vast elevated platform, was situated the Kohan-Dez (Ancient Fortress), which was in fact a collection of royal palaces, mosques, bazaars and schools. The fort, later renamed Arg, was a brilliant jewel set in the middle of a vast oasis of emerald.[23] To weary travellers reaching Bokhara after days passed in the surrounding deserts, the Samanid capital was the image of paradise on earth.

Bokhara was believed to have an infectious charm. Anyone who set foot in it once would be unable to leave it, it was said. On one occasion the recital of a sonnet by the poet Rudaki in praise of Bokhara provoked enough nostalgia in the heart of a Samanid emir for him to instantly order his horse saddled and to set out to return to a capital which he had left in anger a few months earlier.

Rudaki was only one of many men whose talent, scholarship and love of beauty and knowledge gave the Samanid kingdom its unique position in the history of Islam. Born in the village of Rudak near Samarkand, he has been immortalised as one of the two men who created what is known as 'modern' Persian literature some eleven centuries ago.[24]

Another great son of the region was Abu-Ali Sina, known in the west as Avicenna, who was born in the village of Afshaneh, near Bokhara, in 980.[25] He is unique among all Muslim scholars because of the range of his learning and the depth of his understanding of widely different scientific disciplines. He was a philosopher, astronomer, musician, mathematician, doctor of medicine, poet, linguist and writer. He was also an astute politician and rose to become Grand Vizir for some six years.

Avicenna rose to prominence at the age of eighteen when, acting as a doctor, he cured the Samanid emir, Nur Ibn Mansur, from a long illness. In exchange for his services, he asked the emir for permission to use Bokhara's royal library which contained more than 45,000 volumes at the time and rivalled Islam's greatest libraries at Shiraz and Baghdad. He became the author of more than 450 books on medicine, philosophy, music, poetry, politics and a variety of other topics. Of these only 161 volumes survived various 'calamities', including the Mongol invasion, and they are still studied today.[26]

Avicenna's incredible scholarly production earned him the title of Shaikh ar-Ra'is which, roughly translated, means the Master Sage. He is alone in Islam's history to have been thus honoured. His magnum opus *Qanun* (*The Cannon*) is an encyclopedic synthesis of medical knowledge from the earliest ages up to his own time. In it he studies, analyses, codifies and presents research done by Egyptian, Greek, Chinese, Indian and Persian scientists during more than ten centuries. *The Cannon*, which was translated ninety-eight times between the tenth and fifteenth centuries – mostly in Latin, but also in a variety of other European languages as well as Hebrew – offers studies of various human organs from the eyes to the heart, and suggests cures for a variety of ailments ranging from apoplexy to meningitis. Anticipating the much later discovery of bacteria by European scientists, Avicenna writes of 'invisible organisms that are responsible for the transmission of certain diseases'.

The Cannon subsequently became the basis of all teaching in Western Europe's earliest faculties of medicine.[27] In fact, it was only after the great discoveries of the nineteenth century that Avicenna's work gradually lost its central place and came to be treated as part of the history of medical sciences. His contribution to the development of civilisation was not confined to medicine only; nor was he alone in his pursuit of knowledge at a time when Islam in Central Asia offered ample opportunities for scholarship. Having mastered ancient Greek at a very early age, Avicenna set out to translate and/or summarise the works of Aristotle and other great masters into Arabic. It was partly through these versions that ancient Greek philosophy eventually reached Western Europe and helped to sow the seeds of the Renaissance at a time when scholasticism fought hard to limit the frontiers of knowledge to what was permitted under the strictest of theological dogmas.

Another man who stands out among the great scholars of Islam's Golden Age in Central Asia is Abu-Reyhan Biruni (973–1048) who was born in Qath, a village which subsequently grew into the capital of the Kharazmshahi dynasty.[28] Biruni, who like Avicenna wrote his work in Arabic and Persian, was also a multi-discipline scholar; philosopher and mathematician, he was in addition a pharmacist and a historian. He also studied astronomy and, long before Copernicus, described the solar system in surprisingly precise terms. He had his own troubles with Islamic flat-earthers of the time, but no one suggested that he be burned alive.

Biruni's most important work, from a cultural and political point of view, is his extensive comparative study of religions considered as heretical by Islam. While even the study of heretical beliefs was often punished by death, Islamic seminaries in Bokhara and Samarkand had no difficulty in comparing Mazdeen, Manichaean, Mazdakite and Buddhist beliefs with the teachings of the Qur'an. A steadfast defender of freedom of thought and of expression, Biruni studies the rise and development of Islam with a scientific detachment that is almost modern. He rejects the claims of any religious hierarchy to represent 'The Truth' and defends the right of the individual to rebel against any authority – including one exercised in the name of Allah – that he might consider to be unjust and oppressive.

The crucifixion of Mansur Hallaj on a charge of apostasy in Baghdad provoked an energetic reaction from Biruni who denounced the Caliph as a bigot and his agents who organised the murder of the popular dissident as 'veritable criminals'.[29]

Biruni was in a sense a disciple of Abu-Nasr Farabi (872–950), who had actually taught Greek philosophy to the young Avicenna. Farabi, known as *Mua'allem al-Thani* (The Second Master) – meaning after

Aristotle, who is considered the 'first' of mankind's greatest teachers – was born in a village in present-day Uzbekistan and studied in Khorassan, Rey and probably Shiraz. His translations of several ancient Greek philosophers into Arabic and Persian provided the foundation of curriculae in many schools between Transoxiana and Mesopotamia. A lover of music, Farabi ignored Islam's traditional ban on that art and spent many years studying musical modes and traditions which had long disappeared into oblivion. His treatise on the subject revived the ancient music of Persia, which had been inspired by Indian and Chinese musical traditions, and thus paved the way for the development of Arab, Turkish and Iranian classical music. The fact that the obscurantist mullahs of the day were all but powerless in their attempts at imposing their own narrow interpretation of Islamic laws indicates Central Asia's special position as a space of liberty at an age marked by growing intolerance in the Middle East and Europe.

The main reason for the mood of tolerance that allowed for so much scientific and spiritual progress in the region at that time was, arguably, Islam's almost boundless confidence in its own future. For the first time in many centuries, Central Asia did not feel threatened by new invasions either from the east or from the south. The prosperity of Bokhara, Samarkand, Khojand, Khiva, Marv and other cities had gradually reached the countryside also, thus partly upholding Islam's claim of establishing justice and equality in its realm. Peace and stability produced a higher standard of living which, in turn, ensured stability and peace. The region's wealth attracted the best brains of the day from the four corners of the Muslim world; these brains taught at schools which, in turn, attracted the brightest of students from as far away as Andalusia and North Africa.

As already noted, the pursuit of knowledge was not confined to any one domain. Almost at the same time that Abu-Mussa Kharazmi (c.830) completed his invention of 'Algebra', one of his contemporaries Abu-Abdallah Bokhari produced what was to become the most authoritative book on Islamic theology. Bokhari's book under the title of As-Sahih (The Authentic) is considered by the sunnis who form 85 per cent of all Muslims as second in importance only to the Qur'an itself.[30] As-Sahih consists of a painstaking study of all traditions, estimated to number more than a million, to Prophet Muhammad. Separating wheat from chaff, Bokhari has included in his book only those traditions which he has been able to authenticate through historical and theological research. His work not only put an end to potential reasons for schismatic quarrels, but also prevented the endless invention of 'traditions' (hadith) ascribed to the Prophet for the purpose of restricting freedom of thought and of expression.

The stability fostered by the Samanids proved shortlived and, barely a century after it was founded, the dynasty was overthrown by the Chaghtai Turkic tribes who poured into Transoxiana from the northeast. The Samanids were to enter history as the last Iranic family to rule in Central Asia. From then on the entire region was firmly included in the turbulent universe of the Turkic peoples that extended from the Volga to China and from the steppe to the Hindukosh and beyond.

The era of the great Turkic empires was ushered in by the Ghaznavids, a dynasty of mercenary warriors serving the Samanids. After the fall of the Samanids a Turkic mercenary general, Mahmud, son of Sabuktakin, embarked upon an empire-building career of his own and soon conquered most of Iran, parts of Transoxiana and almost the whole of present-day Afghanistan. From his capital at Ghazneh, Mahmud also invaded India and accelerated the process of Islamicisation in the subcontinent.

The new Turkic masters of the region did not see themselves as foreign conquerors, and were quickly integrated into the Irano-Islamic culture of the regions under their rule; they all converted to Islam, and even insisted on perpetuating the fiction of the Caliphate in Baghdad. Mahmud himself, for example, asked for and received the title of 'Sultan', an Arabic word meaning 'the hegemon', from the Caliph. The practice of separating the mosque from the state, theoretically impossible under Islam, had already been started by the Saffarid dynasty of Sistan under Yaqub Laith. Under the Ghaznavids, it was formalised and codified and became a generally accepted part of Islamic statecraft.

Mahmud, a Turkic speaker by birth, became an enthusiastic and generous patron of Persian letters and even tried to write some Persian poetry himself. His court attracted the leading writers and poets of the age including Farrokhi and the Poet-Laureate Onsori. But the greatest of them all, without a doubt, was Ferdowsi whose *Shahnameh* (*Book of Kings*) traced the mythological origins of both Iranic and Turanic peoples.

The Ghaznavid empire did not long survive the death of its resourceful founder, and was soon dismembered and finally defeated by new groups of Turkic conquerors from Central Asia. These groups were led by the Seljuk tribe of Turcomans whose original home had been the southwestern steppe of present-day Kazakhstan to the north-west of the Aral Sea. A section of the Seljuks, under a chief of the same name, had been forced to settle in the region of Bokhara after their defeat by the Samanids. There they converted to Islam, learned Persian and began to encourage other tribes from their original homeland to move into the more fertile lands of Transoxiana.

During Sultan Mahmud's reign two of Seljuk's grandsons, Toghrul and Choghri, gathered an army and, having crossed the Oxus,[31] laid siege to the city of Kharazm.[32] Within less than a decade the Seljuk invaders had become masters of the entire region from Central Asia to Mesopotamia. Toghrul was recognised by the Caliph as the new 'Sultan' and chose Rey, south of present-day Tehran, as his capital.

The Seljuk rulers presented themselves as the legitimate heirs both to ancient Iranian dynasties and to the Abbasid caliphate in Baghdad. They coopted the Iranian elites into their administration and revived some of the Sassanid traditions.[33] The new empire soon extended into Anatolia, where it came face to face with a moribund Byzantium, and extended its realm to the eastern Mediterranean by annexing Syria during the reign of Alp-Arsalan, Toghrul's successor. It was also under Alp-Arsalan that a Muslim army defeated the armies of the Byzantine Emperor Manzikert Romanus at the famous battle of Malazgerd. The Byzantine army included many Russian mercenaries and volunteers who believed they were waging holy war on Muslim 'infidels'.

Seljuk domination did not, however, put an end to the constant emergence of new Turkic conquerors who moved into Transoxiana from the remoter regions of Asia. The Qara-Khata'i tribes established themselves in a vast region that included present-day Kirghizestan and parts of the Chinese Sinkiang, before extending their rule into the region of Samarkand. Other Turkic tribes which carved out kingdoms of their own in the region included the Ghuz Turcomans and the Ghurids who ended up by gaining full control of virtually the whole of Transoxiana.

A far more powerful Turkic kingdom was established by the Kharazm-Shahis, who dominated all lands between the eastern shores of the Caspian and the Oxus. In time the Kharazm-Shahis eliminated the last of the Seljuk princes, conquered Mesopotamia and seized control of eastern Caucasus.

From the eleventh century onwards, the various Turco-Islamic kingdoms that dominated Central Asia and the Middle East were also involved in the Crusades which represented the first concerted attempt by Europe to seize control of the Levant since the fall of the Roman Empire. With their attention focused on the challenge from the west, few Muslim rulers and thinkers gave much thought to potentially far more important threats from the east.

By the start of the twelfth century a new and far more formidable power had already appeared on the Asian scene, although its impact was not to be felt by the Muslim world until nearly a century later. This new power was the Mongol Khanate which gradually pushed numerous Turkic tribes out of their historical habitat in Xiognu, Tujuc, Ruarruan and Mongolia proper and into Transoxiana, Kharazm, Afghanistan, Iran, Mesopotamia, Anatolia and even Egypt. Some of the expelled tribes moved north to Siberia and west to the Volga.

Preoccupied with the European threat to the Levant and busy fighting each other over this or that parcel of Iranian or Mesopotamian territory, the principal Muslim powers of the time all but ignored the gathering storm in the east. They received only scant information regarding the crisis in Mongolia where a demographic explosion, combined with the economy's failure to secure enough food for the local population as well as the tribes which constantly moved in from the colder and less hospitable regions further to the north and east, made war inevitable.

On the eve of the Mongol invasion, two fairly powerful states acted as a buffer between the Muslim world and the Asian heartland where new warrior tribes were already astir. One of these states was the Ghurid kingdom in Afghanistan; the other was the Qara-Khata'i state which had extended its control and now included Bokhara, Samarkand and Otrar, three of the greatest cities of Islam at the time. Both the Ghurid and Qara-Khata'i states were eventually defeated and destroyed by the Kharazm-Shahi Sultan Muhammad. Shahabeddin, the Ghurid emir, and Gur-Khan, the Qara-Khata'i ruler, were both killed in battle. The realm of the Kharazm-Shahis reached the Mongol frontier around 1218.

2

A Storm Strikes From the East

'A darkness chased by a cloud'. This is how Muslim historians have described Mongol armies in operation. Chengiz Khan, the founder of the Mongol khanate that eventually conquered the entire region between China and the Ukraine and between Transoxiana and the Persian Gulf, described himself as 'a punishment sent by the Heavens'. By all accounts, the Muslim peoples of Central Asia who first experienced a Mongol invasion fully agreed with the Khan's view of himself. Even today many Muslim scholars continue to insist that it was the Mongol invasion that marked the beginning of a long process of decline of Islamic civilisation, a process which, according to some, continues even today.

The Mongol invasion did not concern Muslim kingdoms only, and quickly spread to lands inhabited by the Russians. Thus it became the first major experience shared between Russians and Muslims; it illustrated the fact that Central Asia, although it appears as a remote frontier seen from Moscow, is indeed the key to the Volga and thence to the heart of Russia. It was the fall of the Muslim kingdoms of Central Asia and the Kazakhstan steppes which opened the way for the Mongol conquest of the Russian forest zone.

The Mongols were a nomadic people living in the vast and largely empty expanses of southern Siberia. Divided into numerous clans, they were almost constantly at war against one another. The absence of shared economic interests or a common set of religious beliefs prevented them from developing the idea of a single state encompassing all clans. Nevertheless the Mongol clans were eventually united under one Temujin who took the title of Chengiz Khan in 1206. Chengiz had already demonstrated his genius as a leader in war by defeating the Tatars at a battle in 1194, after which many Tatars joined the Mongol armies and took an active part in future conquests. In 1207 the Mongols invaded Tibet and turned it into a tributary. Two years later it was the turn of Minyak to fall. In 1211 the Mongols crossed China's north-eastern borders and four years later they were masters of Peking.

In 1218, almost at the same time that Egypt faced an invasion by Crusading Franks, the army of Chengiz Khan defeated the Qara-Khita'is and conquered their kingdom. This was the first chunk of Muslim territory to fall to the Mongols, but far from the last. A few months later Kharazm was captured and the city of Otrar burned to the ground. In Urgensh, the capital of Kharazm, the Mongols began their rule by five days of massacre. In 1221 it was the turn of Marv (Mari), the former capital of Margiana, to fall. Almost the entire population of the city were put to the sword, only a thousand children and a few dozen master craftsmen were saved. The following year Chengiz entered Samarkand, where he attended a Friday prayer gathering at the Kalan (Cathedral) Mosque. Some Muslim clerics interpreted the Khan's gesture as a sign of his secret conversion to Islam, but Chengiz was not just another Turkic invader who would quickly convert to the Muhammadan faith and usher in an era of peace. He was fully conversant with the basic principles of Islam through a number of Persian adventurers who had joined his court as early as 1210 and, during an extraordinary session at the Samarkand mosque, he was able to hold his own in a theological discussion with the Muslim clerics present. He even made an ecumenical gesture by suggesting that Tengri, the Mongol 'Supreme God', was the same as Allah. Chengiz and his successors were to demonstrate a degree of religious tolerance in sharp contrast with their systematic destruction of the political, administrative and economic foundations of the societies they conquered. The Mongols deprived Central Asia of its political elite and native governmental authorities, but did little to interfere with the activities of the mosque. This policy was to have profound and long-term effects on Muslim society. The belief that all government, outside that of the Caliph, was illegitimate, was reinforced by the presence of foreign and non-Muslim rulers. The mosque emerged as the sole source of religious as well as political legitimacy.

The mosque argued that Islam, having lost the 'battle without', had to fight and win the 'war within'. This meant a systematic attack on freedom of thought and of expression, and the imposition of narrow and dogmatic values on the entire community. Public burnings of books were organised in many cities including Bokhara, Samarkand and Marv. Philosophy was declared anathema to Islam and music was banned. Any individual suspected of harbouring reservations about this or that aspect of Islamic theology was declared a heretic and put to death on orders from the Qadhis (Islamic judges). The Islamic law (shari'ah), which had long fallen in disuse under the Samanids and their successors, was revived with a vengeance. One direct result of the new age of bigotry in Central Asia was the mass exodus of religious minorities – Zarathustrans, Jews and Christians – who found the double yoke of Mongol rule and Islamic fundamentalist pressure too much to bear. Their example was imitated by part of the Muslim intellectual elite and many scholars and artists moved to Persia, Mesopotamia and the Levant.

It was partly in response to the bigotry of the mullahs that secret Islamic societies began to flourish in Central Asia and Khorassan. The tradition of secret societies had been established in the first phases of the Arab invasion in the seventh century as an attempt by a section of the Persian aristocracy to preserve its Mazdeen traditions. These societies had remained hide-outs for Zarathustrans who dreamed of revenge against the Arabs until the ninth century, when Muslim Iranian dynasties established themselves and made it clear that a project of de-Islamicising Iran would have no chance of success. As Iranians converted to Islam en masse, the secret societies were also gradually included into a broader framework of Muslim life. Some Zarathustran ideas and traditions survived in these societies, but by the tenth century they belonged more to Islam than to the Mazdeen faith. Under the Samanids the secret societies had lost part of their *raison d'être*, under the Mongols they offered a private space of liberty within a public life dominated by heathen rulers and dogmatic Muslim theologians. It was from these societies that the *tariqats* (paths) of sufi Islam developed within a tradition that continues to this day.

The initial phase of the Muslim invasion of Central Asia claimed an estimated 1.3 million lives at a time when the total population of the entire region probably did not exceed six million. Cities like Urgensh, Otrar and Marv never regained their importance, while it was many decades before Bokhara, Samarkand, Khojand and Khiva could re-emerge as major centres of economic, political and cultural activity.

The Mongol invasion was not confined to Central Asia. In 1221, at the same time that Marv was being massacred and plundered, a Mongol army defeated a Georgian force in the Caucasus and reached the shores of the Black Sea. Within two years the entire Caucasus had been conquered by Jebe and Subotei, two of Chengiz Khan's generals. In the meantime, Mongol armies had devastated numerous cities and villages in northern Iran. In the Khorassani city of Neishapour, even cats and dogs were put to the sword.

The Caucasus was one of two invasion routes which was to take the Mongols to the heart of Europe. The other route passed through the steppes of Kazakhstan and the Volga region. Soon after the fall of Kharazm, a Mongol army defeated the Bolghars of the Volga and conquered the territory of the Kangli, another Tatar tribe that lived in northern Kazakhstan. Everywhere the defeated Tatars, although

Muslims, joined the armies of their Mongol conquerors. Thus by the time the first Russian outposts were reached by the 'hordes from the east', the Tatars formed a majority of the advancing Mongol armies. In May 1223 a Tatar army, led by Mongol generals, met and defeated a superior Russian force at Kalka. The battle of Kalka was to enter Tatar epics as a great turning point in history. To Russians, however, it symbolised their humiliation at the hands of their traditional Turkic enemies.

The battle of Kalka was initially seen by Russians as an isolated event, and nothing further was heard of the Mongols until the winter of 1236–37 when the appearance of Tatar-Mongol cavalry 'deep in the forest zone ... caused a shock that has never been quite erased from the collective consciousness of the Russian people'.[1] Very soon the Russians realised that this was no ordinary Turkic challenge. The new conquerors, known as Tatars rather than Mongols so far as Russia was concerned, were not simply looking for booty, slaves and additional land to roam in. They had come to change the course of history.

The invading army was led by Batu, one of Chengiz Khan's grandsons who had been assigned the task of conquering and ruling all lands in the direction of the setting sun. Between 1237 and 1241 the Tatar army attacked, ravaged, plundered and massacred almost the whole of Russia. Kiev itself was burned to the ground, and Novogrod escaped only because it had been isolated by massive spring floods. Passing through the present-day Ukraine, the conquerors pushed on into Central Europe and reached Hungary. Their plans to capture the whole of Europe down to the Atlantic Ocean were never put into effect because, in the summer of 1242, news arrived that Ogatai – successor to the legendary Chengiz – had died. Batu had to return home to take part in the inevitable dynastic feuds which follow the death of every great ruler.

Before he returned home, however, Batu founded a new state, the Golden Horde,[2] with the Tatar settlement of Sarai on the Volga as capital.[3] From Sarai the Tatar-Mongol rulers also controlled the affairs of North-east Russia and Novogrod which had become tributaries of the Golden Horde. Thus began the *Tatarchina* (the Tatar Yoke) period of Russian history that was to last nearly two centuries. To most Russians this is the darkest period in their national history. Russian fear of and hatred of the Tatars as historical enemies are probably rivalled only by similar sentiments towards the Germans.

That The Golden Horde did not seek direct rule over Russia must have puzzled the Kievan elites of the time. In Central Asia, Iran and the Caucasus the Mongols had simply established themselves as new ruling dynasties. Russia, however, was to retain a measure of autonomy. There were several reasons for this policy. Unlike Transoxiana, Kharazm and

Iran, the Russian principalities contained no major and wealthy cities which could be plundered and exploited with profit. Nor did Russia contain any rich agricultural land that could be tapped as a source of revenue. In other words, Russia was saved by its poverty as well as its less than attractive climate from direct Mongol occupation – a fate imposed on both China and Iran. All the Golden Horde wanted from Russia was money and slaves: both could be provided by the Russian princes themselves.

In 1257 the Golden Horde, using Chinese experts, carried out the first census ever taken in Russian territories. It was on the basis of the data thus obtained that each village and city was ordered to pay an annual poll tax. In addition a trade tax, very much like the modern western Value Added Tax (VAT) was imposed from 1260 onwards. Tatar tax collectors, protected by armed guards, were stationed in major Russian cities to supervise the task of gathering revenue as well as slaves, mostly children, who were quickly transferred to Sarai. The Tatar officials often went far beyond their duties as tax collectors and intervened in local politics or tried to enrich themselves through additional and illegal levies. The behaviour of some of these officials provoked rebellions which at times engulfed vast parts of Russia. Between 1257 and 1262, Tatar forces had to intervene to crush armed revolts in Novogrod, Kiev and several other cities.

From the 1250s onwards, the Khan of the Golden Horde was considered as the sovereign of all Russia, with the exception of those Russian parts of Lithuania which had escaped the Tatar conquest. Thirteenth-century Russian records refer to the Khan as Caesar or the Tsar, a title hitherto used only to describe the emperors of Byzantium. This was of capital importance in Russia's subsequent political development, since it meant that the final source of state authority lay outside Russia and thus also beyond any control by the Russian people. In other words power, because of its alien nature, had to be violent and arbitrary. During the twelfth century some steps had been taken towards greater popular participation in Russian politics thanks to the formation of the veche, local councils with extensive powers. Under *Tatarchina*, however, these councils all but lost their authority as the Russian princes, constantly using the threat of calling in the Mongol armies, discouraged attempts by their subjects to have a share in decision-making.

Another effect of *Tatarchina* was that Russia, unlike Western Europe, did not experience the so-called 'feudal' period which is now recognised as a major phase in the long and slow development of democratic traditions. By definition, the feudal system excluded the emergence of a single source of authority capable of exercising a monopoly on political power. A feudal lord or prince might pursue tyrannical policies, but there would always be others likely to be more 'liberal'. Individuals who found life unbearable under one despotic prince or feudal lord would always have the opportunity to defend their ideas and work in other principalities. Russia, under *Tatarchina*, had no such scope for pluralism, and by the time it gained its full independence it was already impossible to undo nearly two centuries of experience. Of course, this does not mean – as some Russian and even Soviet historians suggest – that Russia became a victim of despotic rule because it had fallen under an exceptionally savage alien rule. The Tatar-Mongols of the Golden Horde were probably no less culturally advanced than the Russians. Their long contact with such major centres of civilisation as China, Iran and, later, India, meant that they were aware of a variety of religious faiths and political traditions. Russia's failure to develop its politics across similar lines to that of western Europe was, at least in part, due to its own traditions as well as to the role played by the Orthodox Church in ensuring the docility of the peasant masses.

Some Russian princes used the threat of calling in the Tatars as a means of terrorising their own subjects and discouraging all attempts to challenge their arbitrary authority. Princes who dared to lead the masses against alien rule were brutally massacred and, at times, even their children and relatives were put to the sword. The effect of the double despotism exercised by the Tatars and the Russian princes themselves was to encourage general indifference towards all that concerned politics. As time went on, the Russian princes resigned themselves to a fate which had made them auxiliary tax collectors for Sarai. For example Aleksandr Nevsky, who is considered one of Russia's greatest national heroes, was in fact a Tatar tax collector. Russian princes could not claim divine legitimacy since their authority was based on *yarliqs* (charters) issued by the khan at Serai.

Russian experience with the Tatar-Mongol domination was different from that of Central Asia, China and Iran in a number of other ways. In those countries the invaders settled down, intermarried with the natives, adopted local customs and languages, and often even converted to the religion of their new subjects. Vastly outnumbered by the people they conquered, the Mongols were absorbed into larger ethnic groups such as Chinese, the Turkic peoples and the Iranians. No such developments took place as far as Russia was concerned. The Mongols were tatarised and since the Tatars had long established themselves as adversaries of Russia no large-scale mingling with the newly-conquered peoples in the forest was possible. Cultural intercourse between the two sides remained so limited that, after some two centuries of Tatar rule, there were no more than two dozen or so Turkic and Mongol words in the Russian vocabulary – and all these borrowed words had to do with various aspects of oppression: tax, levy, torture, chain, whip etc. The practice of slavery and the death sentence, both alien notions to the Russians, were introduced by the Tatar-Mongol rulers from the thirteenth century onwards.

By the end of the thirteenth century, probably a majority of the Mongols had converted to Islam, and Sarai included several mosques and madrassehs. This gave the hated *Tatarchina* an additional 'black dimension' as far as the Russians were concerned. Islam's proselytising energies were never seriously turned towards Russia, but this did not prevent many Russians from persuading themselves that their unfortunate land had become something of a European rampart against Muslim advance. In later centuries when Islamic armies, now under Osmanli leadership, subjugated many Slav lands and reached the gates of Vienna, the belief that Russia had a special mission to defend Europe against Muhammadanism was further strengthened. Others went even further and spoke of Russia's role in protecting Christendom against the whole of Asia. They referred to the period of Tatar-Mongol rule as *Aziachina*, meaning the Asiatic yoke.

The empire created by Chengiz Khan and his successors through nearly half a century of war collapsed towards the middle of the fourteenth century. The architect of this demolition was Teymur, a warlord from the Tatar clan of Barlas and native of Samarkand. In 1370 Teymur, known to his contemporaries as 'Lang', the Persian word for 'lame', because one of his legs had been permanently injured in combat, declared himself king of Transoxiana and Mongol Emperor. Known to the West as 'Tamerlan' (Teymur e Lang, or Teymur the Lame), Teymur claimed to be a descendant of Chengiz Khan through Jaghtai, one of Chengiz's sons who had become the first Khan of Central Asia in the early stages of the Mongol empire. By the time he died at the age of seventy in 1405, Teymur had fully recreated the empire of Chengiz in an Islamic mould and even extended some of its frontiers. The whole region between China and the Volga and from India to Syria was under his rule. In the process his armies had attacked and looted many cities including Rey, Herat, Baghdad, Alep and Damascus. Sarai was also attacked and conquered and many of its notables put to the sword.

Teymur, as portrayed by Muslim historians, was as barbarous a conqueror as Chengiz had been. Accounts abound of the 'mountains of severed heads' which the Tatar leader left behind in each conquered city. His savage treatment of Bayazid, the defeated Ottoman Sultan who was put in a cage and delivered to public delirium, is often cited as an illustration of the conqueror's sadistic love of cruelty. Nevertheless, this unflattering image of Teymur represents only part of his complex personality, for the Tatar khan was at the same time a very learned man with a taste for poetry and art.

One of Teymur's dreams was to turn his native Samarkand into the most splendid city of its time – and by all accounts he realised much of that dream. Samarkand was turned into a shop-window of the best that Islamic architecture and art could offer. Thousands of master craftsmen brought in from Syria, Mesopotamia, Anatolia and Iran participated in the design and construction of some of the most splendid mosques and palaces ever built in the Muslim world. Even today, Samarkand is an impressive sight and a jewel in the crown of Soviet Central Asia. It was also under Teymur and his successors that Bokhara, Khiva and Khojand were adorned with new mosques, palaces, madrassehs and libraries, the splendid remains of which still attract tens of thousands of tourists each year.

Among Teymur's successors one name stands out: Ulugh Beig (1393–1449). A grandson of the conqueror, Ulugh had little taste for war and instead devoted his energies to science and art. In time he became a considerable mathematician and astronomer; he created an observatory for the study of the stars and, helped by a group of sixty scientists from all over his empire, established an astronomical table that represented the exact position of 1018 stars. He also calculated the trajectory of the stars, and studied and worked out the precise duration of the stellar year.[4] Ulugh Beig's work was to be recognised later by other great scientists such as Bruno and Laplace, who even described the Tatar khan as 'the greatest figure in all history of astronomy'.[5]

Ulugh Beig had a violent end. During a palace *coup d'état* he was captured by a group of plotters led by his own son and his head was cut off. His remains were buried in an unmarked tomb in the royal mausoleum of Gur-e-Emir (the Tomb of the Emir) built by Teymur in Samarkand.[6] For years Soviet historians have tried to present Ulugh Beig's murder as being the result of a plot by fanatical mullahs who disliked his taste for scientific research, the Soviet theory being that his work threatened the foundations of Islamic dogma by trying to offer a scientific rather than a methaphysical explanation of the universe. Ulugh Beig's decision to construct his observatory sealed his fate, according to the Soviet version of events.

However, the Soviet view is difficult to sustain and must be seen as part of a policy of representing Islam as retrograde, anti-scientific and doomed to bigotry. Islam's passion for astrology did not begin with the Teymurid ruler, but could be traced back to the time of the Prophet himself. Under the Seljuks, the various Nezamieh seminaries created by Khajeh Nizam al-Molk all included centres for scientific research. A knowledge of the position and movement of the earth in relation to the stars was necessary for guiding the caravans that linked the Mediterranean to Peking, and Halaku Khan had ordered the construction of an important observatory at Maragheh nearly two centuries before Ulugh Beig had his built at Samarkand. The Tatar ruler was almost certainly more a victim of his son's haste to exercise power than of any anti-scientific outburst by fanatical mullahs.

After Ulugh Beig the Teymurid rulers, who took the title of Emir and described themselves as 'commanders of the faithful',[7] continued to rule for a further half century. It was under one of Ulugh Beig's successors, Sultan Hussein Bayqara, that the first concerted attempts were made at asserting Central Asia's Turkic personality. The architect of what could be described as a veritable nation-building project was one Mir Alishir Nava'i (1441–1501), who served as Bayqara's grand vizir for more than a decade. Born in a prosperous landowning family, Nava'i was able to study at several prestigious madrassehs at Samarkand and Mashad before moving to Herat, where he entered the service of the emir. Soon he rose to become head of a special bureau that dealt with the Turkic-speaking subjects of the emir while another department – much more prestigious – dealt with Persian-speakers. Nava'i, who was fluent in Persian as well as Arabic, soon realised that his native tongue, Chaghta'i Turkic, was treated less than fairly as compared with Persian. The ruling dynasty and much of the local aristocracy were Turkic speakers themselves, but protected and promoted Persian as a language of literature, high culture and politics.

It is difficult to be certain about the relative strength of the various languages used in Central Asia at the end of the fifteenth century. But there is little doubt that outside the principal cities the overwhelming majority consisted of Turkic speakers. Nava'i decided to give his own people their identity and began doing so by creating a written Turkic literature. The language he chose was the Chaghta'i, which predominated in most of Transoxiana at the time. Using Arabic meters and the rules of Persian poetry he composed more than 30,000 lines of poetry of which only a part has survived. His masterpiece was *Farhad and Shirin*, a love epic which he loosely translated from a work of the same title by the Persian poet Nizami of Ganjeh.[8] Nava'i also wrote a number of sonnets in Persian, no doubt to show would-be critics that he could do it. His choice of the Chaghta'i as a medium of expression was not due to his ignorance of Persian or Arabic, the two languages of the literati of his age, but to a conscious political design.

In time Nava'i was to be considered as the father of Uzbek nationhood, a distinction which might have amused him since the Uzbek tribes that subsequently dominated parts of Central Asia arrived on the political scene of the region after the fall of the Teymurids in 1500. During the

1920s Soviet official propaganda – no doubt anxious to combat Uzbek nationalism – found another role for Nava'i; the poet was now described as a fighter for the masses and a leader in the 'class struggle' that supposedly pitted the toiling peasants and the 'national bourgeoisie' against feudal aristocrats supported by fanatical mullahs.[9] However, Nava'i is a poet firmly within the Islamic tradition that includes a rejection of materialism and has certainly nothing in common with the Marxian or any other western interpretation of history.

The end of the Teymurid empire once again turned Central Asia into something of an Islamic backyard which soon fell into oblivion under a variety of clannish rulers. The Shaybani Uzbeks (1500–1599) never really succeeded in creating a credible central authority and the vast region under their nominal rule was plagued by tribal feuds, banditry and political instability. This in turn led to a sharp decline in the number of caravans using the Silk Route which, in any case, was doomed to losing its importance in the wake of the discovery by European navigators of the sea routes to India and thence to the Far East.

The Shaybani clans who won power in Central Asia had first established themselves in the khanate of Tiumen in western Siberia from the middle of the fifteenth century onwards. Loosely associated with the Golden Horde based on Sarai, the Tiumen khanate was in fact part of the White Horde group of Tatar states that occupied the region of eastern Volga to Siberia. Tiumen had at first been drawn into some form of loose association with the Golden Horde based on Sarai. In the early fifteenth century, for example, Yadigar Khan, the ruler of the Golden Horde, managed to exact a tribute from Tiumen.

Tiumen's position as a weak neighbour of a strong state changed under the Shaybanis who claimed descent from Shayban, a grandson of Chengiz Khan. Having already converted to Islam and claiming that they were fighting for the spread of the faith, the Shaybanis began their conquests in two directions. One group, under the leadership of Abolkhair Khan, conquered all lands between western Siberia and Syr-Darya, while a second group, under the command of Haji Muhammad Khan – a warrior who had performed the pilgrimage to Mecca – established control over Tiumen.[10] Under Haji Muhammad Khan's grandson, Ibaq, the khanate began seeking domination over other states of the White Horde. Ibaq enlisted the support of the Nogay (Mangyts) who had not yet fully converted to Islam. Together the Shaybanis and the Nogays helped to accelerate the disintegration of the White Horde and soon began to put pressure on the Golden Horde also. From then on Tiumen began to look like a potential ally of Russia in its fight against its traditional enemies, the Tatars of the Golden Horde. In 1481 a joint Tiumen and Nogay force attacked the armies of the Golden

Horde, under Ahmad Khan, during the latter's retreat from a battle against Russian forces under Ivan III. In the engagement between the two Tatar forces, Ahmad Khan was slain by Ibaq who promptly sent the latter's severed head to the Russian court as a present.

By the middle of the fifteenth century all the Tatar-Mongol states that ruled between Siberia and the Russian forest had undergone the same process of fragmentation already experienced by their kindred states in Iran, Anatolia and Mesopotamia. The large empires created by Chengiz and Teymur failed to turn the many Tatar-Mongol tribes and clans into a single nation, and soon every tribe and clan was trying to have a state of its own. Tiumen's attempts at keeping the White Horde united under its own domination failed and from the middle of the fifteenth century onwards a new khanate, based by the Taybugin clan on the remote settlement of Sibir, in western Siberia, had emerged as an active adversary.

The Golden Horde, meanwhile, had split into three khanates. The largest of these was the khanate of Kazan on the Volga. A second khanate was based on Astrakhan (Hashtar-Khan) on the Caspian Sea, while a third established itself in the Crimean Peninsula with Baghcheh-Sarai (The Mansion of the Little Garden) as its capital. The three khanates maintained more or less fraternal relations with each other, but were at no point capable of pooling their resources either to resist the challenge of other Tatar states from further east or to prepare for Russia's entry on the scene as a major expansionist power.

The weakening of the Tatar states, which led to their eventual fall, was largely due to the failure of the Mongol conquerors to translate their military victories into a durable system of government. In Iran and Anatolia the business of government quickly passed into the hands of the local elites and the conquering clans were rapidly assimilated and absorbed. In Russia the task of administrating the conquered lands had been assigned to the local nobility right from the start. As the Mongol military power declined, so the authority and strength of the Russian nobility increased. The fact that the Tatar-Mongol khanates were constantly involved in internecine wars, often provoked by quarrels over succession, further weakened their position vis-à-vis their Russian dominions. On one or two occasions in the fourteenth century, the Russians even dared to take up arms against their Mongol suzerains. The battle of Kulikovo in 1380 saw Dmitry of Moscow triumph over the Crimean khan; although no more than an exceptional episode in Russo-Tatar relations, Kulikovo was to enter Russian legend as a turning point in the history of the Slav peoples.[11]

The military decline of the Tatar-Mongol khanates was soon matched by a decline in other fields as well. Only Kazan retained some of the prestige which Sarai had once enjoyed as a centre of learning and art. From around 1450, when the Golden Horde was formally dissolved, Kazan was recognised as the centre of Tatar cultural life and an important Muslim outpost facing Europe. Kazan (meaning 'the pot' in Tatar) became Ghazan in Arabic and Persian transcription and thus meant the 'holy warrior city'. In subsequent pan-Islamic literature, Kazan was to be referred to as a 'shining star facing the darkness of the Christian West'.[12]

The decline of the Golden Horde, which had begun after the Teymurid invasion, coincided almost exactly with the emergence of a new Russian power based on Moscow (Muscovy). Under Basil I, Moscow demonstrated its military might by annexing Nizhni-Novogorod in 1392; and by the time Ivan III (1462–1505) had taken over, Moscow was already in a position to interfere with the politics of the Tatar khanates. Ivan III followed a careful policy of intrigue aimed at sowing dissension among the various clan states of western Siberia and the Volga, and claimed a Russian say in choosing the successors of the various khans.

Ivan III's eventful reign was marked by a number of major developments. Probably the most dramatic of these came in 1480 when Russia formally stopped paying tribute to the Golden Horde. This put a final end to more than two centuries of Russian humiliation at the hands of the Tatar-Mongols.[13] However the event also marked a reversal of the balance of power between the two neighbouring peoples, the Russians beginning their ascendancy while the Tatars embarked on a historical decline from which they never fully recovered. Of perhaps more historical importance, however, was the final annexation of Novogorod and the capture of Viatka and Tver by the Moscow principality, as well as the massive expropriations after which a system of conditional land tenure (*pomest'e*) was introduced. This not only turned the ruling prince into the virtual owner of all of Russia, but also set the tone for future conquests of territories beyond the frontiers of Moscow.

By the end of the fifteenth century, the rising Russian power made no secret of its desire not only to drive the Tatars as far away from its frontiers as possible, but also to avenge itself for more than two centuries of suffering and humiliation it had endured.

The fragmentation of the Tatar states during the fifteenth century was not confined to the Golden Horde and the White Horde and their Teymurid successors. In Iran and the Caucasus, too, one Tatar principality after another collapsed under the pressure of new clans which moved in to set their own bloody mark on the history of a tormented region.

Azarbaijan – which had experienced a period of stability under the Il-Khanid dynasty set up by Halaku Khan – was by the middle of the fifteenth century a roaming ground for new Turkic tribes pouring in from the north-western steppes of the Caspian Sea. One of these newcomers was the Qara-Quyunlu (Black Sheep), a confederation of clans which settled in the eastern Caucasus and gradually extended its domination into Azarbaijan. Under Qara-Yussuf (Yussuf the Black), the confederation created a state of its own with Tabriz as capital. By the end of the fifteenth century the Qara-Quyunlu state had been overthrown by another Turkic coalition of tribes known as the Aq-Quyunlu (White Sheep).[14] The Aq-Quyunlu had at first established themselves in northern Mesopotamia and acted as frontier guards for the Teymurid princes. It was under Uzun-Hassan (The Lanky Hassan), a general of exceptional genius, that the Aq-Quyunlu, although numerically small, managed to conquer virtually the whole of the Caucasus plus almost all of Mesopotamia and large parts of Iran. It was also under Uzun-Hassan that the first of many wars between Iran and the rising Ottoman power broke out, marking the start of a duel that was to continue into the twentieth century.

By the middle of the fifteenth century, the various Turkic tribes which had began pouring out of Mongolia and southern Siberia and into the warmer climes of Central Asia, the Volga region, the Middle East and the Caucasus were divided into dozens of small or large principalities constantly at war with one another. The only Turkic state capable of seeking a major role on the world scene at the time being the Ottoman Empire, it was therefore natural that some of the weaker khanates looked to the sultan at Constantinople as a potential protector against the Russian menace from the west.

The Ottoman state, however, was a multi-ethnic empire which could never fully make up its mind as to which aspect of its complex identity to put forward at any given time. It was clear that the vast majority of the inhabitants of Anatolia, the heartland of the empire, were not of Altaic origin; most were in fact of Greek, Armenian, Kurdish and Persian extraction and had been Turkicised without totally losing their own traditions. They would hardly think of describing themselves as descendants of either Chengiz Khan or Teymur the Lame. Thus the Ottoman sultans preferred to play the pan-Islamic card rather than appealing to an indefinable sense of 'Turkitude'.

In Iran and Central Asia as well as Siberia and the Volga region, many of the ruling princes described themselves as the offspring of Chengiz Khan,[15] but they too were often aware of the fact that a majority of their subjects were not of Mongol-Tatar stock.

Even in the khanates of Kazan and Crimea, where the Mongol-Tatar stock was strongly present right from the start, only a small minority of the population had retained their distinct Mongol features. Generations of intermingling between the local non-Mongol peoples and their-Mongol conquerors had led to the emergence of new ethnic types whose 'Turkitude' was largely confined to language and certain old tribal customs.

It was therefore to Islam that all these Turkic-dominated societies looked for a basis for shared values in whose defence the entire population could be united. The threat from Russia was seen as a threat to Islam.

3

The Cross and the Crescent

In 1988 the Russian Orthodox Church celebrated the end of the first millenium of Kiev's conversion to Christianity with sumptuous ceremonies in Moscow. Mrs Raisa Gorbachev, wife of the Soviet leader Mikhail Gorbachev, attended one of the solemn gatherings where the crucial role played by the church in preserving Russia's national identity was emphasised.

This was not the first time that the Orthodox Church was held up as a bastion of Russian nationalism. Between 1941 and 1946 Joseph Stalin, although himself neither a Russian nor a Christian, praised the church as a powerful force capable of helping the USSR win 'The Great Patriotic War'. He rewarded the Russian Orthodox Church for its 'patriotic' stance by ordering the suppression of the Ukrainian Catholic Church which was suspected of having divided loyalties because of its allegiance to the Holy See at the Vatican.

The Orthodox Church's position as a guarantor of Russia's independence was consolidated during the *Tatarchina* and was in contrast with its initial role. Initially, the conversion of Kiev to Orthodox Christianity had linked Russia to the Byzantine empire in more than one way. Basing themselves on the so-called 'symphonia principle', under which the authority of the church and that of the emperor were interdependent, the Byzantine Empire considered Russian Christians as its own subjects. This claimed sovereignty, however, could not be and was not exercised in any coherent way before the Mongol invasion, and during the period of Mongol domination of Russia there was virtually no chance for the emperor of Constantinople to press any of his supposed rights with regard to the subjects of the Great Khan. Nevertheless, Constantinople did retain an important role in Russian affairs thanks to its control over the appointment of high-ranking members of the church hierarchy.

In 1439 the Byzantine Church concluded the famous Florence accord with the Catholics as a step towards unity, but the Russian metropolitans firmly rejected the accord and accused Byzantium of apostasy. From then on all church appointments were made by the Russian hierarchy itself with the approval of the Great Princes of Moscow. The final break with Byzantium came in 1453 when the Ottoman Turks conquered Constantinople; this was Russia's first 'liberation'. The second liberation, as already noted, came in the 1480s when the payment of all tribute to the Tatar-Mongols was stopped by Ivan III.

The fall of Constantinople had profound effects on Russia's development. The princes of Moscow emerged as the only Orthodox Christian sovereigns and were soon propelled into the position of heirs to the emperors of Byzantium. It was no accident that Ivan III began to refer to himself as the Tsar, a title hitherto reserved only for the Tatar-Mongol khans and Byzantine emperors. His new position was further enhanced when in 1472 he married Sophia Paleologue, a niece of the last emperor of Constantinople. Russia began to see itself as a defender of Christendom against an aggressive Islam which all but encircled the Slavic peoples.

Less than a decade after the fall of Constantinople, Russian armies were on the march in an attempt to expand the frontiers of Christianity. By 1472, soon after Ivan III's marriage, they had established control over Perm Veliaka and forced the Tatar tribes living in the vicinity of the upper Kama to convert to Orthodox Christianity. The north-eastern route to Siberia was now open. A year later, another Russian force defeated the Voguly Tatars at the mouth of the Pelym river. Later Muscovite armies, leaving Tiumen territories to their west, struck deeper into Siberia and reached the river Ob where they defeated the Yurga Tatars and forced them to pay tribute to the Tsar. The Russian armies were always accompanied by a host of churchmen whose task was to convert the conquered peoples to Christianity. One of the most energetic of these prosleytisers was one Stephan, the bishop of Perm, who had the habit of ordering those who refused baptism to be put to death. By 1481 the principal trade route between Europe and Siberia had fallen into Muscovite hands and Russian outposts and entrepots were established in north-western Siberia.

Russia's early victories against its Tatar-Mongol neighbours encouraged the Muscovite princes and the Orthodox priests in their belief that Christ himself had bestowed a messianic mission on the Russian people. The fall of the 'first' Rome had been followed by the rise of the 'second Rome' which was Constantinople. Now Constantinople too had fallen to heathen barbarians. Christians should therefore rally around Russian standards and look towards Moscow as the 'third Rome'. In 1510 the monk Philofei, in a letter to Tsar Vasily III, spelled out the doctrine of the Third Rome:

> Of all the kingdoms in the world, it is in thy royal domain that the holy Apostolic Church shines more brightly than the sun. And let thy Majesty take note, O religious and gracious Tsar, that all kingdoms of the Orthodox Christian Faith are merged into thy kingdom. Thou alone, in all that is under heaven, art a Christian Tsar. And take note, O religious and gracious Tsar, that all Christian kingdoms are merged into thine alone, that two Romes have fallen, but the third stands, and there will be no fourth.[1]

Thus Russian nationalism assumed a universal mission right from the start. It saw itself as the sole holder of the truth and the very last defender of the faith. There would be no other Rome after Moscow. These themes were later expanded by the Slavophiles into broader theories regarding the unique role of the Slavs in saving civilisation. Although it later adopted more secular tones, Russian nationalism never quite fully abandoned its theological origins. After the Bolshevik Revolution in 1917 the place of Christian doctrine as the principal component of Russian nationalism with its claim to a universal mission, was, for a while, taken by Marxism-Leninism. Moscow remained the centre of the universe, but this time in the name of international proletarian solidarity rather than Christian unity.

Early Russian conquests in the Volga region as well as north-west Siberia were openly described as the fruits of crusades waged against the infidel. These conquests were accompanied by mass enforced conversion of the conquered people to Orthodox Christianity, followed by the expulsion of those who refused to be baptised. As a result, many clans who had already adopted Islam were forced to move either to Kazan or to go south and seek protection from the Shaybanids in Central Asia. The tactic of mass deportation was used not only against Muslim and shamanist clans; even Slav and other European peoples who refused to adopt the Orthodox version of Christianity ran the risk of being forced out of their homes. In 1510, for example, the army of Tsar Basil III annexed Pskov and forced more than two-thirds of its inhabitants out of their homes and into faraway settlements.

The assumption that Russia had to conquer the world as part of its messianic mission was not the only reason for its policy of aggressive expansionism from the fifteenth century onwards. The desire to avenge two centuries of Mongol rule has already been mentioned, but other economic and geographical factors were also at work. The poor quality of Russia's arable land, combined with the country's harsh climate, meant that agriculture could not feed a rapidly growing population; therefore it was necessary to find new land which could be developed into a source of food. Every Russian conquest was followed by the settlement of Russian peasants in the newly annexed territories. Yet another cause of Russian expansion was the fact that most of the regions which surrounded the heartland of Russia had no natural frontiers. The steppe presented no barrier to conquerors and Siberia was a vast ocean that remained to be mastered. Even the Central Asian plains and desert had no natural defences and could not escape conquest for ever. It was only in the Caucasus that high mountains made the task of the would-be conquerors difficult. In general, geography amounted to an invitation to Russia to move east towards the Pacific Ocean and south to the Iranian Plateau.

The political and military weakness of most of Russia's Asian neighbours was another reason for Moscow's growing appetite for expansion. A land that is easy to conquer will be conquered easily – and this was the case with almost all the Turkic states which had emerged in Asia since the eleventh century. Unlike the west – that is to say in central Europe, where Russian expansion could run into strong resistance – the aggrandisement of Muscovy towards the south and the east did not, with few notable exceptions, present major military problems to the invaders.

By the time he died in 1505, Ivan III had firmly established his duchy of Muscovy as a force to reckon with. But he had not achieved, nor had he attempted to achieve, the supreme desire of virtually every Russian at the time: the conquest of Kazan and the subjugation of the Tatar-Mongols. That task was left to his grandson Ivan IV, who was to receive the nickname of 'Grozniy' or 'the Terrible'.[2]

In 1547 Ivan IV took the title of *Tsar veseia Rossii* or 'The Tsar of all Russia' and also asserted his claim to be heir to the Byzantine emperors by raising the standard of the double-headed eagle. He appointed a special committee to trace his genealogical roots to ancient Roman emperors. As a defender of the faith, he was the successor both of Saint Peter and of Emperor Constantine. Yet another committee was charged with the task of fabricating legends about Moscow's alleged role in early Christian history. The tsar's capital was described as a city with a history of several thousand years and linked to developments in the history of ancient Greece and the earliest days of the Roman Empire. Accounts were even given of various early Christian saints who had supposedly visited Moscow as early as the first century, at a time when the city certainly had not existed.

Ivan also built up Russia's military power. He used a fifteenth-century system of raising levies, known as *datochnye liudi*, to make sure that every part of Russia contributed its share of conscripts to his armies of conquest. This he followed by a series of reforms which strengthened his position with both the peasantry and the aristocracy. It was as an unusually popular ruler that Ivan the Terrible prepared himself for the conquest of Kazan from 1547. Even the growing threat of Polish and Swedish encroachments against Russia's western frontiers would not deter him from his goal of giving the Tatars the *coup de grâce* by seizing Kazan. Determined not to leave anything to chance, the tsar spent virtually the whole of 1547 preparing his plan of action and getting his armies ready for battle.

First making sure of his defences, the tsar had a string of small fortresses constructed south of his frontiers; this defensive line was guarded by regular troops armed with muskets and cannon. In the meantime, six regiments of foot soldiers, known as the *strelitzii*, were raised among freemen who signed lifelong contracts as professional soldiers. They received special training to become elite marksmen. The tsar could also field some 90,000 mounted troops and was thus able to outnumber the Tatar cavalry in any engagement. But the bulk of Muscovy's army consisted of the *possokha*, barely disciplined conscripts often press-ganged in villages and the poor districts of the towns.

Ivan's military plans included two other innovations. He employed large numbers of European mercenaries – Germans, Poles, Swedes and Lithuanians – thus starting a tradition that was to be continued by his successors right to the end of the Tsarist empire. More importantly, he made sure that the command posts in the army went to experienced soldiers and not, as had been the tradition before him, to the often incompetent members of the nobility.

It was towards the end of 1547 that Ivan launched his campaign in the direction of Kazan. But the tsar did not reach Kazan. The icebound Volga gave in under the weight of the cavalry and the army's heavy guns, wreaking havoc among drowning soldiers. Convinced that God was not yet on his side, Ivan ordered a retreat. This gave the Tatars both an occasion and a fresh excuse for resuming attacks on outlying Russian villages where they captured hundreds of men, women and children to be sold as slaves.

It took Ivan two more years to prepare for a fresh campaign against Kazan. Flanked by his brother Yuri and the prince Dmitri Biyelski, the tsar assumed personal command of the operations. The Russian army, hoisting high the banner of 'holy war against the infidel', arrived at the outer walls of Kazan before dawn on Saint Valentine's day of 1550.

The Kazan which faced the armies of the tsar that fateful winter was a city of some considerable importance. With an estimated population of over 100,000, it was at least three times larger than Moscow. The capital of various Tatar khans during more than a century, Kazan had been founded by the Bolghars in the early tenth century. Therefore, it was one of the oldest centres of civilisation in that part of the world.

After a brief decline during the Teymurid era, the city had began to grow again and had become an important link in the east-west trade. It hosted a strong and enterprising merchant class that traded with Russia, China, Central Asia, Iran and the Indian sub-continent. The city's special status as an important centre of Islamic culture was assured through more than 30 madrassehs, some 150 mosques, a public library and an intellectual élite that maintained close and meaningful contact with other major Islamic cities such as Bokhara, Samarkand and even Baghdad and Shiraz.

At the heart of Kazan stood a vast fort containing the Jam'e mosque, the khan's palaces, the main theological seminaries, part of the covered bazaar, most of the industrial workshops and important stores of food and arms. The central square of the fortified city was the venue for annual festivals of songs and plays presented by the *ashiqs*, the Tatar equivalents of the Provençal troubadours. Like other large cities Kazan contained a number of religious and ethnic minorities; Jews, Christians, Buddhists and shamanists lived side by side with Muslims. The over-whelming majority of the people spoke one of the three different dialects of the Tatar language which had developed into a rich and powerful medium of communication by the start of the sixteenth century. The business and cultural elites, however, also spoke and often read and wrote Persian and Arabic. Persian was considered the language of literature while Arabic, the language of the Holy Book, was studied at theological schools and used in mosque sermons. The city's position as a major centre of Islamic studies was illustrated by the fact that its library contained the famous Qur'an of the Caliph Othman, a precious volume believed to be the first manuscript of the Holy Book produced some thirty years after the death of the Prophet.

The Russian attack on Kazan began shortly after sunrise on 14 February 1550 and continued for two more days. The invaders used heavy cannon – hitherto unknown in that part of the world – to prepare the terrain for the advance of the *strelitzii* and the cavalry. They managed to breach the city's outer walls at two points, but failed to force their way into the inner fortress. Gripped by fear, Ivan ordered attempts at seizing the fortress to be abandoned and instead commanded his troops to put 'the infidel' to the sword. Thus began a massacre in which thousands of women, children and old men, all inhabitants of Kazan's poorer outlying districts, were cut down. Over 2,000 boys and young girls were also captured, to be presented to various Russian noble families as slaves. The tsar then ordered his forces to retreat.

The Tatars, their main forces still intact, remained surprisingly inac-tive and made no attempt to attack the retreating Russians, which gave Ivan the chance to present his defeat as a half-victory and to establish a number of Russian garrisons on Tatar territory. One of these garrisons was situated at the confluence of the Volga and the Sviiaga, and was named Sviiazhsk. The small village was quickly built up into a town of some importance where Russian settlers lived together with Chuvash, Mordvia and Cheremis tribes who had a long history of hostility towards the Tatars of Kazan.

Ivan himself might have been content with his half-victory against the Tatars, but the church hierarchy demanded more. The Orthodox Metropolitan, Macare, even went so far as hinting at the possibility of future sainthood for the tsar provided Kazan was conquered. He reminded Ivan that the Catholic princes whose version of Christianity was at best questionable had succeeded in driving the Muhammadans out of Europe; no Orthodox prince worthy of the title of a soldier of Christ could do less.

In June 1552 the army of the tsar was once again on the march. However, before Ivan's forward units had reached Sviiazhsk news came that a Tatar force led by Develt Giray, the khan of Crimea, had attacked Tula and seemed to be planning a march on Moscow itself. The Crimean move was in no way intended as a means of relieving part of the Russian pressure on Kazan. The two khanates had been at odds for a long time and Develt Giray would not have been unduly despondent had Kazan suffered a defeat. All he wanted to do was to seize the opportunity to pillage Moscow while the tsar was away. Nevertheless the Crimean move ended in failure, as Develt Giray's army was defeated by the Russian garrison at Tula. A few days later captured Tatar soldiers were paraded in the streets of Moscow and the local populace, led by their priests, swarmed around to spit on 'unclean Muhammadans'.[3]

Ivan interpreted Develt Giray's defeat as a sign from Christ that the war on Kazan would end in victory for Muscovite forces. On 20 August 1552 the Russian army, this time numbering over 100,000 men and supported by more than 100 pieces of artillery, was once again opposite the outer walls of Kazan. From there Ivan sent a message to Yadegar Muhammad Khan, the ruler of Kazan, inviting him to surrender. The khan's reply was swift and sharp. 'I spit on you and I spit on all Russia,' he wrote. 'Here, everything is ready. We are waiting for you to begin the feast.'[4]

Three days later the tsar unfolded a huge banner adorned with an image of the Christ and ordered the assault to begin. But the ten days of fighting which followed did not produce a quick victory for him. The Tatars fought like raging tigers and killed those of their wounded comrades who might have fallen into Russian hands. It was then that a German engineer attached to the Russian army suggested a plan to blow up Kazan's main source of water; this was carried out but produced no immediate result. Once the shock of the large explosion was absorbed, the Tatars resumed fighting with as much energy as before.

Convinced that he could not return to Moscow without a tangible victory, Ivan finally approved a new German plan for blowing up the whole city. Within a few days a network of underground galleries had been dug beneath the central districts of Kazan. These passages were then filled with as much explosive as the Russians could secure. All that remained was to get the cannon roaring again and leave the rest to the massive explosion of the mined galleries.

The stratagem proved successful and the explosion which followed destroyed much of the city's fortifications. Tatar ranks were gripped by chaos as Russian cannon continued to pound their way towards the heart of the city. History had just witnessed the single biggest use of explosives ever recorded – a fitting baptism for a gunpowder empire that was to continue its expansion for another four centuries.

Declared an open city, Kazan was delivered to Russian soldiers who firmly believed that the massacre of the 'infidel' would draw them closer to Christ. Thousands of tribesmen who hated the Tatars for reasons of their own also took part in the carnage. The Russian and allied forces, four times larger than the Tatar defenders of Kazan, nevertheless, needed six weeks before the city, now little more than heaps of burning debris, was finally subdued. On 2 October 1552 Kazan was declared a Russian city; this prize had been won at the cost of more than 20,000 Russian and allied lives. The Tatars had lost almost as many soldiers, plus some 30,000 women, children and old men who perished in the massacres.

Almost immediately after Ivan's triumphant entry into what was left of the city Orthodox priests began mass conversions of the conquered peoples. Thousands of young widows and unmarried maidens were pronounced 'Christian' and presented to Russian soldiers as concubines. Yadegar Muhammad Khan and a dozen of his companions were taken to Moscow where they too were declared 'Christian'.[5] A ukase of the tsar, meanwhile, announced that only those Tatars who had converted to Christianity could continue to live in Kazan. As a result hundreds of Tatars, especially many of the merchants and members of the Mongol nobility, took the oath of allegiance to the tsar and agreed to be baptised. What were left of the city's mosques and madrassehs were destroyed and the Muslim clerics and teachers who served there were put to the sword or forced to go into exile. Thousands of Tatars who found the prospect of living under a non-Muslim ruler intolerable left with them. Many of the exiles ended up in Bokhara and Samarkand, but some went as far as Iran and thence to the holy cities of Arabia.

Ivan chose the site of Kazan's main mosque as the place where he would build the city's holy church. At a solemn ceremony, he purified part of the site with holy water and laid the first foundation stone of what became the Cathedral of Visitation. No one could have guessed at the time that the tsar's sadistic and mystical love of fire and blood – so tragically illustrated in the martyred city of Kazan – would but a few years later lead to the Oprichnina terror during which many Russian cities suffered fates similar to that inflicted upon the Tatar capital.

The tsar's hopes of turning Kazan into an exclusively Christian city failed, however. The number of Russian settlers remained limited and many of the natives steadfastly stuck to their Muhammadan faith. The merchant classes of Kazan proved exceptionally resilient and the city's famous bazaar was soon bustling with business again. Tempted by the prospect of the revenue that a rebuilt Kazan could bring him, Ivan chose to ignore the gradual revival of the city's Tatar personality including a modest mosque and one or two madrassehs.

Both the tsar and the Orthodox clerical hierarchy were determined to make as much as possible of the Russian victory over the Tatars. The fall of Kazan had enhanced the prestige both of Ivan as a leader and the Orthodox Church as the vanguard of holy war against Islam. To commemorate the fall of Kazan, the tsar and the Orthodox Metropolitan together worked out plans for the construction of a new church in Moscow's Kremlin square. The man chosen to design the edifice was Barma Yakovlev, who had visited Kazan on a number of occasions. The church he designed emerged as an exotic mélange of western architecture as he imagined it, and oriental art, presented with distinctly Russian accents. The extravaganza was to be named after Saint Basil and with its eight unequal cupolas dominated by a pyramid crowned by a golden onion, soon became a symbol of Russia.[6] The entire cost of building the cathedral was borne by the inhabitants of Kazan, who continued to pay war reparations for more than a generation. The Tatars seized every opportunity afforded them for revolting against Russian rule. In a sense, it was not until over a century later that Kazan had been fully pacified and incorporated into the Russian state.

Kazan's two sister states, the khanates of Astrakhan and of Crimea, had remained inactive throughout the Russo-Tatar war of 1552. It was now their turn to be attacked by the forces of the tsar. Convinced that Crimea, under its flamboyant khan, was the harder nut to crack, Ivan focused his attention first on Astrakhan. The smallest of the three khanates, Astrakhan was nevertheless a strategically located and fairly wealthy state. It controlled the mouth of the Volga and claimed an important share of the trade in the Caspian Sea region, the steppe and parts of Russia itself. Founded by Teymur in the fourteenth century, Astrakhan had developed from a small garrison town into the largest trading centre in the region with a population of over 75,000 in 1554.

Its khan could raise an army of more than 25,000 men drawn mostly from among the warrior tribes that lived in the surrounding steppe. But when Russian forces led by Prince Yuri Shemiakin appeared at the walls of the city, the khan had already escaped in a boat; his flight had been so hastily organised that he had left behind most of his treasure as well as his four wives and more than fifty concubines.[7]

Thus Astrakhan fell without much of a fight. This victory meant that Russia now controlled the entire course of the Volga and, for the first time, emerged as a power in the Caspian Sea as well. From Astrakhan, future tsars could contemplate new conquests in the Caucasus, in Iran and – beyond the Caspian Sea – in Central Asia. The annexation of Astrakhan also helped to stabilise Russia's south-eastern borders. From 1556 onwards a massive programme of building stockades in the steppe was carried out with a view to keeping out nomadic warrior tribes and paving the way for Russia's future expansion towards Kazakhstan and southern Siberia.

As with Kazan, the new Russian masters of Astrakhan launched a massive campaign aimed at converting the subjects of the khanate to Christianity. Muslims, referred to as *busurmanin*, a term of insult, were never accepted as subjects of the tsar and received virtually no protection even under the rudimentary laws then in force. Many families were expropriated and their farms and even homes handed over to the Orthodox Church or members of the Russian nobility. In later decades. Russian peasants who wished to escape the scourge of serfdom were also brought in and settled on land that belonged to Muslim farmers. The policy of mass expulsion of Muslims from Astrakhan sent thousands of people into permanent exile in the Caucasus, and even as far as Anatolia and Iran. The Muslims who were allowed to stay in Astrakhan were asked to pay heavy war reparations, including an annual 'gift' of three thousand caviar-bearing sturgeons to Moscow. Much of the city's long-accumulated wealth, mostly kept in the form of silver and gold reserves, was siphoned off to Russia where the Orthodox Church received a part.

The long-term effects of Russia's expansion at the expense of Islam were almost totally ignored by the Muslim authorities in both the Ottoman Empire and Iran. Even the Tatar khanates of Siberia and the Turkic principalities of Central Asia did not fully realise the dangerous consequences of the fall of Kazan and Astrakhan. Only the Crimean khanate, itself directly threatened by Russia, reacted by organising a number of abortive attempts at stemming the tide of Russian expansion. Devlet Giray laid siege to a number of Russian cities including Riazan and Moscow, but each time was roundly defeated thanks to Russia's 'gunpowder superiority'. Unsuccessfully he appealed to the Ottoman sultan to help him in the name of both Turkic and Islamic solidarity. It was only years later, when Russia had already established itself as the supreme power in the region, that the Crimean khanate secured a new status as a protectorate of the Ottoman 'Sublime Porte'.[8]

The fall of Kazan did not produce the same effect on the Muslim world as the loss of Granada sixty years earlier; yet it could be argued that the long-term results of the Russian victory against the Tatar khanate, so far as Islam was concerned, were greater. The fall of Kazan was but the first decisive step towards the destruction of many other Muslim states by Russia and the annexation of substantial sections of territory from the Ottoman Empire and Iran. For more than four centuries Muslim poets and writers have lamented the loss of Granada, the last centre of Islamic civilisation in Western Europe, but the martyrdom suffered by Kazan has inspired few Muslim pens. It is only in the past half-century or so that Kazan's cruel fate has received attention in the context of Islamic revivalist movements.

Unable to destroy the khanate of Crimea, the new Russian power turned its attention to further conquests in the east. In the late 1550s a chain of stockades was constructed along the southern borders of Russia and the conquest of the steppe began in earnest. By 1597 Russian forces were already in contact with the khanate of Sibir, a Muslim Tatar-Mongol state which in the meantime had absorbed the khanate of Tiumen. Sibir was conquered in 1598 and, as usual in Russian conquests, was plundered and then set to fire. Thousands of its inhabitants were put to the sword and thousands more forced to flee as far as Kazakhstan and Central Asia. From then on, no organised state stood in the way of the Russian advance to the Pacific.

The seventeenth century, which saw the Romanov dynasty established in Russia, was dominated by Tsarist attempts at expansion in Europe and punctuated by revolts in various parts of the state. But plans for the conquest of the Crimean khanate were never abandoned, and in 1676 war broke out between Russia and Crimea. The Ottoman Empire, acting as the protecting power for Crimea, was inevitably drawn into the struggle which lasted until 1681. Russia made a number of advances but it was clear that the conquest of Crimea still lay a long way ahead.

The rule of Peter the Great (1689–1725) was marked by the ascendancy of the 'westernisation' movement in Russia. Himself an enthusiastic supporter of the idea that Russia had to reorganise its life along lines set by western European nations, Peter mobilised enough support to usher in a number of reforms. One major result of these reforms was the strengthening of the Russian military power, especially through an increase in its artillery forces, and the creation of a navy. Part of the new Russian navy operated in the Caspian Sea and could thus be used as a means of pressure on Iran as well as for forays into lands to the east of the lake. On a number of occasions the Russian navy landed troops at Astar-Abad (Gorgan) on the Iranian coast of the Caspian, as part of a vague plan by Moscow to launch a conquest of India. It was also under Peter that the idea of Russian expansion towards the Persian Gulf and the Arabian Sea – involving the annexation of Iran and Afghanistan plus the whole of Central Asia – took shape.[9] However, such goals still seemed far too difficult to attain; securing access to the Baltic Sea and the Black Sea seemed a more realistic goal. The defeat of the Swedes in 1709 and the construction of St Petersburg (1712) as the new Russian capital brought the Baltic Sea within reach of the Tsarist state. The Black Sea, however, was controlled by Turks and Tatars.

In 1711 Peter organised a major campaign against the Turks with the aim of paving the way for a Russian presence in the Black Sea. The tsar's forces, however, were roundly defeated at a battle on the river Prut in Bessarabia. The Ottoman Empire had not yet become 'the sick man of Europe'.

During the eighteenth century Russia resumed its expansion towards the east and conquered vast territories inhabited by the Kazakh tribes.[10] A Turkic people, the Kazakhs had converted to Islam after the sixteenth century. Living a nomadic life, they were organised in four tribal confederations known as the Great Horde (Ulus-Juz), the Middle Horde (Orla-Juz), the Little Horde (Kichik-Juz) and Buyuky Horde (Buyuki-Juz). The tactic used by the Russians against the Kazakhs consisted of a slow but persistent nibbling at the pastures used by the tribes. Russian advances into new territory were always consolidated through the construction of forts manned by heavily armed garrisons. Once again, heavy artillery played a crucial role in rendering tribal resistance against Russian forces ineffective in the long run. The fortress town of Omsk was constructed in 1716, to be followed by Semipalatinsk in 1718. A year later Ust-Kamenogorsk was built in the steppe. By 1720 Russia had the springboard it needed for its biggest programme of territorial aggrandisement in Asia.

Russian annexation of Kazakhstan, however, did not come through open warfare. On the contrary, Russia was 'invited' by the four hordes to extend its protection to the Kazakh peoples who had suffered an invasion by Jungar and Kalmuk tribes. These tribes, largely animist and shamanist, were pushed out of their own lands in the Volga region by the Russian advance and forced their way into Kazakh territory in 1723. This marked the start of two years of savage wars which devastated many Kazakh pastures. Thousands of tribesmen were put to the sword or kidnapped by the invaders, who totally ignored the ethnic, linguistic and historical roots they shared with their victims. The Jungar-Kalmuk invasion is remembered by Kazakhs as the era of 'Great Misery' (*Aqlaban shurbundy*). By 1742 all the Kazakh states had been brought under Russian protection. A declared enemy of Islam, the tsar now claimed the mantle of the defender of Muslim tribes against their non-Muslim neighbours. The Kazakhs, in their desperation to escape one wolf, had handed over their fate to an even bigger and hungrier one.

The Russians lost little time in consolidating their Kazakh possessions. The fortress towns of Semirechi and Orenburg were constructed and peopled with Cossacks brought in from the Ural and the Don region. The most fertile lands and the richest pastures were gradually snatched away from the Kazakh tribes and handed over to Russian settlers from the four corners of the empire. The annexation of the Kazakh territories was formalised between 1822 and 1848, when the khans and beigs were gradually deprived of all their political powers and administrative responsibilities. A typically colonial administration was installed with its centre at Orenburg which quickly grew into a considerable city, a window to the vast expanses of the steppe area beyond. The policy applied to the Kazakhs was, however, different from that imposed on the Kazan and Astrakhan Tatars. By the nineteenth century Russia had become a multi-ethnic empire and no longer dreamed of a complete russification of all its non-Slav subjects. Thus, the Kazakhs, unlike the Kazan Tatars before them, were not declared full subjects of the tsar and received the status of *inorodtsy* or 'natives'. As such, they were allowed a measure of internal autonomy and were also exempted from compulsory military service.

Russian attempts aimed at conquering the Crimean Peninsula were resumed in 1736 when an army of Cossacks, led by General Münich, entered Tatar territory and left behind a trail of death and desolation. Münich's murderous campaign was continued a year later by the forces of General Lassy, who spent nearly a year setting fire to Tatar villages and killing as many of their inhabitants as he could. But the complete occupation of the peninsula came only in 1771 when a Russian force commanded by Prince Doloruki seized Baghcheh-Sarai. Three years later the treaty of Kuchuk-Kaynarji put an end to Ottoman protection of the Crimean khanate and opened the way for the annexation of the peninsula by Russia. Under the treaty, Crimea retained its nominal independence while recognising the authority of the Ottoman Sultan as the Caliph of Islam. It was also the first time that Russia acknowledged the Ottoman ruler's claim to be the spiritual head of the entire Muslim community.

From then on Crimean politics was dominated by the constant duel between Russophile and pro-Ottoman factions. In 1782 the pro-Russian khan, Shahin Giray, invited Russian troops to take up position in the

Crimea in order to help him against his anti-Tsar opponents. That meant the end of both factions, and also the end of the Crimea as an independent state. On 9 April 1783 an edict signed by Empress Catherine II (subsequently known as Catherine the Great) announced the annexation of the Crimean state. The edict, a masterpiece of hypocrisy, guaranteed the rights of the Tatars to own property and continue to practise their religion as full subjects of the empire.

However, the Empress lost little time before putting into effect a long-term project for the complete russification of the peninsula. The most fertile lands were instantly seized from owners who were accused of pro-Ottoman sympathies, and handed over to Russian, Ukrainian and Cossack settlers brought in by the army. Wherever they settled the newcomers destroyed mosques, Islamic schools and libraries and generally did all they could to efface the peninsula's Islamic personality which had taken shape during centuries. Soon Baghcheh-Sarai itself was virtually russified as a result of the presence there of Russian civil servants, military personnel and merchants. The Tatars were squeezed into the infertile lands of Central Crimea, while the coastal plains were occupied by Slav settlers. The peninsula's pleasant climate also attracted a growing number of holidaymakers from the rest of the empire.

From early 1780 to the end of the nineteenth century, an estimated 1.2 million Tatars were driven out of the Crimea.[11] The vast majority of them emigrated to the various European provinces of the Ottoman Empire as well as to Anatolia. Those Tatars who stayed behind in the Crimea soon became a despised and miserable minority in their own homeland. It was left to Joseph Stalin to expel the last of them from the Crimean Peninsula in the 1940s.

The annexation of the Crimean Peninsula opened the Black Sea and thence the Mediterranean to Russian naval power for the first time. In 1772 Russia flexed its new maritime muscles by organising a raid on Beirut and defeating its Ottoman defenders. The Tsarist expeditionary force could not, however, constitute a permanent force of occupation, and handed the city over to the warlike Druzes who agreed to conclude an alliance with St Petersburg.[12]

The total elimination of the Tatar states within two centuries ended a long period in which history had seemed to hesitate about bestowing its favours on either a Tatar or a Russian empire. The Russians won for a number of reasons. Thanks to a demographic explosion in the sixteenth and seventeenth centuries, they more than outnumbered all the Tatars from the Crimean Peninsula to Siberia. The tsars could also draw on reserves of populations provided by other Slavs such as Poles, Belorussians, Ukrainians and, later, Bulgarians. The Poles, although victims of Russian domination in their own homeland, played an active role in helping the tsar to annex Muslim countries. Janus Potocki for example, a Polish aristocrat, was one of the first Slavs to travel deep into the Caucasus and Central Asia and to advocate a plan for the annexation of the entire region between the Kuban and Kabul as the first step towards the conquest of India.

The Russian empire-building project was in part financed by western Europe which also sent in mercenaries, technicians and even army commanders to help the tsar expand his realm. The Tatars, however, had no outside sources of financial and logistical support and were largely cut off from Muslim states such as the Ottoman Empire and Iran which might have offered some help.

The Russians were also stronger because they were united under a single autocrat supported by a single church. The Tatars had countless khans and, although Muslims, were involved in a variety of religious schismatic feuds. Thus the various khanates and tribal states could be taken on one by one and defeated without any of the others making a move. From the end of the eighteenth century onwards Russia, partly thanks to French, British and German investment, experienced an unprecedented economic boom that helped to enhance its social cohesion, a precondition for any empire-building enterprise.

Unlike other major European powers looking for colonies overseas, Russia – lacking reliable access to the oceans – directed its imperialist energies against its neighbours. The Russian expansion came at a time when Islam was on the retreat almost everywhere, while Christianity was surging ahead and securing new conquests in Asia, Africa and the New World. The expulsion of the last Muslims from Andalusia came only a decade before the fall of Kazan.

The annexation of the Crimean Peninsula made Russian advances in the Caucasus virtually inevitable. The Russians had long used their base at Astrakhan for expanding into the Kuban plain and the steppes of northern Caucasus. Nibbling at the fertile lands up to the region of the Terek, the Russians reached the Caucasus mountains at the start of the nineteenth century. Their more immediate aim, however, was to seize control of the eastern coasts of the Black Sea.

Russian incursions in the Caucasus had began under Peter the Great and long before the final annexation of the Crimea. In 1722 Peter led an army out of Astrakhan with the declared intention of conquering Persia. The Russian force annexed the coastal town of Derbent (Darband)[13] in August and went on to capture Baku a few weeks later. This led to the signing of a peace treaty between Russia and Iran under which Derbent was ceded to the tsar. But the Russian hold on new possessions in eastern Caucasus remained tenuous until the nineteenth century; furthermore, Russian knowledge of the region remained scanty until the reign of Catherine II.[14]

In 1736 Russia began to apply its policy of consolidation through the construction of garrison towns by building Kizilar and Mozdor as advance posts in the Caucasus. Then in 1768 geographers J. A. Guildenstaedt, S. G. Gmelin and I. Luposhin completed a lengthy mission into the Caucasus and presented Catherine with reports on all aspects of life in the region, together with a number of astonishingly accurate maps. Tsar Alexander I was to describe the Caucasus as 'warm Siberia', but the conquest of this highland sandwiched between the Black Sea and the Caspian Sea was to prove far more difficult than the annexation of the frozen lands of the east.

The Caucasus or 'kuh-e-Qaf' (The Qaf Mountain) features in ancient Persian mythology as 'the other side of the world', a remote region where the bird 'simorgh' builds its nest on top of mountain summits that reach into the sky. To the ancient Greeks, the Caucasus was the home of Prometheus who dared steal the fire from the gods. Jason's Argonauts set out to reach Colchis, present-day Georgia, in their quest for the Golden Fleece, while it was on top of Mount Ararat in the ancient kingdom of Urartu that Noah's ark landed during the Great Deluge.[15]

At the heart of the region lies a range of mountains that stretch for 1,200 kilometres between the Black Sea and the Caspian. Some summits of this range rise to above 5,600 metres. To the north lie the savage steppes of Nogaisk and Kuban, while the fertile plains of Kura and Rion are situated in the south. The fortress-like nature of the Caucasian mountain range made it an ideal hiding-place for a wide variety of peoples driven out of their original homelands because of political convulsions, famines and wars.

The high mountain range is not only a climatic barrier but has also served as a barrage to large-scale human movements. Many parts of the mountain remained virtually cut off from the outside world until the twentieth century and even today only a single major road – constructed in the nineteenth century and known as the Trans-Caucasian (Vladikavkaz) – cuts deep into the heart of the mountain.[16] Numerous ethnic and linguistic groups were able to use the region's isolation from the rest of the world for the purpose of protecting their own exclusive identity. Today the Caucasus includes ethnic and linguistic groups which often number only a few hundred and are each unique in the world.

Although inhabited from the paleolithic times, the region was never brought under a single political authority until the nineteenth century. 'The Mountain of Nations', as the Caucasus was often referred to, was always a mosaic of small, autonomous states. As early as the seventh century BC some of these states, notably Colchis, Iberia and Albania, were in commercial and cultural contact with the Greeks. Later, the Caucasus experienced the passage of countless invaders. From the north came the Scythians, the Sarmatians, the Huns, the Avars and the Khazars; from the south the Achaemenids, the Arsacids, the Sassanians and the Romans sent in expeditionary forces that conquered parts of the region. Later still came the Muslim armies, to be followed by the great Turkic conquerors from Halaku Khan to Teymur.

Throughout the ages, the Caucasus was divided between two spheres of influence from Europe and Asia. Two kingdoms, Georgia and Armenia, had managed to emerge as considerable regional powers between the first and the twelfth centuries of the Christian era. Armenia had converted to Christianity in the first century and Georgia had followed some two hundred years later.[17] The rise of the Seljuk power in the twelfth century, however, put a virtual end to Armenian and Georgian independence. Armenia was forced into decline and ravaged by Turkic troops on a number of occasions; Georgia was spared devastation, but could not escape fragmentation as Islam gradually conquered the mountain.

From the seventeenth century onwards the region became a scene of perpetual power struggle between the Ottoman Empire and Iran. The loosely-structured state of Daghestan (Land of the Mountain)[18] in the north-east was a tributary of Iran until its conquest by the Russians in the nineteenth century. But Iranian influence on the region was never solid and the mountain tribes frequently rose against the distant shahs.

The Ottoman Empire and Iran used the Caucasus as a source of slaves. Especially favoured were Georgian women, who were famed for their beauty; but young Armenian boys also fetched good prices in Turkish and Persian slave markets and many of them ended up as eunuchs in various harems of the sultans, the shahs and members of the Ottoman and Iranian aristocracies. In the eighteenth century the state of Mingreli alone exported more than 12,000 slaves to the Ottoman Empire and Iran each year.[19]

One objective shared by the Ottomans and the Iranians was the de-Armenisation of south-western Caucasus. Whole Armenian cities and villages were razed to the ground and their inhabitants either deported or forced to convert to Islam. In 1603, for example, Shah Abbas, the Safavid king of Iran, ordered the destruction of the city of Nakh-Javan (Nakhichevan)[20] and had its Armenian majority deported to a suburb of his capital at Isfahan. The city of Julfa, on the river Aras, suffered the same fate. The Ottomans, for their part, gradually Turkicised the region around Mount Ararat and pushed Armenians out of south-eastern Anatolia.

The chaos that reigned in Iran through much of the eighteenth century, following the decline of the Safavid power, enabled local dynasties to come into being in southern and eastern Caucasus. With two notable exceptions, Iran had effectively ceased to be regarded as the predominant power in the Caucasus. The first exception was provided by Nader Shah (1688–1747) who, having restored Iranian power from the Punjab to Mesopotamia, also, for a brief period, extended his rule to much of the Caucasus and regained control of Derbent after expelling the Russians. The second exception was the work of Agha Muhammad Khan (1742–1797), who forced the various Georgian states into paying tribute to him and also razed parts of Tiflis (Tblisi) to the ground.[21]

Between the sixteenth and nineteenth centuries, Russia's victories over Muslim states were invariably portrayed as victories of the Cross over the Crescent. They formed only part of Russia's manifest destiny as the master of the whole world. The more enthusiastic of Muscovy's empire-builders were convinced that Russia's domination of the universe would bring about the second coming of Christ.

By the dawn of the nineteenth century, however, Russia's imperialist ambitions were largely discussed in economic, political and security terms. The abolition of the patriarchate by Peter and the decline in the prestige of the Orthodox Church had helped secular sentiments to grow within the Russian state; it was no longer the state that was a servant of the church, but the other way round. One important effect of this change in church-state relations was the effective end to the mass-enforced conversion to Christianity of conquered peoples. In 1782 Catherine even went as far as to publish an edict guaranteeing freedom of religious practice for Muslims. This was almost immediately followed by the reconversion to Islam of thousands of Tatars and Bashkirs who had been forced to adopt Christianity in the preceding decades.

The distinctly secular ambitions of the Tsarist state since Peter did not, however, mean that Russia would not play the Christian card whenever this suited its interests. Not content with posing as protectors of all Slav peoples, many of whom remained under Ottoman rule for centuries, the Tsars missed no opportunity to also act as 'elder brother' for other Christians threatened by Muslim powers. The 1787–91 war against the Ottoman Empire, for example, was unashamedly presented as a move by Russia to protect Christian rights against a Muhammadan power. It was also in the name of defending Christianity that Russia offered protection to Georgia in 1762 before finally annexing it. Georgian mercenaries subsequently helped Russia to complete its conquest of Daghestan in 1796.

The Russian language lacks a distinct equivalent of the word 'people'. The word *narod* designates a religious community rather than a people in general. It was therefore always possible to extend the meaning of *narod* to include other non-Slav Christians, while non-Christians were never covered by the same word until after the Bolshevik Revolution and the emergence of the concept of a 'Soviet people'. At the end of the eighteenth century the only Christian people in the Caucasus not under Russian rule or protection were the Armenians, whose land was divided between the Ottoman Empire and Iran. Not surprisingly, pro-Russian sentiments were strong among Armenian merchants and intellectuals who dreamed of one day having a state of their own; they constantly appealed to Russia for help in the name of Christian solidarity. In time the Armenians were to become strong supporters of Russian imperial projects in the Caucasus, and they were also to pay an exceptionally high price for their collaboration with the tsar's forces.

Russia's confrontation with its Muslim neighbours never quite lost its 'holy war' trappings and was, therefore, often resisted in the name not of secular nationalism but of religion. During the eighteenth and nineteenth centuries Russia had to crush Muslim rebellions far greater than anything experienced by either France and Britain, the other two principal European colonial powers which came in to confrontation with Islam.

To the Muslims who faced Russian aggression, the empire-building ambitions of the tsars belonged to the overall European dream of conquering Islam. Fighting Russia was therefore tantamount to *jihad* or holy war and would be rewarded by an assured entry into paradise. Even the Bashkirs who joined Emelian Pugachev's rebellion in 1773 entered battle with cries of 'there is no god but Allah'.

By far the longest and bloodiest revolt against Russian rule anywhere in the vast empire in the eighteenth century took place in the mountains of Daghestan under the leadership of a Muslim mystic and warrior, Imam Mansur Ushurmah. The rebellion began in 1782 with attacks on Russian military posts. A year later Mansur's forces fought a full-scale battle with a Russian expeditionary unit on the river Sunja in northern Caucasus; that encounter ended with the annihilation of a Russian brigade and complete victory for the Muslim forces.

Mansur then launched a general call for holy war and dispatched emissaries to Circassia and even to Georgian Muslims, inviting them to join the struggle against the infidel. But only the Chechen and Ingush clans joined Mansur's holy war in any large numbers, and the struggle continued until 1791 when the Imam was finally captured in the fortress of Anapa just inside the Ottoman border. He had sought sanctuary in Ottoman territory in the hope of later recovering his strength and pursuing the war with help from Constantinople.

Mansur's prestige among the Chechen was so high that his Russian captors did not dare put him to death as demanded by the military commanders. He was dispatched to the Schlüsselburg fort, where he remained a prisoner until his death two years later. Having crushed the rebellion, the Russian occupation force proceeded to extinguish all possible centres of future revolt. Scores of Chechen *auls* (settlements) in the mountains were totally destroyed and their inhabitants deported. Hundreds were shot, while many more were taken prisoner and dispatched to the four corners of the empire. A number of military roads leading to the heart of the mountains were hastily built, and new garrisons were established at strategic locations.

Military operations against the remnants of Mansur's forces were accompanied by a concerted propaganda campaign against the rebellious Imam. He was described as an Ottoman secret agent sent in to cause trouble among the obedient Chechen.[22] Other accounts even claimed that Mansur was a renegade Italian monk, and that he had devised a religion all his own. He was in turn described either as a Kirghiz or a Bokharan and thus as an outsider in the Caucasian mountains.

The Imam, however, was almost certainly a Chechen and a native of the mountains. He might have spent some time in Bokhara attending an Islamic seminary, but alternatively, could have been a pupil of the Naqshbandi shaikhs who often came to the mountain to teach, to organise the adepts of their *tariqat* and to organise pilgrimages to Mecca. The Naqshbandis had already established their reputation as a fraternity of mystics and holy warriors in the seventeenth and eighteenth centuries by fighting a series of wars against the Buddhist Tatars (Kalmuks) in Kazakhstan. Their holy war against Russia was to dominate the history of the Caucasus during the nineteenth century.[23]

4

A Mountain of Blood

During the nineteenth century Russia was the world's fastest-growing imperial state, with an average expansion of 140 square kilometres per day. In less than a hundred years it had expanded its territory by nearly five million square kilometres, or the equivalent of more than half the total area of the United States. Much of this colonial expansion was achieved at the expense of weak or moribund Islamic states.

The march of the tsars to the heart of Asia and beyond had already captured the imagination of many Russians in the eighteenth century, but it was the conquest of the Caucasus which introduced a true whiff of romanticism to what was a cynical exercise in the superiority of western military organisation and weaponry. Russian poets looked to the Caucasus as a fabulous land of many adventures. Pushkin himself accompanied Count Ermolov, one of the earlier conquerors of the Caucasus, on some of his adventures; the poet, having apparently forgotten that his own maternal grandmother, the Senegalese slave Ibrahim, had been a Muslim, showed absolutely no sign of compassion towards the victims of Tsarist expansionism. He was Russia's national poet and the extension of the frontiers of the empire was a national cause.

Another great Russian poet, Lermontov, went even further and invited the Circassians to be proud of becoming 'slaves of the ruler of the Universe', meaning the Russian tsar.[1] Tolstoy, a prophet of non-violence in his later years, had fought in the Caucasus and used the region as a background for some of his stories. At no point did he question Russia's right to take 'civilisation' to that remote corner of the world. The poet and playwright Griboidev, not content only to write about the imperial adventure, decided to take part in it first as a secretary to Paskievich – nicknamed 'the butcher of the Caucasus' – and later as Minister Plenipotentiary to Tehran.[2]

Russia's southward expansion towards Iran was resumed after the defeat of the Chechen revolt under Imam Mansur Ushurmah in 1791. The principality of Shiravan, covering the entire western coast of the Caspian Sea between Gilan and Daghestan, proved a fairly easy target for Russian expansion. Still loosely linked with the shah in Tehran, it lacked a distinct leadership structure capable of resisting foreign domination.

The population of Shiravan was predominantly shi'ite Muslim and of Iranic stock, but the language it spoke was a form of Turkic. The Turkicisation of the region had started in the thirteenth century, but had become truly deep-rooted under Shah Ismail (1501–1524) when shi'ism was declared the state religion in Iran. The imposition of shi'ism by Ismail forced many Iranian sunni tribes to emigrate en masse to the Ottoman Empire, while a similar movement in the opposite direction brought Turkic-speaking shi'ite clans of eastern Anatolia into Shiravan and Azarbaijan. This enforced exchange of population between the two rival Muslim states strengthened the shi'ite base of the Safavids in Iran but also accentuated the process of Turkicisation in Azarbaijan and Shiravan.

By the start of the nineteenth century, however, shi'ism was no longer a bond sufficiently strong on its own to ensure Shiravan's attachment to Iran. The region's shi'ite clergy remained loyal to Iran, which it considered to be the only truly Islamic state in the world, but at no point was the clergy able to create a political base strong enough to stop the Russian advance.

In 1806 Russian troops captured Baku[3] after largely symbolic encounters with the defending forces. The conquest of Baku led to the first Russo-Iranian war in 1809. The Iranians, commanded by the Crown Prince Abbas Mirza, put up a brave fight on a number of occasions and even briefly regained control of Baku after a battle in which the Russian general Sissisanov was killed. Outnumbered and outgunned by the Russians, the Iranians however had little chance of restoring their suzerainty over the Caucasus. The Treaty of Golestan, named after a village in Qara-bagh[4] where it was signed by Iranian and Russian representatives through British mediation, recognised the tsar's sovereignty over Georgia, Derbent, Baku, Shiravan, Qara-bagh, Ganjeh and Sheki. Under the same treaty, Iran also renounced its right to maintain a navy in the Caspian Sea.

The growing Russian menace did not persuade the Ottoman Empire and Iran to bury their centuries-old feud and establish a common front to resist the enemy from the north. Religious hatred between sunni and shi'ite Muslims was so strong that both sides almost preferred defeat at the hands of the Russians to an alliance with each other. The two

Muslim neighbours sapped each other's military strength by fighting an exceptionally bloody war over the control of Armenia and parts of Mesopotamia.

The second Russo-Iranian war was provoked by the shi'ite mullahs of Baku, Qom and Najaf (in Mesopotamia) who declared *jihad* on Russia after accusing the Tsarist authorities of mistreating Muslims and forcing them to convert to Christianity. This time, too, the Iranians were roundly defeated after a promising start which saw the shah's forces capture several cities held by the Russians. By 1827, however, the Russians had captured the cities of Yerevan and Nakhichevan and, crossing the river Aras, had entered Azarbaijan. They pushed on to Khoi and later also seized Tabriz, the capital of Azarbaijan and the official residence of the Crown Prince. Once again with British mediation, a humiliating treaty was imposed on Iran, under which Iran ceded to Russia all territories to the north of Aras and agreed to pay heavy war reparations. The Russians also gained control of part of the Talesh mountains where the population was predominantly sunni Muslims. A curious item in the treaty of Turcoman-chai, named after the Azarbaijani village where it was signed, obliged Iran to hand over to Russia all the volumes in the Royal Library at Ardebil. The library, created in the fourteenth century, had been expanded under the Safavids and in 1828, when it was emptied, contained thousands of volumes including hundreds of precious manuscripts which today adorn many Soviet museums. After Turcoman-chai, Iran was not only unable to regain its lost territories but was gradually turned into a semi-colonial state in which Russia and Great Britain exercised hegemonistic powers. The Russians secured the right of veto on the choice of a crown prince by a reigning Iranian monarch, and in 1854 they forced the shah to recognise total Russian control over the Caspian Sea despite the fact that the entire southern coast of the inland sea belonged to Iran.

The Russians had tried their hand at gunboat diplomacy on a number of occasions since the reign of Peter the Great; at least three naval expeditions sent to various Iranian ports on the Caspian in the eighteenth century had ended in defeat and disaster for them. By the end of the nineteenth century, however, the Caspian had become a Russian lake. Russian companies controlled the region's trade and even determined Iranian fishing quotas. A few years later, the Caspian region became the chief source of oil supplies for the Tsarist empire.

With Iran eliminated as a contender for power in the Caucasus, the Russians turned their attention to the Ottoman Empire. Barely waiting for the ink to be dried on the Turcoman-chai treaty, they attacked Ottoman positions in 1828. The war lasted nearly a year and was mostly fought in the Balkans, but it was in the Caucasus that the Russians achieved their victories; they captured the cities of Kars and Erzerum and penetrated deep into eastern Anatolia. The hostilities ended with the Treaty of Edirne (Adrianapole) in which the 'Sublime Port' virtually abandoned all claims of sovereignty over Circassia.

As far as the Circassians were concerned, this was a most strange outcome. They had not been involved in a war which had not even taken place on their territory, yet suddenly they found themselves put under the sovereignty of an 'infidel' ruler. Large numbers of Circassians simply refused to live under non-Islamic rule and organised mass emigration to the Ottoman Empire. Within the following four decades an estimated sixty per cent of the entire population either left voluntarily or were deported by Russians. Those who remained decided to fight, and they made sure that Russian sovereignty over Circassia remained largely nominal until the very end of the Tsarist empire. The Russians had to conquer their new possession virtually inch by inch.

In 1835 General Veliaminov was charged with the task of establishing order in the Circassian territory, and opened his campaign with a series of atrocities that included the beheading of many local leaders in conquered villages. The Russians tried their customary tactic of consolidating their conquests by building a string of fortresses deep inside conquered territory, and had between 12,000 and 30,000 troops – including many Georgian and Armenian mercenaries – committed to the region. But the forts built by the conquerors quickly became isolated islands in the middle of a hostile sea.

Thanks to Circassia's long-established trade links all along the Black Sea, the rebels were able to receive arms, ammunition and other supplies from the Ottoman Empire for a very long time. The Russian navy constantly proved unable to interfere effectively with these vital links.

In 1841, an expeditionary force of 600 Russians and 2,000 Georgian mercenaries was soundly defeated near Sochi by a Circassian army led by Haji Barzaq Dukmah Aqa, a Circassian prince then aged over seventy. That battle ended Russian attempts at conquering Circassia through the force of arms for over a decade.

News of Circassia's dogged resistance against Russian rule quickly spread to St Petersburg, Moscow and other major cities of the empire. To many Russians the Circassians appeared as savage warriors who were determined to refuse the beneficial effects of civilisation. One Russian writer went even further:

> The Circassians are like ... American Indians – as untamable and uncivilized ... and owing to their natural energy of character, extermination only would keep them quiet or ... if they came under Russian rule, the only safe policy would be to employ their wild and warlike tastes against others.[5]

The Circassians were not the only Muslim people to fight the Russian domination of the Caucasus. Daghestan, in north-eastern Caucasus, was also the scene of a major revolt against the Tsar which had begun in 1824, more than five years before the Circassian uprising. Unlike Circassia, where the revolt was led by traditional chieftains, the Daghestanis united behind their religious leaders who, rising to the occasion, combined their duties as spiritual leaders with the tasks incumbent on military commanders.

A year after the revolt had begun more or less spontaneously, the Naqshbandi order seized its leadership with a call for *jihad*. The call came from Ghazi Muhammad Yuqur-Yaraq (Heavy Shield) who used the tiny khanate of Kurin as his base; but it was under one of his successors, Imam Shamil, that the revolt of Daghestan developed into a truly major war which sapped the energies of the Tsarist empire for more than a generation.

The Naqshbandis had appeared on the Caucasian scene in the early nineteenth century by establishing a number of bases in Shiravan. They penetrated into Daghestan from 1820 onwards and soon found strong support from the various peoples of the mountains, specially the warlike Chechen.

The Russian entry into Daghestan and Chechen country came at a time when Islam had gained fresh vigour and vitality thanks to the activities of the Naqshbandis. Thus the strong ideological base needed for any national resistance movement was already in place. The region was an ideal setting for guerrilla warfare against a foreign invader since the steep mountains of Daghestan, often inaccessible except through narrow passes that could be easily isolated, offered ideal hiding-places for any would-be rebels. The dense beech forests of Chechnia offered equally attractive safe havens to guerrilleros. The revolt of Shaikh Mansur Ushurmah had already demonstrated Chechnia's propensity to revolt.

The Muslim uprising needed a charismatic leader capable of mobilising the broadest sections of the population regardless of class distinctions. Such a leader was soon found in the person of Shamil. Born in the village of Ghimri in north-eastern Daghestan towards the end of the eighteenth century, Shamil was initiated into the Naqshbandi order by Ghazi Muhammad probably in the 1820s.

Shamil established his position as the leader of the national resistance in 1831, when his forces attacked the Russian stronghold of Vnezapnaya (Fort Surprise) and routed its garrison. Unable to absorb the shock of this setback, the tsar ordered an immediate punishment of the rebels. Within a few months a Russian force of ten thousand soldiers, backed by Georgian mercenaries and equipped with heavy guns, besieged Shamil's stronghold at Ghimri. The 500-man garrison of the village resisted the Russian attack for more than a week. In the end, however, only two Muslim warriors managed to escape from the death-trap that Ghimri had become. One of the two was Shamil himself. All the other holy warriors were killed in battle or subsequently shot by the Russians.

The disaster at Ghimri did not affect Shamil's position adversely; on the contrary, his movement now had an abundant number of martyrs to avenge. In 1834 Shamil declared himself Imam and commander of the faithful and appointed scores of *nayebs* (deputies) to represent him in various parts of Daghestan and Chechnia. He established a government of his own, complete with Islamic courts and a system of tax collection based on *zakat*. His imamate also sought to establish diplomatic relations with other nations, notably the Ottoman Empire, Iran, Egypt and Great Britain.

In 1837 a Russian force of five thousand seasoned troops launched a campaign aimed at cleaning up the mountains and the forests of Chechnia, but everywhere they suffered defeat. The Muslim holy warriors used hit-and-run tactics which drove the Russian commanders, always anxious for a classical battle, to desperation. The following year Shamil transferred his headquarters to Akhulgo, which was attacked and besieged by the Russians in 1839. The imam's stronghold was captured after a week of fighting, but Shamil himself managed to escape once again; this time he chose the Chechen forests as a hiding-place and continued to act as if he was still the leader of an independent state at war with a foreign invader.

The Russians spent the year 1840 on the construction of three new forts in the mountain, not realising that in a guerrilla war such strongholds could easily be ignored by the guerrilleros. By 1841 the newly-completed forts had become veritable death-traps for them. Two years later the Russians launched a fresh attack against Shamil's positions in the forest and the mountains, but once again the soldiers of Allah triumphed. The Russians lost some thirty heavy cannon, which were instantly used by Shamil as the nucleus of an artillery he had long dreamed of. By the end of the year the imam's forces had gained control of part of the Caspian coast as well.

In 1845 the Russians returned with an even larger force as part of an expedition led by the Count Mikhail Vorontsov, a relative of the tsar. This time the invaders suffered an even bigger disaster: the count's army was ambushed and dispersed with the loss of four thousand men who were killed, wounded or taken prisoner.

However, there was no question that the tsar would simply renounce his plans to offer the Caucasus a taste of civilisation. An empire that had defeated Napoleon and sent its Cossacks marching in the heart of Paris could not be expected to flee in the face of the challenge posed by a small army of semi-savage rebels. Tolstoy had seen Napoleon as an agent of fate whose task solely consisted of kicking Russia out of its deep sleep. Victorious Russia was now fully awake and recognised no rival even in Europe. Shamil had to be put down no matter what the cost.

In 1847 the Russians, bringing in a force of ten battalions backed by heavy artillery, tried to capture Shamil's stronghold at Gharghebil near the Sular river. But this time, too, Shamil emerged victorious; he fought his way through Russian lines and went deep into Chechnia, where he chose the strategic village of Veden as his new headquarters. Veden had the advantage of being close to Dargo and the border with Daghestan.

The Russians were already planning fresh expeditions against Shamil when they became involved in the Crimean War (1853–6). For some three years Shamil was left virtually free to run his imamate the way he wished, but the Crimean War underlined the dangers inherent in Russia's weak position in Daghestan. The region could have been used as part of a second front against Russia and, indeed, Shamil had written urgent letters to Constantinople and Cairo demanding help to do precisely that. His dream of creating a pan-Islamic alliance aimed at driving Russia out of the Caucasus and later pushing into the Volga region to 'liberate' Astrakhan and Kazan never appealed to either the Sublime Port or the pashas of Egypt. But the potential for staging a general revolt of the Muslims against Russia, with Daghestan as its initial base, continued to haunt the high command in St Petersburg.

In 1853 Prince Alexander Baryatinski was appointed Viceroy of the Caucasus and Commander-in-Chief of Russian armies in the south. High on the list of orders he received from the tsar was the ending of the rebellion led by Shamil. Baryatinski had no desire to repeat the experience of his predecessors. Knowing that an early victory was impossible and that patience was the name of the game, he launched a major programme of building roads deep into the mountains and the forest, nibbling slowly at the area under Shamil's control. Within a few years Shamil was forced into a shrinking patch of territory around the river Arghun, where he established a stronghold at Veden.

By the time it was besieged by the Russians in February 1859, Veden had achieved an almost legendary status in the minds of the Daghestanis and the Chechen. It was seen as the capital of the imamate, the shining heart of Islam and a place where angels descended from the heavens to communicate with Shamil. No one could dream of Veden falling into the hands of the *kafir* (heathen) Russians ... and yet Veden did eventually fall. On 1 April 1859 a force of forty thousand Russian troops supported by some fifty of the heaviest guns available anywhere in the world at that time launched their final assault on Veden and captured its charred corpse. Once again, however, Shamil and his closest aides slipped through the Russian net. Although shot and wounded, Shamil was able to cross the enemy lines at night after cutting down a number of Russian soldiers.

After a few weeks in hiding, Shamil surfaced again in the high mountain village of Gunib in his native Daghestan. Baryatinski, for his part, was not prepared to allow the imam enough time in which to recuperate and raise a new army of fanatical warriors. Therefore Gunib was quickly isolated and subjected to almost continuous bombardment by heavy guns. For years Shamil had promised his supporters that he would soon receive reinforcements from the Ottoman Empire and Egypt as well as Arabia and Yemen. Now, under siege in Gunib with no access to the sea, he could no longer rely on such promises to keep morale high.

Early in August Shamil agreed to open negotiations with Baryatinski and a truce was concluded under which the count guaranteed the safety of Shamil and his companions. There were to be no acts of revenge against the population, and Muslims were to be allowed to practise their religion in the way they wished. On 21 August 1859 Shamil, riding his grey horse, emerged in front of the Russian lines. He was received with full military honours by Baryatinski and handed over his sword to the count.

Shamil's surrender did not mean the end of Russia's troubles in the Caucasus. The Naqshbandi-led revolt had been a heavy burden on Russia's treasury and a drain on its military power, but it was only one of a number of revolts. The Circassians continued to fight on until 1865, while other uprisings shook the mountain as well as the forest country well into the 1880s. In fact, it was only after 1887 that the Viceroy of the Caucasus could inform the tsar that the region was quiet and living in peace.

The taming of the Caucasus was an essential step towards consolidating Russia's new position as a world power. The few western European and American travellers who visited the Caucasus during the revolts of Circassia and Daghestan came back with dramatic reports of Russian cruelty towards the local population; in many instances the Russians employed scorched-earth tactics and destroyed villages and even towns which they could not hope to hold. Observers also found in Russia's savage determination to impose its rule on that rebellious land a foretaste of what the empire of the tsars might do to future conquests in Europe and elsewhere.[6]

During the nineteenth century hundreds of thousands of people fled their homes in the Caucasus simply because they found life under the Tsarist yoke unbearable. Most of them went to the Ottoman Empire but many, especially from Shiravan, also ended up in Iran where they became known as the *muhajer* (immigrants). Some – especially among the Chechen and their kindred folks, the Ingush – committed suicide rather than submit to Russian domination. Accounts abound of men murdering their own wives and children to prevent them from being captured by Russian troops. The presence of Georgian and Armenian mercenaries alongside Russian forces only aggravated matters so far as the Muslims were concerned. Georgians and Armenians proved all too keen to avenge centuries of humiliation at the hands of Muslim Iranian and Ottoman rulers.

However, not everyone wanted to or could leave. The sentiment of those who stayed, confident that the Russians would one day depart, was put by Haji Ali, a rebel leader bidding farewell to a British supporter:

> Happily for you, you have a country to go to where you may live in peace and where there is no dread of Muscovy. We, alas, have no other home to fly to; nor, if we had, would we leave that of our forefathers, in which we were born, which Allah has given us, and for which it is our duty to die.... Tyranny can never long prevail, or freedom be forever suppressed in the Caucasus; the tide of conquest may, for a while, submerge its valleys, but the time will come when, in spite of all the forts that Russia can erect there, it must recede even from them.[7]

Unrest in the northern Caucasus did not end with Shamil's surrender. Many of the supporters of the fallen imam soon joined a new rebel movement led by another religious leader: Kunta Haji Kishiev, a *murshid* (guide) in the Qaderi order of sufis, who had spent some time travelling in various Muslim countries including Egypt, Arabia and Turkey. The Qaderis had established their reputation as a militant order by converting the warlike Ingush tribes of the mountains to Islam between 1850 and 1865.

Kunta Haji, a Kalmyk by birth, had spent his earlier years as a shepherd but had soon distinguished himself through his piety and aptitude in mastering difficult theological concepts. He was also a good fighter and a natural leader of men. These qualities helped him to organise a mass uprising against Russian rule in 1862. Many of his closest aides were former companions of Shamil who came out of hiding to join the new call for holy war.

This time, however, the Russians were much better prepared to deal with any revolt and their forces, strongly entrenched in the mountains, succeeded in quelling the rebellion within eighteen months. Kunta and most of his companions were deported to Kazakhstan. This led to mass demonstrations throughout the Chechen and Ingush country, and Russian troops were forced to fire on the crowds on a number of occasions. At such an incident in the village of Shali on 18 January 1864, a unit of the Russian army fired on some 4,000 demonstrators, killing more than 200 and wounding a further 1,000. The 'massacre of Shali', as the incident is known, was to become part of the Chechen mythology of heroic struggle against the 'infidel'.

A year after the Shali incident more than five thousand Chechen families gathered what they could of their belongings and emigrated to the Ottoman Empire. The Russians made no move to stop them; the fewer the Chechens in the Caucasus, the safer the Tsarist domination of the region. In 1867 news of Kunta Haji's death in a Russian prison provoked further unrest; he was elevated to the status of a saint who had fought and then died under torture in the service of Allah.

In 1877 the Qaderi and Naqshbandi orders in northern Caucasus united their forces for yet another desperate attempt at forcing the Russians out of the mountains. This time the combined force of the fighting *murids* was led by the Naqshbandi shaikh Muhammad Ibn Adbul-Rahman Shuhratli and lasted only a few months. More than six thousand *murids* were deported to Siberia, never to return; those of them who escaped the Russian net either went underground or emigrated to the Ottoman Empire and Bokhara, although a few continued to fight by forming bands of *abreqs* (highwaymen) who attacked and robbed Russian convoys and distributed the proceedings among the poor. The *abreqs* were not completely eliminated until the end of the tsarist empire in 1917.

The return of calm to the Caucasus released Russia's energies for fresh advances in Central Asia. Russian conquests there were resumed in 1865 when a force commanded by General Chernayev, operating out of the fortress town of Verny,[8] attacked the holy city of Turkestan[9] before capturing the town of Chimkent – both of which belonged to the khanate of Kokand. A few months later another Kokand city, Tashkent, was captured. The way was open for an attack on the emirate of Bokhara, the principal Muslim power in Central Asia at the time.

The emirate of Bokhara dominated the valley of the river Zar-Afshahn (Gold Sprinkler) in the territory now divided between the Soviet republics of Uzbekistan and Tajikestan. It was founded by Muhammad Rahim, a Mangitid tribal chief who defeated the Astra-Khanids in 1753 and established his own dynasty. One of Rahim's successors, Haydar, felt himself to be strong enough to call himself 'Emir' in 1800, and by 1826 had repudiated all of Bokhara's tributary accords with the Shah of Iran.

The Russians attacked Bokhara in 1868 and quickly captured Samarkand, the second most important city in the emirate. In May of that year they inflicted a heavy defeat on the emir's army at the battle of the river Zara-Bulaq. In June of the same year the emir signed a treaty which turned Bokhara into a Russian protectorate.

The next Muslim state to be attacked was the Khanate of Khiva, which covered part of the territory of the old kingdom of Kharazm (Khorezm) in lower Amu-Darya. Under the Iltuzer ruling family the khanate had become a veritable centre of the slave trade; every year thousands of Russians, Bokharans and Persians were captured by special raiding parties and sold to slave merchants from as far away as China and Arabia. The Russian troops entered Khiva in August 1873 and forced the khan to sign a treaty that put him under the protection of the tsar.

Two years later the Russians resumed their operations against Kokand. This khanate, which covered the Ferghana Valley and parts of the present-day Soviet republic of Kirghizestan, had been founded by Alim Khan of the Min dynasty in 1798. A veritable armed camp rather than an ordinary state, the khanate of Kokand was considered by the Russians to be their most dangerous enemy in the region. Thus when Russian troops entered its capital there was no question of any negotiations. Kokand was simply declared 'abolished' as a state and incorporated into the Russian General Government of Turkestan in February 1876.

These new conquests in Central Asia brought four million more Muslims under Russian rule, but St Petersburg had no intention of ordering a halt. The next target for Russian aggression was provided by the Turcoman tribes who lived in a vast region between the Caspian Sea and the desert of Karakoum. A first operation against the Yammut confederation of tribes was launched in 1873 and led to some of the bitterest fighting ever seen in the region. Once again Russian heavy artillery was greatly superior against largely nomadic tribes who fought with swords and bows and arrows or, failing that, with their bare hands.

The Turcoman town of Qizil-Arvat (Golden Oasis) was captured in 1877 and some of its inhabitants massacred. Many Turcoman fighters, however, managed to escape and reached the Iranian frontier. In 1879 the Russians arrived at the Turcoman stronghold of Geok-Tappeh near the river Atrak on the present-day frontier with Iran. The settlement was defended by the Takkesh tribes, who routed the invading force commanded by General Sokobelev. The battle of Geok-Tappeh was to become an important event in Turcoman national history and a symbol of Muslim resistance to colonialism. Nevertheless, the Turcomans could not have expected to hold on for ever against a far superior force. Iran and Afghanistan, two Muslim states directly bordering on Turcoman territory, were neither able nor willing to help in any way. Geok-Tappeh was finally captured and destroyed.

In 1884 it was the turn of the oasis city of Marv (Mari) to fall to the Russians, and by the end of the century Russia had reached the borders of both Iran and Afghanistan. Many of the Turcomans who did not wish to live under Russian rule crossed the river Atrak and entered Iran, where they settled at Sarakhs and Bojnurd. Further east, thousands of Kirghiz and Tajik families crossed into Afghanistan while others sought sanctuary in Chinese Turkestan which was also inhabited by Muslims.

The relative ease with which the Russians conquered Central Asia could be explained by a number of factors. To begin with the region, mostly flat, does not offer much opportunity for guerrilla warfare on the same lines as fought in the Caucasus. Russian gunpowder superiority made nonsense of tribal resistance in the long run. Further, the various Muslim states of the region had been fatally weakened as a result of decades of wars amongst themselves. The local rulers, never popular among their subjects, were unable to mobilise the same kind of fierce resistance against the invader that the *murshids* of the Caucasus brought about in the 1850s and 1860s. The fight against the Russians was never presented as a struggle by Islam against the 'infidel' empire. Emirs and khans who lived lives of idle luxury and were notorious for their love of wine and disdain for Muslim values were hardly credible when they spoke of *jihad*.

Resistance against the invader could not be organised with reference to European-style nationalism either, since Central Asia was inhabited by a wide variety of ethnic and linguistic groups whose one common bond was their adherence to Islam. The ruling elites in Bokhara and the khanates had established such a record of corruption and cruelty that, when the time came, they could not pose as genuine leaders of their peoples. The Russian invasion was preceded by more than half a century of economic decline and social unrest throughout the region. At times the people rose in major revolts which led to virtually endless armed clashes with the forces of the state. In 1825, for example, a local incident involving the emir of Bokhara's tax-collectors and a group of shepherds led to a tribal revolt by the Qypchaq Uzbeks, who continued to fight until 1862. In 1826 it was the turn of Samarkand's artisans and merchants to stage riots against the emir, while the following year was marked by clashes between peasants and the army of Khiva. In both incidents hundreds of people were killed or subsequently hanged in public. Between 1856 and 1869, the khanate of Kokand was shaken by tribal uprisings in the Kazakh territory under its control.

The economic decline, social unrest and political instability of Central Asia was in sharp contrast with Russia's growing stature as a major world power. Between 1800 and 1890 when the conquest of Central Asia was virtually complete, the number of industrial enterprises in the tsar's empire rose from under 2,000 to more than 25,000. This rapid industrialisation – which turned Russia into the world's fourth major economic power in the world by 1905 – led to an equally dramatic increase in demand for raw materials, while Russian exporters also began to look for new markets.

The treaty of Paris (1856), concluded after the Crimean War, practically shut Russia out of the Balkans and the Mediterranean and thus indirectly contributed to Tsarist expansion in the east. Many Russians had the feeling that they had been excluded from Europe for a long time to come. This was how they saw the situation in the wake of the Crimean War:

> Russia's future is not in Europe; it is towards Asia that she should direct her attention. In the years to come industrial development, especially manufacturing, will necessitate (access) to important sources of raw material. While sources of western supplies will diminish or become difficult to attain as a result of antagonism among nations, Russia must turn towards Asia and develop her exchanges with (that continent).[10]

It did not take long for that view to be borne out by developments far from Russian frontiers. The American Civil War (1861–65) underlined the unreliability of sources of raw material not controlled directly by the tsarist state itself. In 1862 Central Asia supplied more than forty per cent of the raw cotton needed by Russian mills, while the rest came from the United States and Egypt. During the next two decades, however, Russia had all but stopped buying foreign cotton thanks to its control of Central Asia.

Russia's eastward march, often compared with the American advance towards the Pacific, also provided the empire with new markets. By 1854 Bokhara and the khanates purchased no less than twenty-seven per cent of all of the manufactured goods that Russia exported. The fortress city of Orenburg, built by Peter the Great as an outpost against Kazakh marauders, was by 1865 established as an important entrepôt for trade with Asia.

Some historians have tried to show the Russian conquest of Turkestan as an almost incidental and totally unplanned result of developments in the Tsarist empire. True, the forces of General Kauffmann achieved remarkably speedy victories in Central Asia, but their success had been made possible as a result of more than a century of patient Russian preparation for the final assault. Incursions into Central Asia had followed shortly after the annexation of Astrakhan in the sixteenth century, but it was from the middle of the eighteenth century onwards that Russia began making its way towards the heart of Asia.

In 1834 a Russian fortress was constructed on the north-east coast of the Caspian Sea as an observation post for Central Asia.[11] Five years

later an expedition led by General Perovsky used the fortress as a base
for launching an attack on Khiva. The force, consisting of 5,000 Russian
troops and 2,000 Kazakh auxiliaries and supported by a train of more
than 10,000 camels, was decimated by the armies of the khan. Only a
few hundred Russians survived and succeeded in returning to the fort.

In 1850 the Russian Geographical Society dispatched a special mission
to Central Asia under P. I. Nebolsin; it returned with an abundance of
maps which were later used by Russian invading forces. Nebolsin also
recommended the linking of the Aral Sea and the river Amu-Darya with
the Caspian, as a means of creating a waterway linking the Volga region
to the borders of Afghanistan. One direct result of the mission was the
establishment of several import-export and transport companies which
specialised in trade with Central Asia. The Russian Royal Family held
important parts of some of these companies.

Finally, Kazakhstan and Central Asia had for long been considered
by Russian empire-builders as a region capable of absorbing Russia's
own excess population. The settlement of thousands of Russian muzhiks
and ex-serfs in Kazakhstan and Central Asia helped to relieve pressure
on the overpopulated rural zones of western Volga and the Ukraine. In
some cases peasants were transported to Kazakhstan and Central Asia
as part of an attempt to prevent rural revolts in the European areas of
the empire. The newly-conquered territories were also used as a place
of enforced exile for political opponents, as well as common criminals.
Kazakhstan and Turkestan had become colonies of an empire without
being formally recognised as such.

5

The Imperial Prison

Described as 'The Prison of the Peoples'[1] by its opponents, on the eve of the First World War the Empire of the Tsars was a multi-ethnic state in which Russians formed barely 40 per cent of the population. At that time Muslims, who numbered more than 16 million, were the largest religious minority.

United by their faith in the message of Muhammad, Russia's Muslims were nevertheless divided into many different ethnic groups.[2] Of these, the single largest consisted of the Kirghiz-Kazakh peoples who numbered some four million.[3] Their distinct Mongolid features and many of their tribal customs underlined their 'Altaic' origins. The next major ethnic group among Russia's Muslims consisted of the various branches of the Tatar people. The Tatars spoke an 'Altaic' or Turkic language which shared common roots with the languages spoken by the Kirghiz-Kazakhs. Nevertheless, the Tatars could not be described as a purely Mongolid people; they had developed into a distinct racial type as a result of centuries of intermingling between European and Mongol peoples. Numbering just under four million in 1913, the Tatars were present throughout the empire. By far the most dynamic and best-educated of all of Russia's Muslims, they were destined for a position of leadership among all the Muhammadans of the empire. From their heartland in the Volga they had spread into Central Asia and the Caucasus, where they acted as messengers of modernisation amongst peoples still groping in the darkness of the Middle Ages.

The first of the Muslim peoples to fall under Russian domination, the Tatars were the only one to be declared full subjects of the tsar and subjected to a programme of russification from the sixteenth century onwards. Ivan the Terrible and many of his successors had done all they could to destroy the Tatar identity and, above all, convert the Tatars to Orthodox Christianity. But the Tatars continued to defend their language and culture and, every time their mosques were razed to the ground or burned down, returned to build new places of Muslim worship. Even the seventeen-year-long campaign of the Orthodox Archbishop of Kazan in the eighteenth century to remove all traces of Islam from the Tatar city eventually failed, despite the fact that not a single mosque was left standing.[4]

Kazan continued to attract prominent Muslim scholars from all over the world and, in the last decades of the nineteenth century, emerged as one of the most buoyant centres of Islamic revival worldwide. The presence of a strong and experienced merchant class, on the other hand, helped enhance the economic role of the Tatars in the booming trade between Russia and Asia. Almost everywhere the Tatars acted as intermediaries or partners for Russian industrialists and Central Asian landlords. Alone among the Russian Muslims the Tatars had developed a native middle-class fully capable of participating in economic progress and social change. It was only a matter of time before the Tatar intelligentsia, heavily influenced by its Russian counterpart, began to flirt with nationalistic and, later, socialist ideas. Some Tatar intellectuals began to think of the power Russia's Muslims might wield if and when they were united. The question of unity was to dominate Islamic political debate throughout the nineteenth century and beyond. The advantages were apparent to all; what caused division was the means needed to achieve the desired goal.

More than three centuries of living with Russians had not left the Tatars totally unaffected. A good part of the early Tatar aristocracy had converted to Christianity and risen to positions of prominence in all walks of life; such distinguished 'Russian' families as Turgenev, Yussupov and Bassanov were of Tatar origin. The poor Tatars, however, had reconverted to Islam at the first opportunity, but they too had not been able to completely escape Russian influence. Kazan was a bilingual city and many Tatar families did not hesitate to send their children to Russian schools and universities. The Tatars came into contact with the west through Russia and, in turn, became the pioneers of various scenarios for westernisation in the Muslim world.

The third largest ethnic group among Russia's Muslims consisted of the various Uzbek or Sart clans and urban settlers who had emerged as a distinct people as a result of more than four centuries of interbreeding of Iranic and Turkic stocks. Mostly farmers, the Uzbeks also had an educated class but – unlike the Tatars who had succeeded in opening windows towards the west – the Uzbek intelligentsia remained cloistered in the Islamic madrassehs and maktabs almost to the end of the empire. Most Uzbeks spoke a Turkic language, while Persian remained the language of literature.

The most numerous Muslim people after the Uzbeks were the Shiravanis, referred to as 'Caucasus Tatars' until the 1870s. Predominantly shi'ites, the Shiravanis were an Iranic people who over the centuries had adopted a Turkic language and a number of Tatar customs. Their affective links with Iran remained strong despite systematic efforts by the Tsarist government to de-Persianise the region as thoroughly as possible. It was to that end that the use of Persian as the language of all courts of law was formally banned throughout Shiravan after 1873; a year later all the Persian-language schools in the region were closed and the mullahs ordered to give their sermons either in the local Turkic language or in Russian. From the 1880s onwards a ban was imposed on Iranian mullahs wishing to visit Shiravan, while Shiravani *talabehs* (theological students) were no longer allowed to study in Iran.

The Shiravanis numbered around 1.2 million in 1913 and over the years were weaned away from Iran but – much to the disappointment of the Russian authorities in the Caucasus – did not transfer their sentimental loyalty to the tsar. Instead they began to look to the Ottoman Empire as a source of inspiration and further emphasised their Turkic identity. In time the region began to be called Azarbaijan, after the province of the same name in Iran. The Shiravanis and the Azarbaijanis were of almost the same ethnic and historical background; they were all shi'ites and spoke three dialects of the same Turkic language. Disappointed in an Iran which was seemingly doomed to perpetual decline under corrupt and incompetent shahs, and determined not to allow themselves to be russified, the people of Shiravan – who now described themselves as Azeris – were anxious to forge a distinct identity of their own.

The development of the oilfields of Baku which were, for a time in the early part of the last century, the largest in the world, turned the centre of Shiravan into a cosmopolitan industrial city where a Muslim industrial working class came into being alongside the deeply conservative bazaaris and mullahs. Baku, together with Kazan, was one of only two Muslim cities in Russia where the Social Democrats had a constituency.

Other ethnic groups completed the galaxy of Muslim peoples in Russia. The Bashkir, Finnish tribes who had been Turkicised after conversion to Islam, numbered over a million. They were in the process of being fully absorbed into the larger Tatar community with which they shared a language as well as many customs and traditions.

The Turcomans, arguably the least developed of all Muslims under Russian rule, numbered around 300,000 in 1913. They continued to live a largely pastoral life and, ignoring international frontiers, moved back and forth between Central Asia and Iran. With under half per cent of the adult population able to attend school, the vast majority of Turcomans were illiterate. For intellectual leadership, the Turcomans had to look to neighbouring Uzbeks and, beyond them, to the Tatars. A deeply devout people, the Turcomans tried to keep their contacts with the 'infidel' Russians to a strict minimum.

The Tajiks, forming a substantial part of Bokhara's urban population, were also present in the highlands of Pamir. They numbered around a quarter of a million and had emerged as a distinct people as a result of intermarriage between Iranic and Mongolid stocks. They all spoke Persian, a language which was also widely used by Kirghiz-Kazakh and Uzbek intelligentsia and served as the medium of instruction in the maktabs throughout Central Asia.

Finally, the various Caucasian and Iberian peoples who inhabited the northern and western Caucasus accounted for the remaining 1.2 million Muslims of the empire. Daghestan, in northern Caucasus, was the only Muslim region of the empire where Arabic was used as a lingua-franca by the literate strata of more than a dozen different ethnic groups.

The tsars did not pursue a uniform policy towards their Muslim subjects. Most seemed to have no policy at all, beyond making sure that the regions inhabited by Muslims remained calm and open to Russian trade and economic exploitation. The policy of russification was never applied with any degree of finesse and at times led to events which recalled the savage deportations recorded in ancient history. The Crimean Peninsula was a glaring example of genocide combined with the forcible transformation of an entire region's historical and cultural personality.

Muslims who had been officially absorbed into the empire were put under the spiritual jurisdiction of a mufti (religious authority) appointed by the tsar and operating from the Bashkir city of Orenburg. The rest of the Muslims of the empire, in Turkestan and the Caucasus, were free to organise their own religious life and select their own religious leaders.

Despite the adverse conditions inherent in life under alien rule, Islam in Russia remained self-confident and dynamic. It continued its proselytising mission right up to the time of the Bolshevik Revolution. Many tribes, both in Kazakhstan and in the high mountains and dense forests of the Caucasus, were converted to Islam after their lands had been absorbed into the tsarist empire.

In 1913 there were 24,600 Muslim 'parishes' in Russia. Of these, 5,500 belonged to Central Asia (Turkestan), while the Bashkirs claimed 2,000. The Tatars of the Volga region were organised in over 1,000 parishes, the figure for Daghestan was more than 2,000. The number of mosques and other places of worship in the empire was also impressive; there were over 26,000 mosques, almost one for every 700 Muslims in the empire. This contrasted with the figure of one church for every 10,000–12,000 Christians under the tsar.[5]

The Muslim clergy represented an important spiritual and political force. Numbering nearly 46,000 in 1913, the shi'ite mullahs and sunni muftis and mawlavis represented the only legitimate power in the eyes of the vast majority of the Muslims. They applied the *shari'ah* (Islamic law), taught at maktabs and madrassehs, officiated at circumcision, marriage and burial ceremonies and set the general social and political orientations of the community. The Muslim clergy also wielded considerable economic power thanks to its control over *waqf* (endowment) land and buildings which, as was the case in Shiravan and Daghestan, represented a major part of the local economy. The Islamic theological schools, especially strong in Turkestan and Daghestan, were entirely financed by local donations and in 1913 they boasted more than 17,000 pupils, all of whom received regular stipends for studies that could last up to twenty years.

The empire also included an estimated 9,000 Islamic holy places. These ranged from the tombs of Muslim saints such as Fakhr Razi, or especially pious kings such as Shah Ismail Samani and Sultan Sanjar, to mythical places of worship associated with the prophets of the Old Testament or legendary kings and princes of the Iranic and Turkic peoples. The city of Turkestan, considered by many Kirghiz-Kazakhs and Uzbeks as Islam's second holiest centre after Mecca itself, each year attracted tens of thousands of pilgrims from all over the empire. In Daghestan a number of villages associated with Imam Shamil had become popular places of pilgrimage and worship as early as 1860. The interest many Muslims showed in holy places and other objects of veneration, such as sacred trees, led some Russian and other Europeans into making hasty assertions about the alleged 'paganism' of Tatars, Bashkirs, Kirghiz-Kazakhs and the people of the Caucasus.[6] It is as if one ceased to be a Christian simply by lighting a Christmas tree at home or performing a pilgrimage to Lourdes. One German traveller went even further and, having observed the love of Tajiks for the evergreens that covered the lower slopes of the Pamir, concluded that Central Asia was the veritable birthplace of 'Indo-Germanic peoples'.[7]

Some Muslim writers have constantly refused to recognise the division of Muslim societies into social and economic classes. One often reads that there are 'no classes in Islam'. Muslim societies, however, have always had class structures of their own which, although they did not exactly correspond to class divisions as described by Karl Marx and Friedrich Engels, were no less real for that. The Muslim communities within the Russian empire had class divisions of their own compounded by the presence of an alien administrative and commercial elite, especially in urban areas.

The base of the Muslim society was provided by the vast mass of poor peasants or nomads who owned neither land nor animals and often worked in exchange for payments in cash or in kind sufficient only to ensure bare subsistence. Much of the land under cultivation, as well as the sheep and goats reared by the nomadic tribes, belonged to khans, beys and their associated zamindars who, especially from the end of the nineteenth century onwards, often lived in towns.

The rapid development of cotton as a cash crop in Turkestan introduced a new type of absentee landlord in parts of the region: the Russian or Tatar investors who often did not even visit Central Asia. The fourfold increase in cotton production in Turkestan and the emirate of Bokhara created a new class of landless peasants who received cash wages.

The rural economy supported still other strata: there were the administrators and tax collectors working for the khans and beys who, in turn, handed over part of the proceeds to the Russian authorities. People in charge of the maintenance of the irrigation canals, craftsmen producing the tools needed for farming, moneylenders who provided a form of rudimentary banking, usurers who financed carpet-weaving workshops, speculators who pre-purchased whole harvests, private militamen of landlords acting as an unofficial police and middlemen who sold the crop to the bazaar merchants – all these had to be supported by a fairly backward agricultural sector. And that was not all. The rural sector also financed the mullahs and muftis, the fortune-tellers, witch-doctors, snake-charmers, dervishes, fakirs and an assortment of other vagabonds who always showed up at harvest time and on religious occasions.

Few women worked, except on the farms. And girls had to wear the Islamic veil – *chador* in Shiravan (Azarbaijan), *parndja* in Turkestan and headscarves among the Tatars and Bashkirs from the age of four. With few exceptions amongst the wealthier classes, girls were not allowed any schooling at all. On the eve of the Bolshevik Revolution, no more than half a dozen Turcoman women knew how to read and write.

The community's elders, known as ishan, wielded much power and enjoyed great prestige. Consulted on private as well as public matters, their advice often assumed the force of law. Age conferred a certain degree of authority on both sexes. The *aq-saqals* (literally: white-beards) and the *khatuns* (old ladies) were listened to with respect and obeyed on most occasions. Family and clan loyalties were extremely strong and there was little room for individual initiative and innovation. A person was his or her father's offspring and would have to define his or her identity in terms of clan and tribal background. The individual was protected by the extended family, the family by the clan and the clan by the larger tribe. There were hardly any 'national' sentiments except, maybe, among the western-educated intellectuals. It was only when one wished to distinguish oneself from the Russians that the term 'Muslim' or 'people of the Qur'an' was used.

Most Muslim communities in the empire were poor by any standards and often lacked even basic infrastructural equipments such as roads and postal services. But, contrary to claims made by Soviet writers in later years, these were for the most part solidly-based and united communities. Muslim communities within the empire at no point experienced violent class struggle; there were many reasons for this. For one thing, Islam offers its adepts a strong sense of belonging to a wider community transcending class barriers. Classes do exist in economic and social terms, but relations between them are harmonised through religious structures.

Moreover, the fact of foreign occupation promoted a feeling of interclass solidarity against an alien and 'infidel' power. The many revolts staged against Russian rule show that it was against foreign domination that most of the Muslim communities' pent-up hatred would be directed at every possible opportunity.

The savage repression of Muslim revolts in the Caucasus and the brutal use of force demonstrated by General Kauffmann in Turkestan imposed a deadly calm on all Muslim regions of the empire from around 1890 onwards. The Volga had been pacified after the crushing of a revolt led by Shaikh Bahauddin in Kazan in 1861. The Naqshbandi leader's call for *jihad* had not produced the mass uprising of the tribes he had hoped for.[8] In 1898 another call to *jihad*, this time in the Uzbek city of Andijan, led to a bloody battle between Russian troops and tribal Muslim warriors. Suppressed with the customary violence, the revolt was followed by the deportation of hundreds of Uzbeks to Siberia. The Russians also used a new tactic by blowing up the homes of people suspected of having led the uprising. This was followed by the confiscation of thousands of hectares of exceptionally rich farmland belonging to the Uzbeks. The land thus seized was quickly distributed among Russian and Ukrainian settlers brought in for the occasion.

The Muslims' inability to shake off the Russian yoke through revolts did not, however, end all attempts to find a way out of what most Muslims saw as an unjust and intolerable situation. Even those who resigned themselves to remaining under Russian rule and referred to the Tsarist empire as their own country, had little doubt that Muslims ought to shape their own specific destiny and preserve their cultural identity.

In the early stages of Russian occupation it was possible for many Muslims, especially in the rural areas, simply to ignore the course that 'outer history' had taken. This 'outer history' consisted of events and developments in this world which, if the Muslims knew how to defend their own 'inner history', would end up by having little or no effect on the future of the faith. What happened in the world of empire politics consisted of nothing more than mere fact, while the Truth remained completely Islamic. Nevertheless this 'ostrich attitude'[9] could not be pushed too far; other ways had to be found.

Russia's domination of so many Muslim peoples was only part – albeit an important part – of the broader challenge faced by Islam as a result of Europe's ascendancy. Turks, Arabs, Iranians and Indian Muslims had faced that challenge even earlier than many of Russia's Muslims. The sentiment that Islam needed to revive its forces had grown steadily stronger since the end of the eighteenth century. In Arabia a desert Qur'anic teacher, Muhammad Abdul-Wahhab, had founded an ascetic order which preached the strict observance of the *shari'ah* and a total rejection of alien values. Later Istanbul, Cairo, Beirut, Tehran and Aligarh (in British India), had developed into centres of debate regarding reform and revival in Islam.

The Muslim intelligentsia in Russia, especially in Kazan, was fully aware of the efforts made in other countries to stop Islam's historical retreat in the face of western imperialism. Broadly speaking, two different analyses were offered with regard to the reasons and circumstances that had led to Islam's defeat on virtually all fronts. The traditionalist elements, including the vast majority of the clergy, argued that all the misfortunes which had befallen Muslims were due to their gradual but steady drift away from a truly Islamic way of life. According to them, all that was needed was for Muslims to return to their sources, reassert their identity and strictly apply the rules of the *shari'ah*. In time, supporters of this point of view came to be known as the *qadim'iyn* (literally: the precursors) or simply the *qadims*.

Rejecting the analysis of the *qadims*, a number of prominent Muslim intellectuals argued that Islam's decline and defeat were due to its failure to catch up with a changing world. Islam, they insisted, had to reform itself or face the prospect of becoming a macabre shadow of its glorious past. To reject all that the West had to offer was foolish at best and suicidal at worst. The root of all present-day problems in Muslim societies had to be found in tyrannic government supported by clerical obscurantism. Those who defended these positions came to be known as the *jadid'iyn* (renovators) or simply the *jadid*. Their overall attitude to contemporary life was described as *tajaddud*, which, translated loosely, could mean 'modernisation'.

A survey of Muslim political literature in the nineteenth century might give the impression that the *jadids* were virtually alone in thinking and writing about the basic issues of the day. *Jadid* thinkers and propagandists gained audiences far beyond their native countries. Jamaleddin Assadabadi (al-Afghani), Abdul-Rahman al-Kawakebi, Mirza Agha Khan Nuri, Shaikh Hassan Ruhi, Sir Sayyed Ahmad, Namiq Kemal, Shaikh Muhammad Abduh, Amir Ali, Abdul-Haqq Hamid, Shahabeddin Marjani and Haji Aghush Selim who propagated the idea of reform and modernisation from Egypt to Indonesia, were widely known and their work was discussed over the Muslim world. It is important to note that they were all sincere and practising Muslims, none of whom believed that secularism, the separation of religion from the state, would solve Islam's problems. Many were evidently fascinated by the development of parliamentary government in parts of Western Europe and became enthusiastic constitutionalists. Almost all of them were the products of Qur'anic schools and Islamic theological centres, but also had direct access to European political thought thanks to their command of one or more western languages.

The *jadids*, however, seldom succeeded in taking their message directly to the Muslim masses, since the mullahs provided an effective barrier through which very few new ideas could infiltrate. Led by the *qadims*, the Muslim clergy produced its own literature which, unlike the work of the *jadids* which was presented in journals and newspapers, circulated from madrasseh to madrasseh in manuscript form. They produced almost as much as the *jadids* did, but their work has been virtually neglected by students of Islamic history. It would be all too easy to dismiss the *qadims*, as do most Soviet historians, as 'fanatical reactionaries' interested only in protecting their own corrupt privileges. Many of the *qadim* thinkers were genuinely concerned about the future of Islam and tried to find solutions within the teachings of the Muhammadan faith itself.

The *jadids* addressed their work mainly to the ruling classes. The *qadims*, on the other hand, were persuaded that reform from the top was at best an illusion and at worst would lead only to a further increase in the power of the state. The Ottoman experience with the Tanzimat reform in the nineteenth century showed that the crisis in Muslim societies was far deeper and more complex than many of the more starry-eyed renovators seemed to believe.

Neither the *jadid* nor the *qadim* movements were monolithic. The basic difference between the two was that one wished to embrace the modern world, as shaped by the West, while the other tried hard to ignore or reject it. Beyond that, each camp represented a wide variety of political ideologies. Some of the *jadids*, notably al-Afghani, had somehow managed to persuade themselves that it was possible to create a synthesis of masonic ideas and pan-Islamic dreams.[10] Others were attracted by the ideas of western social democracy. Still other *jadids* tried to mix the teachings of Muhammad and the ideas of Jean-Jacques Rousseau, arguing that the true meaning of *jihad* was 'war on ignorance'.

To its credit the Tsarist regime, unlike the Bolsheviks who eventually succeeded it, never really tried to stop all contact between its Muslim subjects and the rest of the Muslim world. Many Muslim families, especially in Turkestan and the Caucasus, sent their children to finishing schools in Istanbul, Beirut, Damascus and Cairo. At the same time, Turkish and Persian newspapers and periodicals were freely and regularly imported from the 1870s onwards.[11]

The idea of social and political reform from the top did not have much relevance in Russia, where Muslims had no share in governmental power. As a result, the *jadids* of Russia focused their attention on cultural and educational reform. The creation of a western-style network of schools, where religious education would be only part of a syllabus mainly centred on sciences, became a major item in the *jadid* project for Islamic revival. The *jadids* also studied the position of women and often urged a better deal for them, but few would go as far as preaching the full legal equality of the sexes. They paid little attention to the problem of a more egalitarian distribution of income and the matter of opportunities for social and economic advancement. To them education was the magic key that would open all doors and solve all riddles.

Most *jadids* in Russia seemed to believe that the problems of the Muslim community in the empire could be solved almost in isolation from the state. This was why, whenever there was an opportunity for open political activity, the Muslims rushed to form distinct organisations of their own. A few wealthy Muslim families joined the Constitutional Democrats (Kadet) party and an even more limited number of Muslim intellectuals became members of the Russian Social-Democratic Party (RSDP). As for the *qadims*, they would have nothing to do with any Russian institution whether sponsored by the government or opposed to it.

Russia's defeat in the 1904 war with Japan went a long way towards undermining the prestige of the Tsarist state in the eyes of its Muslim peoples. The mighty empire which had defeated and humiliated the Ottoman Empire – Islam's 'superpower' – and reduced Iran to the status of a buffer state was now forced to bow to the superior arms of an obscure Asian state considered by many Muslims to be totally heathen.[12]

The revolution of 1905 dealt yet another blow to the tsar's prestige and exposed its long-term vulnerability, but the Muslims were totally unable to exploit the consequences of the Russo-Japanese war and the 1905 revolution. Even the few Muslim intellectuals – especially in Shiravan (Azarbaijan) – who had participated in the events of 1905 were not quite sure whether they fought for a parliamentary system in Russia as a whole or wanted independence from the empire. The constitutionalist movement in Russia greatly inspired those Iranian intellectuals who helped to lead the 1906 revolution to victory against the shah. Both the Caucasus and Turkestan had for decades served as centres for encouraging political agitation in Iran and Afghanistan. The writings of such Muslim thinkers as Mirza Fath-Ali Akhund-Zadeh of Shiravan and Ahmad Taleb-Zadeh (Talebov) of Turkestan were widely read in Iran.[13]

The inherent long-term weaknesses of the *jadid* movement soon became apparent. Unable to offer a credible and coherent set of ideas capable of uniting the intelligentsia with traditionalist elements and, through them, the Muslim masses, the *jadid* movement continued to beat around the bush with such topics as adopting the Latin alphabet and promoting Western styles of clothing for both men and women. In time the *jadid* movement in Russia was sucked into the empire's broader politics and divided across roughly the same lines as the Russian political parties.

The *jadids* did not reject all hope of self-determination for Russia's Muslims, but believed that this could be achieved only if Muslims became as like Russians as possible. Although they rejected russification, the programme they offered would almost inevitably lead to that. Often the energy of their anger was more directed against what they saw as Islamic obscurantism rather than against Russian colonialism which had denied the Muslim peoples the basic right of choosing their own system of government.

The *jadids* sought to render relative and susceptible to revision values that, only if regarded as absolute and immutable, could be counted upon to mobilise the defensive energies of Muslim societies against foreign domination. They began to dress in European styles and shaved their beards, often allowing their womenfolk to discard the veil. They developed a taste for Western music and literature and hardly ever went to the mosque. Many of them remained members of semi-clandestine sufi fraternities and took much pride in certain folkloric aspects of their own traditional cultures. They found the temptation of adopting solutions already found in the West too strong to resist. Islam did not have to re-invent the steam engine and could therefore also adopt wholly developed and fully packaged political ideas offered by the West. With every step the *jadids* took, they distanced themselves further from their fellow-Muslims whose progress and prosperity they so ardently desired.

The *jadids* had set out to produce a synthesis of the east and the west, but had ended up by simply becoming confused. They were neither Western nor wholly Islamic. In the final analysis they served as a Trojan horse for Russian political domination of the captive Muslim peoples of the empire – first under the tsars and later under the Bolsheviks. Their indecision and confusion often reflected Russia's own gropings in the dark. Russia's fascination for different Western ideas, ranging from the concept of the enlightenment to positivism and faith in scientific progress as the answer to all of humanity's problems, were – often with a delay of several years – shared by Muslim renovators.

Russia's identity crisis was reflected in the duel between the slavo-philes and the westernisers, whose divergent views of the origins as well as the destiny of the Russian people dominated political debate from the seventeenth century onwards. The slavophiles, or pan-slavists, saw Russia as a country chosen by providence for the task of creating a universal system of justice and piety under its own rule. To Alexander Pushkin, Russia was like 'an ocean' in which the many 'Slav rivers' would find their permanent home. Pan-slav ideas were closely linked with the Orthodox mythology in which Russia was described as 'the Northern Star' guiding mankind and the 'third Rome'. Russia's victory in the Napoleonic wars greatly enhanced the influence of pan-slav thinkers throughout eastern and central Europe.

In fact pan-slav thinkers such as N. I. Nadezhedin, M. P. Pogodin, S. P. Shevirev and A. S. Khomiakov[14] produced an impressive literature which appealed to both the elites and significant sections of the masses. Their ideas were taken to the poor peasants by Orthodox priests who shared many of the goals of the pan-slav movement. To pan-slavs, Europe appeared as 'old and sick' with nothing to offer Russia which was 'young and healthy'. Much was made of the assertion that Russia, unlike other nations of Europe which had been converted to Christianity by the sword, had adopted the faith of its own free will. The poems of F. I. Tiushev sang Russia's praises as the earthly expression of the promised Christian kingdom.

Pan-slav ideas were later further reinforced by massive borrowings from German romantic nationalism which led to the National Socialist upheaval of the twentieth century. Schelling's theme that Europe's negative rationalism leads to the destruction of the faith was taken out of context and used as an excuse for Russian despotism. The fact that Europe never really considered Russia as one of its own further reinforced the position of the slavophiles, who argued that Russia must carefully tread a tightrope on one side of which lies the danger of

Westernisation while on the other can be seen the inferno of Tataris-ation.

The westernisers, for their part, rejected Napoleon's formula about Russians being Tatars hidden beneath a European skin. The most energetic of all westernisers was of course Peter the Great himself; he had no time for slavophiles whom he considered to be responsible for Russia's backwardness. P. Y. Chaadaiev (1794–1856), a tireless west-erniser, wrote about Peter the Great that 'he found a blank slate named Russia and on it he wrote: Europe and the West. And since then we belong to Europe and the West.'[15] Alexander Herzen and Ivan Turgenev, each in his own different way, also rejected pan-slavism and advocated the Europeanisation of Russia.

Throughout the nineteenth century the Tsarist government often encouraged slavophile groups as a force to counterbalance the rise of the left. The various brands of socialism preached in Russia could be seen as part of the broader westernisers' movement at that time. The slavophiles were never entirely eliminated from the Russian political debate even after the 1917 revolutions which represented historical victories for the westernisers. Some slavophiles even tried to represent the Bolshevik coup d'état as 'the resurgence of the Russian race against the foreign Tsar', a reference to the non-Russian origins of the Romanovs.[16]

The Muslim intelligentsia in Russia closely followed the seesaw battle of ideas between westernisers and slavophiles with keen interest. Of the two it was the latter that seemed more attractive to the Muslims. An outright advocacy of westernisation, with secularisation as the central theme, appeared doomed to failure amongst peoples who seemed to cling to their religion as if to life itself. The great racial and ethnic diversity of Russia's Muslims at first encouraged pan-Islamic projects directly inspired by pan-slav models. It was clear that the overwhelming majority of Russia's Muslims believed that the most important charac-teristic which they all had in common was their religion. This fact was clearly stated by Russia's leading Islamologist: 'The settled peoples of Central Asia regard themselves first as Muslim and then as inhabitants of any given town or region; ethnic concepts having virtually no sig-nificance in their eyes.'[17] This was even more true in the case of the Muslim-inhabited regions of the Caucasus which represented a veritable mosaic of peoples and languages.

Of all the Muslim peoples of Russia only the Tatars, divided between the Volga and the Crimea, could be said to have most of the charac-teristics of a modern, European-style nation. It was therefore no accident that the Tatars developed the idea of pan-Turkism as an alternative both to pan-Islamism and westernisation. As noted earlier, the Tatars enjoyed a prestige that transcended the borders of Russia. Their capital Kazan was one of the four or five major centres of Islamic learning until the Bolshevik Revolution. In 1913 the Islamic University of Kazan had some 12,000 students, including hundreds from all over the Muslim world. More than 400 books, with a total circulation of over four million, were published in Kazan each year. The Kazan central library was one of the largest in the Muslim world. The Tatar intelligentsia could easily see the Tatar nation claiming on behalf of all the Turkic peoples the same status as Russia sought for itself among the Slavs. Pan-Turkist ideas had already surfaced in the Ottoman Empire and even in Egypt, but it was left to the Tatars to give it a structure and an abundant literature.

The first Tatar thinker to give pan-Turkism a more or less coherent ideological basis was one Yussef Aq-Churaoghlu, a Kazan teacher who was a founder of and contributor to the periodical *Turk* published in Cairo from 1902 onwards. In 1904 he published his famous article 'Three Political Systems',[18] in which he tried to provide 'scientific proof' that all the Turkic peoples 'from Egypt to China' formed but one nation. Aq-Churaoghlu's pan-Turkism was not, however, presented as a rejection of Islam. One of his disciples, the Caucasian Ali Hussein-Zadeh, made this abundantly clear by launching a slogan that was to gain wide currency: 'Turkicisation, Islamicisation, Modernisation.'[17] Another pan-Turk theoretician, Ziauddin Geok-Alp, was even more specific: 'We belong to the Turkish nation, the Muslim religion and the European civilisation.'[19]

Thus pan-Turkism offered an ambitious programme in which only one essential goal was conspicuously absent: the throwing off of the Tsarist yoke. The pan-Turk movement was to focus its energies on imposing itself within the Muslim communities of the empire. The 'Turkicisation' referred to by Hussein-Zadeh[20] meant the gradual elimination of non-Turkic languages used by Muslims in Russia. The prime target in this campaign was of course Persian which, apart from being a language of literature and religious education in Central Asia and Shiravan, was widely spoken in the cities of Turkestan as well as in the Caucasus and the foothills of present-day Tajikestan. Next, the pan-Turks were determined to eliminate the old languages of the northern Caucasus and replace them by a common Turkic language. Such a language remained to be invented, however. The many varieties of Turkic spoken from the Balkans to the borders of China were as different one from the other as French is from Rumanian. Even the Tatars of the Volga did not all speak the same language.[21]

The presence of different languages amongst the Muslims of Russia and the emergence of increasingly diverse versions of Turkic was seen by other reformers – who were not necessarily pan-Turkists – as a threat to Islamic unity. The task of trying to blend the many different versions of Turkic into one super-language common to all Muslims of Russia and beyond was left to a Crimean Tatar aristocrat named Ismail Hasbarli (Gasprinski) (1841–1914). A man of many talents, Gasprinski was a linguist, a poet, a historian and a statesman. He founded the newspaper *Terjuman (Interpretation)* in his native Baghcheh-Sarai in 1883 to propagate the cultural and political unity of all Turkic peoples as the first step towards a pan-Islamic revival under Turco-Tatar leadership. His doctrine he summed up in a simple slogan: 'Unity of language, unity of thought, unity of action.'[22]

To achieve the unity of language, Gasprinski adopted a simplified version of Ottoman Turkish and purged it of as many of its Arabic and Persian loan words as possible. The place of the 'foreign' words thus omitted was given to words borrowed from the Chaghta'i version of Tatar, a literary language since the fourteenth century, as well as dialects spoken by the Turkic peoples of Central Asia and the Caucasus. Gasprinski's campaign met with immense success and at one point *Terjuman* achieved a circulation of more than 5,000. Each copy of the paper was of course read by dozens of different people, thus assuring a much wider audience.

The goal of creating a single Turkic language, however, had to be abandoned after 1905 when it became clear that different Turkic dialects had already developed into fully autonomous languages. The process of fragmentation was later further encouraged by Stalin, who saw pan-Turkism as a serious threat to his own 'socialist' empire. Gasprinski's call for 'unity of thought and action' also went largely unheeded, but his teachings helped to speed up educational reform in Turkestan, Bokhara and the Caucasus.

Aq-Churaoghlu's call for the Islamicisation of those of the Turkic peoples who had either remained shamanist or had been forcibly converted to Christianity fared no better than Gasprinski's quest for a single Turkic language. Many Kazakhs continued to convert to Islam or to deepen their attachment to the Muslim faith. But attempts to persuade the Finns, and even some Lithuanians, to rediscover their supposedly Turkic origins bore little fruit.[23]

It was in the field of educational reform that the pan-Turks registered their most enduring achievements. The model school created by Gasprinski in Baghcheh-Sarai became a place of pilgrimage for educationalists from all over Russia as well as the Ottoman Empire, Egypt and Iran. By 1916, more than 5,000 reformed schools were in operation in the Muslim regions of the empire. These schools offered a complete curriculum that included the study of the Qur'an and Islamic traditions plus Russian and modern sciences, especially mathematics. The language of instruction in most cases was the Turkic as developed by Gasprinski, written in a very simplified version of the Arabic alphabet. In Shiravan (Azarbaijan) and Daghestan many schools also taught Arabic, while Persian was part of the curriculum in Turkestan.

Some of the *jadid* schools achieved a justly deserved reputation throughout the Muslim world. The Husseinieh (Orenburg), Muhammadieh (Kazan), Aliyeh (Ufa), Rasulieh (Troitsk) and Zinjirli (Baghcheh-Sarai) rivalled the best educational centres in Cairo, Beirut, Istanbul and Tehran. However, the *jadid* schools could not penetrate into the emirate of Bokhara which, nominally independent from Russia, retained a traditional system of education under the control of the *qadims*.

Having devoted their energies to the internal reform of Islam, the various strands of the *jadid* movement did not address the problem of political self-determination. Many of them implicitly accepted Russian domination as an inalterable fact of life and some even referred to Russia as 'the motherland'.[24] To them the real enemy was not Russia, which offered the possibility of progress and modernisation, but the mullahs who tried to keep the people in the dark while they themselves indulged in every depravity of which the West was accused. A *jadid* thinker wrote that in the West 'everything is open. We [ie the Muslims] shroud everything in secrecy. If in Islamic centres such as Kazan, Orenburg, Ufa and Troitsk there are no libraries, no scientific, literary or cultural societies, in every single one of them there are houses of ill-repute operated by genuine Muslims and staffed by Muslim girls.'[25]

Part of the critique made by the *jadid* of the traditional structures of Islam was no doubt reasonable and sound. Some mullahs, largely financed by landlords and sections of the middle classes, did use Islam as a barrier to social progress and the perpetuation of undeserved privilege. The premise of the *jadid* critique was right: Islam had to accept a measure of reform in order to enhance the material and spiritual life of the community. The conclusions drawn by most of the *jadids*, however, could not appeal to many Muslims. Few were prepared to accept Russian domination as a necessary evil. As in the case of Afghanistan in the 1980s, most of Russia's Muslims were not prepared to gladly submit to foreign rule in exchange for becoming 'civilised'. Even fewer could persuade themselves that Russia – and, beyond it, Europe – were worthy models to emulate. Nineteenth-century Europe with its many wars and revolutions seemed more like a warning than a model, despite its undoubted material progress and military strength.

The idea of trying to reform Islam through the mobilisation of its own potentials for change had many advocates in the Ottoman Empire, Iran, Egypt, India and other Muslim countries throughout the nineteenth century. Among Russia's Muslims the idea found a formidable exponent in the person of Shaikh Shahabeddin Marjani (1818–1889) of Kazan, who argued that Islam was fundamentally strong enough to benefit from a critical re-examination of some of its practices. Marjani had been associated with Shaikh Bahauddin's anti-Russian campaign of 1862 and was certainly convinced that the Tsarist model of society was far from the best that Muslims could emulate. A disciple of Shahikh Abu-Nasr Kursavi, Marjani was one of the last veritable *hakims* that Islam produced.[26]

Marjani's proposed reform was based on the suggestion that *aql* (i.e. man's critical faculty) should prevail over *naql* (i.e. religious traditions inherited from the past). Rejecting narrow scholasticism, Marjani proposed a fresh reading of the Qur'an from the point of view of the modern man whose needs, experiences and ambitions are different from his predecessors. His attacks were especially directed against the Bokharan mullahs, who in practice attached more importance to often apocryphal traditions linked with the Prophet than to the text of the Qur'an itself.[27] Marjani also rejected the principle of *taqleed* (emulation) current among the shi'ites as a tradition that annihilates man's critical faculty and general ability to develop a judgement of his own regarding the basic issues of life.

Marjani's work was continued by two of his disciples Riazeddin Fakhreddinoghlu (1859–1936) and Mussa Jarallah Beygi (1875–1949), who went so far as calling for the abolition of Qur'anic schools so that believers could discover the truth of their faith as a result of direct access to the Holy Book. They also echoed one of the most celebrated slogans of Wahhabism, which regards Islam as 'a religion without priests'. Needless to say, both Fakhreddinoghlu and Jarallah Beygi were declared 'impure' by the mullahs of Bokhara and Samarkand and sentenced to death as 'enemies of Islam'.[28]

While the *jadids* remained under the limelight, the *qadims* consolidated their position. They remained in full control of the muftiate of Orenburg and enjoyed mass support thanks to the presence of numerous clerics in the countryside. They sought no publicity and were content to keep Islam out of Russian political developments until a more favourable time. The backbone of the *qadims* consisted of the various sufi orders established in Turkestan, the Volga region and the Caucasus for centuries. Using the time-honoured tactic of *khalvat dar anjuman* (solitude among the crowd) and 'inner immigration', these orders tried to keep Islam's physical contact with *kufr* (apostasy) as represented by Russian institutions, to a minimum. They did not feel in any hurry and seemed to operate on two different levels of time. At one level they were prepared to see the Muslim community dominated by Russia and, beyond it, the

West in general. However, at another, inner level, time was supposed to be under the total control of the faithful. The history of Islam did not always have to coincide exactly with Islamic history. What really mattered was to anathemise the power of *kufr* and withdraw from it.

The various strands of jadidism, also known as the Islahist movement, in fact represented the tip of an Islamic iceberg in Russia. The tsars' secret police, the Okhrana, could keep an eye on their activities, but the clandestine sufi orders remained off-limit to Okhrana and the Russian government in general. The *qadims* believed that any attempt to confront the tsarist state from a position of political weakness and cultural inferiority could only lead to defeat. They were not even prepared to exploit the apparently favourable climate for political activity which had followed the revolution of 1905. The *jadids*, however, were prepared to give it a try. One of them – Abdul-Rashid Ibrahimov, a disciple both of al-Afghani and of Gasprinski – negotiated a deal with the authorities under which he was allowed to organise a pan-Islamic congress.

The congress, the first of its kind in Russia, was instantly opposed by the *qadims* including Sayyed Bayazidov, the Mufti of Ufa, and the Mufti of St Petersburg Muhammad Yar-Sultanov. Both saw it as a Russian device for interfering with the affairs of the Muslims. Eventually the congress was held on a yacht in Nizhni-Novogrod under the watchful eyes of the Okhrana for fear that participants might be murdered by fanatical partisans of the *qadims*. More than 120 *jadids* from all over the empire took part and announced the foundation of the Ittifaq Moslemeen (Alliance of Muslims).[29] The congress made five demands: the unity of all Muslims of Russia, equal rights for Muslims in the empire, the establishment of a constitutional monarchy complete with a system of popular participation, freedom of education, of expression and of cultural association for Muslims and, last but not least, respect for private ownership of land and the end of expropriations of Muslim landlords in favour of Slav settlers. The congress also decided to create sixteen regional *majlises* (assemblies) covering all regions of the empire inhabited by Muslims. There was also to be a supreme *majlis* based on Baku in Shiravan (Azarbaijan). In the event only one *majlis* was created in the upper Volga.

The following year a second congress was convened, this time in St Petersburg and with Gasprinski as chairman. This turned out to be more of a pan-Turk gathering than a pan-Islamic affair and most of its time was spent on a discussion of terms under which Muslims could cooperate with the Kadets in the Duma elections and in the subsequent parliamentary sessions. The third congress, held in Nizhni-Novogrod in August 1906, decided to turn the alliance into a fully-fledged political party with a complete programme that read very much like the election manifesto of the Kadets. This was also a largely Tatar affair with some representation from Shiravan (Azarbaijan). Eleven of the fifteen members of the party's central committee, elected at the congress, were Tatars from the Volga. The sole representative of Turkestan on the central committee, Aminjan Elhamjanoglu, was also of Tatar origin. Only one non-Tatar played a key role in all three congresses; he was the shi'ite Ali-Mardan Tupchibashi (1862–1934) who was a press magnate in Baku.[30]

The deep divisions which existed between the westernised Muslim intelligentsia and the traditional clerics prevented Russia's Muslim communities from assuming a significant role in the development of the revolutionary atmosphere that engulfed the empire from 1905 onwards. Lacking mass support the islahists had to enter into unequal alliances with the larger Russian parties, while the *qadims* continued to wait for the divine signal of revolt that failed to materialise. Nevertheless, the Russian domination did not go totally unchallenged.

The confusion created by the disorders of 1905 encouraged a number of peasant revolts, especially in Turkestan. Some historians have presented these revolts as mere acts of banditry,[31] and it is true that the rebels attacked a number of Russian convoys and goods trains in the period 1905–7. The advent of the railways, which later culminated in the famous Turkestan-Siberia (Turksib) line, was seen by many of the local peoples as a double disaster. First it gave the Russians easy military access to the remotest parts of the region's forbidding deserts, the Karakoum (Black Sands) and the Qizil-Koum (Golden Sands) which had hitherto acted as natural barriers against fuller control of the entire region. Also the railways destroyed the camel caravans which had provided local merchants with an important source of revenue for over 2,000 years.

The unrest in Turkestan, however, was not confined to bands of robbers and included peasants, especially in present-day Uzbekistan and Tajikestan. The revolts were aimed against both local Muslim landlords and the Russian military authorities supporting them. Assured of support among the mass of the peasantry in the region, a number of guerrilla groups began to operate in southern Turkestan as well as in the territory of the emirate of Bokhara. One guerrilla leader, Namaz Piri, soon became a legend in his lifetime; years later, Lenin himself praised Piri as a 'Robin Hood of the desert' and a veritable 'revolutionary leader of his people'.

The peasant movement in Turkestan continued right up to the fall of the tsars without ever becoming truly linked with the various movements headed by Muslim intellectuals. Nor were the largely illiterate and politically inexperienced peasant leaders capable of linking their movement with agitations among urban workers and middle classes, notably in Bokhara. It was not until 1916 that a number of Bokharan and Kirghiz-Kazakh intellectuals succeeded in forging a synthesis of revolutionary energies capable of uniting virtually all classes of Muslim society in a desperate attempt to secure independence.

Bokhara, because of its special status as a theoretically independent state, was destined to play a crucial role in posing the issue of independence for Russia's Muslim lands. The ruler, Emir 'Alim Khan, meted out a medieval justice and generally acted as an agent of the tsar; he prided himself in being an honorary officer of the Russian Imperial Army, on which he counted as an ultimate recourse against rebellious pulsations in his realm.

The emirs of Bokhara had tried to face up to the double challenge of pan-Islamism and pan-Turkism in two ways. They strengthened their links with Russia, including the Okhrana which helped to keep an eye on potential dissidents, and at the same time they tried to reduce the influence of Uzbek and Kirghiz-Kazakh chiefs by promoting more Persian-speaking shi'ites to positions of prominence in the emirate. Although almost everyone in the city of Bokhara itself spoke or at least understood Persian,[32] not all Persian-speakers were shi'ites. In fact, shi'ites represented under 25 per cent of the total population of the emirate.[33]

The policy of 'Persianisation' had reached its peak in 1910 under Emir Abdul-'Ahad and had provoked violent riots organised by Uzbek and Kirghiz-Kazakh sunni tribal chiefs and intellectuals. Hundreds of shi'ites, including women and children, were massacred by riotous youths who rampaged through the streets and burned down shops and houses owned by members of the 'heretic cast'.[34] Pan-Turkist ideas, far from promoting the creation of a united front against Tsarism, had reopened ancient rifts within Islam itself. The massacres were so savage that even the Russian authorities were shocked and, for a time, considered the full annexation of the emirate.

The sunni-shi'ite clashes strengthened the *jadids'* belief that only educational reform could help Muslims break out of the stranglehold of fanaticism and backwardness. Shortly after the massacre a number of middle-class intellectuals, sunnis as well as shi'ites, created a secret society called Jam'iyat Tarbiyat Atfal (Association for the Education of Children) which rapidly developed into a blanket organisation for more than a dozen other clandestine groups active in the emirate and beyond. The leadership of the society included Osman Khajeh'ev, Hamid Mehri and Mirza Abdul Vahidev. Their thinking brain was Ahmad Makhdum Danesh known as *kalleh* (The Brain). In a sense, they were all disciples of Abdul-Ra'uf Fetrat who, as one of the most formidable Muslim intellectuals of his age, dominated the political debate in Bokhara and Turkestan well into the 1920s. In 1910 Fetrat, chased away by *qadim* mullahs, was in exile in Istanbul, but he had already sown the seeds of enlightenment in his own native Bokhara through scores of essays, plays, short stories and poems.[35]

The Tarbiyat, as the secret society came to be known, had by 1914 included in its ranks virtually all of Bokhara's more or less westernised intellectuals. The society, almost certainly influenced by Freemason traditions as well as ceremonies associated with the Young Turks, quickly adopted a strong anti-clerical attitude partly borrowed from the teachings of Bab.[36]

The Tarbiyat had the good fortune to be supported by three of the region's wealthiest families: Mansur-Zadeh, Yaqub-Zadeh and Araboghlu. These families financed the creation of schools and offered scholarships to students sent to complete their education in Europe and the Ottoman Empire. In 1912, members of Tarbiyat even managed to persuade the Russian Political Agent to pressure the emir into granting permission for the publication of a daily newspaper. This paper, *Bokhara-ye-Sharif* (*Noble Bokhara*), appeared in the spring of 1912 in Persian. It was edited by Jalal Yussef-Zadeh, a journalist specially imported from Baku. In July of that year, the same editorial staff began to produce a supplement in Uzbek which appeared twice a week.[37]

The Muslim countries annexed or dominated by Russia during more than three centuries of expansion had stayed out of the mainstream of Russian life until the First World War. In the nineteenth century Russian capitalism, supported by German, French and British finance, succeeded in including most Muslim regions into the economic system of the empire. The construction of roads and railways as well as rudimentary manufacturing units encouraged a measure of capitalist development in the Volga, the Caucasus and Turkestan. A few major enterprises, such as the oilfields of Baku and the huge coal mines of Qara-Khandaq (Karaganda = the Black Ditch) in Kazakhstan achieved international importance. For the vast majority of Muslims, however, economic life continued along traditional lines. In Crimea, the Volga and Turkestan, as well as Kazakhstan, peasants and nomadic tribes suffered the consequences of Russian colonisation as a result of massive and totally arbitrary expropriation measures enforced against the Muslim population and in favour of Slav settlers brought in from Europe.

Russia's chief instrument of control over Muslim regions was the naked use of force. It could not claim legitimacy in the name of a religion or an ideology, since Islam rejected intervention by non-Muslims in the government of Muslim communities. Nor could Russia offer its Muslim subjects the prospect of a better material life. Most Russians remained poor and the Muslims were generally even poorer. The best lands were often reserved for the Slavs, as well as the best jobs. Even the gold rush which created so much excitement in Turkestan in the early years of this century left the 'natives' behind; Slav and German 'colons' poured in to exploit the gold reserves while Muslims only watched.

On at least two points, however, Russian rule was more bearable than that later imposed by the Bolsheviks. Despite periodical attempts at russification and enforced conversion of Muslims into Orthodox Christianity, on the whole the tsars did not try to destroy Islam as a religion. Also, the empire allowed contact between its Muslim possessions and the independent Muslim states to continue in some domains. Thus, Russia's Muslims were not completely shut out of broader developments in the Islamic world as a whole.

The outbreak of the First World War might have left Russia's Muslims largely indifferent had it not been for a Tsarist decision to order massive recruitments among Muslims in Turkestan. The decision, announced in June 1916, could not have come at a worse time for the Russians, for a few weeks earlier a secret assembly in Samarkand had decided to organise an armed uprising against Tsarist domination in Turkestan. Led by Abdul Rashid Behbudi, Osman Khajeh'ev, Munavvar Qari and Pahlvan Niaz, the conjurors, mostly *jadid* intellectuals, had achieved the rare feat of establishing contact with the Kirghiz-Kazakh chiefs on the one hand and some *qadim* mullahs on the other. Thus they hoped to be in a position to create a broadly-based united front capable of taking up arms against Russia. Believing that the Tsarist Empire would not emerge out of the world war in one piece, they were determined that Muslims should set up independent states of their own.

The armed uprising began on 13 July 1916 with attacks on Russian military posts in Samarkand. The mullahs declared *jihad* on Russia. Scores of Russian civilians were murdered and many others taken hostage. The revolt, strongly encouraged by Ottoman as well as German agents, was brutally crushed by the Russian army within a week, but the Kirghiz-Kazakh tribes continued to fight until the fall of the empire in February 1917.

6

Red Star Over the East

In February 1917, what many Muslims had hoped and prayed for happened: the empire of the tsars collapsed in the confusion of revolution and war. The Muslims had virtually no part in the revolution which led to the formation of a provisional government headed by Alexander Kerensky, the leader of the Social Revolutionary (SR) party. Any illusions that Russia's Muslims might have had regarding the new regime were quickly dispelled by Kerensky's announcement that he was committed to the territorial integrity of Russia and determined to pursue the war until the fall of Constantinople. The message sent to Muslims, and other minorities in Russia, was clear: there will be no change.

By the time Kerensky formed his government, however, the idea of independence had captured the imagination of some Muslim intellectuals especially in Bokhara and among the Kirghiz-Kazakhs. In June 1916 a Muslim delegation had even attended the Third Congress of Nationalities in Lausanne to inform world public opinion of 'the sufferings of our peoples at the hands of Russia'. The delegation was divided into two groups. One, led by Abdullah Baghjun, spoke on behalf of 'the Chaghta'i peoples', a label used to designate almost all of Russia's Turkic-speaking peoples. This group wanted an immediate end to Russian domination and full independence for Bokhara and other undefined territories inhabited by Muslims. The second group, led by Ahmad Saffar, claimed to represent the Kirghiz-Kazakhs and formulated more limited demands which included equal rights for Muslims and the restoration to them of all land handed over to Slav settlers.

Russia's Muslims discovered classical-style nationalism at a time when Russian politics was rapidly coming under the domination of socialist ideas. In 1917, when the various brands of socialist ideology were in dispute over the leadership of the revolution, there were few Muslims who could describe themselves as socialist. The non-Marxist brand of socialism had reached Kazan late in the 1890s when a group of Tatar intellectuals led by Sadri Maqsudi, Ayaz Eshaqi, Fuad Touqtar and Shahabeddin Mohammadayarov created a secret society and published the periodical *Tarraqi (Progress)*. But even they were ideologically closer to the Young Turks' movement than to any European Social Democratic Party.

The number of Tatar Marxists was even smaller in February 1917. Nevertheless, they decided to create the 'Kazan Socialist Committee' and immediately established contact with the Bolshevik (majority) wing of the Russian Social Democratic Party.[1] The committee was dominated by Sultan Ali Sultan Aliev, known to Russians as Sultan Galiev, and Nur-Muhammad Vahidov. Both men had attended Qur'anic schools and Vahidov had also served as a Muslim cleric for a while. Both had also spent some time with *jadid* ideas. Neither could be described as Bolshevik, although both had a fairly good command of the Marxian doctrine.

In Shiravan (Azarbaijan) Muslims had become acquainted with socialist ideas in the early 1900s. In 1904 a wealthy Baku aristocrat, Amin Rasul-Zadeh, created a socialist study circle.[2] He was soon joined by a number of other aristocratic or middle-class intellectuals, notably Nariman Bey Narimaonoghlu,[3] Mashadi Azizbegoghlu,[4] Sultan Majid Efendi-Zadeh and Dadash Bonyad-Zadeh. Together they created the *Himmet* (Effort) Party in 1905. Banned by the tsarist police in 1912, the party maintained a clandestine existence and resurfaced in 1917 to preach a synthesis of socialism and Islam.

Soon after the February revolution a Muslim Congress (*shura*) was convened in Moscow in the hope of working out a common strategy. Instead the congress only revealed wide divisions among the various Muslim parties and the old disputes between *jadids* and *qadims* were once more brought into the open. The congress failed lamentably in its stated hope of offering Russia's Muslims a coherent plan of action at a difficult but highly promising time. In Turkestan groups that had attended the congress quickly divided into two camps. The *jadids*, now able to act openly, created the 'Shuray-e-Eslami' (the Islamic Council), while the *qadims* set up a rival organisation named 'Shuray-e-Ulemayee-Eslam' (the Council of Islam's Ulema).

Some members of the Islamic Council seemed prepared to go along with part of the programme so heatedly discussed in Petrograd and Moscow by Russian Social Democrats regarding the distribution of land among poor peasants and the expropriation of big landowners and capitalists. The rival Council of Islam's Ulema, however, rejected all notions of class struggle and concentrated on its demand that Russian imperial law should be instantly replaced by Islamic *shari'ah*.

The Kirghiz-Kazakhs, who had largely avoided being drawn into the *jadid-qadim* dispute, created their own political organisation under the name of 'Alash Orda' (the Camp of Alash).[5] The Kirghiz-Kazakh party put the restoration of Kazakh lands handed over to Slavs at the head of its demands, reflecting in that the interests of the landless peasants and the nomadic tribes. In later years Alash Orda was to be described by Soviet authors as a grouping of 'feudal chiefs and tribal warlords'.[6] But in those dramatic days of 1917, Alash Orda appeared to most Kirghiz-Kazakhs as a nationalist movement aimed at securing dignity and independence for a nation suffering under a foreign yoke. The fact that thousands of Kirghiz-Kazakhs who had chosen exile in neighbouring Chinese Sinkiang returned to join Alash Orda indicated the hopes that the new movement created throughout Kazakhstan and the Chinese Turkestan.

The February revolution also shook Bokhara, where the emir could not believe that his protector and master – the Tsar of all Russias – had become a mere prisoner. The *jadids*, helped by ethnic Russians who lived in the emirate, came out into the open and began to challenge the authority of 'Alim Khan. The most active of the *jadid* groups was 'The Young Bokhara Society' led by Sadruddin Ayni.[7] Here too the *jadids* were divided among themselves, but none could be even remotely described as 'socialist'. The leadership as well as the bulk of the mass support for the *jadids* came from aristocratic and middle-class urban elements. Young Bokhara had virtually no foothold in rural areas where more than eighty per cent of the population lived.

In Daghestan the events of February caused hardly a stir. The peoples of the mountains did not believe that the abdication of the tsar would in any way loosen Russian rule over Muslims. A number of *Himmet* propagandists did tour parts of Daghestan in the hope of stirring the mountain people to revolt; but in Daghestan the effective leadership of the masses was provided not by middle-class intellectuals but by clandestine sufi fraternities.

At a time when Russian politics was rapidly moving towards a sharp right-left confrontation, most of Russia's Muslims could be described as being on the right of national politics on virtually all major issues.

The relative weakness of the socialist movement among Russia's Muslims reflected the industrial underdevelopment of Tatarstan, Turkestan and the Caucasus. Even where modern industrial units existed on Muslim land, as was the case in Baku and Kazan, the bulk of the working class consisted of Russians and other Slavs. In Turkestan and Bokhara not a single native socialist could be found to help set up local branches of the SR or the Bolsheviks.

The seizure of power by the Bolsheviks in October 1917[8] speeded up the pace of events to such a degree that political activity based on patterns of the past seemed both irrelevant and dangerous. Lenin's coup d'état in Petrograd created an almost tropical political climate in which parties and groups had either to grow at the speed of events or risk being left behind. Galiev was among the first Muslims to understand the new situation. He knew that Muslims had to take sides in the civil war unleashed by the Bolshevik revolution and he had no hesitation; he would side with the Bolsheviks. The so-called 'Whites' who declared war on the new Soviet power under Bolshevik domination made no secret of their determination to restore the empire though without the tsars. The Bolsheviks, on the other hand, promised an end to the war, land for the peasants and self-determination for all the peoples of the empire.

The Bolsheviks had announced their colours on the very day that the Kerensky government was toppled. The second Congress of the Soviets of Workers', Peasants' and Soldiers' Deputies, attended by 650 members, was convened on 7 November only hours after the Bolshevik *coup d'état*. The gathering included representatives from soviets in a number of Muslim regions including Samarkand, Tashkent and Trans-Caucasia. Dominated by Lenin, whose Bolshevik Party controlled two-thirds of the delegates, the congress approved two important resolutions. One called for immediate peace. The second envisaged land distribution among the peasants.

The majority of Muslim political organisations agreed with the first resolution of the congress of soviets, but no such consensus existed on the issue of land reform. Lenin was determined to secure the support of Russia's Muslims for his regime or, failing that, at least to make sure that Muslims would not enter the civil war on the side of the Whites. On 15 November the Council of People's Commissars, as the new Soviet government described itself, published a text headed 'Declaration of the Rights of the Peoples of Russia'. It proclaimed: 1) equal sovereignty for all the nations of the former tsarist empire; 2) their right to self-determination up to and including the right to secede and form independent states; 3) the cancellation of privileges and limitations of a national or religious nature; 4) recognition of the right to development for all national and ethnic minorities.

These decisions could not but confirm Galiev's view that only the Bolsheviks could offer Muslims a chance to break out of their underdevelopment and poverty. That hope was further strengthened on 3 December 1917 when an appeal jointly signed by V. I. Lenin and J. V. Stalin, the commissar for nationalities, was addressed specifically to Russia's Muslims. The text read:

Muslims of Russia! Tatars of the Volga and the Crimean! Kirghiz and Sarts of Siberia and of Turkestan! Turks and Tatars of Trans-Caucasus! Chechens and mountain peoples of the Caucasus! And all you whose mosques and places of worship have been destroyed, whose customs have been trampled under foot by the tsars and the oppressors of Russia! Your beliefs, your customs, your national and cultural constitutions are from now on free and safe. Organise your national life freely and with no hindrance. You have the right to do so. Know that your rights, like the rights of all the peoples of Russia, are guaranteed by the all-powerful Revolution and its organs, the Soviets of workers, soldiers and peasants' deputies ... Comrades! Brothers! Let us march together towards an honest and democratic peace. On our banners is inscribed the freedom of all oppressed peoples ...[9]

Could the Bolsheviks be trusted? Were they sincere in their promise of full self-determination for all nations of the fallen empire? These questions were heatedly debated then and have continued to be debated since. It is clear that at first Lenin did not really believe that his revolution would remain long in power; his original hope was for his government to last as long as the Paris Commune of 1871. Thus he was anxious that the Soviet power should produce as much progressive and egalitarian legislation and in as short a time as possible. It was as if he wanted to work for the record so that, once his government had fallen, he could defend it as having been the most progressive and revolutionary in history. In any case, the new Soviet government did not even control Petrograd and Moscow fully when it promised independence to Turkestan and the Caucasus.

There is little doubt that Lenin, the architect of democratic centralism and of the dictatorship of the proletariat, could not have viewed such bourgeois concepts as national self-determination as anything more than a tactical device. He had made this abundantly clear back in 1913 in a note he wrote about the 1903 decision by the Russian Social-Democratic party to admit the right of 'self-determination' (*Samo-opredelenie*) for all peoples. In this he explained that the promise of self-determination to all nations was no more than a tactical move against the tsarist enemy,[10] and went on to state that the self-determination he supported was 'self-determination not for peoples or nations but for the proletariat of each nationality'.[11] To him nationalism was one of the many manifestations of capitalist ideology. The proletariat could not but operate as an international force.

Lenin even rejected the concept of national culture which he said was of interest only to 'the bourgeois and the priests'. 'Workers cannot but talk of the international culture of the universal labour movement.'[12] He also rejected the assertion that subject nations had to choose only between assimilation and complete secession.

Lenin's thoughts on the question of nationalities were further developed by Stalin, who emerged as the Bolshevik Party's specialist on the subject from 1903 onwards. In 1913 Stalin tried to fill a major gap in Lenin's theories by offering a definition of the 'nation', to which end he had to coin the word *natsiya* to distinguish the concept of the nation from that of *narod* (people and religious community). He defined the nation as 'a stable and historically developed community based on the community of language, of territory, of economy and of psychology manifested in a community of culture'.[13]

However, Stalin's definition suffered from a number of limitations. Pan-Turkists did not like it because it did not allow for 'the same nation living in different territories'. It also angered many Marxists, who found it subjective and strongly objected to the absence of any mention of class struggle. Nevertheless, in 1917 Stalin – in his capacity as head of the Commisariat of Nationality Affairs (Nar-Kom-Nats)[14] – was in a strong position to test some of his theories in practice. Some national minorities were encouraged by Stalin's appointment; he was after all a Georgian and thus better able to understand the hopes and aspirations of the subject peoples of the now defunct empire. Few people could have guessed at the time that the 'little Georgian' would in time prove to be a 'Great Russian chauvinist'.[15]

Stalin faced numerous difficulties in carrying out his task. In the Caucasus, only Baku had a local Bolshevik base – an island in a hostile sea. Georgia was under the influence of the SR and the Mensheviks while Armenia, which had only just re-emerged as a geographical and political expression, followed the nationalist Dashnag Party. Daghestan remained under sufi political domination, while in Turkestan only symbolic signs of Bolshevik influence were visible in Tashkent and a few other cities. Bokhara was closed to Bolshevism and Kazakhstan was the exclusive domain of the Kirghiz-Kazakh nationalists who headed a vast tribal movement that also included the Uighurs. It was only amongst the Tatars of the Volga that serious allies seemed present. One of them was of course Galiev, who was chosen by Stalin as head of the Muslim section of the 'Nar-Kom-Nats'.

But Galiev also had his own ideas and pursued his own project for a universal Muslim revolution under the leadership of the Tatars. Part of his true ambitions became clear in November 1918 during the first Congress of Muslim Communists in Moscow. Galiev was in the chair and Stalin represented the Bolshevik leadership. The congress, heavily dominated by Kazan Tatars, nevertheless included delegates from the Crimea, Shiravan and the Caucasus. The congress was held against the background of the civil war which had immensely enhanced the importance of the role that Muslims were expected to play in future developments. The civil war was almost entirely fought on Muslim territory, and Muslim support was keenly sought by both the Whites and the Bolsheviks.

At the congress Galiev developed his idea of full autonomy for the Muslim Communist Party, which he saw as a force capable of taking the revolution to Iran, Afghanistan, India and China. Stalin was evidently unhappy about Galiev's stance and emphasised the need for democratic centralism within a single, unified party capable of acting as the vanguard of the international proletarian revolution. Under Stalin's influence the congress rejected all of Galiev's ideas and went on to elect Stalin himself as the representative of Muslim Communists in the Central Committee of the Bolshevik Party.[16] Galiev was retained as an official of 'Nar-Kom-Nats' with a much diminished status.

A shadowy figure who seemed to have emerged into prominence as if out of nowhere, Galiev is something of an enigma even today. He remained a close associate of Stalin for a few more years, but was eventually 'purged' from the party and thrown into prison in the 1930s. The exact circumstances of his death have never been established. He gave his name to one of the heresies Stalin combated with the greatest vigour: Sultangalievism!

What did this oddly-named heresy consist of? Did Galiev preach a nationalist version of Communism? Stalin had no doubt that this was the case. To him Galiev appeared to be trying to revive the old dream of Kazan Tatars of creating an empire that would include all the Turkic peoples of Russia before expanding its domain to cover all other Turkic nations and, beyond them, the Muslim world. Galiev disputed two of Lenin's main contentions: that the Bolshevik revolution would spread to Europe, and that the Russian proletariat was fully prepared to play a selfless internationalist role.

Galiev was certain that Europe, ravaged by war, had no energy to invest in a world revolution. The world revolution had to come from the oppressed peoples who, in fact, formed 'proletarian nations'. The Western working classes, he further argued, were partners of their national bourgeoisie in the plunder of the colonies and the weak states of Asia and Latin America. In terms later echoed by Mao Tse-tung and Enver Hoxa, Galiev disputed Lenin's claim that the Russian proletariat was the principal vehicle of revolutionary Marxism. As far as the East was concerned, the Russian working class had at best an auxiliary role to play. Galiev was perfectly prepared for the Tatars to become Russia's junior partners in a universal revolution, provided they could have the leading role in the Muslim world and Asia.

Galiev's point of view was strongly put by one of his Tatar associates during the Congress of the Peoples of the Orient in Baku in 1920:

> The western proletariat will not come to the help of the Russian revolution. We
> must, without losing time, get the Orient organised in a rational way and in
> conformity with religious, social and economic conditions that obtain there. There
> is no other way out for Soviet power.[17]

What the speaker did not know was that by the time the Baku congress
met, the Orient had also grown out of its revolutionary fever.

Galiev and his friends took their ideas further and soon began to
speak of a 'Colonial International' in which all subject peoples would
unite to prepare a revolution of their own. The object of that revolution
would not be solely to achieve decolonisation, but to reverse the roles
and have colonialist powers dominated by their former colonies in an
act of historical justice. Even Soviet Russia would not be spared such a
fate. Galiev wrote:

> The old Russia which continues to develop under the name of the Union of Soviet
> Socialist Republics cannot last long. Soviet Russia is a transient phenomenon and
> the hegemony of the Russian people over other peoples will, inevitably, be replaced
> by the dictatorship of these peoples over the Russian people.[18]

Soviet Russia, being an industrial power, had to be excluded from the
'Colonial International'.[19]

The leadership of the new 'international' would be assumed by a new
revolutionary 'Republic of Turan' which would be Islamic in religion,
Tatar in culture and Marxist in politics.

What is surprising in Galiev's attitude is that during the civil war he
steadfastly stood by the Bolsheviks and even took part in combats
against the Whites and the Muslim units that supported them in the
early stages. Logically, Galiev should have let the Russians fight it out
amongst themselves and applied his energies to the organisation of his
own people, and the other Muslim peoples of Russia, as a means of
asserting their specific identity and political demands. He must have
been aware of the fact that the Bolsheviks had virtually no influence in
the Muslim regions of Russia and that the few Bolshevik committees
created in Verniy, Tashkent, Semirehchi and Samarkand consisted
largely of Russian 'White Trash' which saw Lenin as a new tsar capable
of preserving Russian privileges in Asia.

The civil war began almost instantly after the birth of the Soviet state.
The standard of revolt was first raised by Admiral Kolchak, who
declared himself commander-in-chief. He was quickly joined by the
forces of the Cossack *Ataman* (Chief) Dutov who captured Orenburg,
thus severing all contact between Russia and Central Asia. A few days
later Alash-Orda declared the creation of an 'autonomous government
of the steppe' under the Kazakh chief Muhammad Buyuki-Khanev. In
January 1918 a Rumanian force captured Bessarabia. In March French,

British and American expeditionary corps seized the port of Murmansk and set up a new 'Government of Northern Russia'. A few days later it was the turn of the Japanese to land a task force at Vladivostok while waiting for American, British, French and Italian units also to arrive. But the most formidable threat to the new Bolshevik power came from the Czechoslovak war prisoners who organised themselves into a veritable army in Siberia and, armed by Britain and France, began to move across the steppe towards the Volga. Moving along the trans-Siberian railway line, they captured Samara, Kazan and Simbirsk.

In November 1918, exactly a year after the start of the civil war, Kolchak declared himself 'Supreme Regent of Russia' and lost no time in making it clear that he would settle for nothing less than a full restoration of the empire, possibly without the Romanovs.

In the meantime, a British expeditionary force operating out of Iran had conquered Shiravan and entered Baku in the summer of 1918. The British intervention had been explained as a move to protect the Baku oilfields which were partly owned by British capital, but the expeditionary force did not stop at merely policing the oil installations. It helped to install a government of the independent republic of Baku consisting entirely of members of the Mussavat (Equality) Party. A strongly nationalist movement, Mussavat was at the time by far the most popular political party in Shiravan and might have won a majority in any fair election. But that was not a time for electoral politics. The British force – no doubt encouraged by Mussavat – arrested and later executed the 28 members of the Baku commune who had cooperated with the Bolsheviks. Many of those shot were members of the *Himmet* and shared much of the nationalist aspirations of the Mussavatists.

British intervention in Russia's stormy politics was also extended to Central Asia. An army of Cossacks assembled around the Iranian town of Bojnurd launched an invasion of present-day Turkmenistan in summer, but did not go far. By September 1918 more than two-thirds of the former tsarist empire was out of Bolshevik control – a control which, in any case, had never been even nominally respected.

Foreign military intervention combined with the chauvinistic attitude of the White leadership, however, led to a gradual change in the attitude of Russia's Muslims to the new Bolshevik power. As the tide turned in favour of the Red Army, created and led by Leon Trotsky, various Muslim organisations began to abandon the White camp to join the Bolsheviks. Before the end of 1918 a number of Tatar, Uzbek, Tajik and Kirghiz units were fighting alongside the Red Army. Many of those who volunteered to fight were nationalists who saw Kolchak and Denikin as remnants of an oppressive empire rather than as harbingers of a better world.

By the end of 1920 the White armies had all but been defeated and foreign forces expelled from Siberia, Turkestan and the Caucasus. The Red Army entered Baku in April 1920, ending the brief Azarbaijani independence. In September Bokhara was captured and the rule of the emirs abolished.[20] The Crimean Peninsula was conquered in October and in December Khiva was brought under Red rule. Now almost all the major Muslim political parties decided to join the Bolsheviks en masse. Himmet (Azarbaijan), Alash-Orda (Kirghiz-Kazakh), Milli-Firqah (National Sect) (Crimea) as well as the Young Bokhara and Young Khiva parties led the way.

Among the new recruits to Lenin's party were a number of prominent Muslim nationalist politicians: Ahmad Bey-Tursun (Kazakh), Fayzallah Khajeh'ev (Uzbek), Veli Ibrahimov (Crimean) and Sadruddin Ayni (Tajik). The new members made several inconclusive attempts at securing permission to organise either an autonomous Communist Party for Muslims or, failing that, to control the regional branches of the Bolshevik Party. Stalin, however, was adamant: there could be no concession on absolute party unity. The argument which had led to the expulsion of the Bund[21] could not be allowed to surface in the name of Islam or 'Turkic' identity.

The civil war had not spared any part of Russia's Muslim territories and many Muslim towns had suffered atrocities at the hands of both the White forces and the Red Army. Dutov had begun his anti-Bolshevik campaign by cutting the throats of a number of Muslims in Orenburg. Bolshevik forces had pillaged and burned the Turkestan city of Kokand. In the Crimean Peninsula, the destruction of the Tatar government at Baghcheh-Sarai by Bolshevik forces had been accompanied by mass executions and arbitrary arrests. The conquest of Baku by the Red Army had been accompanied by the massacre of at least 3,000 Muslims, including women and children. Hundreds of Muslims living in predominantly Armenian areas had also been murdered as an act of revenge for the massacre of Armenians by an Ottoman Expeditionary Force in 1918. Mikhail Frunze's conquest of Bokhara and Khiva had also been marked by acts of terror including mass executions, the burning of homes and shops as well as schools and mosques, and the deportation of scores of suspected anti-Bolsheviks.[22]

Throughout the civil war Muslim political leaders of almost all shades of opinion failed to devise a policy that could unite them, first among themselves and then with the Muslim masses of Russia. They watched Muslims massacred and Muslim villages and towns burned and looted by both the Whites and the Reds, but continued to think only in terms of siding either with one or the other camp in the Russian civil war. The ideological fragmentation of the Islamic leadership prevented the

Muslims, on whose land the civil war was principally fought, from defining and defending their own specific interests and aspirations. The westernised intellectuals, the various strains of jadidism, lacked mass support, especially among the peasant majority, and could not break out of the dialectics of choice between the two principal actors of the drama. Thus they condemned themselves to playing only a supporting role in the civil war.

Despite their reactionary politics and association with the exploiting cliques, the Muslim clerics could mobilise mass support. But once this support was mobilised, they themselves were the first to become frightened by it. A mere call for holy war was no longer enough to lead the faithful to battle and victory. Even the most backward peasants knew that something dramatic was taking place and that change was very much the order of the day. The intellectuals who might have been able to give the masses – mobilised by the ulema – a political programme were branded by the clerics as 'enemies of Allah' and even at times sentenced to death.

A rare example of unity between the ulema and intellectuals was provided in Daghestan where a 'Muslim Council of Defence' was created against both the Whites and the Reds. The ulema on the council were represented by Shaikh Uzun Haji, a sufi guide and Imam Ali Aq-Usha. During the period of struggle against Denikin's White forces, the council was also supported by the local Bolsheviks and other intellectuals of the left such as Ahmad Zalikov.[23]

The Bolshevik victory against the Whites enabled the new Soviet power to turn its attention to the only major potential source of challenge to its authority: a united Muslim community. The Soviet policy, shaped by Stalin with – until 1922 at least – advice from Sultan Galiev, was aimed at depriving the Muslim community of its independent leadership. As far as Stalin was concerned this leadership was divided into two broad categories: the various groups of westernised intellectuals on the one hand and the ulema on the other.

Stalin was determined that the Muslim leadership must be either co-opted into the Bolshevik Party or eliminated. The policy of co-option proved efficient and hundreds of non-Communist Muslim leaders joined the new Soviet power and provided it with a base it would otherwise have lacked in large areas of the country. Until 1922 almost the entire success of Soviet presence in Kazakhstan and Central Asia was due to help from local Muslim intellectuals. Many of the *jadids* had even participated in the military conquest of their native towns by the Bolsheviks. The policy of co-option was far less successful with the ulema; only a few more ambitious clerics joined the Bolsheviks, among them the Tatar Galimjan Ibrahimov and the Kabard Mussa Qat-Khanev.

Convinced that the ulema would prove difficult to co-opt, the Soviet government launched a major campaign against them especially in the Caucasus. Thousands of ulema fled to Iran and Turkey in 1921. The campaign coincided with the announcement of the New Economic Policy (NEP) approved in the Tenth Party Congress as a means of repairing the damage done in the civil war and preventing a collapse of the economy.

In 1922 Stalin was elected Secretary-General of the Bolshevik Party and the foundation of the Union of Soviet Socialist Republics was formally announced. Almost at the same time the purge of Muslim intellectuals from positions of power began in Kazakhstan and Central Asia. Like other fellow-travellers before and after them, the *jadids* who had joined the Bolsheviks had to be discarded by a triumphant revolution that did not wish to owe anyone anything. Some of the *jadids* instantly crossed over to the Basmachi rebellion which had started in Turkestan in 1919; others fled to Afghanistan and ended their lives in exile in the Middle East or Europe.

In 1923 the Constitution of the USSR was promulgated to give the new state a complete legal system. The Constitution of the Soviet Socialist Republic of Bokhara and Khorezm, set up the same year, was remarkably liberal as far as the individual practice of Islam was concerned. Muslims were guaranteed the right to maintain Qur'anic schools and mosques. At the same time, however, the new government of the newly-created republic consisted exclusively of Bolsheviks, even *jadid* fellow-travellers being eliminated from the administration.

The arrest of Sultan Galiev in the same year indicated Stalin's determination to combat all attempts at ideological sectarianism or organisational factionalism within the party and the government. It was not for nothing that one of the Russian proverbs Stalin liked to quote most was: 'Two bears in the same den cannot agree!'

The real threat to Soviet authority did not, however, come from the *jadids* or national-communists. The westernised intellectuals had cut themselves off from the masses by their readiness to sacrifice Islam and the national sentiments of their peoples in an imaginary pursuit of progress and justice. They had falsely assumed that the poor and illiterate masses would become instruments of reform and modernisation simply by being promised a better life.

On the one hand the *jadids* asserted that Muslim masses had been kept at a sub-human level of existence by 'feudal chiefs and mullahs', while on the other they looked to these very same masses to assume the responsibility of creating the new world, a task that required imagination, generosity and courage – qualities which no 'sub-human' could demonstrate.

The *jadids* ignored the fact that the mass of the poor and illiterate had almost always been instruments of oppression rather than of liberation, that they were good at burning libraries and not building them, and were best at forming lynching mobs rather than societies for the protection of individual freedom and well-being. Moulded by centuries of ignorance and injustice, the same poor and illiterate masses would understand hate better than love and xenophobia better than international solidarity.

To these poor and illiterate masses of Central Asia and Kazakhstan the new Soviet power, at first so enthusiastically supported by the westernised elites, was not to be judged solely by its promises – which, to be sure, were tempting – but by the brutal reality of its determination to change traditional patterns of life in Muslim communities.

Many Kazakhs and Central Asians made the same choice that the Afghans were to make some sixty years later. They rejected the party of progress because it was associated with foreign rule and chose the party of reaction because it promised independence. The mountains of the Tajik and Kirghiz countries had become strongholds for anti-Bolshevik resistance from 1919 onwards. Within a few months the warriors of the mountains had been joined by tens of thousands of peoples from the plains and the cities, where famine and Bolshevik domination rendered life difficult.

In September 1920, the emir of Bokhara decided to withdraw from his capital and pursue the holy war in the mountainous eastern regions of the emirate. The emir's move was encouraged by the strong support shown for his *jihad* by Tajik and Turcoman tribes. Two of the emir's generals, Ibrahim Beig[24] and Dowlatmand Beig[25] soon raised an army of some 20,000 fighters mainly consisting of elements from the Ghuzz tribe of Logha'i. They were joined by hundreds of city-dwellers who did not feel they could bear life under an un-Islamic government.

The Bolsheviks instantly named the rebels *Basmachis*, an injurious term. In the Turkic languages the word *basmah* signifies 'fake' and, by extension 'false', while the suffix *chi* means 'maker' or 'doer'. Thus *Basmachi* means 'one who fabricates fakes'. The term also describes bandits, highwaymen who posed as regular troops in order to rob caravans. But once the rebellion had spread from the borders of China to the Iranian frontier, the term *Basmachi* had become synonymous with courage and dedication to Islam. By the end of 1921 the movement had developed into a veritable anti-colonial uprising. The emir had fled to Afghanistan and lost almost all his influence with the Basmachi leadership. At the same time the guerrillas had attracted large numbers of peasants who fled the Bolsheviks like a pest. Even some *jadids* now joined the Basmachis, among them Ahmad Zaki Validov,[26] Muhayuddin

Maqsum[27] and Abdul-Qader Muhyuddin.[28]

Unlike the Afghan resistance of the 1980s, with which it shared numerous characteristics, the Basmachi movement was nevertheless doomed to failure right from the start. It attracted virtually no support from the outside; even neighbouring Afghanistan and Iran refused to help. In fact, the two states went even further and became the first in the world to recognise and sign treaties with the USSR. The Basmachi did not enjoy a fall-back position and were soon left without adequate money and arms. They also remained deeply divided among themselves and totally failed to create a unified political and military command or, at least, coordinate their military operations against the Bolsheviks.

Hopes for Basmachi unity rose to fever pitch in 1921 when the Turkish General Enver Pasha,[29] who had created a 'government' of his own in the port of Batoum, was told by Moscow to leave the Caucasus after the conclusion of a treaty between the new Turkish government of Mustafa Kemal in Ankara and the USSR. Enver, an ambitious general, obeyed and soon moved to Moscow where he became acquainted with reports regarding the Basmachi revolt. He put himself forward as the man capable of persuading the Basmachis to make peace with the new Soviet power. Stalin agreed, but once Enver had reached Turkestan he suddenly decided that fate had chosen him as the architect of a new Tatar empire that would extend from China to Central Europe. Enver quickly forgot his earlier flirtations with the Bolsheviks and, having gathered a small army of his own, declared himself to be Commander of the Faithful and 'Emir of Turkestan'. His dream of repeating the exploits of Chengiz Khan whom, against all logic, he described as his racial ancestor, deepened the divisions within the leadership and caused confusion among the masses who were prepared to fight for Islam but not for pan-Turkism. Defeated at the battle of Beyssum by the Red Army, Enver was gradually isolated and, by the spring of 1922, had become the head of a small armed band relentlessly hunted by the Red Army across the vast expanses of Central Asia. On 5 August 1922 he was killed in an engagement with Soviet troops near the Afghan border just before he could escape across the frontier.

The Red Army was less successful against another Basmachi chief with high ambitions. Qurban Muhammad, a Yamut Turcoman[30] had returned from his Afghan exile in 1916 and, exploiting the confusion that reigned in the tsarist empire at the time, had conquered Khanki, Gurlan, Urganch and Khiva and declared himself Khan of Khans of the Turcomans. Chased out of Turcoman territory by the Russian General Golkin, Muhammad had fled to Iran only to return at the end of 1917. In 1918 he established the independent khanate of Khiva with himself as khan. Two years later he was evicted once again by the Red Army, but he declared himself king of the Karakoum desert and continued to fight the Soviets until his final defeat in the autumn of 1928.

The Basmachi movement had all but faded away from the scene by 1924, although various armed bands continued to fight the Red Army as late as 1939. In at least one incident in 1953 Soviet reports spoke of a Basmachi attack on a settlement in Turkmenistan. The Soviet authorities claimed that the attack had been launched by clans based on the Iranian side of the border.

The end of the Basmachi movement intensified efforts to settle nomadic Kazakh and Kirghiz tribes. This was the start of a long and tragic struggle that caused the nomads tens of thousands of lives. It was a tragic irony that at the time when the Red Army was hunting down the nomads, in 1924, the creation of an autonomous Kazakh Republic based on Alma-Ata was announced. The same year saw the creation of Soviet Socialist Republics of Uzbekistan and Turkmenistan. Hopes for a single republic of Turkestan were all but buried as the process of 'balkanisation' under Bolshevik rule was put in motion.

The Soviet government combined its energetic persecutions of the ulema that forced thousands of them into exile between 1920 and 1930 with an imaginative policy of reforms aimed at securing support among the peasantry on the one hand and the urban middle classes on the other. The Bolsheviks also knew where and when not to push ideology too far. In 1926, for example, they agreed to exempt Central Asia and the Muslim region of the Caucasus from the provisions of a new socialist family code that gave guaranteed full equality of rights between men and women. Riots in various cities of Daghestan, Azarbaijan and Central Asia had shown that the revolutionary reform enjoyed no popular support, not even among women. Nevertheless this did not prevent the Soviet government from decreeing the abolition of the veil and an end to the practice of *kalym* (purchase of wives), polygamy and the repudiation of wives between 1926 and 1928.

The new Soviet power used its programme of land distribution among the peasants as a means of destroying the economic foundation of the ulema's power. The ulema, thanks to their control of endowment (*waqf*) land and other property, had for centuries played a major role in shaping the economies of Turkestan, Daghestan and Shiravan (Azarbaijan). The emergence of the ulema as a vested interest in the preservation of the established economic order also turned them into partners of the ruling families who rejected all change and reform.

This alliance in defence of stagnation was nowhere better illustrated than in Bokhara and Khojand. There the ruling classes, which included the ulema, believed that their societies had somehow discovered the perfect, the ideal form of an Islamic state. Thus politics for them could have no other role except in preventing change. Anything that even remotely threatened the established order would be punished by imprisonment or death. Economic change was avoided by even more astonishing methods. Increased agricultural or artisan production would be instantly translated into useless luxuries for the ruling rich. Trade guilds were forced to keep their numbers strictly limited regardless of the demand for skills. If for example the demand for carpets rose, the supply would be maintained at its previous level by preventing an increase in the number of weavers. And if it was discovered that the market did not need so many cobblers, the unwanted individuals would be simply chased out of the country.

It was assumed that the existing order and the borders of the state would be protected by the numerous saints buried in Central Asia. To many ulema it was a veritable shock to see that Russian forces and, later, Bolshevik troops could simply move in without being struck down by the anger of the dead Muslim saints.

On the eve of the Bolshevik Revolution Bokhara alone had an estimated 60,000 mullahs for a population of around two million. In addition, there were at least 2,000 talabehs at theological schools. Islam was the emirate's largest industry, after the emir's army of courtiers, personal bodyguards and administative representatives. Thus what could be described as the non-productive sectors of the economy represented an exceptionally heavy head on an increasingly weak base.

Danesh, Fitrat and Ayini have left graphic and dramatic pictures of life before the Bolshevik Revolution and portrayed the almost unbelievable sufferings of their people under a fossilised regime of tyranny and terror. Islam's attitude towards the problem of poverty facilitated the task of emirs, khans and ulema who were not prepared to abandon any part of their ill-gained privileges in order to improve the lot of the poor. Islam is full of flattery for the poor, who are constantly assured of Allah's love and told that they have a strong chance of entering paradise. Islam also upholds thrift, the simple life and contentment with a minimum of material comforts as laudable virtues. In other words, Islam does everything to help the poor and to please them – everything, that is, except changing their status and helping them to stop being poor.

The early stages of Bolshevik rule therefore appeared to many poor people, especially in Central Asia, as a rather pleasant surprise. Contrary to claims made by the mullahs, the Bolsheviks did not establish a system of wife-sharing, nor did they roam the Muslim villages with the intention of raping the local womenfolk. Instead, they distributed land controlled by the ulema or the khans among the peasants. The measure was at first rejected as un-Islamic because the ulema were able to persuade many peasants that prayers said on 'usurped' land would not be acceptable by Allah, and that eating the fruit of distributed *waqf* farms would lead to madness or strange diseases.

Gradually, however, the peasants began to appreciate the ownership of their own farms, unaware that this was no more than a brief parenthesis preceding the era of Stalinist dekulakisation and collectivisation. The peasants and the urban poor also appreciated the truly massive anti-illiteracy campaign organised by the Bolsheviks. The number of schools, though often of low quality, multiplied, and enabled the children of the poor to enter a marvellous world which had never been opened to their fathers.

However, the Bolshevik power did not see its historical role as an instrument of improving the lives of the downtrodden of this world. Contemplating its own image in the mirror of messianic illusions, it regarded its mission as one aimed at making sure that historical development conforms with the ideological pattern set first by Karl Marx and then by Lenin and Stalin. Giving land to landless peasants was a good deed only as long as it served the purpose of making the promises of ideology come true. And if and when required by ideology it became necessary to expropriate the peasants, there was no question of Bolshevik power having any qualms about forcibly withdrawing what it had given. It was not ideology that had to serve life and real people, but the other way round.

As was the case with numerous other forces with which it came into contact, Bolshevism had no intention of making any concessions. Lenin's celebrated dictum 'one step back, two steps forward' remained the motto of the USSR leaders. The kid gloves with which the Islamic community had been treated after the defeat of the Basmachis were soon removed. In 1925 the Movement of the Godless[31] was formally launched under Stalin's influence, its aim being to rid the USSR of all religious faith. Marx was misquoted to describe religion as 'the opium of the people'[32] and attacks were launched on places of worship throughout the country. The Muslim regions suffered far less simply because the 'Godless' lacked a sufficiently strong base in Central Asia, Daghestan and Azerbaijan, as well as in the Muslim regions of the Volga and Crimea. Even in 1927 Muslim Communists represented less than 1.6 per cent of the fifteenth Congress of the Communist Party of the USSR. Ethnic Russians formed more than 70 per cent of all party members; the Slavs as a whole accounted for more than 96 per cent of the party's total membership.

The reasons for the low number of Muslims in the party were not limited to the absence of a veritable proletariat in Muslim-inhabited regions and the lack of a tradition of socialist activities there. Equally important was Stalin's wariness about opening the doors of the party and its youth wing 'Komsomol' to individuals and groups of doubtful ideological loyalty. The same reason subsequently motivated the successive purges of the party ordered by Stalin. The mistrust felt by him towards Muslim intellectuals was largely shared by other Bolshevik leaders. If anything, leaders like Trotsky and Zinoviev were even less enthusiastic about opening the doors of the party to 'hordes' of Asiatic Muslims. Zinoviev, who had become leader of the Communist International (Comintern) thought so little of Muslim Bolsheviks that he often used non-Muslims as Comintern's contacts with Communist movements in various Islamic countries.[33]

The Bolshevik power recognised that Islam could be a far more dangerous adversary to the projected socialist society than almost any other religious faith. Islam did not recognise a separation of the mosque and the state and assumed responsibility for every aspect of individual and social life. Further, Islam specifically stipulated respect for private property, the very cornerstone of all types of society that Bolshevism wished to abolish. The fact that Islam could operate without a formally structured priesthood made its control far more difficult in comparison with the Orthodox Church, for example. All this meant that the Soviet approach to Islam provided for a mixture of caution and brutality.

The destruction of the ulema through executions, imprisonment and exile had been followed by the implementation of similar policies towards non-Bolshevik Muslim intellectuals. By 1927 it was the turn of Muslim farmers to be 'liquidated'. The attack on the 'enemies of the people' in Muslim rural areas began with a massive literacy campaign which combined a genuine educational programme with the biggest propaganda drive ever witnessed in Central Asia and the Caucasus. This campaign was to reach its crescendo in 1929. In the meantime, however, units of the Red Army were dispatched to numerous villages, especially in Kazakhstan and Uzbekistan, supposedly to root out the remnants of the Basmachi movement but in fact to requisition reserves of grain and livestock needed to feed Russia's famine-stricken cities.

In 1929 the NEP was officially abandoned and the first Five-Year Development Plan inaugurated by Stalin who now assumed the title of *Vozhd* (Supreme Leader).

The war on the 'kulaks' was on. The term 'kulak' was never seriously defined and could be applied to almost anyone. People could be branded 'kulak' not only because they owned land and livestock, but also because their real or imagined political beliefs did not exactly coincide with party doctrine. The officials at times spoke of controlling or limiting 'the parasitical activities of the kulaks'. More often, however, they openly called for their 'liquidation' and 'elimination'.

The de-kulakisation drive had as its most immediate consequence a revival of the Basmachi movement. Bands of rebels poured into Central Asia from Afghanistan, the Chinese Turkestan and Iran to wage holy war on the 'infidel'. Apart from taking on regular military units, the rebels also carried out a large number of terrorist attacks throughout Central Asia. The victims of these attacks were principally Bolshevik officials directly involved in the collectivisation project; but many school-teachers, leaders of women's associations, pro-Bolshevik writers and poets and even doctors were also murdered by the Basmachis.

Between 1930 and 1933, more than 95,000 households were de-kulakised in Kazakhstan and Kirghizestan alone. In Turkmenistan more than 2,100 kulak households were deported, often to Siberia.[34] In Taji-kestan, where there were very few farms of any size at that time, the creation of the *kolkhozes* (collective farms) affected a smaller number of farmers. The bitter pill was further sweetened for the Tajiks by the creation of a separate Soviet Socialist Republic of Tajikstan in 1929. The new republic's capital of Doshanbeh was instantly renamed Stalin-Abad as a mark of special favour from the *Vozhd*.

The scale of resistance to the collectivisation programme was only hinted at by the Uzbek party leader Ahmed Ikramov in 1932; he reported more than 77,000 anti-Kolkhoz 'incidents' for the two preceding years alone. During the same period there were no fewer than 164 recorded cases of attempts at mass uprising in the Uzbek republic.[35] Many of these incidents were in fact caused by the arrival in Uzbek *auls* (settlements) of bands of armed militia, at times backed by regular army units, to empty the stores of the village and take away whatever livestock was available.

In parts of Uzbekistan as well as Kirghizestan and Kazakhstan, farmers preferred to burn their stores of grain and breeders chose to kill their livestock rather than let the Bolsheviks 'steal' the fruit of the *aul*'s labour. Between 1929 and 1933 the three republics of Central Asia most affected – Kazakhstan, Kirghizestan and Uzbekistan – experienced the loss of nearly half of all their livestock. Whole clans fled into China, Afghanistan and Iran. In one incident in Kirghizestan, the entire popu-lation of a frontier *aul* crossed into China, taking with it 30,000 sheep and 15,000 head of cattle. In some regions which had been traditional centres of animal husbandry for thousands of years, all trace of livestock vanished in but a few months.

The human cost of collectivisation was even greater. The 1926 census had estimated the Kazakhs to number nearly four million, but thirteen years later the 1939 census put their number at just over three million. Allowing for natural growth the 1939 figure should have shown a Kazakh population of at least 4.6 million; in other words, more than 1.5 million Kazakhs simply disappeared as a result of collectivisation and the policy of enforced settlement of nomads that accompanied it.

To be sure, not all of those who had 'disappeared' had been killed by the Bolsheviks as some anti-Soviet authors have suggested. Large numbers of Kazakhs fled into Uzbekistan, the Tatar republic, Turkmenistan and Sibera, while many managed to escape to China via Kirghizestan. The heaviest toll was almost certainly taken by famine. Deprived of their principal sources of food and with their traditional economy savagely disrupted, the Kazakhs died of hunger and disease. Nevertheless, thousands must have been killed in clashes with the Bolshevik forces.

The fate suffered by the Kazakhs has often been compared with the tragedy of American Indians. But there are major differences. The Kazakhs were victims of a centrally planned, organised and led genocide in the name of ideology. Unlike the American Indians, they were largely unarmed and seldom given a chance to defend themselves against the invaders. Moreover, they were not originally hostile to the dominant Whites and had not taken up arms to stop the settlement of Europeans in the northern parts of their ancestral territory. Further, the *Vozhd* had been amply warned by scientists and experts that Kazakhstan was not ready for collectivisation and that the steppe which formed large parts of the republic's territory was better suited to animal husbandry than to growing grain. They had also emphasised that the enforced settlement of the tribes would lead to untold human suffering with little or no economic benefit to the USSR as a whole.

Stalin's reasons, however, were ideological. He could not allow so large a part of his empire to live under a parallel authority provided by tribal chiefs, heads of clans and the network of elders. To break the traditional social system, it was necessary to destroy its economic infrastructure.

In Uzbekistan the principal aim of the collectivisation was to impose state control on cotton farms which provided the republic with a major source of income. Left on their own, Uzbek cotton-growers might have easily developed into a wealthy and powerful class of farmers quite capable of offering the basis for a non-socialist pattern of economic development in the region. The party was committed to the elimination of all vestiges of 'feudalism' and the *Vozhd* was determined to turn the entire peasant population of his empire into 'proletarians'. Thus a totally new relationship with land had to be established.

The 1930s, which witnessed the edification of what was arguably the best organised and the most brutal totalitarian state in history, are now described by many Soviets as the era of *Stalinchina*, which in the horrors that it unleashed against the people far surpassed the periods of terror registered under the Mongols and Ivan IV, the 'Terrible' tsar. Stalin was determined to achieve two goals: to concentrate all economic power in the hands of the state and destroy any set of beliefs capable of challenging the Communist doctrine. It was in the spirit of 'historical materialism' that he first attacked the economic structure of the society before dealing with the religious and cultural 'superstructure'.

The final assault on superstructure was launched in 1932 with the unveiling of a five-year plan to eliminate religious beliefs. The Union of Godless was given control of all mosques and Islamic seminaries – as well as churches and synagogues – throughout the union. In Central Asia and Azarbaijan many mosques were turned into night-clubs, cinemas, dance halls and social centres. The payment of Islamic taxes and alms, needed for the maintenance of religious edifices, was declared illegal and Muslims were no longer allowed to go to Mecca on pilgrimage.

The plan also included a ban on printing and distributing the holy Qur'an. More than 3,500 books were black-listed for 'propagating Islamic superstition' and taken out of libraries and burned. In 1934 and 1935 mammoth auto da fe sessions were organised in Kazan, Ufa and Orenburg where piles of Muslim books, including copies of the Qur'an, were set on fire in public squares. These ugly scenes provoked the anger of the Muslim clergy and a protest march led by Nihat Kazemjanev, the Mufti of Ufa, was ruthlessly suppressed by the militia, the Mufti himself being arrested and deported to Siberia after being accused of espionage for Germany and Japan. Thousands of mullahs and muftis were also arrested in Daghestan, Azarbaijan, Uzbekistan and Tajikestan. Many Muslim clerics in Turkmenistan escaped into Iran.

This new wave of repression was accompanied by the creation of two new union republics: Kazakhstan, with Alma-Ata as capital, and Kirghizestan centred on the outpost town of Pishpek, renamed Frunze after the Bolshevik war leader who reconquered much of Central Asia. The 1930s also witnessed the massive expansion of communication lines in all Muslim territories of the union, which enabled Moscow to establish a network of military control that discouraged any further attempt at armed rebellion.

Having deprived the Muslim peoples of the former tsarist empire of their autonomous economic base as well as their religious leadership structures, Stalin turned his attention to the destruction of all nationalist potential in the Muslim-inhabited regions of the union. The new wave of repression struck in 1938 with Bolshevik leaders in Central Asia, Daghestan and Azarbaijan as the main targets. In Azarbaijan, almost all the top leaders of the local Communist party were executed or deported to Siberia after being accused of harbouring Islamic and nationalist sentiments. Thus Moscow resumed the anti-nationalist campaign of the 1920s during which many prestigious Muslim Bolsheviks such as Veli Ibrahimov, Kashshaf Mansurov, Ra'uf Saberov, Veli

Ishaqov, Mahmud Budeyli, Ali Ferdows and Meqdad Burundukov had perished.

Victims of the new wave of terror against Muslim intellectuals came from virtually all shades of opinion. Among them were former partisans of the 'Great Turan' such as Hassan Sabri Ayvaz, Ibrahim Velikhanov and Osman Aq-choqraqli. The worst hit region, however, was Azarbaijan, where the purge began by the brutal murder of over a hundred intellectuals associated with Mahmud Khan-Budaghev's group of 'crypto-nationalists'. This was followed by the execution of Dadash Bonyad-Zadeh, Hamid Sultan-Zadeh, Majid Effendioghly (Efendiev) and many others. Even Nariman Narimanov, who had already died, was given a posthumous death sentence as 'enemy of the people'.

In Central Asia the list of those purged and shot read like a who's-who of Turkic intellectuals. Hassan Cholpan, Abdul-Rashid Fitrat, Munavvar Qari, Akmal Ikramov and Fayzallah Khajeh'ev were among those shot. The newly-created Kazakh republic had its own share of executions; between 1935 and 1939 more than ninety per cent of the republic's leading intellectuals were executed or deported. Even such early converts to Bolshevism as Ellam Sefiev, Ryskulov and Sadvakasov were not spared.

Stalin's anti-nationalist campaign in non-Russian republics was accompanied by a strong dose of russification. In 1939 the Russian alphabet was imposed on all languages of Central Asia, Azarbaijan and Daghestan. The study of Russian was also declared a compulsory subject throughout the educational system of the union. With the storm of the Second World War gathering on the horizon, Stalin was determined to unite the many different peoples of the USSR under the leadership of the Russian 'elder brother'.

Deprived of their elites, the Muslim regions of the union were in no position to put up effective resistance against the new wave of russification. It was only the outbreak of the war that stopped the process and forced Stalin to offer some concessions to the Muslims. The *Vozhd* needed the manpower resources of the Muslim regions and knew that Muslims would not gladly fight on the side of their oppressor. The widespread resistance manifested in Central Asia, especially among the Kara-Kalpak (Black Bonnet) tribes against conscription in 1940, persuaded Stalin to a halt in his anti-Islam campaign. Shortly after German forces invaded the USSR in 1941, the Union of the Godless was virtually disbanded and pressure on Muslim clerics reduced. A few mosques were also allowed to re-open, notably in Moscow. In 1942 a pan-Islamic conference in Ufa called on Muslims throughout the world to side with the allies and help the USSR defeat Nazi Germany.

7

Parallel Lives

The invasion of the USSR by German forces in 1941 led to an almost instant end to the war which had been waged against Islam in Soviet territory for more than two decades. Unable to fight on two fronts, Stalin decided to turn Islam into an official church that could be controlled by the state. Reviving a policy devised by Catherine the Great, he created three 'Spiritual Directorates' charged with the task of supervising the religious aspects of life in the union's Muslim-inhabited regions.

The first directorate to be set up was based on Ufa, the capital of the Bashkir autonomous republic, and was put in charge of Muslims in all European territories of the USSR. Kazan might have been a better choice as the seat of the directorate, but Stalin was determined to limit the role of the Tatars as much as possible and also did not wish to antagonise the Orthodox Church by restoring part of Kazan's position as an Islamic centre. Nevertheless, the Ufa directorate was allowed to use the Kazan Tatar as its official language.

The second directorate was centred on the Uzbek city of Tashkent and covered the Muslims of Central Asia and Kazakhstan. The official language chosen was Uzbek.

The Muslim peoples of Soviet Azarbaijan, Armenia and Georgia were covered by a third directorate based on Baku. Unlike the first two directorates which dealt exclusively with sunni Muslims, the Baku authority covered both shi'ites and sunnis.

A fourth directorate was added in 1944 to cover the sunni Muslims of north Caucasus. Based on the town of Buynaksk, it covered the autonomous republics of Kabard-Balkar, Chechen-Ingush and Northern Ossetia in Daghestan, as well as the autonomous regions of Karachai-Cherkess and Adygh.

The question as to which official languages to choose for the directorates of northern Caucasus and Transcaucasia was resolved by Stalin himself. The Baku-based directorate could use Azari Turkic, but the Buynaksk directorate had to select a neutral language so as to prevent discord among various ethnic groups each determined to defend its own dialect. The *Vozhd* would have liked Russian to be chosen, but in the end agreed that Arabic be used as the official language of the muftiate of Buynaksk.

The role played by the official structure created by Stalin has been the subject of much debate during the past forty years. Some Muslim writers, as well as a whole host of Western anti-Soviet scholars, have tended to dismiss the directorates as mere tools of tyranny in the hands of Stalin and his successors. The Soviet Muslims, however, have expressed far less negative views.

The directorates were created at a time when Stalinist purges and policies had deprived Soviet Muslims of an effective leadership. Hundreds of Muslim intellectuals had been shot and thousands deported, while many more thousands had fled into exile. Those who remained had been divided into three groups. A small minority – people like Ayni, Lahuti and Tarsun-Zadeh – had joined the Stalinist regime and become its loyal servants.[1] They justified their act by reference to the undoubted material benefits brought about by the new Soviet system in the poorer regions of the USSR.

A third group of intellectuals, among them many mullahs, decided to have recourse to a long-established Islamic tradition. They chose *khalvat dar anjoman* (privacy in the crowd) or 'internal immigration'. The Soviet society was dominated by Taghut[2] and the Muslims were for the time being not strong enough to overthrow him. History was not Islamic, but Muslims could have their own history. Movements and ideologies based on western models – ranging from pan-Turkism and pan-Iranism to pan-Islamism itself – had failed. It had become clear that Islam could not beat Communism on terms set by the latter, which was a western product. Islam had to withdraw behind its own traditional defences. The Bolsheviks had made spectacular advances in achieving the goals of Stalin's policy of *Korenizatsiya* (striking roots) in Muslim regions. It was necessary to sap these roots from underground.

The tradition of going underground had first been established by the Persians in the early stages of the Arab occupation in the seventh century. Later it had been revived as an Islamic defence mechanism against the heathen Mongols. Scores of *tariqats* (paths) have been offered by *murshids* to seekers of the truth. In the nineteenth century members of the various *tariqats* had put up a heroic resistance against European domination. Imam Shamil and others had shaken the tsarist empire in northern Caucasus. In the Sudan, the Mahdi and his *ansars* (companions of victory) had stood up to the British. In East Africa the *tariqats*, inspired by the sufi Shah Hassan, had fought the Italians in Somalia.

From 1930 onwards there was little chance of the *tariqats* and their *ghazis* (Holy Warriors) defeating the Red Army in battle. The *tariqats* were nevertheless able to offer an alternative to the Soviet society, a life 'within' that could proceed alongside the life of oppression offered by the heathen power.

Four *tariqats* had been firmly established among the Muslims of Central Asia and the Caucasus long before the advent of Russian rule. After a long period of decline between the 1880s and the 1920s they were all revived and assumed growing importance in the life of the community.

The smallest *tariqat* was known as *Kubrawwyah* (followers of Kubra), named after its founder Shaikh Najmeddin Kubra.[3] This *tariqat*, a continuation of the *dehghan* (farmer) movements of the early Islamic era, was especially powerful among the Kara-Kalpaks and the Turcomans.

The oldest *tariqat* was the Qaderiyah, named after Abdul-Qader Gilani who founded it in Baghdad in the twelfth century.[4] The Qaderiyah dominated Islamic life in Central Asia in the thirteenth and fourteenth centuries and were strongly established in Bokhara and Khojand.

The Yassawwiyah, named after their founder Shaikh Ahmad Yassawi,[5] was also an old-established *tariqat* in Central Asia and present-day Kazakhstan. A deeply mystical and apolitical movement, the Yassawwiyah assumed a militant anti-Soviet stance after 1917. Two branches of the movement known as the Lachis[6] and 'The Hairy Elders'[7] took up arms against Bolshevik forces in the Ferghana valley in the 1920s.

The fourth and the largest *tariqat*, the Naqshbandiyah, was named after Shaikh Bahaeddin Naqshbandi[8] and was strongly present in Central Asia and Kazakhstan as well as among Tatar and Bashkir Muslims.

In Daghestan and Shiravan (Azarbaijan) only two *tariqats* were present: the Naqshbandiyah and the Qaderiyah. The Naqshbandiyah order was introduced in the mountains of the Caucasus by a Kurdish prince, Ismail Kurd-Emir, in the seventeenth century, and later spread to Shiravan under another *murshid*, Khas Muhammad. The order produced some of the most outstanding warrior-saints of the region including Shaikh Muhammad Yuquri-Yaraq and, of course, Imam Shamil. The last *murshid* of the order in Daghestan had been Haji Muhammad of Sogratl, who was hanged by the Russians in 1879. After 1917 the Naqshbandis made a strong comeback in the Caucasus, this time in a decentralised organisational structure. Probably as many as twenty-five different *murshids* led various more or less autonomous branches of the movement in Daghestan, the Chechen country and parts of Azerbaijan.

The Qaderiyah had been established in the Caucasus from the middle of the nineteenth century. Their first *murshid*, Kunta Haji of Kishiev, had been a prophet of non-violence but had ended his life in a Russian prison. After his death, the order was divided into three groups. The first and probably the largest used the name of Kunta Haji and remained strong among the Chechens and the Ingushs as well as Ossetian Muslims and Kabards. The second group, known as Bamat Giray,[9] offered a traditional, almost quietist version of Naqshbandi teachings. The Batal Haji group[10] was the most radical of all and preached constant preparation for an eventual *jihad* against the Russians and the Bolsheviks.

In the 1930s a fourth group of Qaderiyeh appeared in the Caucasus with special influence in Soviet Azerbaijan, Armenia and Georgia. Known as the *wird-e-pir*[11] it obeyed the *murshid* of the city of Maragheh in Iranian Azerbaijan.

A fifth Qaderi group known as the 'Drummers' (Barabanshchiki) was distinguished by its scrupulous avoidance of politics.[12]

The various orders saw themselves as so many paths leading to the summit of the same mountain, considering each other not as rivals but as complementary visions of Islam's single, unalterable and eternal truth. Moreover the orders were not in conflict with the official structure of Islam; it was considered perfectly possible for the same man to be part of the government-controlled structure of Islam and at the same time belong to a secret order. Indeed, some of the leaders of official Islam in the USSR were – and are today – members of various sufi orders. Mufti Ziauddin Baba-Khan of Tashkent, a long-time associate of various Soviet leaders from Stalin to Brezhnev, for example, belonged to the Naqshbandi order until his death in 1982. The various sufi 'paths' also recruited many of their members from Muslims who had joined the Communist power and served as high-ranking party, state and even army leaders in the Asian republics.[13]

With their strict rules of initiation, the orders offered Soviet Muslims a private and protected space beyond the reach of a totalitarian state that wished to control all aspects of a man's life. The order was a haven of peace where one found oneself amongst friends and where it was possible to be free and speak without fear. The order also created many links with the past at a time the new Soviet order was bent on destroying the old to build the new. All orders offered elaborate ceremonies that included ritual incantations (*zikr*), dances, music and sessions of silent vibrations inspired by the quest for the truth.[14] Inside the *wird* or the group of *murids*, time assumed a different rhythm from the pulsations of the outside world. Here one came into contact with the Truth, whereas what went on outside was nothing but facts – pedestrian, transient and ultimately insignificant facts. The new Soviet order could burn the Qur'an, desecrate Islam's holy places, turn mosques into dance-halls, unveil women and even deport and kill tens of thousands of believers, but it could never capture that inner space, that *harim* (the forbidden zone) that was for ever closed to the infidels thanks to the magnetic relationship between the *murids* and their *murad*.

The *wirds* did not limit their activity to the provision of solace to sensitive Muslims at especially difficult times. They acted as custodians of Islamic culture, art, tradition and even law. Islamic judges (*qadhis*) ruled on all matters referred to them within the fraternity and regardless of Soviet law and practice. Their judgement was respected and obeyed willingly, whereas Soviet courts had to impose sentences by force or the threat of its use. Marriages already registered with secular Soviet authorities could be given the proper Islamic blessings by the shaikhs within the *wird*. Soviet power occupied the streets, the public buildings and, of course, the army garrisons and police stations. Islamic power, however, reigned supreme at homes, in tea-houses and bazaars and inside the often illegally-organised madrassehs and Quranic classes.

While Soviet power celebrated its domination of time and space through frequent ritual ceremonies linked with the October Revolution and the cult of the *Vozhd*, Islam marked out its own space by keeping alive popular traditions which at times even predated the message of Muhammad. Mass celebrations were each year organised on the occasion of the Prophet's birthday anniversary, the Ba'athat feast,[15] the Feast of the Sacrifice (Id-e-Qurban) also known as Bayram (Festival), and in shi'ite Azarbaijan the Ghadir-e-Khom.[16] The tradition of cele-brating the spring equinox as the start of a new year, the Nowruz feast, was also largely observed.[17] Nowruz was in fact so successful that Stalin decided to confiscate it as part of the revolutionary calendar. Renamed the Feast of Spring, it was dedicated to 'the toiling rural masses' and celebrated throughout the union. The sufi fraternities played a crucial role in defending the Islamic calendar against attacks by a secular, indeed atheistic, power.

The role of the various sufi movements, described by some scholars as 'parallel Islam',[18] must not be exaggerated however. The fraternities were not mass organisations but highly exclusive secret societies to which only the chosen few could gain access. Some Western researchers estimated the strength of 'parallel Islam' in the USSR at the beginning of the 1980s at around two million people.[19] This is without a doubt an exaggeration. The principal *murshid* of the Naqshbandi order, by all accounts the largest segment of parallel Islam in the USSR, has offered more plausible figures. In 1983 he estimated the total number of Naqshbandis throughout the Muslim world at 'around three million', with the Soviet Union accounting for no more than 'sixty to sixty-five thousand *murids*'.[20] Thus the total number of *murids* involved in the activities of various fraternities in the 1930s to the 1950s could not have exceeded 100,000.

The Naqshbandi spiritual leader described the *wirds* as 'centres for the few who wish to devote their entire life to the search for the Truth'.[21]

Even so, the presence of tens of thousands of highly-motivated and tightly-disciplined *murids* was a crucial factor in helping Islam preserve as much of its identity as possible in the face of multi-faceted aggression by the Communist state. The importance of the *murids* as leaders of society becomes more apparent when one recalls the fact that the number of Muslims who joined the Communist Party did not exceed a few thousands until the 1950s. And many of those who secured a party membership card did so largely out of opportunistic calculations. Some continued as members of the *wirds* as well, a tradition that persists to this day. It is not unusual to find high-ranking Communist Party officials and even officers of the KGB[22] who are at the same time members of a sufi fraternity.

The 'double-game' played by some Muslims against Soviet power was part of the defence mechanism developed by Islam under especially difficult circumstances. In Soviet Azarbaijan the shi'ite tradition of *taqiyeh* (dissimulation) permitted people to play the role of dedicated Communists in public and remain fanatically opposed to Communism in all its forms in private. This tactic is described by a 'committed Communist of Muslim origin' in the following terms: 'The practitioners of the art of *taqiyeh* secure this world through the Communist Party and the next by belonging to a sufi underground cell.'[23]

It is almost certain that Stalin and some of his closest associates, notably the infamous Beria,[24] must have had some knowledge of the influence exerted by sufi movements in Muslim regions of the union. But the various secret police organisations, from the Cheka to the GPU and MVD, never quite succeeded in infiltrating any of the *wirds*. It is possible that the secret police persuaded Stalin that underground Islam was no more than a ghost from a dead past. Nevertheless, vigilance against the slightest sign of a resurgence of pan-Islamism remained a constant concern of the *Vozhd*.

To eliminate once and for all the danger of pan-Islamism, Stalin decided to turn the various Muslim peoples of the union into as many Western-style nations as possible. Between 1924 and 1940 the Muslim peoples of the USSR were divided into no fewer than 39 nations, nationalities and ethnic groups. The procedure was simple enough. Any ethnic group capable of manifesting at least some distinctive features would be marked out for 'promotion' to the rank of a nation or a nationality. The objective in almost every case was to prevent the establishment or consolidation of large Islamic nations.

The first victim of this 'divide and rule' policy was the Tatar nation, whose intellectuals had nurtured dreams of one day rivalling the might of Russia by uniting under their own flag the entire Muslim population of the union. Most of the Tatars lived in the Volga region, but Tatar communities also existed in the Crimean Peninsula, Transcaucasia and Central Asia. Denied territorial contiguity, the various parts of the Tatar nation could not be grouped together within a single political unit. The creation of a single Tatar republic in the Volga region, however, seemed both perfectly logical and feasible. Indeed, the Bolshevik Revolution had promised the establishment of a Tatar state in the Volga region.

By 1919, however, Moscow had changed its mind. Now the Tatars were to be divided into as many small units as possible. Moreover, all these units were to remain parts of the Russian Soviet Federative Socialist Republic (RSFSR). In 1919 an autonomous Bashkir republic was set up with Ufa as its capital. A year later, the Tatar autonomous republic came into being with Kazan as capital. The creation of a Bashkir republic, however, necessitated the invention of a Bashkir nation as well. The trouble was that the Bashkirs, who represented less than a quarter of the population in their newly-created state, did not feel themselves to be separate and considered themselves no more than a branch of the Tatar nation.

In 1920 Stalin appointed a special committee of historians, linguists and ethnologists charged with the task of turning the Bashkirs into a nation. The committee spent three years on the task and fabricated a Bashkir literary language complete with a national mythology and history derived from Tatar traditions but sufficiently tampered with to appear different. Despite this the Bashkir language remained adamantly linked with Tatar of which it had been a dialect.[25]

Also in 1923, Stalin tried to turn several other Tatar groups into distinct nations. The Mishars, the Teptyars, the Noghay-Begs and the Qryashens were all given the status of 'nationality' and forced to develop and use 'national' languages of their own as distinct from the Tatar language which they already used. The experience continued until 1939, after which all the invented 'nationalities' were once again classified as Tatars and allowed to continue to use the Tatar language.[26]

The Tatars were further cut down to size with the establishment of the Udmurt, the Mari, the Mordovian and the Chuvash autonomous republics. All these various groups might have been described as part of the Tatar nation and united within a single political structure.

Stalin's anti-Tatar campaign, no doubt at least in part motivated by the hatred of the Russians for the Tatars, was taken still further.[27] Contacts between the Tatars of the Volga and of the Crimea, also grouped in an autonomous republic, were reduced to a minimum. And in Central Asia, Kazakhstan, northern Caucasus and Soviet Azarbaijan, where the Tatars had always formed part of the intellectual elite and the urban middle class, every effort was made to 'dissolve' them into the local populations. Tatar schools were shut and the number of Tatar newspapers and books constantly reduced. The idea was that the only Muslim nation sufficiently developed to promote the idea of pan-Islamic unity against Soviet power should be so fragmented as to have little or no major impact on future political developments of the union.

Another major blow was struck against the Tatar nation in 1944 when Soviet forces recovered control of the Crimean Peninsula after pushing the German armies out. In a special decree in which the Tatars as a whole were accused of aiding and abetting the enemy at time of war, Stalin declared the abolition of the Tatar autonomous republic of the Crimea. This was followed by an operation that recalled the exploits of Nabuchodonosor in ancient Babylon: the entire Tatar population of the Crimea, estimated at around 250,000, was rounded up in a series of raids on towns and villages and deported to Central Asia and Kazakhstan. Thousands perished on the way, cut down by epidemics, hunger and despair. The deported population was deprived of its leadership as the majority of Tatar intellectuals were arrested and dispatched to labour camps in Siberia. Many never returned.

The divide-and-rule policy adopted by Stalin towards the Muslim peoples of the USSR did not end with the fragmentation of the Tatar nation. It was quickly extended into the steppes and Central Asia where it emerged as an ambitious project for the creation of new 'nations'. The Kazakh-Kirghiz family of tribes was divided into two groups each dotted with its own language. Soviet linguists took great care to make the Kazakh and Kirghiz languages – essentially dialects of the same Turkic lingua-franca – as distinct one from the other as possible. Both languages were given the Russian alphabet and presented with new vocabularies of Russian loan words. Sometimes two Russian synonyms would make their separate ways into the Kazakh and Kirghiz languages to express the same thing. The idea was that the Kazakhs and the Kirghiz should in time cease to communicate directly in their own native languages and be forced to use the Russian instead. To drive in the wedge even further, the common mythology of the Kazakh-Kirghiz people was divided between the two newly-created nations. Some folk tales were edited to give the impression that the Kazakhs and the Kirghiz had even been rivals and enemies since the dawn of time and until the October Revolution.

The Kazakhs and the Kirghiz ended up by having their own union republics, but a third branch of the same family – the Qara-qalpaqs (Karakalpak = Black Bonnets) – was later detached from the Kazakh territory and given an autonomous republic of its own as part of the Uzbek Soviet Socialist Republic. Once again the authorities accompanied their nation-building exercise with the invention of a language and the fabrication of myths supposed to spell out Karakalpak history.

The 1924 administrative reform (*razmezhevanie*) which abolished the wider-based republics of Turkestan, Kharazm and Bokhara – all of which bore territorial and not ethnic titles – enabled Stalin to pursue his nation-building plans still further. The Soviet Socialist Republic of Uzbekistan and the Soviet Socialist Republic of Turkmenistan were established. The new Uzbek identity was designed to replace the broader concept of the Sart people which had encompassed peoples of many different races and languages. The Sarts represented a synthesis of Turkic and Iranic peoples with Jewish, Arab and other minority groups also added. Their common language was a branch of Turkic, while Persian provided them with their literary language. The new Bolshevik power, however, was determined to eliminate both Turkic and Persian from the region.

The Turcomans, now also turned into a nation, were in fact a confederation of tribes whose principal bond was Islam. After 1925, however, they were provided with a unified national language and given a distinct history of their own. In the process both Persian – the literary language of the Turcomans – and Arabic – the language used at Quranic schools – were locked out of the newly-created republic.

Finally, the last remaining Persian-speaking regions of Central Asia were detached from Uzbekistan and turned into the Tajik Soviet Socialist Republic. The 'nation' was confined to a remote mountainous region and denied geographic contact with Iran. At the same time a substantial number of Tajiks who lived in the cities of Samarkand and Bokhara were turned into subjects of Uzbekistan, while almost as many Uzbeks were left behind in Tajikestan.

The process of dividing the region into smaller and smaller 'national' units came to a halt on the eve of the Second World War. Thus a number of other potential 'nations' were left without a geographical expression of their identity. The Arabs, the Persians (called Ironi or Persik), the Hazarahs,[28] the Baluch, the Pushtuns, the Pamiris, the Dungans[29] and the Koreans were in fact doomed to assimilation in the long run. A number of Turkic peoples, notably the Tatars, were also deprived of the means needed for protecting their own cultural identity in Central Asia as a result of Moscow's decision to close all Tatar schools and restrict Tatar publications in the region. The Qypchaq and Kuramas tribal groups[30] and the urban Turks of the Ferghana Valley were also denied the status of 'nationality'. The Uyghur Turks, however, were dotted with languages and alphabets of their own and allowed to preserve their cultural identity.

Stalin's nation-building exercise in the steppes and Central Asia was a comparatively smooth undertaking in comparison with what the *Vozhd* had to face in the Muslim regions of the Caucasus. The consensus among the region's intellectuals, including the few who had adopted Bolshevism, pointed towards the creation of at most two republics after the October Revolution: one to cover the many different peoples of the north and another to represent the Azaris. In 1919, however, the new Soviet power announced the creation of two republics in northern Caucasus. Both were called 'republic of the mountain' but in two different languages. The 'Gorskaya Avtonomnaya Respublika' (the autonomous republic of the mountain) covered the Kabards, the Chechen, the Ingush, the Cherkess (Circassian), the Ossetes, the Balkars and the Karachais. The autonomous republic of Daghestan covered twenty different national groups divided into three linguistic families: the Ibero-Caucasian, the Turkic and the Iranic.

The two new republics did not only represent veritable mosaics of peoples and languages but also lacked economic unity. Some of the nationalities in the region were still trying to emerge out of the feudal era, while others had come into contact with the modern industrialised world through a number of cities and seaports. The only unifying factor among them was Islam, and it was precisely Islam which Stalin was determined to banish from the region. One of the first decisions taken by the new Bolshevik power regarding northern Caucasus was to ban the study of Arabic, which was described as 'the language of decadent feudalism'. Arabic books were taken out of the few libraries that existed in the region and burned, while more than 200 Quranic schools where Arabic was the language of instruction were closed down and their teachers deported to Siberia or forced to flee into exile. In his hatred of Arabic, Stalin was even prepared to lend support to a pan-Turk project aimed at imposing Azari Turkic as the lingua franca of the educational system of Daghestan. By 1928, however, it had become evident that Azari had virtually no chance of striking roots in that part of the Caucasus. Another Turkic language, the Kumyk, was also tried in the mountains but failed to gain ascendancy.

The 'Gorskaya' republic fell apart almost before it could be fully established as a credible administrative unit. Between 1920 and 1938 Central and Western Caucasus were divided into a number of smaller units, each based on an ethnic group with a language or dialect of its own. Soviet linguists were put to work to provide tribal dialects with alphabets, invent new vocabularies and make sure that basically similar languages became as different from one another as possible. The region was divided into five administrative units. The autonomous republic of Chechen-Ingush had two national languages.[31] The autonomous republic of Kabard-Balkar was also given two national languages.[32] The autonomous republic of Northern Ossetia and the autonomous region of Adygheh had one national language each.[33] Finally, the Karachai-Cherkess autonomous region had three national languages.[34]

The division of the region into so many 'national units' led to 'the creation of micro-nationalities of a tribal type. It rendered impossible the consolidation of that land into three groups of Muslim peoples whose languages were very close to one another: the Chechen-Ingush group, the Adygheh group . . . and, finally, the Turkic group of Karachais and Balkars . . .'[35]

The policy of linguistic division was equally absurd in Daghestan where eleven 'official' languages, representing four families of languages, were decreed by Moscow in 1930.[36]

Some Soviet authors and officials describe the creation of so many 'national' languages in the Caucasus as one of the 'greatest achievements of the October Revolution'.[37] 'The Soviet state gave so many nations a chance to retain their identity and to produce their own literature,' says one top leader of the Communist Party of the Soviet Union.[38] But it is virtually impossible not to detect other motives in the policy pursued by Stalin in the northern Caucasus. Known for its fanatical attachment to Islam, the region had fought Russian domination harder and longer than any other part of the Tsarist empire. It had raised the banner of revolt against the Bolshevik power also, and had been subjugated only thanks to massive doses of brutal force. It was essential to divide the warlike peoples of the mountain and make sure that they grew as far apart from one another as possible.

The failure of the Bolsheviks to rally the peoples of the mountains to their cause was amply illustrated during the Second World War when various Muslim groups welcomed Hitler's armies as liberators. This was not because they had any special affection for the Nazi Fuhrer who, being an atheist, was equally damned in the eyes of the Muslims. But the Muslims of the Caucasus 'under the slogan: "Stalingrad is but a step away from the Mountain" were hopeful that a Russian defeat would give them a chance to become independent – a chance they had missed in the first major European war.'[39]

The German defeat at Stalingrad, however, ended Muslim hopes in the Caucasus, and in 1943 decrees were issued to abolish the Karachai and Kalmyk and the Chechen-Ingush autonomous republics. The Kabard-Balkar autonomous republic was reconstituted to exclude the Balkars, who were accused of collaboration with the Nazi invaders.

Chechens, Ingushs, Kalmyks, Karachais and Balkars, totalling more than 800,000 people, were deported to Asia and deprived of a home base.

That Soviet policy towards the Muslims of northern Caucasus was not motivated by concern for the preservation of the identity of the 'nations' living there can be illustrated by at least two points. First, all the various autonomous republics and regions created there were included in the Russian republic and remained largely ruled from Moscow. This was in sharp contrast with the status of union republics which, under the various Soviet constitutions, enjoyed the right of secession. That the exercise of this right was well-nigh impossible did not change the fact that those republics which had at least theoretical access to it enjoyed a higher status than those which did not. The second point is that Soviet power pursued an entirely different policy in Transcaucasia, where the stated aim of policy was to unite rather than divide.

There were several reasons for the different treatment which Stalin reserved for Shiravan (Azarbaijan). This region, especially the city of Baku and its environs, represented the only part of the USSR where a sufficiently credible Bolshevik base existed amongst the Muslims. Thus a concession given to Azarbaijan was in fact a concession to 'comrades' who could then assume the task of exporting the revolution to Iran and Turkey. The Azarbaijani union republic could also be built up against union republics in Armenia and Georgia where nationalists and Mensheviks respectively retained much influence even after being purged by the Bolsheviks.

Soviet Azarbaijan was dotted with just one 'national' language: the Azari, a Turkic language with a half-Persian vocabulary. The official version of Azari, as developed by Soviet linguists between 1922 and 1936 when the Russian alphabet was adopted, absorbed the four dialects of the language which had been steadily drifting apart under the Tsars. The linguists also purged Azari of as many of its Persian, Arabic and Turkish words and expressions as they could without making the language virtually unusable by the masses.[40] Many of the purged words and expressions were replaced by new coinages or loans from Russian. The fact that the Azari Bolshevik elite took pleasure in adorning their speeches and conversations with Russian words further helped to 'russify' the language.

The Azari Bolshevik leaders used their special relationship with Moscow partly for the purpose of promoting chauvinistic policies of their own. They first turned their attention to the task of 'absorbing' the non-Azari minorities within their republic. A determined campaign was waged against Persian, especially in urban areas, while Arabic was banned from all schools and libraries. Next it was the turn of the Taleshis – an Iranic people professing sunni Islam as opposed to the Azaris who are shi'ites – to come under attack. The few Taleshi schools which had opened between 1905 and 1920 were closed down and all Taleshi publications were made illegal. The Baku government also pursued a policy of establishing Azari settlers in Taleshi territory in sufficiently large numbers so that Taleshis would become a minority in their own native country. By 1940 the Taleshi port of Lenkoran, on the Caspian Sea, had acquired an Azari majority. Although they numbered over 200,000 in 1945, the Taleshis were simply left out of Soviet statistics and absorbed by the Azaris after the war. This was in sharp contrast with Moscow's insistence that even tiny groups, such as the Lezgis in northern Caucasus, should retain their national identity and language.

Another Iranic group to gradually disappear in Soviet Azarbaijan consisted of the various Tat tribes and urban families. Many of them immigrated to Iran and some went to Daghestan where they could have an identity and language of their own. Others who stayed behind, probably numbering over 150,000 in 1989, were simply not mentioned in Soviet statistics.

The third Iranic group deprived of its identity in Soviet Azarbaijan was that of the Kurds who inhabited the south-western parts of the republic. The Kurds were also strongly present in Nakhichevan (Nakh-Javan) which was turned into an autonomous republic within Soviet Azarbaijan. But this did not imply any recognition of the status of the Kurds; Nakhichevan only acknowledged the presence of various Turkic tribes including the Shahsevans and Qara-Papakhs.

The policy of absorption practised by Azari leaders was also applied to Georgian (Meskhetian) and Armenian Muslims living within the republic. The Azari minorities who lived in the neighbouring republics of Armenia, Georgia and Daghestan nevertheless retained their national identity and enjoyed access to Azari schools and publications.

One major group that could not be absorbed by Soviet Azarbaijan consisted of the Christian Armenians in the mountainous enclave of Nagorno-Karabakh (High Black Garden). This was turned into an autonomous region as part of the Azari republic against the expressed wishes of a majority of its inhabitants.

The map of the Caucasus as it was finally established on the eve of the Second World War was not free of anomalies. Substantial ethnic, religious and linguistic minorities remained within the borders of the various autonomous or union republics created. The assumption was that the process of 'drawing-together' (slibzhenie) would efface the differences and lead to the emergence of a common Soviet identity. Some Soviet theoreticians believed that nationalism was a transient aberration marking the passage of a society from the stage of feudalism to that of industrial society complete with the emergence of a capitalist class. The USSR's Asian peoples could escape that process by moving directly from feudalism to the classless communist society. Stalin promised the definite end of all nationalism by the end of each five-year plan that he unveiled, but he was intelligent enough not to believe his own propaganda. And the struggle against nationalism has remained an important element of Soviet policy up to the present.

The successive purges of the Azari leadership in the name of the struggle against nationalistic tendencies did not put an end to the attempt by some sections of the Azari intelligentsia to try to create a mini-empire of their own in the name of Communism and with support from Moscow. The Azari party chief, Mir-Ja'afar Baqer-Zadeh (Baqerov) became a close associate of Stalin and Beria and played a crucial role in involving the USSR in the abortive attempt at detaching the provinces of Azarbaijan and Kurdestan from Iran in 1944–46. Baqerov had hoped that those two provinces would eventually be annexed by Soviet Azarbaijan, thus enabling Baku to emerge as the capital of the USSR's third most populous republic after the RSFSR and the Ukraine.[41]

Soviet policy in the Caucasus, Kazakhstan and Central Asia offered an original experience in the administration of former colonies by a European power. The Soviet leaders retained a firm grip over the party apparatus, which was dominated almost exclusively by Russians and other Slavs, but opened the doors of governmental bureaucracy to 'natives' in an unprecedented scale. The policy of 'nativisation' (*korenitzaya*) saw thousands of Kazakhs, Uzbeks, Tajiks, Turcomans, Daghestanis, Azaris and others – some of them barely literate – assume administrative tasks at virtually all levels. As time went by the peoples of Kazakhstan, Central Asia and the Caucasus gained the impression that they had indeed become masters in their own land. Very few were able to see through the façade and recognise the reality of Russian domination at virtually all levels of decision-making. Soviet propaganda made much of the fact that Russian and other Slav waiters served at restaurants in Tashkent and Frunze where Uzbeks and Kirghizes dined. How could Russians be 'colonialists' when they worked in the kitchen?[42]

Stalin's policy, pursued in different ways by his successors, was based on a number of important stratagems. By imposing the cyrillic alphabet on all Muslim peoples, the Soviet state virtually made them illiterate at a blow. They all had to learn to read and write again. The change of alphabet also meant that there could be no immediate access to the literary heritage of centuries. The Soviet authorities would decide which books to re-issue in the new alphabet. Over the years scores of classical writers and poets whose work was labelled 'feudalistic' or 'reactionary' have simply ceased to exist except for a few specialists.[43] Instead, poets and writers identified as 'progressive' are often forced upon a captive readership as part of promoting the proletarian culture.

The adoption of the cyrillic alphabet also cut off the Muslims of the USSR from the wider Islamic world. Turkey had adopted the Latin alphabet in the 1920s, while Iran, Afghanistan, Egypt and other Middle Eastern states used the Arabic script. The Muslims of British India also wrote some of their languages in the Arabic alphabet.[44] The injection of thousands of Russian words into the Muslim languages of the USSR, often replacing Persian and Arabic words, also widened the gap of understanding between Soviet Muslims and their neighbours.

The USSR's frontiers with Afghanistan, Iran and Turkey were sealed after 1921 except for selective items of trade. Even divided families were not allowed to visit each other after 1925 and this led to much hardship especially among the Azaris and the Turcomans on both sides of Soviet borders with Iran. The Turcoman case was especially tragic, as many clans were suddenly divided by a frontier imposed by Tehran and Moscow. This provoked numerous raids across the frontier in both directions well into the 1970s.[45]

While all ethnic Russians lived within the borders of the USSR, many of the Muslim peoples of the new Soviet states represented part of larger ethnic groups which inhabited several different countries. The Tatars, for example, were present in Turkey,[46] Bulgaria and even Rumania.[47] The Turcomans also lived in Afghanistan, Iran and Iraq. The Uzbeks, the Kirghiz, the Uyghurs and the Tajiks had branches in Afghanistan and China. The imposition of Soviet rule severed all human, cultural and economic links among the various peoples thus divided. Regions which had once played a central role in the development of Islamic thought and culture were reduced to the level of backyards of an atheist state. Alma-Ata, Tashkent, Bokhara, Samarkand, Marv, Doshanbeh, Pishpek (Frunze), Ashkabad and Baku became windows that opened only towards Europe as represented by Russia. Kazan, Ufa and Orenburg were in a still more exposed position as the number of Slav settlers continued to grow, together with Russian cultural and political domination of highly vulnerable Muslim societies.

The reality of Russian domination was also reflected in a variety of other ways. Hundreds of cities and thousands of villages underwent name changes that indicated a change in their status. The capital of Tajikestan was named Stalin-Abad after the *Vozhd*. Frunze, the Bolshevik general, gave his name to the capital of Kirghizia, although few Kirghizes could pronounce that word properly.[48] In the Caucasus, many cities were named after Orjokinidze and Kirov, two of Stalin's closest associates whose brutality had become proverbial in the region. The ancient city of Ganjeh, once one of Islam's most important cultural centres, became Kirov-Abad after having briefly regained its name during the revolution.[49]

In the Caucasus and Central Asia even the summits of mountains, rivers and waterfalls were named after Marx, Engels, Lenin, Stalin and other Communist leaders. In some regions the names of Islam's prophet and saints were removed from towns, monuments and public places to make way for personalities and events associated with Russia. In ancient Rome conquering generals often adopted the name of places or peoples they subjugated, but in Communist USSR the reverse happened: conquerors gave their names to conquered lands and peoples.

The death of Stalin and the campaign launched against his 'personality cult' by Khrushchev did not bring about any dramatic change in the policy of nationalities as practised by Moscow since the 1930s. If anything, Khrushchev intensified two aspects of Stalin's policy in Muslim regions. First he speeded up the settlement of Slavs in Kazakhstan, Central Asia and the Caucasus as part of an ambitious programme aimed at mobilising the natural resources and agricultural potential of the peripheral republics.

In 1954 Khrushchev inaugurated his 'Virgin Lands' programme which was supposed to make the USSR self-sufficient in basic food items within two decades. The programme eventually led to the settlement of more than a million Slavs, mainly Russians and Ukrainians, on Kazakh land. By the end of the 1960s the Kazakhs had become a minority in their own republic; it was not until 1989 that the situation was reversed to give them a slight numerical advantage over ethnic Russians in Kazakhstan.[50]

The second aspect of Stalin's policy pursued by Khrushchev with renewed vigour was the anti-Islamic campaign. A foretaste of this came in 1955 when the Young Communist League (Komsomol) spearheaded a wave of attacks on women wearing the veil in Kazakhstan, Central Asia, northern Caucasus and Azarbaijan. Veil-burning ceremonies were organised in villages and on collective farms and, in some cases, led to violent clashes between Komsomol zealots and the local population.

In 1958 Khrushchev assumed the post of prime minister, after ousting Marshal Bulganin, and almost immediately revived the Union of the Godless which had been pushed into the background since 1940. The Union launched concerted attacks on Islamic schools, mosques and monuments.

In Azarbaijan attacks were made on shi'ite mourners in February, leading to at least three deaths.[51] Some monuments were partly or wholly destroyed. In Shemakhi, Azarbaijan, a mosque dating to the fourteenth century was razed to the ground to make room for a party youth club.

During Muharram and Safar, the two months of shi'ite mourning, concerts and dance festivals were organised in city squares as a direct insult to the feelings of the faithful majority. In 1959 the end of the 'era of the veil' was officially announced, and what was presented as 'the last veil' was burned in public at an official ceremony in Bokhara.

Khrushchev's anti-religion campaign was not aimed exclusively against Islam but also hit other faiths. The campaign was accompanied by a new programme of russification. The educational reform of 1958 made Russian a compulsory subject at virtually all schools throughout the union; it gave families the option of sending their children to Russian-language schools in regions where Russian was not the official national language. This was an open move to deny many vernacular schools of their base. The effect of the reform was particularly dramatic in the Tatar and Bashkir autonomous republics. The natives were often in a minority there and Tatar and Bashkir schools could not have continued to function without attracting some Slav children. The net result of the new policy was the closure of many native schools and the absorption of Tatar and Bashkir children into Russian schools.

The Anti-Islam campaign and the russification drive that accompanied it drew a wedge between official Islam and the Soviet authorities for the first time. The *modus vivendi* worked out since 1941 was shattered and official Muslim leaders did not hide their sympathy for 'acts of protest'.[52] These acts at times assumed a violent aspect. In 1962, for example, Karakalpak tribesmen clashed with the militia after an official attempt at closing a village mosque. Some of the coal miners who joined the strike at Karaganda in Kazakhstan also complained about the fact that their halls of prayer had been shut.

A side effect of Khrushchev's policies was the revival of age-old hostility between the Azaris on the one hand and Armenian and Georgian Christians on the other, especially in Baku and Sumgait where ethnic riots broke out in 1963.

The removal of Khrushchev in 1964 and the end of his anti-religion campaign did not remove all of the bitterness that had been created. The new collective leadership under Leonid I. Brezhnev took a number of steps aimed at reassuring the Muslims. Russian racists who had attacked Chechen and Ingush deportees in Grozny were brought to justice, and a committee was set up to organise the return of deported Meskhetians (Georgian Muslims) to their homeland in 1965. The reconstruction of Tashkent, destroyed by earthquake in 1966, also provided the new leadership with an occasion for wooing 'official' Islam. A number of new mosques were included in the reconstruction project, a move that completed the policy of restoring Islamic monuments which had been unveiled in 1964.

In 1967 the Presidium of the Supreme Soviet, the country's highest law-making institution, published decrees exonerating the Crimean Tatars, Turks, Kurds and Khemshins (Armenian Muslims) of charges of treason during the Second World War. A year later, the muftiate of Tashkent was allowed to publish the magazine *Muslims of the Soviet East* in five languages.[53] This was followed by the granting of scholarships to some 50 Soviet Muslim students who wished to read theology and Islamic law (*shari'ah*) in Cairo and Damascus.

The new status of official Islam was further highlighted when the mufti of Tashkent, Ziauddin Ibn Ishan Baba-Khan, organised an international conference in the city in 1970. The conference was above all a political show, and speaker after speaker attacked 'Imperialism' and 'Zionism'. Nevertheless, it marked the return of official Islam to the Soviet political scene in a manner unprecedented since the early 1940s. Throughout the 1970s official Islam was called upon by Moscow to play an active role in promoting Soviet diplomatic objectives in the Middle East. Did this mean that the masters of the Kremlin cynically exploited Islam for their own purposes? There is no definite answer and the debate continues among those who believe that official Islam had become a tool of Soviet imperialism and those who are convinced that it was right and proper for the muftiates to occupy whatever space was relinquished by Moscow.

Relations between official Islam and the parallel movements that kept the faith alive, although not fully free of conflict, remained on the whole stable throughout the 1970s. Frequent visitors to the Muslim regions of the USSR detected no sign of major tension between the two until the advent of militant fundamentalism symbolised by Iran's Islamic Revolution in 1979. But by then other sources of resentment, notably the growing corruption of officials in Central Asia, Kazakhstan and the Caucasus, had been shaped and undermined the tenuous peace established between Islam and the Soviet power under Brezhnev.

8

Islam: Faith, Culture and Identity

Ivan IV (The Terrible) had vowed that after his triumph over the Kazan Tatars no Muslims would be allowed to enter Moscow except in chains. More than four centuries later, however, the Moscow mosque is one of the busiest places of worship in the capital of the USSR. And thanks to Mikhail Gorbachev's policy of *glasnost* (transparence) a number of Islamic books and cassettes are openly on sale in the Izamilovo Park as the faithful – sporting the traditional Muslim beard and accompanied by their womenfolk who wear a variety of colourful head-dresses – discuss matters of interest to the umma. Not far from the park a huge portrait of the Prophet Muhammad, woven into a carpet of exquisite patterns, hangs from the wall of the select Baku restaurant.

Officially, however, there are no Muslims in Moscow or anywhere else in the Union of Soviet Socialist Republics. There are people, 'an increasingly small minority' according to officials, who practise 'Islamic rites'. But they too have no right to describe themselves as Muslims. Yet some high-ranking Soviet leaders admit that the country is faced with 'a serious problem' in the shape of an Islamic revival.[1]

Because it does not have a formal hierarchy complete with baptism and regular masses, Islam could assume an ethereal existence: it could be everywhere and yet nowhere at the same time. Anyone born of at least one Muslim parent is automatically considered as a Muslim unless and until he expressly renounces his links with the community. But even then one is not totally excluded from the umma since Islam has no system of excommunication. It is not rare to encounter people who describe themselves as 'Islamic atheists', and one distinguished example of this seemingly unlikely combination was the famous Azarbaijani composer Fikrat Amirov. A high-ranking member of the Azarbaijani Communist Party and a member of the Supreme Soviet for several years, Amirov was a veteran Bolshevik and a firm believer in 'the superiority of science over metaphysics of which religion is a part'.[2] And yet it is with some pride that he added, 'I am also a Muslim.' He described the rosary he always carried with him as 'my link with my Islamic culture'.[3]

Soviet statistical data contain no mention of religion. It is therefore by reference to the ethnic identity of the USSR's 153 different 'nations', 'nationalities' and 'ethnic groups' that one could identify the Muslims and estimate their numerical strength. The 1897 census, taken under the tsars, clearly stated the religious identity of all the subjects of the empire. Since the Muslim peoples then identified have not renounced Islam so far, it is possible to consider them as nations, nationalities and groups that, at least culturally, belong to the Islamic universe.

Using the 1979 census as a base, it is possible to estimate the number of various Muslim nations, nationalities and groups in the USSR today. The largest Muslim nation in the USSR is the Uzbek, which has its own Soviet Socialist Republic (SSR) where it forms more than 70 per cent of the population. Uzbeks throughout the USSR were estimated to number 15 million in 1989.[4] The Kazakhs, who also have their own SSR where they constitute just over 40 per cent of the total population, number more than 7.2 million. The third largest Muslim nation in the USSR is represented by the Tatars who have an autonomous republic (ASSR), but who are also present in almost every republic of the union; their numerical strength could be put at around seven million.

The fourth largest Muslim nation of the USSR are the Azaris, who form more than 80 per cent of the population of the Azarbaijan Soviet Socialist Republic. Also present in Armenia, Georgia, the Russian republic, the Baltic states and Central Asia, they number just over 6.2 million. The Tajiks, who form more than 60 per cent of the population in their own SSR, are also present in Uzbekistan, Kirghizestan and Turkmenistan; they number just over 3.3 million and have registered one of the highest demographic growth rates in the world. The Turcomans constitute about 70 per cent of the population in their own SSR and are also present in Uzbekistan, Tajikestan, Kirghizestan and Kazakhstan; they number more than 2.5 million. They are followed by the Kirghiz, also organised in an SSR where they form just under 50 per cent of the population; also present in neighbouring republics, they are estimated to number 2.5 million. Next the Bashkirs, organised in an ASSR where they form just over half of the population, number 1.9 million.

Four autonomous republics and two autonomous regions (AO) within the Russian republic (RSFSR) include Muslim populations. The Daghestan ASSR has a Muslim majority that consists of various ethnic and linguistic groups; together they are estimated to number around 1.8 million. Also in the Caucasus, the Chechens who number 750,000 share an ASSR with the Ingushs who are no more than 150,000. The Kabard–

Balkar ASSR has some 450,000 Muslims who form 60 per cent of the total population.

The Adygheh autonomous region contains just under 100,000 Muslims. In the Cherkess-Karachai autonomous region, Muslims number 200,000 and form more than half of the population.

The Georgian SSR includes several Muslim minorities. In the Abkhaz ASSR Muslims number around 65,000, while the Adzhar ASSR contains some 200,000 Georgian Muslims (Meskhetians). The South Ossetian AO, also part of Georgia, includes 20,000 Muslims.

The Armenian SSR hosts more than 180,000 Muslims, mostly Kurds, Turcomans and Tatars.

The various peoples of Finnish origin converted to Islam[5] probably number around 650,000. Organised in their autonomous republics of Udmurt, Mari and Chuvash they fall under the administration of the RSFSR.

Finally, the city of Astrakhan and its environs represent a Muslim stronghold with a population of over 600,000.

Thus Muslims, representing some 53 million people out of a total population of more than 290 million, form the second largest group in the USSR after the Russians.[6] To be sure, Soviet writers make every effort to underestimate the number of Muslims in the USSR, while some Western anti-Soviet writers blow the number of Muslims in the USSR out of all relation to reality. The two extremes offer us numbers ranging from 38 million to more than 70 million!

Whatever the exact number of Soviet Muslims, there is one point on which everyone agrees: Muslims have the highest birth rates in the USSR and, if the present trends continue, they might well outnumber ethnic Russians within the next two to three decades. Muslims already provide the USSR with its biggest reservoir of labour and by 1990 no less than 45 per cent of all new entries into the labour market will be of Muslim origin. While the European population of the USSR is ageing and static – if not actually on the decline as is the case in Belorussia – the Muslim republics project an image of youth and vitality. In the academic year of 1988–89, no fewer than half of all children attending primary school in the USSR were from a Muslim background.[7]

The Muslims' demographic 'explosion', especially in Central Asia, has already provoked problems in the field of employment. The region's economy, geared to the needs of a top-heavy system, is not sufficiently dynamic to create the jobs needed. If the policy of 'social market', advocated by the Moscow leaders since 1986, is fully implemented, hundreds of thousands of people in Central Asia might find themselves without jobs.

One solution to the problem would be to encourage Muslims to leave their native lands and emigrate to Siberia, where an acute labour shortage has persisted since the 1970s, or to the European republics where an ageing population could make way for newcomers in the job market. Soviet Muslims, however, have consistently proved reluctant to leave their native countries. Central Asia and the Caucasus represent the USSR's 'sunbelt' where the rigours of Siberian and Russian climates are only talked about. The easier pace of life, an abundance of food and a traditional pattern of life which offers emotional and material security, are factors militating against mass immigration by Soviet Muslims.

The Muslim populations refuse immigration for at least one other reason. A majority still live in rural areas, while in European USSR more than 55 per cent of the population is already urbanised. What energy there is for immigration in the Muslim republics is spent on moving from the rural areas into the cities within the borders of each republic. Until the mid-1980s European settlers – notably Russians, Ukrainians and Belorussians but also Germans – formed a majority of the population in Tashkent (USSR's fourth largest city), Baku (USSR's fifth most populous city), Alma-Ata, Doshanbeh, Frunze and even Makhachkala. Kazan, Ufa and Orenburg appeared like Russian cities with Muslim minorities. Only smaller cities such as Samarkand, Bokhara, Marv, Astrakhan, Shemakhi and Kirova Abad had retained a Muslim majority. There are several factors which have contributed to a change in the situation that is likely to alter the demographic composition of the Central Asian, Kazakh, Azarbaijani and north Caucasian cities within the next one or two decades.

The various Soviet constitutions enacted since 1918 describe religion as a purely 'private' affair; yet the government has constantly tried either to eradicate all religions or to bring them under some kind of control. In 1943 Abdul-Rahman Rasuloghlu (Rasula'ev), the Mufti of Ufa, reached an agreement with Stalin under which Muslims were given permission to set up an administrative structure capable of attending to the needs of the faith. The structure, consisting of four 'directorates', has survived many ups and downs and still represents the most immediately recognisable sign of Islam's presence as an organised force in Soviet society.

The first of the four directorates is the muftiate of Tashkent which covers Kazakhstan, Uzbekistan, Kirghizestan, Tajikestan and Turkmenistan. It is headed by Shaikh Haj Shaikh Muhammad Muhammad-Yussuf[8] with Shaikh Yussuf Khan Shakirov as Vice-President. The official language is Uzbek. Because it covers a majority of Soviet Muslims, the muftiate of Tashkent is often considered as the centre of official Islam in the USSR, while the man heading it is at times referred to as 'The Grand Mufti'.

The Mufti of Tashkent is responsible for Muslims of the sunni-hanafi persuasion who form a majority of Muslim believers in the USSR. In charge of between 700 and 2,000 mosques and shrines[9] throughout Central Asia and Kazakhstan, the muftiate is also the guardian of the Qur'an of Othman, believed to be the oldest copy of the Holy Book.[10] The muftiate has published six editions of the Qur'an, which were quickly sold out.[11] Two prestigious madrassehs are administered by the muftiate; the Madrasseh Mir-Arab in Bokhara has between 70 and 80 pupils at any given time, selected from among hundreds of candidates.[12] The course offered at Bokhara could be completed in seven years. There are no formal examinations and the work of each pupil is individually assessed over the years not only by his professors but also by fellow-students.

Graduates from the Bokhara school can apply to enter the Madrasseh Imam Isma'il Bokhari in Tashkent, which is the highest centre of Islamic learning in the USSR. In 1988–89 the madrasseh had 22 students and 25 professors and teachers including the mufti himself. Students leave the madrasseh when they and their teachers feel that the time has come for them to do so. This could take between three and six years. Some graduates go to the al-Azhar University in Cairo for further research and study.

The curricula offered at both Bokhara and Tashkent remain strictly traditional. The study of the Qur'an, which necessitates the study of Arabic language and literature, is the basis of all instruction. Islamic law (*shari'ah*), although officially condemned by the Soviet system, is assiduously studied, together with the *hadiths* (traditions attributed to the Prophet). Theology, the science of men,[13] mathematics, philosophy, comparative law, English, Persian literature and Russian are also included in the curricula. It is largely up to the pupils themselves to determine the best pattern of studies they wish to pursue. The graduates become teachers, researchers or Imam-Khatibs – that is to say mullahs who administer mosques, lead prayer gatherings and attend to other religious needs of the community.

The mufti himself readily admits that the number of graduates is nowhere near enough, especially now that the pressure exerted by the party and government on all religions has been substantially reduced. The muftiate puts the number of various 'servants of the faith' in its employ at under 1,500 people for a total Muslim population of around 40 million.

The muftiate of the Muslims of Russia and Siberia, based on the Bashkir capital of Ufa, is the oldest of the four directorates. Founded in 1783 by Catherine II, it was revived under Stalin in 1941. Headed by Shaikh Tal'at Taj-eddin, a young and dynamic cleric, this muftiate has tried to establish new points of contact with the Muslim world since 1982.[14] The official language of the muftiate is Tatar and it covers the Tatar ASSR, the Bashkir ASSR, Lithuania, the RSFSR, the Ukraine and Siberia. The important mosques of Moscow, Leningrad, Rostov-on-Don and the strong Muslim community in Astrakhan fall under the authority of Ufa. The muftiate is also responsible for preserving a number of major Muslim monuments and libraries in Kazan, Astrakhan, Orenburg and other cities. Like the one in Tashkent, the muftiate of Ufa follows the sunni-Hanafi school of Islam.

The Ufa directorate employs some 400 servants of the cult but does not offer educational facilities of its own. However, plans to open two madrassehs were completed in 1989 and Shaikh Taj-eddin hopes to begin training future mullahs in Ufa and, perhaps, in Moscow itself within the next two years. He sees the future as bright and promising and is convinced that the Gorbachev policy of *perestroika* will enable Soviet Muslims to 'fully live their own lives'.[15]

The third muftiate of the USSR is based on Makhachkala, the capital of Daghestan. Originally created in 1944, it was at first centred on the city of Buynaksk but moved to Makhachkala in 1975. The muftiate is headed by Shaikh Muhammad Guekkiev, a Balkar, who is highly respected in the Muslim world for his wide reading in Islamic theology. The language of the muftiate is Arabic, a choice largely dictated by tradition.

The Makhachkala directorate offers services both to Hanafi sunni Muslims of northern Caucasus and the Shaf'ei sunni Muslims who predominate in Daghestan.

Finally, the directorate of Baku covers Soviet Azarbaijan where duo-decimain shi'ites form a majority together with the sunni Muslims of Georgia and Armenia. Headed by Ayatollah Haj Allah Shukur Pasha-Zadeh, an Azari mullah, this directorate uses Azari as its official language. No estimates regarding the number of mullahs working under the directorate or mosques administered by it were available in 1989. Of all the four directorates which together represent official Islam in the USSR, the one based on Baku seemed to have the most difficulty in ensuring a popular base for itself.

The total number of officially open mosques and other places of Muslim worship in the USSR has been the subject of controversy for more than half a century. According to an official of the muftiate of Tashkent, there were no more than 200 official mosques throughout the USSR,[16] nearly half of which were located in the city of Tashkent and its environs. The rest of Uzbekistan and the other three republics of Central Asia had no more than 35 mosques including four in Bokhara. Ashkabad, the capital of Turkmenistan, had just one official mosque.

Mosques in Kazakhstan did not exceed 12 and the remaining number was accounted for by Daghestan (30 mosques), Azarbaijan (17 mosques), European USSR and Siberia.

The four muftiates who control the official mosques, however, readily admit that they do not represent the whole of Islam in the USSR. Most Muslims could meet their religious needs without recourse to an official clergy. Any literate man capable of understanding the Qur'an and following Islamic rites could officiate at especially important ceremonies such as marriage and burial. Believers could gather together on a regular basis to study the Qur'an, discuss points of Islamic history and exchange views on various issues of contemporary life. Any believer who is adult, sane and capable could lead his fellow-Muslims in prayer. Strictly speaking, Islam could do without clerics. According to many *hadiths* the Prophet himself was in fact opposed to the emergence of a professional group of religious officials. On one occasion when he wanted to dispatch a group of disciples to take the message of Islam to the Yemen, he made it clear to them that they should instantly return to their original employment after the completion of their mission.

Thus Muslims in the USSR are perfectly capable of going their own way, regardless of what the muftiates say and do. The muftiates play their role by helping to preserve Islamic monuments and by arranging the publication of Islamic texts. Their rulings on controversial issues could also be of some significance in so far as Soviet lawmakers might take them into account.

All the muftiates have adopted conservative positions on such issues as abortion, artificial insemination and the transfer of human organs. However on some issues, including illegitimate birth and adoption, they have gone along with general trends in Soviet jurisprudence.

When asked whether or not a 'parallel' Islam exists in the USSR, officials at the muftiates respond with enigmatic assertions such as 'Islam is where believers are'. In more private conversations, however, they admit that the unpredictability and the harshness of Soviet policy over more than 70 years have led many Muslims to wall themselves in and build a spiritual life beyond the reach of the totalitarian state.

The recent loosening of controls exerted by the state and the party has allowed parallel Islam to gradually come into the open. Everywhere, new mosques have been constructed or are under construction by individuals and groups not connected with any of the muftiates.

Some Soviet writers do not hide their apprehensions regarding the growing presence of unofficial Islam. Igor Beliayev, a leading journalist, has called for 'energetic action' aimed at stemming the tide of Islam in the USSR. He writes:

Everyone knows that in the USSR the state and religion are separate and that no one bans others from believing in Allah. But here a number of unexpected developments take place – developments to which we have to pay attention. In Central Asia and Azerbaijan, in the Volga region and the Ural and in other traditional centres of Islamic presence, a number of 'parallel mosques' have began to function. They number more than 1,800! Only Allah knows what sermons are read in those mosques and who is in charge of them. We have to recall that organising a small mosque in one corner of a private residence is not a difficult task. All that is needed is a copy of the Quran and a few simple rules regarding prayers. It is possible for a mosque to operate in a Kazakh village or an Uzbek 'Qichlaq' (hamlet) without the neighbours finding out for a long time.[17]

The same writer suggests that the construction of mosques be made legal so that the activities of parallel Islam could be brought under official scrutiny. 'Would it not be wiser to authorise the construction of mosques where there is a need for them? Things would be much clearer both for the faithful and for local authorities.'[18]

Another Soviet writer, the Azarbaijani Abdul-Farid Dashdamirev[19] identifies Islam's revival as 'a serious issue' for the Communist state. He writes: 'Religion still exists in parts of the population (in Soviet Azarbaijan) and there are self-appointed mullahs and holy places ... We must make serious efforts to understand what makes religion able to survive, why it can still influence people.'[20] Dashdamirov tries to provide an answer: 'Religion is trying to find its place in the sphere of national relations ... In recent years the interest of our intellectuals and masses in national culture, in the sources of our culture and in the traditions and customs of our people have increased noticeably. The confusion between the national and the religious, the replacement of one by the other, takes place mainly on the level of mass consciousness. The idealisation of religion, the overestimation of its role in the life of the nation, generally accompany nationalistic attitudes and the glorification of the national style of life.'[21]

Since 1986 official and parallel Islam have been engaged in an undeclared competition over repairing mosques and shrines and building new centres of worship. Soviet press reports with dismay the 'vast sums' spent by private citizens on the building of new mosques. One mosque in a fairly modest village in the Jizak oblast reportedly cost over half a million roubles (around £400,000). 'The local party committee knew about this and did nothing,' reported one paper.[22]

In 1988 the muftiate of Tashkent organised a series of ceremonies to mark the restoration and inauguration of one of the most important Muslim holy places in the USSR. The monument, in the city of Turkestan (Shavkar) in southern Kazakhstan consists of several buildings including a mosque. But its claim to fame is based on a mausoleum built under Teymur in the fourteenth century. The mausoleum – which contains the mortal remains of Shaikh Ahmad Yassawi, the founder of one of the most prestigeous sufi orders in Central Asia – had been an important centre of Muslim pilgrimage until it was closed down and isolated by barbed wire under Khrushchev. The then mufti of Tashkent, Ziauddin Baba Khan, was subsequently forced into issuing a number of *fatwas* (edicts) against acts of pilgrimage other than the performance of *haj* at Mecca.

In 1986 the guardian of the monument, one Shaikh Sultan Hamra, launched an appeal for a major renovation project to be carried out. Within a few days an association was founded and enough money raised to begin the task. Then an appeal was made to the local authorities, headed by Muslims, who instantly agreed to provide material and technical assistance. The new Jam'e Mosque and the renovated mausoleum were opened to the public in the summer of 1988 with the blessings of the muftiate of Tashkent. Here, both wings of Islam – official and parallel – could take pride in a joint venture. Official reports indicate that the association which helped carry out the project consisted of people from many different walks of life including factory workers and university students.[23] The re-opening of Yassawi's mausoleum to openly organised pilgrimage in 1989 must be seen as a sure sign that, provided the policy of *glasnost* continues, clandestine Islam might well be persuaded to emerge into the open in the pursuit of legitimate goals.

The division of Soviet Islam into 'official' and 'parallel' has led to a number of errors in analysing the exact role played by the muftiates on the one hand and the sufi fraternities on the other. Some Western writers have automatically assumed that official Islam is nothing but a tool of Soviet domination and a few have even gone as far as accusing the muftis and their closest associates of being KGB agents. Communist writers, on the other hand, have had no hesitation in labelling parallel Islam – even under the tsars – as agents of this or that foreign power. Imam Shamil was presented as a British agent and the American Central Intelligence Agency (CIA) is now credited with the visible rise in the fortunes of clandestine Islam in the USSR. We also know that on different occasions both the USSR and the United States have tried to turn Islam into a weapon with which to fight each other during the Cold War.

The difference between official and parallel Islam in the USSR, however, is certainly not about the ends but the means. The muftis would instantly cease to be effective if they were even remotely suspected by the believers of being more loyal towards the Communist state than the faith of Muhammad. In other words, Soviet official Islam must be genuinely Islamic in order to have any significance at all, and once it becomes genuinely Islamic it can no longer serve the long-term interests of the Soviet state. Keeping Islam alive in any form and virtually at any level remains a direct and potent challenge to Soviet rule, especially in the more totalitarian phases of its existence.

The division of Islam into official and parallel is not confined to the USSR. It exists in all Muslim countries, even in the Islamic Republic of Iran where the mullahs have directly ruled since 1979. The reason for this is that Islam recognises no separation of mosque and state and seeks the establishment of the 'perfect state' in this world. Since none of the governments in power could achieve a consensus as to their status as fully legitimate representatives of Allah on earth, the Islam they profess, finance and foster – the official Islam – is not considered to be perfect in the eyes of the majority of believers. But imperfect Islam does not mean anti-Islam, and relations between official religious organisations and the mass of the believers – who continue to demand a fuller application of Islamic rules – could continue at levels of mutual acceptance.

In the final analysis, however, unofficial Islam, because of its roots among the masses, can control and discipline the official structures, as was amply demonstrated in Iran when officially-approved mullahs did not hesitate to side with the Islamic revolutionaries against the shah in 1979. A less dramatic example of this was witnessed in the USSR itself when Shamsuddin Ibn Ziauddin Khan Baba Khan, the Grand Mufti of Tashkent, was forced into resignation in January 1989. The young mufti, a very learned theologian but also a man of the world, had to step down after a series of demonstrations organised by parallel Islam demanded his departure. Mufti Shamsuddin was accused of anti-Islamic habits including 'drinking alcholic beverages, spending time with many women and playing snooker'.[24]

Mufti Baba Khan had been identified by some Western writers as a major player in a Soviet strategy for the domination of the Muslim world. The supposed strategy was described by one of the West's leading experts on Soviet Islam in the following terms:

> For some 20 years, since 1967–68 to be more precise, when Yuri Andropov became head of the KGB, the USSR has practised a strategy of infiltration of the Muslim world through the official hierarchy of Soviet Islam. . . . In 20 years the Soviet Union has succeeded in gaining a foothold in the Muslim world while the West is still trying to define its position vis-a-vis Islam.[25]

Anyone who has spent some time talking to the various muftis and their principal advisers would know that their first loyalty is to Islam and not to the Soviet state which they consider only as the least of all evils under the circumstances.

Soviet official Islam has never conceded, in fact could never concede, the supremacy of Marxist-Leninist ideology. At best it considers Communism as a method of managing the economy and running the administration. Even on such vital issues as the Soviet invasion of Afghanistan, the muftiates singularly failed to come out in support of Brezhnev's policy. Even when some muftis discover that Communism contains a number of Islamic ideas, it is to emphasise the superiority of Muhammad's teachings over Marxism. Islam's ambition is to unite the entire universe under its own banner. It cannot accept the role of a Trojan horse for Soviet infiltration in Muslim countries. While the West sees official Islam as a branch of the KGB, many Soviet scholars and propagandists return the compliment by portraying parallel Islam as a Western creation. This is how one Soviet writer exposes this strange idea:

> Brzezinski[26] developed an Islamic 'Kriegspiel' against the Soviet Union. ... The objective was to create an 'Islamic bomb' in the Soviet republics of Central Asia. The idea took flesh when an official report was prepared in 1979. [It] indicated that specialised, secret Muslim organisations should be created with the aim of undertaking subversive operations in our country. They would use Soviet citizens living in regions where Islam has traditionally been propagated.[27]

The same article speaks of a mysterious 'Islamic conference' held in the United States during which a plan for 'the creation of an Islamic republic in Soviet Central Asia' was approved.[28]

Adepts of the theory of conspiracy on both sides would, presumably, not change their opinion, but it is necessary to reassert a few facts. The muftiates were created in the eighteenth century before the Communist ideology was born; they were suppressed by the Bolsheviks and their revival was an important demand of Muslims between 1918 and 1942. When Stalin finally agreed to let the muftiates resume work he did this as a concession to Islam, and also at a time the Soviet state was in a position of weakness. Official Soviet Islam may – indeed almost certainly does – include a number of KGB agents. But on the whole it must be regarded as part of Islam and not of the Soviet state.

The assertion that the USSR has pursued a carefully planned policy towards Muslim countries is equally open to question. It is based on the assumption that the USSR was specially knowledgeable about developments in Muslim societies, yet the Soviet experience in Afghanistan showed that this was not the case. Despite a strong diplomatic presence in Kabul for more than sixty years, the Soviets were 'maliciously deceived' by Afghan Communists. 'We were fooled by Nur-Muhammad Taraki and his followers,' one top Soviet leader says. 'We believed what these people said and were gradually sucked into the Afghan quagmire.'[29]

During the two decades in which Moscow was supposedly wooing the Muslim world, the Soviets were expelled from Egypt, lost much of their influence in Iraq and were caught in a civil war in South Yemen.

The Soviet 'infiltration' plan was so badly organised that individuals known for their anti-Islamic activities were appointed as ambassadors to a number of Muslim countries.[30]

Soviet official Islam has certainly taken part in the campaign against Israel and the United States, but to see this uniquely as a result of KGB manipulation is wrong. Hatred of Israel and enmity towards the United States, partly because of its support for the Jewish state, are popular themes throughout the Muslim world. There is evidence that Soviet official Islam has exerted what pressure it could on Moscow to adopt an even tougher stance on the Palestine issue.

That Soviet power never fully trusted official Islam is also illustrated by the fact that the financial and manpower resources allocated to anti-Islamic propaganda in Muslim regions have always been many times higher than allocations made for the four muftiates. In Alma-Ata alone, for example, the local House of the Godless employed no fewer than 540 lecturers and 1,300 'agitators' for the purpose of combating Islam through 'scientific and atheistic propaganda'.[31] This is higher than the total number of people working for the muftiate of Tashkent, the largest of the four.

The theories according to which parallel Islam has been created or sustained first by the British and then by the United States are equally devoid of any serious content. The sufi fraternities represent the continuation of a tradition that began in Khorassan in the eighth century. The various orders were established in their present form between the twelfth and fourteenth centuries. It would be a unique feat for any foreign power to control such a vast network of believers throughout the USSR. In any case the sufi orders, strong and well-organised as no doubt they are, do not represent more than part of parallel Islam in the USSR.

Sufism does not, and never did, represent a monolithic movement. And not all forms of sufism could be expected to encourage or at least sanction militant Islam. Sufism has in fact often been a means of escape from the real world into a universe of mystical asceticism. Some Soviet anti-Muslim specialists recognise the diversity of the sufi movement and one such specialist writes: 'Historical sufism had two trends: 1. progressive sufism whose leaders advocated asceticism as social protest; and 2. reactionary sufis whose leaders themselves became the people's oppressors and feudal lords ... Present-day ishans belong to the second category. They have no beauty, no spirituality, no humanity.'[32]

The author concludes: 'Our atheism must be militant, and we must conduct a pitiless war against the ishans and self-appointed mullahs ... It is necessary to link the fight against religion with the fight against the activities of the believers, especially reactionary believers...'[33]

The difficulty faced by the Soviet state in coping with unofficial Islam is that Soviet ideologists have not yet succeeded in gauging the phenomenon which they perceive as a long-term threat but are totally incapable of adequately defining. Thus they fire their shots in the dark and in all directions. Islam is attacked as a manifestation of nationalism, chauvinism, feudalism, class advantages, superstitions, individual deviations and political opportunism all at once.

One Soviet author has this to say: 'Just go to a mosque when Qurban Id (The Feast of the Sacrifice) is celebrated, or a *rowzah* (Muslim mourning ceremony) is in progress. . . . Are the young people present in those crowds believers? Not at all. They are attracted by the smell of nationalistic pestilence.'[34]

Another Soviet writer blames Islam for the persistence of 'inhuman, feudal customs'. He writes: 'Despite the fact that family relations, especially regarding the attitude to women, have undergone tremendous changes, the family (in Uzbekistan) still remains a closed world. . . . The authority of the elders and their influence on younger generations remains strong and plays a substantial role in preserving tradition.'[35] The author then offers a list of 'feudal customs' still respected in Tashkent: '*sovchilik* (formal betrothal), *kelim salam* (payment for a fiancée), *pol-chokhi* (distribution of money among the guests), *sushanla kirish* (hiding the would-be bride behind a curtain), *yuz-ochdi* (ceremony to uncover the face of the bride) and *nan-sindimish* (breaking the bread).'[36] The fact that none of these traditions is necessarily Islamic or deliberately anti-Soviet does not seem to interest the new zealots of the Godless movement.

Until the mid-1980s, visitors to Soviet Central Asia and Azarbaijan might easily have reached the conclusion that Islam there interested the older generations only. A majority of those who attended mosque prayers and performed pilgrimages at various holy shrines were aged sixty or over. The impression that Islam was a 'dying faith' was confirmed by a number of Soviet studies which also showed Islam to be stronger among the rural, less-educated and poorer sections of the society. The Soviet phrase 'formerly Muslim peoples', used to describe the Muslims of the USSR, was uncritically adopted even by some otherwise keen observers of the Soviet scene.[37]

A Soviet study completed in 1979 claimed that out of every 100 'formerly Muslim peoples' no fewer than 50 per cent were no longer believers. Only 30 per cent described themselves as believers, while the remaining 20 per cent said they were 'hesitant'.[38] The same study claimed that the majority of believers were old, rural and only partly educated.

The traditional Soviet theory according to which Islam thrives only on ignorance, poverty and underdevelopment has been thoroughly questioned, however, partly thanks to *glasnost*. Many Muslims now feel that they no longer need to practice *ketman* and hide their religious beliefs. A survey carried out among undergraduate students at Tashkent University in 1987 portrayed a different picture of Islam; more than 60 per cent of the students polled described themselves as 'Muslims' and fewer than seven per cent said they were 'atheists'. The remaining 33 per cent said they were from Muslim families but not practising.[39]

It was with some surprise that the Godless discovered that Tashkent's ultra-modern telecommunications centre had been turned into a veritable stronghold of Islam. The director of the centre, Sa'eed Taherov, a prominent member of the Communist Party, was denounced as the organiser of semi-clandestine sessions of Quranic studies together with Sabur Tarsuenov, leader of the local Komosmol (Young Communist League).[40]

That Soviet Muslims have experienced impressive advances in virtually all aspects of material life during the past 70 years is undeniable. They have twelve times as many doctors of medicine per head of population as the Afghans, for example. They have six times more students at university level than the Moroccans, and produce four times more electricity than the Turks. Leaving aside the oil-rich states of the Muslim world, the USSR's Muslim republics enjoy a far higher standard of living than virtually any other Muslim country.

That material progress need not necessarily mean a death of religion – or indeed of nationalism which, in Central Asia and Azarbaijan, is inextricably linked with Islam – is shown by a growing number of studies carried out since 1985. One study makes the point directly:

> The young show a continuously increasing interest in the folkloric aspects of culture (sic). This is probably not only due to attempts to assert national identity, but also represents a search for social and moral fulfilment ... It is important that truly humanistic ideas prevail in this basically positive tendency, pseudo-national elements must not be presented as popular ones, the national must not be mixed with nationalism and a seeking after God.[41]

Another study suggested that religion appealed to 'peoples at two ends of the educational spectrum: those with only rudimentary schooling on the one hand and those who have acquired an advanced modern education'.[42] Yet another study suggests that the 'Islamic custom' of having large families is today more popular among younger and better-educated Muslim women in Ubzekistan than among their elders.[43] One explanation for this unexpected result, according to the authors of the study, is the existence of 'ethnic differences between Russians and Uzbeks' living together in the same republic.

Many Muslims are aware of the role that demography can play in reordering the balance of political and economic power especially in

Central Asia where large numbers of European settlers still live in the bigger cities. In Tashkent, Frunze, Alma-Ata, Doshanbeh and Ashkabad, Muslim women – on the average – produce three times as many children as their European counterparts. It is the steady increase in the number of Muslim children born during the past 20 years, rather than immigration from the rural areas, which has turned Muslims into the largest groups in virtually all major cities in Kazakhstan and Central Asia with the possible exception of Frunze.[44]

Visitors to Tashkent are presented with statistics that show a growing number of mixed marriages in the city. A closer examination of the data, however, shows that in more than 95 per cent of the cases mixed marriages do not cut across ethnic and religious boundaries. Uzbeks, Tatars, Tajiks, Turcomans, Kirghizes and other Muslim ethnic groups greatly intermarry in the larger cities. The same is true of Russian and Ukrainian settlers in Central Asia and Kazakhstan. But the number of marriages between Muslims and non-Muslims remains strictly limited. In fact, data for the past decade shows a marked decrease in the number of inter-ethnic marriages in Kazakhstan and Central Asia. Curiously, this decrease does not concern Muslims and Slavs alone; the German communities of Kazakhstan and Central Asia have also been more reluctant to marry into other ethnic and religious groups.[45]

Stalin's dream of leading Soviet Muslims into a cultural identity that would be 'national in form and proletarian in content' had no chance of being realised even in the heady days of the revolution when the progressive message of Marxism-Leninism held a certain appeal for a section of Muslim intelligentsia. If anything, the culture one now witnesses in Soviet Muslim societies is essentially Islamic in content and only partially proletarian in form. The spread of education has enabled more and more Muslims to gain access to their own history and traditions, and the rise in living standards has created the security and self-confidence necessary for the assertion of a community's cultural and religious identity. In a sense, it is the very success of some seven decades of economic development which has prepared the ground for an Islamic revival in the former empire of the tsars.

The Soviet state, however, has remained confused about how best to cope with the Islamic heritage of nearly 20 per cent of its subjects. Under Lenin, Islam was looked upon as a potential ally of Bolshevism in a worldwide crusade against colonialism and imperialism. Lenin professed much admiration for some Islamic folk heroes such as Niaz Piri and Dedam-Kurkud whose legendary struggle against the Christian oppressors still captures the imagination of Turkic-speaking Muslims. Even Imam Shamil was praised as a 'hero of national struggle' and had streets and schools named after him in Daghestan.

Stalin, however, saw Islam as 'a relic of feudalism' and Muslim heroes as 'bandits and barons'. To him people like Shaikh Ibrahim Gotso (Gotsinski) who tried to repeat the exploits of Shamil and raised the standard of revolt against the Bolsheviks were 'leeches and thieves'. Khrushchev largely shared Stalin's views and organised a ruthless attempt at de-Islamicisation especially in Soviet Azarbaijan and Kazakhstan. The Bolsheviks continued the Tsarist tradition of describing the Russian people as 'saviours' of the Muslim peoples of the empire who had supposedly lived under the oppressive rule of khans, emirs and shahs before being delivered from their bondage. To be sure, Stalin and his successors did not directly refer to the Russian nation as 'saviour', but they emphasised the role of the proletariat as the 'vanguard' of justice and progress. And where was the proletariat to be found? Naturally in the industrial regions of the empire, the Slav lands.

Russian conquerors like General Kauffmann and Marshal Paskievich who had been described as 'butchers and blood-suckers' by the Bolsheviks in the early days of the revolution were quickly restored to the status of historical figures who had helped save Muslims from Ottoman and Persian oppression. The openly nationalist attitude of Soviet leaders towards their non-Russian subjects could not but lead to the emergence of nationalism among the various peoples of Asia and even the Baltic region. The seeds of the nationalistic tensions of the 1980s were sown in the 1920s.

9

The Mafia of 'Real Socialism'

The most immediately striking feature of the USSR and a key factor in shaping the policies of its rulers is its sheer size. Spreading across eleven time zones the USSR is no ordinary country; it is truly an empire on which the sun never fully sets. Covering an area of 22,402,200 square kilometres, the Soviet Union accounts for nearly one-sixth of the world's total land surface. The country stretches some 10,000 kilometres from west to east, and half that distance from north to south. Seventy-five per cent of Soviet territory lies in Asia and only 25 per cent in Europe. The total length of Soviet borders exceeds 60,000 kilometres.

The country's geographical hugeness is matched by its ethnic and linguistic diversity. Almost all human groups, except the Africans, are present in the USSR where over a hundred nationalities are officially recognised. Some nationalities, like the Negidalsky, number fewer than 500. Others, like Uzbeks or for that matter Ukrainians, are larger than many full members of the United Nations Organisation. Over 130 different languages are daily used in the USSR, where no fewer than 53 'literary' languages have been 'created' since 1920. At least five alphabets are still used in the country.

The USSR is divided into 15 union republics, 20 autonomous republics, eight autonomous regions, ten autonomous areas, six territories, 123 regions and 3,225 districts. There are 2,176 cities and towns in the USSR, five of which have populations of more than two million.

Despite its size and diversity the USSR is a highly centralised state. The economy is centrally planned at Moscow, the capital, where all major decisions are taken. It is perhaps to emphasise the importance of the centre that all train, bus and airline schedules are given only in Moscow time. The over-centralised structure of the state was not invented by the Bolsheviks; they inherited it from the tsars. But they perfected and extended the machinery and methods needed for administering and controlling the whole of the country from Moscow.

The tsars had treated their territory, outside the Slav-inhabited regions and notably Russia itself, as classical colonies to be used as sources of raw material and markets for manufactured goods. They did not organise any large-scale settlement of Slavs in the conquered territories. The Russians present in the 'colonies', especially in the Caucasus and Central Asia, were fully aware of their status as temporary residents. They were administrators, soldiers, teachers and travelling salesmen; they did not wish to strike roots in those alien lands, nor did they wish to see the 'natives' change their religious beliefs and way of life.

The Communists who took over from the tsars, however, preached *slibzhenie* (drawing-closer-together) as the necessary condition for the eventual emergence of homo-sovieticus, a new brand of human being who would transcend racial, ethnic and religious differences. The absence of native Communists in Kazakhstan, Central Asia and the Caucasus did not prevent Lenin from trying to administer former colonies through local elites at least in the immediate aftermath of the revolution. Very quickly; however, the native elites proved unreliable or frankly hostile to the Communist project. Under Stalin, the Muslim regions of the USSR were put under police rule. Almost all the leaders of the party and government in the Caucasus and Central Asia were members of the Soviet secret police which functioned under different labels from 1919 onwards.

Under Khrushchev a massive programme of direct European colonisation, especially in Kazakhstan, pushed the natives on to the defensive until the 1970s. Khrushchev's successor as party leader, and later head of state, Leonid Illiych Brezhnev, became the first Soviet ruler to use the Muslim regions as a power-base for himself.

These regions contained solid assets that could be used in a power struggle in Moscow. The importance of Asia as a source of wealth for the Soviet state had been underlined by such leaders as Zinoviev as early as 1920. 'Baku's oil and Turkestan's cotton can ensure the industrial future of the Soviet state,' Zinoviev had said. 'In exchange our revolution will give those regions justice and civilization.'[1]

Baku's oil, brought to the market from the 1860s onwards, continued to account for nearly half of all Soviet oil production until the 1950s. The so-called 'second Baku' oilfields which were later developed are also situated in Muslim lands. Oil is also produced in Kazakhstan and Central Asia. As for cotton, the four republics of Central Asia and Kazakhstan account for virtually the whole of Soviet production and make the USSR the largest grower of the crop in the world.

Kazakhstan alone encompasses an estimated 35 per cent of the agricultural land of the USSR. No less than 14 per cent of all of the union's grain output comes from there. When Uzbekistan, Turkmenistan, Kirgh-izestan, Tajikestan, Azarbaijan, Daghestan and other Muslim regions of the union are included, the share of the Muslim republics in the USSR's agricultural production as a whole reaches more than 50 per cent. In other words these regions produce more than twice their statistical share of total farm output. In such areas as fresh fruits, garden vegetables, meat, milk, dairy produce and wool, the share of the Muslim regions in total production is even higher.

Kazakhstan's coalfields at Karaganda and Ekibasutz make it the USSR's third largest producer with an annual average of more than 110 million tonnes. The republic is also a major producer of oil in Emba and Manqyshlaq.[2] In addition Kazakhstan supplies European USSR with an average of five billion cubic metres of natural gas each year.

Natural gas deposits also exist in Uzbekistan and Turkmenistan, where such fields as Gazli, Uch-Qyr and Jarkak are among the largest in the world. Central Asia was in fact the largest producer of natural gas in the USSR until 1976, when it was overtaken by Western Siberia. In 1989 Central Asia accounted for 28 per cent of all natural gas production in the USSR.

Central Asia and Kazakhstan also provide virtually inexhaustible deposits of many minerals which have helped to make the USSR a superpower.

Leaving aside Kazan and Ufa where a number of advanced industries have been located since the 1950s, most Muslim regions of the USSR still have a long way to go before catching up with the industrialised parts of Russia, the Ukraine and the Baltic states. Oil refineries, petrochemical plants and coal-processing units exist in Azarbaijan, Central Asia and Kazakhstan, but the share of industrial production in all those republics is only half of the national average for the entire USSR. In 1989, more than 70 per cent of the union's cotton was processed in the European republics which grow no cotton at all. Some prestigious sites such as the Baykanur 'cosmodrome' from which Soviet spacecraft are launched[3] might give the impression that Kazakhstan and Central Asia are established as modern economies. In reality, however, this vast region remains primarily a source of raw material for the industrialised parts of the USSR. The transfer of some factories to Central Asia and Kazakhstan, as a means of putting the Soviet industrial heartland beyond the reach of Nazi bombers and advancing armies, did not lead to a sustained project of industrialisation.

Brezhnev's long involvement with Kazakhstan and Central Asia began in 1954 shortly after he had emerged as one of Khrushchev's closest allies in the power struggle against the so-called 'anti-party group' of Stalinists. He was dispatched to Kazakhstan to supervise the 'Virgin

Lands' projects from his position as the party's second-in-command in the republic. Within a few months Brezhnev established himself as the veritable ruler of Kazakhstan and acted as a dictator who took all decisions.[4] He had quickly 'understood that it was nonsense to try to reply on proletarian solidarity to run the place. Kazakhstan had to be run like a khanate and Brezhnev proved specially cut-out for the role of the khan.'[5]

Promoted first secretary of the party in Kazakhstan within a few weeks of his arrival in Alma-Ata, Brezhnev quickly created a network of Kazakhs and Uzbeks who were personally loyal to him. One of them was Din-Muhammad Kuna'ev who became his lifelong ally and friend.[6] It was Kuna'ev who reportedly persuaded Brezhnev to accept 'honorary membership' of a Kirghiz-Kazakh clan known as Qizil-Juz (Red Horde) and supposed to be a grouping of Asian communists. The clan included among its rules a number of initiation rites such as 'exchange of blood' with other members.[7] It is not known whether or not Brezhnev performed all the rites, but there is little doubt that he was considered by many of his Asian associates as a Kirghiz-Kazakh nobleman.

The initial success of the 'Virgin Lands' projects, symbolised by one extraordinary harvest in 1955, speeded up Brezhnev's ascent towards the summit of power in the Kremlin. His brutal suppression of Kazakh riots against the 'Virgin Lands' project in 1962 enhanced his image as a decisive leader.

Once established as the master of the Kremlin, Brezhnev could fully implement his own 'nationalities' policy' vis-à-vis the Muslim republics. He knew that Moscow would never be able to make Soviet rule acceptable on grounds of ideology alone. It was necessary to win the loyalty and support of at least a section of the local intelligentsia to prevent any mishaps. To achieve this, Brezhnev scrapped the harshest aspects of Khrushchev's anti-religion campaign and gave 'official' Islam a greater role to play not only in the USSR itself but also in helping promote Moscow's foreign policy objectives in the Middle East. But being the cynic that he essentially was, Brezhnev believed that 'a certain degree of corruption' was part of 'the national character' of the peoples of Kazakhstan, Central Asia and Azarbaijan. He had already practised a policy of favour distribution in Kazakhstan and now his examples could be emulated throughout the union.

The dramatic increase in world oil prices in the 1970s turned the oil-rich regions of the USSR into centres of an economic boom based on a cash windfall rather than genuine development. Throughout the Brezhnev era, income from oil and natural gas saved the economy from major crises, but it also encouraged widespread corruption.

Brezhnev described his oil-financed economic policy as 'real socialism', but in practice 'real socialism' became known as the rule of Mafia-style organisations that dominated various sectors of economy and public life.

One region which had already experienced Mafia-type pressures was Soviet Azarbaijan. Groups of smugglers, influence-peddlers and other 'parasites' had began to establish themselves in Baku, Kirov-Abad, Karabakh and other parts of Soviet Azarbaijan from the late 1950s onwards. Ferries moving under the cover of darkness brought smuggled goods from Iran to the Soviet port of Lenkoran on the Caspian. The autonomous republic of Nakhichevan was turned into a veritable entre-pôt for contraband trade. The otherwise heavily-guarded border between Iran and the USSR turned out to be full of holes when it came to illicit trade. Luxury and consumer goods – notably washing machines, tape-recorders and television sets – smuggled into Soviet Azarbaijan were then sold as far away as Latvia and Estonia.

No doubt inspired by Brezhnev's example in Kazakhstan, the Azar-baijani party leader Muhammad Akhund-Zadeh quickly turned corruption into an instrument of government. He allowed the entire bureaucracy including the various branches of the omnipresent police to demand and receive a share of the cake. A system of bribes was established, under which various public services were offered at clearly specified prices. A place in the Baku faculty of engineering, for example, could be purchased for around £3,000. A £2,000 bribe could help one jump the ten-year-long queue for an apartment by almost half.

Under Brezhnev the situation in Azarbaijan became so grave that the entire republic was put under the control of the KGB whose local chief, Heydar-Ali Reza Aliev, took over as party leader after the ousting of Akhund-Zadeh and the purge of a further 2,000 party members. The crackdown also included the execution of 24 party and government officials, including two republic ministers.

But the crackdown did not mean an end to corruption; it only became more sophisticated, better concealed. The Azarbaijani model was quickly adopted by neighbouring Georgia where even ministerial posts were offered for sale. One could become Minister of Commerce for the equivalent of £350,000! The new wave of corruption under 'real socialism' went far beyond the limits long set by the Nomenklatura.

Most leaders of the 'real socialism' Mafia in the Muslim republics made a point of attacking Islam at every opportunity. They wished to cover their involvement in financial corruption under a mask of ideological purity and combative communism. All protégés and associates of Brezhnev, one such outspoken enemy of 'reactionary Islam' was Mrs Yadegar Nassreddinova who rose to become Speaker of the Soviet of Nationalities, the second chamber of the USSR parliament.

Yadegar, a close associate of Sharaf Rashidov, the Uzbek party chief, served in various ministerial and party posts both in Uzbekistan and at union level until her exclusion from the Communist Party of the Soviet Union in 1988. Despite serious charges brought against her, she has not been prosecuted and continues to live in a sumptuous apartment in Moscow. Among the charges are: ordering the release of 59 'big crooks' in exchange for bribes, building several dachas at government expense and spending more than £100,000 of public money on her son's wedding.[8]

One could imagine the public's feelings when Yadegar, in one public meeting after another as well as in articles published in party journals, lashed out against 'the Islam of feudals who hate to see women play their full role in the construction of Socialism'.[9] Her aggressive, vulgar and at times deliberately provocative manners did not help the image of Socialism as 'the only system fit for human beings'.

Yadegar was by no means the only champion of 'real socialism' to use her position for self-enrichment in Uzbekistan, the largest Muslim republic of the USSR. Rashidov, who became party first secretary in 1959 while also holding the post of 'head of state', created his own Mafia of several thousand peoples from all walks of life. A close friend of Brezhnev since the 1950s, Rashidov constructed no fewer than thirty magnificent mansions, described as 'hunting lodges', to house Brezhnev and members of his entourage on private visits to Uzbekistan. In the event Brezhnev did not visit the republic more than half a dozen times and the 'hunting lodges' were sold to the local rich for £500,000 to £1,000,000 each.

Rashidov's network, described by the Soviet press as the 'Uzbek Mafia', was brought to the attention of the Kremlin leadership in 1983 shortly after Brezhnev's death. An investigation was ordered by Yuri Andropov, the long-time KGB chief who took over from Brezhnev as CPSU leader and head of state. But it was not until September 1988 that the Soviet press finally published limited accounts of what must be described as one of the largest cases of public office corruption in contemporary history. Rashidov himself died under suspicious circumstances in 1983; some of his friends even claimed that he had committed suicide to defend his 'honour'. At least twelve other Russian and Uzbek officials involved in the Rashidov operations committed suicide between 1983 and 1989, among them Nikolai Shchelokov, the Deputy Interior Minister who killed himself and his wife in 1984.

According to evidence cited at the trial in Moscow in September 1988 of Yuri Churbanov, Brezhnev's son-in-law, who was found guilty of having received a cash gift of £700,000 from the Rashidov Mafia, the Uzbek scandal involved no fewer than 780 separate prosecutions brought against more than 4,500 people.[10] It could take more than twenty years before all those accused of wrong-doing are brought to justice. The Uzbek Mafia is accused of having embezzled more than £5,000 million of public funds over a period of fifteen years.

The Uzbek Mafia made part of its fortune by falsifying official records regarding the production of cotton. Within ten years more than four million tonnes of cotton simply disappeared. Directors of textile companies were then bribed to purchase the stolen cotton and turn it into fabrics which were also sold on the black market.

Cotton was only part of the business of the Rashidov empire. Every post had to be bought and, once purchased, had to be kept only in exchange for regular payments (to the Mafia). This system was in operation at all levels, from the boroughs to provinces and right up to the level of the republic itself. In this race for making money, those who had to pay bribes in turn exacted bribes from their subordinates.

Rashidov, who made frequent presents to Brezhnev – including more than half a dozen luxury sports cars bought in Europe – received no fewer than ten Orders of Lenin, one of the highest decorations in the USSR. A generous man, Rashidov never forgot the birthday anniversary of Galina, Brezhnev's favourite daughter who had a soft spot for diamonds.

The death of Rashidov, followed by the execution of Mehmet Osmanov, the minister in charge of the cotton trade, in 1986, did not bring the Uzbek Mafia to an end however. Rashidov's successor Imamjan Osman-Khaje'ev and Ihsan Khoda-Verdiev, who took over as prime minister, continued the same policies and practices. Both were removed from their posts at the start of 1988, but continue to live ostentatious lives in Moscow and Tashkent. Khoda-Verdiev is under investigation for the sale of union honours including the highly-coveted title of Hero of Socialist Labour to highest bidders.

The 1979 Islamic Revolution sent tremors throughout Soviet Azarbaijan and Central Asia. The various Mafias of 'real socialism' were divided in their assessment of the Iranian cataclysm and the best means of limiting its after-shocks in the USSR. While Rashidov and Yadegar Nassruddinova continued to violently attack Islam, others sought a new dialogue with militant Muslims. In Soviet Azarbaijan, Aliev began to speak of 'common objectives' which bound Islam and 'the international workers' movement' together.[11] The KGB was ordered to turn a blind eye to the activities of unofficial mosques unless they threatened public order. This attitude was condemned by Muhammad-Nazar Ghafurov, First Secretary of the Turkmen Communist Party in 1981 as 'giving bribes to Khomeinists'.

In Uzbekistan, and probably also other Central Asian republics, the local Mafias went even further and – the verbal violence of some leaders notwithstanding – began to finance a number of activities by the mullahs. One man who adopted this policy was Abdul-Vahid Karimov who served as Bokhara party leader between 1977 and 1984. Charged with giving and receiving bribes, Karimov was brought to trial in 1987 and condemned to death, the highest-ranking party member to receive the penalty under Gorbachev.

Karimov's fall, followed by the most extensive purge of the party carried out in Uzbekistan since Stalin's times, was no doubt the opening scene in the Rashidov drama. What was especially significant, however, was that Karimov and some of his associates were also accused of 'complacency in the face of moves by chauvinist and obscurantist elements', code terms for Islam in Soviet propaganda language.

Attacking Karimov, *Pravda* hinted at the existence of a possible understanding between the Uzbek Mafia and certain Islamic circles in Bokhara and Samarkand. It said:

> Among the serious problems faced by the party organisation in Uzbekistan is the need to improve anti-religious propaganda and atheist education; it is essential that we act decisively against backward habits and traditions which, assuming popular colours, spread ideas and values that are foreign to our society.[12]

The publication of details of the various activities of the Uzbek Mafia has provided the Soviet press with a fresh opportunity for launching direct or indirect attacks on Islam, which they wish to portray as a medieval system of values that sanctions cruelty and corruption. The case of one Ahmad-Jan Adelov has been specially seized upon by Soviet propagandists for attacks on supposedly Islamic customs.

Adelov, a close friend of Rashidov, was the head of an agro-industrial complex with more than 30,000 employees in the Ferghana Valley. He had turned the complex into a little khanate of his own, complete with his harem, located in a sumptuous villa in the middle of a nine-hectare garden, and a personal bodyguard recruited from among the Sovkhoz workers. Adelov also applied his own laws and organised trials at which he was the prosecutor and the only judge. His khanate even had a prison of its own where those 'sentenced' would serve their term in a dungeon divided into solitary cells with steel bars.

Adelov's victims were often whipped before being thrown into prison. The prison terms meted out by the little 'khan' varied between a few days and a year, but on one occasion he sentenced a Sovkhoz official to seven years imprisonment plus the confiscation of his property. Among those whipped in public on Adelov's orders were several local party leaders who had displeased the 'khan'.[13]

Soviet media have presented Adelov's case as just another example of Muslim people's inability to liberate themselves from the Middle Ages.[14] Soviet Muslims, however, have a different view, seeing the roots of corruption in the system itself – a system that concentrates all political and economic power in a few hands and gives the people virtually no say in matters of public interest. Rashidov, Karimov, Adelov and others are both hated and admired by many Soviet Muslims. They are hated because they were part of the Soviet system which, in the minds of many Muslims, symbolises Russian domination. They are admired because they were able to cheat the Russians out of billions of roubles. Arkady Warberg, a lawyer involved in uncovering the activities of the Uzbek Mafia, put it like this: 'To the average Uzbek the corruption did not appear as a disease in the body of the region's politics but as the body itself. . . . It was the rule not the exception.'[15]

Throughout Central Asia and Azarbaijan one comes across giant posters showing the 'heroic' Soviet people busy constructing socialism. The models presented in the posters are almost always of European type with blond hair and blue eyes. Every now and then an Uzbek, Tatar or Azari face is added for good measure in the same way as 'Asiatic' actors are given supporting roles in Soviet TV serials. But the overall impression remains: the system in place belongs to the Russians and their European kin. It is no accident that the share of the Muslim republics in the membership of the Communist Party of the Soviet Union is more than 50 per cent less than the average for European republics, Armenia and Georgia.

In some regions membership of the CPSU has become a veritable handicap, especially since Gorbachev's policy of *glasnost* has brought many of the misdeeds of party leaders into the open. Application for membership of the Komsomol is at its lowest for more than twenty years in Kirghizia and Tajikestan, where people associated with the CPSU even complain of 'feeling physically threatened'.[16] During riots in Doshanbeh in March 1989, a number of party members were beaten up by the Muslim crowd. These riots followed demonstrations aimed at making Tajik-Dari the official language of the republic.[17]

Unhappiness with the presence of Europeans in large numbers is certainly not a result only of Muslim dislike for Communism. Part of the growing tension is due to racist attitudes on both sides. To many Muslims in the USSR, all Europeans appear as 'black-marketeers keen just on restaurants and prostitutes'.[18] The Slavs are generally portrayed by 'Asiatics' as lazy, alcoholic and totally lacking in moral values. Even Muslim university students see 'European women as loose, easy preys who could be used and discarded. . . . But would go mad if an Uzbek woman went out with a European.'[19]

The Slavs return the compliment by describing the 'Asiatics' – often called 'blacks' – as inferior people who have no scruples. 'He is quite an Uzbek' is a new, fashionable expression in Moscow. It means: 'he is ready for all manner of corruption.' Another expression – 'like a Baku man' – implies that the person referred to is a crafty opportunist who can talk a donkey into giving up its four legs. 'Give a Baku man half a chance and he will take the other half,' says a Soviet proverb that does not displease the Azaris. For more than half a century Soviet propaganda and education have tried to eliminate the scores of proverbs, expressions and folk tales that depict the Tatars as bloodthirsty savages. Some Russian mothers still try to frighten their offspring by threatening to call 'the Tatar who will eat you'.

A constant theme of Soviet propaganda is the supposed emergence of the new 'Soviet Man' (*sovetskii chelovek*) who is free of all religious, ethnic, nationalist and, of course, class prejudices. In reality, however, the USSR has remained a multi-national state in which nationalist sentiments continue to sharpen and, occasionally, lead to violent conflict. In multi-national cities, Tashkent or Moscow for example, it is rare to see Europeans and 'Asiatics' mixing together outside their places of work. Even in factory and office canteens, different ethnic groups prefer to be served at separate tables. In some restaurants Slavs and 'Asiatics' are received in different salons. Gorbachev's decision in 1986 to launch a campaign against alcoholism gave restaurants owned and managed by Muslim cooperatives in a number of cities, including Moscow, a good excuse for imposing an alcohol-free regime in the name of party purity rather than Islamic *shari'ah*. The ideal of the new 'Soviet Man' received a serious blow in December of 1986 when Alma-Ata, the capital of Kazakhstan, was shaken by two days of bloody rioting which left some thirty people dead and hundreds injured.[20]

Alma-Ata was for long presented by Soviet propaganda as an excellent example of the Soviet 'melting pot' where more than forty different nationalities lived together. Founded in the nineteenth century, the old garrison town had by the 1980s developed into a city of more than a million people, with a number of prestigious faculties and a lively cultural and scientific life. The man largely responsible for the city's progress was Din-Muhammad Kuna'ev, a scientist who was an early convert to Bolshevism and who, as already noted, became a lifelong friend of Brezhnev. Kuna'ev also became the first Muslim to join the Politburo as full member under Brezhnev.

As Kazakhstan party chief Kuna'ev, who was born into an aristocratic Kazakh-Kirghiz clan, seized the opportunities offered by the policy of 'advancement for the locals' (*menstnichestve*) for the purpose of giving the Kazakhs greater scope for social and economic advancement. Between 1970 and 1985 he achieved spectacular results. The number of

Kazakh students attending university rose from less than 12 per cent to over 70 per cent. A variety of administrative rules was used to keep the Slavs, especially the Russians, out of the university. The policy of 'kazakhization' was also applied in industry, the media and the party structure. Kazakhs were not especially encouraged to join the Communist Party, but those who had already joined were helped to assume greater responsibilities. Between 1970 and 1985 the Communist Party machine in Kazakhstan came to be controlled by what Soviet propaganda refers to as the 'Kazakh Mafia'. Kuna'ev and his close associates such as Abdul Ramazanov, Ibrahim Asgarov Orhan Rajab-Janov and Karim Naribeyev were at the centre of a vast network of favour-distribution that tried to combine the search for private profit with a genuine desire to make the Kazakhs masters of their own land.

To most Kazakhs Kuna'ev was a 'nationalist' who tried to help the Kazakh nation escape the danger of assimilation and loss of identity. Muhammad Arghun-Beyev – who held the chair of 'History of Party and Soviet Journalism' at Alma-Ata University until 1986 – saw the campaign launched by Moscow against Kuna'ev as 'pure character assassination'. 'Is nationalism automatically wrong?' Arghun-Beyev asked. 'It is not wrong when the aim is to strengthen a weaker nation against stronger ones. Even in five centuries the Kazakh nation would not be in a position to threaten the great Russian nation. But the Kazakhs could become strong enough to hold their own, to decide their own destiny.'[21]

This view was disputed by some Kazakh intellectuals who openly admit that their first loyalty is to the CPSU and not to any 'mythical Kazakh nation'. The Kazakh novelist Abdul-Jamil Nurbeysev saw Kuna'ev as a clan chieftain, from the Ulus-Juz (Great Horde) tribes of southern Kazakhstan, who simply wanted to 'install his own relatives and friends at all key posts'.[22] Since Ulus-Juz was the last Kazakh state to fall under Russian rule in the last century, the assumption is that people descending from it still harbour anti-Slav sentiments.

The Alma-Ata riots, however, took place on such a scale and were led in such a way as to make it difficult to believe that nothing more than a desperate defence of unfair privileges was at issue. Although Soviet propaganda labelled the Kazakh demonstrators 'bandit mobs' and 'ignoramuses', the first group of marchers to the confrontation with the forces of order on 17 December were students at the Faculty of Architecture and the Institutes of Economic Science, Agriculture and Natural Sciences. Shouting such slogans as 'Justice for the people' and 'Kazakhstan for Kazakhs', the demonstrators moved towards Brezhnev Square in the centre of the city where they were joined first by secondary school pupils and then by hundreds of office and factory workers who poured in at around lunch-time. According to most eyewitness accounts there was no sign that the demonstration was organised by any particular clan or tribe. Many of those who took part were members of the party and the Komsomol. Nor was the demonstration directly presented as a protest against Kuna'ev's dismissal from the Politburo and his replacement as Kazakh party first secretary by a Russian on Gorbachev's orders.

The demonstrations could not have been promoted by partisans of 'the period of stagnation' – as Gorbachev calls the Brezhnev years – for another reason. One of the first targets attacked by the demonstrators was precisely Brezhnev's bust at the entrance to the university compound, while later in the day slabs of marble from the monument in the centre of Brezhnev Square were pulled out and smashed into pieces.[23] Police and militia attempts at breaking up the demonstration later in the day led to scuffles and then to pitched battles between students and police. At least nine students were killed in the encounters and about 500 arrested.

The following day, 18 December, the demonstrators returned to demand the release of their comrades and an enquiry into police tactics which had led to loss of life. This time, however, the forces of order – no longer taken by surprise – were deployed in full strength and the demonstrators were denied access to the centre of the city and the university compound. This provoked a series of localised riots in which a number of official buildings, including a party ideological training centre, were attacked. Scores of official cars were set on fire. The demonstrators burned tyres, broke windows of official buildings and burned piles of documents seized at a register office. Hit-and-run engagements between demonstrators and forces of order continued well after sunset in sub-zero temperatures. At least seventeen people, including three militiamen, were killed in the encounters and scores seriously injured by gunshot. The authorities, claiming that some demonstrators had used firearms, imposed a dusk-to-dawn curfew on the city of nearly one million people on 18 December. Hundreds of suspected 'troublemakers', mostly university students, were rounded up and transferred to prisons in northern Kazakhstan. A blackout on all news from Alma-Ata was imposed and access to the city was limited to officials only.

Nevertheless, news of the riots did filter out of the beleaguered capital and provoked trouble in other parts of the republic. Mass demonstrations were organised at Jambul and Chimkent, in southern Kazakhstan. In Jambul at least four people including a woman doctor[24] were killed by the police in clashes with demonstrators. Contrary to official accounts which try to present the events as limited only to southern Kazakhstan, protest marches and riots also took place in the mining centre of Karaganda and the industrial centres of Tselinograd and Petropavlosk in the north. That demonstrations were larger and more violent in Alma-Ata and Jambul was not solely due to the imagined domination of the anti-Russian Ulus-Juz. The Kazakhs form a majority in the south of the republic, which has also retained much more of its Islamic personality than has the north.

Alma-Ata, Chimkent and Jambul remained under virtual martial law well into February 1987 and 'volunteer militia detachments' consisting mostly of Russians and Ukrainians continued to patrol the main city streets until the end of the year.

Official Soviet propaganda remains undecided as to who was to blame for the riots, which cast doubt on many basic political assumptions in the union. The fact that the riots began a day after a Central Committee plenum in Alma-Ata during which Russian domination of the republic was once again fully restored shows that 'nationalism' was a crucial factor in fomenting public anger. Anvar Alim-Janov, a Kazakh journalist and a veteran Communist, has few doubts regarding the source of the troubles. He writes:

> Some people managed, by mean of persuasion, deception and threats to bring inexperienced, politically illiterate young people out into the streets and squares. Nationalistic slogans appeared, drawn from the darkest depths of history. ... Hooligans, drunkards and other anti-social elements joined the crowds. Wild rowdies, armed with metal rods, sticks and stones, beat up and insulted citizens, overturned cars and set fire to them and broke the glass in stores, hotels and other public buildings.[25]

Another writer, Victor Melman, a Ukainian, however saw 'the hand of Islamic fanaticism at work' especially in the city and region of Jambul. He writes: 'Extensive work is carried out to spread the practice of Islam in some places. Former roving mullahs have been invited back. Pseudo-mullahs organise funeral ceremonies on their own and the practice of other religious rites can be noticed.' He then relates an encounter between an official of the Kazakh 'House of Atheism' and a local mullah who is caught in possession of a number of Arabic books. The books, we are told, turned out to have 'absolutely nothing to do with the religion'.[26] Were the books political manuals published in Arabic?

The authorities' belief that 'Islamic fanaticism' did have a key role in provoking and leading the Kazakhstan riots led them into taking a number of measures against what they saw as 'the rise of medieval sentiments'. A series of seminars on how best to spread atheism were organised in Alma-Ata, Chimkent, Jambul, Kordai, Zavod and other major centres in the republic during the months that followed the unrest. Once again, the rise of Islam in Kazakhstan was blamed on 'foreign enemies'. The many hundreds of new 'atheistic lecturers' brought in from outside Kazakhstan to cover the republic were told: 'Foreign

Muslim organisations pin their hopes on the slogan of the "Islamic factor" influencing ignorant people in our country. ... Atheists have much work to do to liberate the minds of people from the web of religion.'[27]

The riots in Kazakhstan not only dealt a serious blow to Gorbachev's standing as a champion of liberalisation, but also underlined the real nature of political power in the Muslim republics. Gennadi Kolbin, the new Kazakhstan party boss, quickly appeared as a Russian satrap in an outlying province of an empire. Branding all opponents as parasites, Kolbin fixed a delay of eight weeks in which 'all centres of parasitism should be cleared out'.[28] By March 1987 a thorough purge of the party, universities, secondary schools, kholkhozes and industrial units had been carried out involving thousands of 'parasites'. Scores of 'places of parasitism' were closed down, among them the two remaining mosques in Alma-Ata and the small mosque at Jambul. Five private Quranic classes were also shut in Chimkent and their organisers – described as 'fake mullahs' – arrested. A large number of Kazakh writers, teachers, film-makers and scientists lost their jobs and many others were transferred to lower posts.

The trials of those arrested during the riots were all held in camera. Most prisoners were released after receiving a strong warning, but some exceptionally savage sentences – probably intended to serve as examples – were also passed. For instance, on 7 January 1987 the Kazakh supreme court, chaired by a Russian judge, sentenced an Alma-Ata teacher, Mrs Jamila Sabetova, to five years imprisonment with hard labour at a 'special regime colony', to be followed by a further five years during which she would not be allowed to teach. The charges levelled against her were 'unfurling a provocative banner and distributing leaflets with which she attempted to inflame international enmity and incite young people to act illegally'.[29] The banner in question carried a simple message: 'Let us be Kazakhs in Kazakhstan!'

Kolbin, referred to by some Kazakhs as *rus-kepi* (Russian dog), moved on to carry out a number of measures aimed at 'cleansing' the universities which had become veritable centres of Muslim agitation. Thousands of undergraduates were asked to re-enroll after undergoing lengthy interviews clearly aimed at testing their political beliefs. From 1987 all those who wished to enter university were required to spend at least one year 'doing socially useful work' before sending in their applications. This additional year turned out to consist of atheistic lecture series and regular sessions in Marxism-Leninism, followed by a number of written examinations.

One immediate effect of the new policy towards the universities was a drastic cut in the number of Kazakh undergraduates. Official propaganda maintains that Kazakh pupils remain intellectually and academically 'less prepared' than their Slav peers for higher education. It is interesting to note that the ethnic Germans in Kazakhstan generally sided with the Russians and Ukrainians against 'the blacks', despite long-standing enmity between the Germanic and Slavic communities in Alma-Ata. Instead other Muslim communities, especially the Kirghiz and the Uzbek, rallied to the Kazakh side from the first day of the troubles. A number of rallies were also organised in support of the Kazakhs in Tashkent and Frunze in January 1987.

In Jambul and Chimkent ceremonies marking the death of demonstrators continued until the summer of 1987 and provided 'parasitical mullahs' with a number of occasions to 'spread their anti-Socialist venom in the name of religious faith'.[30] Attempts to incite 'official' Islam against Kazakh 'troublemakers' were also made, but produced little result. The muftiate of Tashkent, which also covers Kazakhstan, issued a number of vague statements condemning 'attempts at leading the youth astray', but it was clear that the muftis did not wish to endorse the imposition of direct and brutal Russian rule over a traditionally Muslim land. Tashkent's statements, though they offered little comfort to Kolbin and his masters at the Kremlin, nevertheless provoked much anger and resentment among Muslims not only in Alma-Ata but also throughout Kazakhstan and the Central Asian republic. An *Islamizdat* leaflet accused the then Grand Mufti Shamsuddin Baba Khan of 'not knowing what is the right path to take'.[31] It added. 'It is not enough to go abroad and speak out against the injustice of Zionist occupation of lands that belong to Muslim Arabs and to deny the right of Muslims to reign in their own homeland here. ... Every advantage is today for others and for Kazakhs there is only disappointment.'[32]

Moscow, however, saw the root of the troubles in attempts at 'excessive Kazakhisation' of life in a multi-national republic. The CPSU's central organ, *Pravda*, devoted a number of articles to attacking Kazakh newspapers and writers for 'nationalist survivals in their consciousness and behaviour'.[33] In a lengthy review of the situation in the republic *Pravda* said that Kazakh papers 'contain only Kazakh names and the photographs in them largely feature representatives of the indigenous nationality. This kind of one-sided coverage of life in a multi-national republic is scarcely conducive to instilling an awareness of the unity of the Soviet people's interests.'[34]

The paper also attacked the Kazakhs' lack of interest in Russian literature and the focus put by Kazakh literary magazines on works by 'native authors'.

A far more serious threat to 'the spirit of a proud sense of belonging to the united socialist homeland', according to *Pravda*, was the growing popularity of exclusively Kazakh kindergartens and schools. The paper suggested that such schools be closed down and replaced by Kazakh-language sections in multi-ethnic centres of education where the principal language of instruction would, of course, be Russian.[35]

Pravda was also 'scandalised' by an article in the weekly *Kazakh Adebiyati* (*Kazakh Literature*) which discussed demographic trends in the republic.[36] The article forecasts that the Kazakhs, thanks to their high birth-rate, will form 65–70 per cent of the total population in their own republic by the year 2,000. Then *Pravda*, which saw the article as opposed to 'the spirit of internationalism', went on to attack another Alma-Ata paper, *Bilim Janeh Enbek* (*Knowledge and Work*) for devoting space to studies on the origins of peoples living in Kazakhstan.[37] In other words, the CPSU organ wanted the Kazakhs to stop being interested in their own past and not to be overly enthusiastic about their language and literature. The Kazakhs were also required to stop trying to bring up their children as Kazakhs only because they lived in a multi-national republic.[38]

Kazakhstan's bloody events provoked a number of 'incidents', albeit on smaller scales, in Uzbekistan, Turkmenistan, Tajikestan and Kirghizestan. This confirmed the generally-held view that developments in the Asian republics were deeply interrelated.

The most serious incidents took place at the university of Frunze in February 1987, when Kirghiz students attacked and sacked the dormitories of European undergraduates. The students then marched through the streets of the city chanting 'anti-internationalist' slogans; they were mainly protesting against the abolition of quota systems which reserved fixed numbers of places in various faculties for undergraduates of Kirghiz origin. The abolition of the quotas was defended by the Kirghiz Communist Party leader A. M. Masaliev at a special session of the Central Committee. In a lengthy attack on 'troublemakers', he said:

> At the time that the problem of creating a national intelligentsia existed, the young people of the local nationality justifiably enjoyed priority in admission to central and republican higher education establishments. ... The practice ... engendered national egoism and self-conceit in a certain number of students and created a foundation for nationalistic phenomena, which occurred in the university in particular.[39]

Masaliev, however, contradicted himself by admitting that since two-thirds of Kirghiz families were still working in agriculture, their children were at a disadvantage for gaining admission to higher education. He also revealed that a majority of Kirghiz school-leavers had only 'a poor command of Russian', a language needed for entry into most of the more highly-coveted faculties.[40] Because most scientific subjects are taught only in Russian, the average Kirghiz student is at an automatic disadvantage compared to his Russian and Ukrainian peers.

The crackdown against students at Frunze continued throughout 1987–88, with an estimated 150 undergraduates expelled for 'unpatriotic' activities. The discovery of a number of Arabic books in one of the dormitories in December 1988 led the authorities to claim that some 'alien elements' were involved in inciting 'fanatical feelings among the inexperienced students'.[41] The number of students from Muslim countries admitted at Frunze was subsequently reduced.[42]

Muslim 'troublemakers' have also been blamed for a number of 'indecent scenes' at the city of Osh, the capital of southern Kirghizestan. Osh, often referred to as 'Second Mecca' – a title it shares with the holy city of Turkestan in Kazakhstan – is one of Central Asia's most important centres of Islamic faith. It contains a number of ancient monuments, notably the Takht-e-Suleiman (Solomon's Throne) and each year attracts tens of thousands of pilgrims and tourists from all over Central Asia. In 1987 the local Intourist (Soviet Tourism Office) decided to profit from the booming pilgrimage business by offering its own organised tours of the 'Second Mecca', which led to a series of clashes between genuine Muslim pilgrims and Europeans brought in by Intourist. The city was then taken off the circuit of organised tours offered to Russian and East European tourists. A number of people were arrested and charged with undermining public order and preaching 'discarded ideologies', i.e. Islam.

The official press accused Muslim militants of spreading 'wild rumours' about the alleged torture of Kirghiz children and young people by Russians and the desecration of holy places by Europeans. According to one article, 'It became clear that some active ideology was behind all that.'[43]

That 'active ideology' is seldom named, but officials drop enough hints to make it clear that they blame Islam. Mikhail Gorbachev himself pointed the finger at Islam as 'enemy of progress and socialism' in a speech made in Tashkent shortly before the Alma-Ata riots in 1986.[44] He called for 'effective and decisive action against religion in all forms that its influence takes in society'.[45] The long-sustained fiction according to which material progress had rendered religion in general and Islam in particular redundant had to be discarded by party leaders as a new and more militant Islam made its presence felt.

One immediate result of a new anti-Islamic campaign that followed the riots in Kazakhstan was a rather clumsy attempt by the Soviet authorities to prevent Muslim pilgrimages from taking place in Uzbekistan, Turkmenistan, Tajikestan and Kirghizestan. In one incident on 30 April 1987, the militia intervened to disperse a praying crowd in the park surrounding the mausoleum of Nebi-Ayub (The Prophet Job) near Jalal-Abad in the region of Osh. The mausoleum and the park, among the most sacred monuments of Islam in Kirghizestan, were turned into a tourist recreation centre in 1959 and closed to pilgrimage. Under Brezhnev, however, the pilgrims were allowed to return on special days and public prayer sessions were organised.

In another incident, on 26 January 1987, the mausoleum of Ishan-Qal'ah (Castle of the Elders) where a number of sufi saints are buried[46] was closed by the local party officials after a ceremony was organised to mark the fortieth day of the deaths of Kazakh Muslims in Alma-Ata. The incident began when a small group of Kazakhs organised a prayer session at the mausoleum and were joined by several hundred Karak-alpaks, Uzbeks and Tatars. The ceremony was broken up an hour later when a number of 'thugs' attacked the believers.[47] In a similar incident at the mausoleum of Khajeh-Sabzpush (The Master in Green) in Taji-kestan,[48] seventy-three people including many old women were arrested after a prayer session in February 1987.[49] The mausoleum – opened to pilgrims under Brezhnev – was closed once again and did not reopen until September 1988. However, another gathering a few days later at the mausoleum of Mullah Junaid, in the village of Hessar near Dosh-anbeh, was not interfered with.[50] This probably indicated differences of opinion within the party as how best to handle the situation.

The largest memorial gathering for the Kazakh 'martyrs' took place on 4 June 1987 in the courtyard of the Shah-e-Mardan (King of Men) mausoleum at Hamzah-Abad, in the Ferghana district of Uzbekistan.[51] According to eyewitness accounts several thousand people, including many young students and workers, attended a 'well-ordered ceremony' led by Qulibey Atabeyev, an 'illegal' mullah who was subsequently arrested but later released.[52] An attempt at organising a similar ceremony at the mausoleum of Shaikh Bahauddin in Bokhara, a few days later, was however aborted after the streets leading to the monument were closed by the authorities.

By all accounts the Kazakhstan riots had a traumatic effect on Soviet leaders at both republican and union levels. The commission of inquiry formed on Gorbachev's orders a few days after the Alma-Ata riots never came out with its report. Official accounts of what happened, and why, continue to diverge widely. The Kazakhstan Prosecutor-General, Halim Yelemisov, claims that there were no casualties among the 'trouble-makers' and that only one militiaman, S. A. Savitskii, was killed in the riots.[53] According to Yelemisov, 'persons in an aggressive mood rampaged for more than ten hours'.[54]

The prime minister of Kazakhstan, Nur-Sultan Nazar-Bayev, however, put the number of casalties at 'two killed and more than 200 injured'.[55] He also agreed that the rioters had 'voiced some legitimate grievances including food and housing'.[56] He further made it clear that an important cause of the disturbances had been popular 'unhappiness' with the selection of Gennadi Kolbin as party boss. Kolbin himself had rejected suggestions that his nomination had caused any resentment, and blamed the riots on 'provocative moves by bankrupt ideologies'.[57] But Kolbin's decisive defeat in the general election of 26 March 1989 showed that he enjoyed virtually no support even among Communists in Kazakhstan.

The Kazakhstan 'event', as official propaganda continued to describe what was a popular uprising, underlined a number of important facts. They showed that a great deal of pent-up resentment exists in the predominantly Muslim republics. Also they brought into the open the true nature of Moscow's domination of peripheral republics; in the final analysis, it was naked force that kept the 'international proletarian order' in place.

The 'events' and their after-effects in other republics also revealed the existence of deep and legitimate social and cultural grievances which have not yet fully discovered how best to express themselves. In most Muslim societies, anti-state agitation begins at social and cultural levels long before spreading into the domain of politics. Economic grievances, although acutely felt and important at the level of individuals, seldom lead to political protest on their own. Muslim societies begin to boil when they feel they are being humiliated by non-Muslims or their associates and that Islam itself is being threatened by its enemies. Seventy years after the October revolution, the USSR has not succeeded in changing these basic facts of life in its Muslim regions, especially in Kazakhstan, Central Asia, Daghestan and Azarbaijan.

10

Explosion in the 'Black Garden'

Until the winter of 1988, few people outside Transcaucasia had ever heard of Nagorno-Karabakh, one of the most isolated regions of a vast empire that stretches from the heart of Europe to the Pacific. The last time the region had been in the news, so to speak, was in 1797 when Agha-Muhammad Khan, Shah of Iran, was assassinated at the fortress of Shusha, the capital of what was then a province of the Persian empire. Before that Qara-Bagh (The Black Garden) had served as a hunting ground for various Tatar-Mongol khans including Teymur (Tamerlane).

Nagorno-Karabakh (High Qara-Bagh) covers 4,400 square kilometres of the original 'Black Garden' which in its heyday stretched from Yerevan, today the capital of the Soviet Republic of Armenia, to the mountains of Talesh that dominate the Caspian Sea. Although ruled over by Muslim shahs, khans and sultans since the eighth century, Karabakh[1] always remained an Armenian region. Periodic attempts at converting the population to Islam failed, as the Karabakh Armenians clung to their church, language and national traditions with a rare degree of tenacity. At specially difficult times the Armenians adopted the largely Islamic tactic of *ketman* (hiding one's religious identity), and even adopted Muslim names in order to escape persecution.[2]

In 1987 the population of Nagorno-Karabakh was estimated to be around 200,000, with ethnic Armenians accounting for 90 per cent of the total. The Muslim Azaris who made up the rest of the population were mostly concentrated in the region's capital of Stepanakert which until 1923 had borne the name of Khan-Kendi (The Khan's Village). Nagorno-Karabakh, an enclave in the Soviet republic of Azerbaijan, is separated from Armenia by a stretch of mountain paths that cover a distance of less than 10 kilometres. Yet it is virtually impossible to reach Nagorno-Karabakh directly from Armenia except on foot. Successive Soviet Azerbaijani governments have pursued a deliberate policy of isolating Nagorno-Karabakh from Armenia and, indeed, from the outside world as a whole.

Karabakh had become part of the ephemeral republic based on Yerevan which had emerged after the disintegration of the Tsarist empire in 1918, the first Armenian state for more than 2,000 years. In 1936, however, the redrawing of borders in Transcaucasia led to the inclusion of Karabakh – with the Russian prefix of *nagorno*: 'high' now added to its name – into the Soviet republic of Azarbaijan. The decision, taken by Stalin, was not only just another sign of the dictator's displeasure with the Armenians who had tried to stay out of the USSR and maintain an independent state; it also reflected the greater influence that Azarbaijani leaders wielded in Moscow at the time. Baku had been the only important Bolshevik foothold in the Caucasus in the crucial days of Civil War, and on the eve of the Second World War Stalin could count on Soviet Azarbaijani leaders to help mobilise Muslim support for the USSR in any future conflagration in Europe.

Soviet Azarbaijan, itself considered by some Azaris to have suffered from Russian and Soviet 'colonial domination', treated Nagorno-Karabakh as a veritable colonial possession. Large sections of the enclave were left without electricity, despite the fact that the hydroelectric complex of Madaghiz on the Terter river produced more than twice the needs of Nagorno-Karabakh. The electricity produced was transported away from the enclave and used as far away as the Caspian coast.

Although technically an autonomous region, the enclave was directly administered from Baku, with the local soviet at Stepanakart serving as a largely ceremonial body. Nagorno-Karabakh in 1987 lacked 'anything resembling a health service and did not have a single paved road'.[3] 'The leaders of Azarbaijan did not see that an explosion was coming,' reported an Azari writer.[4] Every effort was made in Baku to make life as difficult as possible in Nagorno-Karabakh, in the hope that the Armenian population will, in time, leave the enclave for Soviet Armenia. During the early 1980s, in fact, the inhabitants of some villages did leave for the 'Armenian homeland'. Some even emigrated to the United States.

Enmity between Armenians and Azaris had a long history dating back to the tenth century when the process of 'Turkicisation' of Transcaucasia and Anatolia first started. Under the Tsarist empire the Armenians generally preferred Russian Christian rule to domination by Muslim states such as Iran or the Ottoman Empire. Soviet historians still boast that it was inclusion in the Russian empire that saved Armenia from being totally absorbed by its Muslim neighbours. No doubt the claim is wildly exaggerated. The Armenians had held their own against the Parthian, Sassanian, Roman, Byzantine and Islamic empires for more than twenty centuries and might well have continued to do so without being annexed by the tsars. But it is certain that the involuntary association with the rising power of Russia did help to give the Armenians a better chance especially against the Ottomans.

During the First World War many Armenian nationalists cooperated with Russian armies against the Ottomans and participated in massacres of Turks and Kurds in eastern Anatolia. This was in part an attempt at revenge for earlier Ottoman pogroms against Armenians in the nineteenth century. The Turks, strongly supported by Kurdish tribes, seized the opportunity provided by the disarray in the Tsarist empire and committed a series of fresh atrocities against the Armenians between 1915 and 1921. The Soviet power preferred secure borders with Turkey to any glory that might have accrued from defending the Armenian cause. Several predominantly Armenian districts were ceded by the Bolsheviks to Turkey against the express wishes of nationalists in Yerevan.

The Armenian community in Transcaucasia is situated in an extremely vulnerable part of western Asia. Its geographical expression, the Soviet republic of Armenia, interrupts what would otherwise have been a continuous galaxy of Islamic communities from the Mediterranean to China. 'Armenia is like a dagger in the heart of the Islamic world and the universe of the Turkish peoples,' wrote one early prophet of pan-Turkism.[5] Modern pan-Islamic writers compare Armenia with the state of Israel which also 'interrupts' the Islamic continuum of peoples and states from the Atlantic Ocean to the Persian Gulf. A third 'interrupting factor' in the Islam world is of course India which, despite the fact that it has nearly 100 million Muslims, is seen as an 'alien intruder'.[6] Any project aimed at eliminating India is bound to appear rather unrealistic, but the same is not true of either Israel or Armenia, tiny states with small populations.[7]

The division of the Caucasus into three Soviet republics – Georgia, Armenia and Azarbaijan – and a number of autonomous republics and regions attached to the RSFSR did not create political units where administrative boundaries exactly coincided with ethnic and religious divisions which have made the entire land mass a veritable mosaic of nations and civilizations.

In 1989 there were an estimated 600,000 Armenians in Soviet Azarbaijan, including Nagorno-Karabakh and the autonomous republic of Nakhichevan. This was partly counterbalanced by the presence of an estimated 300,000 Azaris in Armenia. There were 500,000 Armenians in Georgia, which also hosted 250,000 Azaris. Soviet Armenia in addition hosted some 100,000 Kurds.[8] The Azarbaijani capital of Baku, the USSR's fifth largest city with a population of nearly two million in 1989, included more than a quarter of a million ethnic Armenians. Some

Armenians regarded Azerbaijan in general and Baku in particular as home regardless of centuries of discord largely provoked by religious differences.[9]

Centuries of tension between Armenians and Muslims in the Caucasus did not disappear after the October Revolution. The Armenians distanced themselves further from their 'Asiatic' habitat which had brought them so much suffering for so long. They began to see themselves as a European people and turned their eyes more intensely towards the West. Many emigrated and ended up in France and the United States, but new immigrants also arrived from Iran, Iraq and Lebanon where ethnic Armenians looked to Yerevan – and more particularly the Echmiadzin cathedral – as the core of their civilisation.[10] Compared with their Azarbaijani neighbours, the Armenians played a more active role in the CPSU and took special pride when Anastas Mikoyan, an Armenian, became the USSR's head of state.[11]

Inclusion in the USSR did not however deal a death blow to either Armenian or Azari nationalisms. It is possible to argue that nationalism remained the principal political force in Armenia. In 1968 a group of Armenian intellectuals, some of them with old Dashnak backgrounds,[12] formed the Armenian United National Party (AUNP) with the clearly stated aim of creating an independent Armenian state. Although passionately anti-Soviet, the AUNP wished to achieve its objective within the constitution of the USSR that recognises the right of all union republics to secession.

One of the first steps taken by the AUNP was the compilation and publication of a political map of 'Greater Armenia'. This included virtually the whole of eastern Turkey, parts of north-west Iran, Nagorno-Karabakh, Nakhichevan and the southern coastal steppes of Soviet Azarbaijan. 'Greater Armenia' would be a large state between the Black Sea and the Caspian. AUNP found some support among Armenians in the diaspora, especially in Los Angeles and Tehran.[13] By 1970, however, the KGB had rounded up virtually all AUNP's activists and leaders. Two of them – Tzaven Baghdassarian and Stepan Zatikian – were found guilty of 'anti-state conspiracy' and executed in 1971, the first political opponents to be shot under Brezhnev. A number of other AUNP activists, however, escaped the KGB net and went underground.

Mikhail Gorbachev's policy of 'transparence' enabled AUNP to resume its activities though without establishing a formal party structure. It was apparently decided by the leaders that a more decentralised organisation would be less vulnerable when and if Gorbachev was overthrown or forced to change his policies. Armenian nationalists from Baku and Sumgait began to pay regular visits to Nagorno-Karabakh from the middle of 1987. The idea was to foment an active nationalistic atmosphere in the isolated enclave where Azari domination had always been deeply resented.

Nationalist propaganda in Nagorno-Karabakh had as its most immediate effect a sharp increase in the sense of fear which has formed a major part of the Armenian national psyche for so long. Armenian nationalist propaganda deftly exploits that fear by recalling real or invented 'pogroms' and keeping alive the memory of the 'genocide'. In recent years new concerns have added to the Armenians' sense of insecurity about their future. For one thing, Armenia is suffering from low demography. The Azaris inside Soviet Armenia produce three times as many children as the Armenians, while in neighbouring Azarbaijan the rate of population growth is twice as high as the average for the USSR. The Armenian position is made even less secure by the fact that more than a million ethnic Armenians prefer to live in other parts of the USSR. Moreover the 'Californian dream' continues to drain large numbers of Armenians, especially the young and the better-educated, towards the diaspora. The Azaris, on the other hand, do not emigrate and prefer to stay in their own republic where their share of the total population has steadily increased since 1940. Soviet Azarbaijan's relative prosperity – largely due to the oil boom of the Brezhnev years – also added to Armenian resentments, not least because Nagorno-Karabakh received virtually no share of the bonanza.

It was against this background of tension that a number of clashes broke out among Armenians and Azaris in Stepanakart towards the end of January 1988. A band of Armenian nationalists attacked Azari districts of the town and came to blows with Azari militiamen. According to most accounts, the incidents – although the first of their kind for many years – were not serious enough to lead to any violence on a larger scale, but they came at a time when at least a section of the Azari party leadership was looking for an opportunity to vent its hostility towards Gorbachev's policies of transparence and re-structuring.

When news reached Baku and Sumgait that Azaris had been mistreated by Armenians in Karabakh, it instantly led to cries for revenge among the Muslims. At first the reaction in Baku did not go beyond the preparation of petitions addressed at local authorities. In Sumgait a number of fist-fights among bands of Azaris and Armenians were reported through much of February. Surprisingly, nothing was done to stop further escalation towards greater violence, which negligence gives some credence to Soviet accounts that the Azarbaijan Communist Party leader Kamran Baqerov wished to exploit the situation as part of his own campaign against the Gorbachev line.

This is how one Azari writer put the thesis: 'At first we faced only local scuffles but soon we witnessed pogroms throughout the Caucasus ... Who was responsible? The leaders, the tycoons who lived on bribes and corruption ... They deceived the people and incited Azaris and Armenians to riot against each other. Unfortunately even intellectuals took part (in the pogroms) ...'[14]

This analysis was also echoed by Gorbachev himself, who accused 'enemies of *perestroika* ... those whose interests are threatened by reform' of being responsible for disturbances in both Armenia and Azarbaijan.[15] The fact that Gorbachev also carried out a thorough purge of the party and government apparatus in both republics showed that the Soviet leader saw the turmoil in the Caucasus as part of the power struggle against him. But this is a simplistic, not to say naïve view of a problem with deep historical, political and religious roots.

In the city of Sumgait a number of social factors helped to complicate the situation further. Founded in 1936 on a wasteland, Sumgait is still a new city with all the problems that this implies. More than 60 per cent of the working population is engaged in industrial work; most are young and single men who live in beehive-like dormitories. Drunken rows are frequent and competition between Azaris and Armenians for girls is rife. News of Azari-Armenian clashes in Karabakh, therefore, came as a lit match applied to a powder-keg. The 'explosion'[16] occurred on 26 February 1988 when bands of Azari youths roamed Armenian districts in Sumgait and set fire to Armenian shops and homes. The Armenians quickly organised themselves into defence committees, but were beaten back. Busloads of Azaris later arrived from Baku to help crush what had been presented as an Armenian attempt at seizing control of Sumgait.

What was subsequently labelled 'the Sumgait pogrom' by Armenians continued throughout the night and much of the following day. By the time Soviet army units – backed by 37 tanks and over 100 armoured cars – had entered Sumgait, many scenes of massacre had been enacted. Armenian sources put the number of Armenians killed during the 'pogrom' at between 300 and 1,500. Official Soviet accounts published in Moscow, however, speak of 90 dead and over 1,500 injured, mostly Armenians.

Reports published by Armenians depicted scenes of horror. In one incident Azari youths allegedly beheaded an Armenian and played football with the severed head. In another, a pregnant Armenian woman was 'opened up by Azari knives' and her 'inside and what was left of her unborn baby' pulled out. In a third incident, one is told, a band of Azari youths attacked the home of an Armenian family and raped all the females there, 'including the eighty-year-old grandmother and a girl aged only four'. These horror stories, and many more, are regularly presented to foreign journalists by professional 'eye-witnesses' who offer interviews at Moscow's Armenian cemetery almost every day.

These horror stories, magnified and published throughout the world thanks to the strong presence of the Armenian diaspora in Europe and the United States, bear virtually no relation to the truth. They are not countered because the Azaris do not have a diaspora to lobby on their behalf or at least to give their side of the story. A section of the Western media echoed the stories without further investigation because they confirmed the image of Islam as a violent faith and of Muslims as bloodthirsty savages.

The horror stories are important because they indicate the depth of bitter feelings which have accumulated between the Armenians and the Azaris. The root cause of the enmity between the two nations is not religious bigotry on both sides. The Armenians and the Azaris are basically from the same human stock and share very close common roots. They are divided by language and religion, but these differences need not on their own lead to enmity and violence. Nationalism, which is the translation of fear into violence, transcends language, religion and cult. Under Soviet rule, both Azari and Armenian nations have felt threatened and insecure. The Azaris have seen their mosques closed and their religious ceremonies banned. The Armenians have seen their churches turned into 'Houses of Atheism' and their national monuments vandalised in the name of Marxism-Leninism. The Azaris have lost their alphabet and have to work with a script which cannot render the real sounds of their language. In such a context any additional threat, especially if it comes from an adversary considered to be vulnerable, is bound to lead to violence.

The Sumgait riots were followed by a year of violence in both Azarbaijan and Armenia, during which at least 400 people died. The majority were Armenians, but this did not mean that the Azaris did not suffer as well. According to Soviet officials no fewer than 250,000 people have been turned into refugees in the two republics as Azaris and Armenians continue to leave each other's territories and seek refuge in their respective 'home' republics. The massacres of 1988, accompanied by widespread 'pillaging' of property,[17] sharply increased the sentiment of fear in both republics and thus further strengthened nationalistic feelings.

Moscow's initial reaction to the events in Transcaucasia was one of disbelief. Azarbaijan and Armenia had long been regarded as model republics. The Azarbaijani communist elite had established a reputation for loyalty to Moscow and a militant commitment to the CPSU since the 1940s. During the 1970s and much of the 1980s, Baku had emerged as a veritable political power-house under Heydar Ali-Reza Aliev[18], a

KGB creature who had built up his image as an incorruptible revolutionary. Aliev had supposedly 'cleansed' Azarbaijan by putting it under direct KGB rule between 1970 and 1980. He later became a member of the Politburo, the first Azari ever to reach so high a position, and also served as Deputy Prime Minister under Tikhonov.[19] Under Aliev, many party and state officials were executed after trials that lasted only a few hours. In one instance, a twenty-minute-long 'trial' led to the execution of Ibrahim Baba-Zadeh (Baba'ev), a Baku high court judge.[20]

The leadership in the Kremlin had assumed that Aliev's 'iron hand' had all but destroyed the last vestiges of Muslim and nationalistic presence in the southern republic. But when almost all major Azarbaijani towns were put under martial law in 1988 a different picture began to emerge. The Soviet military authorities who took control of Azarbaijan quickly found that the local branch of the KGB had all but ceased to exist except as a club for Azari elites determined to protect their own privileges and eliminate their personal enemies.

The army crackdown led to the discovery of some 30,000 firearms in Baku, Sumgait, Lenkoran, Shemakhi, Sheki and Kirov-Abad, and to the arrest of over 1,500 people in 1988.[21]

The dusk-to-dawn curfew imposed on Baku, Sumgait and Yerevan enabled the army and the militia to organise a series of raids on nationalist strongholds in both republics. A number of illegal printing presses were seized and large quantities of anti-Soviet literature were discovered and destroyed.

The Soviet authorities have never published the full list of those arrested together with the exact nature of charges brought against them, but a number of secret trials were organised throughout 1988 and hundreds of people were condemned to various terms of imprisonment. One military tribunal in Baku sentenced two Azari Muslims to death in December 1988 after finding them guilty of endangering the security of the state.[22] The two men, Qanbar Qadarov and Murad Zaynal-Zadeh, were the first political opponents of the Soviet regime to be shot since Gorbachev assumed the leadership of the CPSU in 1985.

The treatment of Armenian dissidents was markedly more lenient. Paruir Ayrikian, who had emerged as the most effective spokesman for the Armenian cause, was deprived of his Soviet nationality and forcibly expelled to Ethiopia in July 1988. Ayrikian's close associates, all members of the Karabakh Committee created in Yerevan, were arrested on a number of occasions and released before being seized once again in November 1988 and transferred to Moscow.

In November 1988 Armenia was hit by a major earthquake which claimed more than 50,000 lives and made a further 200,000 people homeless. The cities of Spital and Leninakan were almost completely destroyed. The natural disaster did not, however, bring about ethnic peace as was at first expected. Passions were further inflamed by a campaign of rumours partly fomented by extremist elements in both Armenia and Azarbaijan. Tracts claiming to contain the texts of two telegrams allegedly sent by the Azaris to the Armenians after the earthquake were widely circulated in Yerevan and provoked fresh violence.[23]

One alleged cable read: 'We are ready to complete the task so graciously began by nature.' The second alleged telegram simply read: 'Congratulations on your earthquake. Nature saved us from doing the job!' Although widely reported by the Soviet media, the cables were almost certainly forgeries designed to provoke further unrest at a particularly tense time. A number of more directly anti-Soviet rumours were also circulated, one of which presented the earthquake as the result of an explosion in a nuclear power station in Armenia.

The anti-Azari campaign in Yerevan provoked fresh anti-Armenian outbursts in Azarbaijan. Yerevan Radio deliberately exaggerated reports of violence. In one broadcast, for example, it claimed that 'the situation in Azarbaijan is out of control ... Armenians are being killed and the authorities are just watching.'[24] This was at a time that Baku was under Soviet army occupation and all assemblies of more than three people were banned in most Azarbaijani cities.

The appearance of Armenian priests at the head of mammoth anti-Azari marches and demonstrations in Yerevan gave the ethnic conflict an additional religious dimension. On both sides, in fact, religion remained the principal ingredient of nationalistic feelings. Compared with Armenian priests, however, the Azari 'official' mullahs had played only a minor role during the crisis until the autumn of 1988. In October the official head of shi'ite Islam in the USSR, Ayatollah Allah-Shakur Pasha-Zadeh, who had been bitterly attacked for his cautious attitude throughout the crisis, felt obliged to intervene with a strong attack on 'enemies of Islam' and called for 'mobilisation and vigilance of the faithful'.

This was not quite the call for holy war that the more militant Muslims wanted, but it was sufficiently strong to persuade many hesitating Azaris that the nation had to close its ranks and put itself on a war footing. Ayatollah Pasha-Zadeh's move coincided with the start of the shi'ites' mourning months of Muharram and Safar. On Tassu'a, the ninth day of Muharram that marks the start of the final cycle of martyrdom in the shi'ite calendar, a series of mass demonstrations took place in Baku, Kirov-Abad, Sumgait, Shemakhi, Sheki and Lenkoran. Tens of thousands of men, all dressed in black, followed by women wearing the Islamic *hijab* for the first time in decades, marched through the streets.

They carried flags and banners associated with the rite of mourning the martyrdom of Hussein Ibn Ali, the third imam of shi'ism.[25] At intervals the crowds stopped to listen to mullahs' sermons recalling the tragic events of Karbala in the eighth century. In parts of Baku, portraits of the Iranian shi'ite leaders Grand Ayatollah Abol-Qassem Mussavi-Kho'i[26] and the late Grand Ayatollah Muhammad-Kazem Shariatmadari and the standard of 'Lion and Sun'[27] were carried by the demonstrators. According to some reports, a number of portraits of Grand Ayatollah Ruhollah Khomeini were also shown by the demonstrators, together with the green flags of Islam.[28]

The series of mourning demonstrations led to a number of clashes between shi'ites and the Soviet forces. More than 600 people were injured and some 2,000 Azaris were rounded up. A meeting between Ayatollah Pasha-Zadeh and the local party leader, Abdul-Rahman Vazirov, on 27 November led to a compromise under which the authorities allowed the holding of mourning ceremonies at private homes and a number of former mosques and *takiyehs*,[29] in exchange for an undertaking by Muslims not to organise fresh street marches. The Soviet military presence throughout Azarbaijan was strengthened and the curfew extended to a number of other cities besides Baku and Sumgait.

Throughout the crisis Iran continued its pressure on the USSR by waging a bitter radio war principally aimed at Azari shi'ites. The main theme of the Iranian propaganda was that Muslims should be allowed to perform their religious duties and conduct their life in accordance with the teachings of the Quran and not of Marx and Lenin. This was spelled out by Iranian Deputy Premier Ali-Reza Moayyeri at a press conference in Paris at the end of November. 'It is perfectly normal for the people of Soviet Azarbaijan to want to live their lives as Muslims,' he said. 'We did not send them any pictures (i.e. of Khomeini) since they are fully capable of securing whatever they need in their fight to remain Muslims and live a truly Islamic life.'[30]

Soviet official media revels in the theme of corruption in the Muslim republics where local 'Mafias' have supposedly installed a system to 'rip off our socialist economy'. The average Russian, Ukrainian or Georgian has been persuaded that Muslims in the USSR contribute to the national economy far less than they benefit from it. Muslims are portrayed as backward, superstitious, dirty and, at the same time, crafty and opportunistic. It is never mentioned that all the words associated with corruption – such as bribery, embezzlement, favouritism, connection, graft, fraud and hoarding – are directly borrowed from Russian by all Muslim languages of the USSR.

The fiction that the Muslim republics are in fact subsidised by other union republics is sustained in the face of numerous facts to the contrary.

The Muslim republics provide more than 60 per cent of the raw material needs of Soviet industry and remain captive markets. In an economy where all prices are fictitious, it is difficult to be sure who is ripping off whom. But, accepting official rates of exchange, Central Asian cotton fetches a price which is less than half of that offered on international markets. And cheap oil, gas and coal from the Muslim republics were the principal elements in the so-called 'boom years' of the Brezhnev era. The Soviet economy is centrally planned and as such cannot allow the different republics to make full use of their relative advantages.

The introduction of a market economy may, in an initial phase, put the Muslim republics at a disadvantage vis-à-vis the more developed industrial economies of European USSR. In the longer term, however, the Muslim republics would certainly have a far better chance of achieving sustained growth. The farming season in Russia and much of the rest of European USSR is limited to three to four months a year, while in the Muslim republics it is at least twice as long. An abundance of mineral resources and relative demographic advantage are further factors in favour of the economies of Kazakhstan, Central Asia and Azarbaijan.

With the exception of Azarbaijan, Tatarstan and Bashkirestan, the Muslim republics of the USSR remain the least urbanised in the union. There, the number of students admitted to universities and other institutes of higher education is among the lowest of any ethnic group in the USSR.[33] Instead of speeding up the industrialisation of the Muslim republics, Moscow had devised and implemented a number of projects aimed at turning these regions into sources of cheap labour for the rest of the union. These projects had proven ineffective. 'Cultural, familial, linguistic and religious ties tend to keep Central Asians in their native regions.'[34]

In the early years of Brezhnev, some attempts were made to equalise living standards throughout the union by helping the less developed republics along the path of industrialisation. The USSR was accordingly divided into economic regions that cut across national-republic boundaries. The measure was strongly opposed by many republics which saw this as the first step towards the absorption of all nationalities in a Soviet 'melting-pot' dominated by the Slavs. Brezhnev's policy was also opposed by party leaders in Leningrad, Moscow, Kiev and the Baltic republics on economic grounds. These regions did not wish to surrender part of their own development budgets in favour of industrialisation in the Muslim republics.

In the early 1980s the Muslim republics seemed to have achieved an unprecedented degree of influence in Moscow. For the first time in Soviet history two politicians of Muslim origin, Din-Muhammad Kuna'ev and Heydar Aliev, were full members of the Politburo with a third – Sharafuddin Rashidov, Uzbek party leader – as candidate member. This Muslim lobby was not strong enough to attract the massive investments needed to turn Central Asia and Azarbaijan into veritable industrial poles, but it did have sufficient influence to force the party to put some major development projects related to Central Asia and Kazakhstan on the economic agenda.

The most important of these projects, and certainly the most ambitious, was the Ob-Irtysh river diversion plan designed to prevent an envisaged shortage of water in Kazakhstan, Uzbekistan and Turkmenistan during the 1990s. Leaving aside Tajikestan, with its more than 1,000 rivers and huge glaciers containing endless sources of water, the rest of Central Asia depends essentially on two large rivers, Amu-Darya and Syr-Darya, both of which are fed from the snow reserves of the Pamir mountains and flow into the Aral Sea. Because of over half a century of savage development and neglect of the rules of nature both rivers are under tremendous pressure. Amu-Darya has been subjected to over-exploitation plus change in its traditional course caused by the systematic destruction of forests that mark out its banks from the surrounding desert.

Many Central Asians claim that their beloved river, which is regarded with almost divine reverence in folk traditions, has begun a period of long agony which is bound to end in death. 'When God loved us he gave us the Amu-Darya,' says one Uzbek poet. 'And when he stopped loving us he sent us Russian engineers.'[35] Result-oriented agricultural projects, especially the 'Virgin Lands' campaign launched by Khrushchev, had stretched the region's water resources to breaking point. The constant fall in the level of the Aral Sea and the shrinking of the Caspian Sea, largely through the evaporation of its waters in the Qara-Boghaz Gol, are further threats to ecological balance in Central Asia and Kazakhstan.

The Ob-Irtysh project was aimed at diverting part of the waters of the massive Siberian river, Ob, to the river Irtysh and south to Kazakhstan and Central Asia. The project required the construction of a 2,300-kilometre-long canal, the longest ever planned anywhere in the world, which would feed the Siberian water into the Aral Sea. Early feasibility studies estimated the cost of the project to be around £30,000 million. In the oil boom of the 1970s, the USSR felt confident of being able to finance the project. In 1976 the Twenty-Fifth Congress of the CPSU gave the go-ahead for preliminary work to be done on the project. This was a major success for the 'Muslim' coalition led by Kuna'ev and supported by Rashidov, as well as the Turkmen party leader Muhammad-Nazar Ghafurov. In 1978 the project was formally approved by a special commission of the Gossplan (the Central Planning Ministry) in Moscow.

Brezhnev's death, however, gave opponents of the project – including Yuri Andropov and his closest associate Mikhail Gorbachev – a chance to delay the work needed. Gorbachev, who was in charge of agriculture within the Politburo, favoured further investment in the non-black earth European regions of the USSR (*nechernozem*) which enjoy dependable rainfall. Andropov's death and the return of the Brezhnevites under Konstantin Chernenko led to the revival of the project in 1985.

After Chernenko's death, opponents of the scheme renewed their campaign to have it cancelled. During the Twenty-Seventh Congress of the CPSU in 1986 Gorbachev's principal economic adviser, the Armenian professor Abel Aganbegiyan, strongly attacked the Ob-Irtysh project. The subsequent dismissal of Kuna'ev, Rashidov and Aliev from leading positions in the CPSU and in their respective republics meant that the project was left with no influential supporters. When its formal cancellation was announced by Gorbachev himself in 1988, the decision was received with enthusiasm by the Russian environmentalist movement which emerged as the principal expression of Russian nationalism after 1985. In Kazakhstan and Central Asia, however, the cancellation of the Ob-Irtysh project was seen as a 'betrayal'.[35] Asghar Kuna'ev, the younger brother of Din-Muhammad, was removed from his position as President of the Kazakhstan Academy of Sciences after criticising Moscow for adopting an 'anti-Asian posture'.[36]

Muslim suspicion that the cancellation of the project was a direct result of 'European chauvinism' was partly based on the fact that the newspaper *Sovetskaya Rossiia*, the organ of the Russian republic, conducted a long campaign against 'wasting money in the deserts of Central Asia' and in favour of more investment west of the Ural mountains.

The cancellation of the Ob-Irtysh project was not the only sign that the economic needs of the European republics will receive greater priority under Gorbachev. Between 1986 and 1989, no fewer than 170 development projects aimed at resource development in Azarbaijan, Turkmenistan, Kazakhstan, Uzbekistan, Tajikestan and Kirghizestan were scrapped on orders from Moscow. The Soviet official media tried to justify the decisions by blaming the Muslim republics for over-ambitious development goals and inability to absorb fresh investment.

Insufficient investment in higher education, industrialisation and agricultural development is only one of many reasons for the economic backwardness of the USSR's Muslim republics. Unable to foster normal trade relations with Turkey, Iran, the Arab Middle East, Afghanistan, Pakistan and China, these republics have to gear their economies to markets and sources of imports thousands of miles away in Europe.

The Baltic states have developed extensive trade links with Finland and the Scandinavian countries. The RSFSR and the Ukraine have direct access to the COMECON countries in eastern and central Europe. Commercial exchanges and tourism between the European USSR and Western Europe, and North America, have steadily increased since the mid-1970s. Regular air, rail, road and water transport links between the European USSR on the one hand and the rest of Europe on the other have developed dramatically during the past two decades.

The Muslim republics nevertheless remain isolated from the rest of their natural economic region. The city of Nakhichevan on the river Aras, for example, could be reached from the Iranian river-port of Qizil-Qishlaq in a motor-boat in about ten minutes, yet the inhabitants of the two cities have absolutely no chance of encountering or trading with each other. The border remains sealed and the river is heavily guarded as a military zone. An Azari from Tabriz who might wish to visit Baku would have to go to Tehran, then fly to Moscow[37] and from there fly to the capital of Soviet Azarbaijan.

Access to world markets for the Muslim republics of the USSR could be assured through rail and road links via Iran, Afghanistan and Pakistan. A number of projects aimed at making this possible were in fact discussed between Moscow and Tehran in the 1970s. One proposal envisaged the construction of a railway line connecting Central Asia to the Gulf of Oman via Afghanistan and the Iranian province of Sistan and Baluchistan. The Islamic Revolution in Iran and the Soviet invasion of Afghanistan in 1979, however, buried that and other similar projects. In 1986 Moscow quietly shelved a plan for building a hydroelectric complex on the river Atrak which forms part of the border with Iran; this meant that large parts of Turkmenistan, including the capital city of Ashkabad, might face a shortage of water and power in the 1990s.

Geographically and historically part of Asia, the USSR's Muslim republics have not been allowed to develop economic ties with the rest of the continent. At the same time, however, they have not been fully integrated in a larger European context of economic development and trade. Most Muslim regions of the USSR have been opened up to European and North American tourism, but still remain closed to tourists from the Muslim countries. Muslims can visit Central Asia and Azarbaijan only with special permission or as guests of the 'official' organs of Islam in the USSR. Soviet Muslims are allowed to visit central and eastern Europe as tourists or on business, but cannot travel to Muslim states except on official duty. While Soviet Muslims have a quota of 55,000 pilgrims for the Haj rites at Mecca, between 1980 and 1989 no more than an average of twenty pilgrims – all officials – were allowed to go to Arabia.[38]

Mikhail Gorbachev has stated that helping to foster peace and prosperity in the 'common European home' is one of his principal objectives for the remaining years of this century. But 75 per cent of the USSR's territory and some 30 per cent of its population belong to Asia. Soviet Muslims do not feel part of the 'common European home' and are becoming increasingly aware of their position as junior partners in an unequal partnership. Gorbachev's notorious lapsus in Kiev in 1987 when he kept referring to the USSR as 'Russia' was regarded by some Soviet Muslim intellectuals as a significant revelation as to the new leader's deepest-felt sentiments.[39] These intellectuals share the view held by many Russian nationalists that Gorbachev is a representative of the old 'Westernisers' school' built on a dream of making Russia part of Europe. The Slavophiles' rejection of Gorbachev's European ambitions is shared by many Soviet Muslim intellectuals who feel that by becoming part of Europe the USSR will have to relinquish all pretension of a special relationship with its Muslim nations.

Blaming the Muslim republics for 'narrow-minded nationalism' was a fashionable pastime in Moscow's elite circles in 1989; but it was in the Baltic states and Russia itself that nationalism, albeit in a less threatening form, seemed to be the strongest. The Soviet authorities – who did not tolerate ceremonies at Muslim holy shrines in Central Asia and the Caucasus – permitted and to a certain degree even encouraged religious and nationalistic demonstrations in Russia and the Baltic states. On 28 February 1989 more than ten thousand Russian nationalists attended a public mass during which the Tsarist national anthem was played after the Metropolitan of the Orthodox Church blessed 'the children of Russia' in an elaborate ceremony.

Muslim fears that Gorbachev's policy of 'Westernisation' may lead to greater discrimination against the Asian republics were increased as a result of what appeared to be double standards in dealing with nationalistic movements. In the Baltic states where 'popular fronts' came into being after 1987, nationalists have been allowed to revive many pre-Soviet symbols and traditions. The 'bourgeois' flags of Latvia, Lithuania and Estonia are no longer banned and the three republics, annexed by Stalin in 1940, have been allowed to celebrate their traditional national days. The KGB seems to have been ordered to adopt a low profile in the Baltic states, and Gorbachev has also allowed unprecedented scope for the activities of various Christian churches in the European republics. In the Muslim republics, however, the KGB is still omnipresent and few of the rules against religious education and rites have been relaxed.

The Muslims' view that Gorbachev looks down on the Asian republics as potential enemies of his modernisation plans is only partly attributable to fear of change in essentially conservative societies. There are many reasons for Soviet Muslims to believe that he might not understand their problems. He is the first Soviet leader since Lenin to have had no experience outside the Russian republic. He was born in Stavropol, in northern Caucasus, where the Russians form the largest ethnic group among more than fifty different nationalities.[40]

In the early 1940s Gorbachev witnessed first Nazi occupation and then the mass deportation of Kalmuk Muslims who were accused of collaboration with the Germans. Was he not marked by his personal experience? Did he not think that Muslims were inherently anti-Soviet and that Russians were naturally meant to lead a wide variety of nationalities in the building of socialism? The fact that Gorbachev's highly influential wife, Raisa, is an ethnic Ukrainian is also considered by some Soviet Muslims as another sign that the new master of the Kremlin is more inclined to look West rather than east.

Gorbachev's refusal to act against the semi-fascist *Pamiat* (Pledge) movement which advocates unmistakably racist policies in the name of defending the Russian 'motherland' has angered many Muslims and others. *Pamiat* publications are full of insulting remarks about Tatars and other Muslims who are described as 'blacks in the heart and the colour of skin'.[41] While Muslims are attacked as 'barbarians', Jews are described as 'the cosmopolitans ... the enemy within'.

Under Gorbachev the Slavs have dramatically strengthened their hold over the CPSU and the governmental machinery of the USSR. Out of the twelve members of the Politburo in 1989, only two were non-Russians. For the first time in 25 years, not a single Muslim figured among the members or candidate-members of the Politburo; none of the sections of the Central Committee was headed by a Muslim. Of the 500 men and women who formed the highest echelon of party and government leadership in the USSR in 1989, more than 400 were Russians, Belorussians and Ukrainians. Stavropol, Leningrad, Moscow, Latvia and Kiev were strongly represented, but the Muslim republics had virtually no high-ranking representation. This was in sharp contrast with the line-up of leadership in the Bolshevik Party in 1917, at which time no fewer than sixty per cent of the leaders were non-Russians. Forty per cent were Jews, but no Muslim figured among the principal leaders. Seventy years later, the CPSU appeared as a pan-Slav set-up on a scale never before known.

Kazakhstan was the only republic where a non-native headed the local party structure. In other republics Russians usually occupy the position of second secretary of the party and in most cases the second secretaries – together with KGB and army commanders who are also Russians – control the real levers of power. Nevertheless the presence of 'natives' at the top of the party and state pyramids is appreciated by a majority of the population.

Gorbachev blames the Brezhnev era, which he describes as 'a period of stagnation', for distancing the USSR from the West. Brezhnev's power-base in Kazakhstan and Uzbekistan is therefore perceived by Gorbachev as essentially a dead weight likely to slow down the process of reform.

The problem of nationalities was extensively discussed during the Nineteenth Conference of the CPSU in 1988. The resolution adopted at the end of the conference committed the party to 'enlarging the rights of federated republics and autonomous entities ... through decentralisation, by the transfer to local level of certain administrative functions and by reinforcing autonomy and (regional) responsibility in matters of economic, social and cultural development and the protection of nature.' The same resolution further pledged support for 'the principle of financial autonomy in the republics'.

The CPSU's new policy was instantly applied to Estonia which, in April 1988, was given the right to be solely responsible for managing its own economy. The session of the Politburo which approved the move in favour of Estonia made it clear that it was in the Baltic States that *perestroika* will be applied more fully.

The Muslim republics, however, had to remain content with promises. In April 1988 when Gorbachev addressed a session of the Central Committee of the Uzbekistan Communist Party, this turned out to be no more than a pedagogic exercise in which the Uzbeks were advised to abandon 'old practices' and support the programme of reforms. But Uzbekistan was not offered any of the privileges which Estonia had received and in 1989 remained much the Russian-dominated republic as it had always been since the 1920s. The situation was still more dramatic in Soviet Azerbaijan, where Moscow's military presence was in sharp contrast with Gorbachev's promises of pluralism, democracy, decentralisation and greater autonomy for the many nations that go to make up the USSR. Gorbachev released many European and Jewish dissidents from prison or internal exile but filled their places with Muslims, especially from Azerbaijan. The decision of the Supreme Soviet to put Nagorno-Karabakh under direct rule from Moscow in January 1989 further indicated Gorbachev's determination to remain 'tough' towards Muslims in general and Azaris in particular.

Godless in Search of God

Seventy-two years after a revolution which boasted that it would 'bury all religion', God is alive and increasingly popular in the USSR. Everywhere old and long-abandoned churches and mosques are being restored and reopened. They are quickly filled with the faithful who come from all walks of life and represent all generations. In many parts of the union new churches and mosques are under construction, all financed by the faithful.

The seemingly sudden popularity of religion in the Soviet Union, however, does not represent the return of God from the dead. Religion never died in the USSR, but had to hide itself as best it could in order to escape some of the cruellest forms of persecution ever recorded in history. Mikhail Gorbachev's policy of *glasnost*, which began to make a real impact after 1986, gave religion a chance to resume something resembling a normal life in the USSR.

The new leadership under Gorbachev seemed to have little difficulty in coping with the various Christian churches. As mentioned earlier Raisa, the president's wife, attended ceremonies marking the end of the first millenium of the Orthodox Church in Russia. The Catholic church in Estonia is accepted as a central national institution. Church ceremonies and programmes dealing with various aspects of the Christian faith are broadcast by radio and television in various European republics. 'The Christian heritage is part of our national culture,' said one top ideologist of the Communist Party of the Soviet Union. 'It is not in contradiction with the socialist character of our society.'[1]

When it comes to Islam, however, the Soviet leaders do not demonstrate the same degree of generosity. Christianity accepts the separation of church and state as a matter of course; the kingdom of Christ is not of this world, and what is Caesar's must be recognised and respected as such. Soviet ideologists now say that the initial clash between church and state after the 1917 revolution was due to Stalin's 'stupidity and greed'. Had it not been for this, the Orthodox Church would have readily agreed to coexist peacefully with the new state just as it had lived under Mongol domination and during many reigns of terror inaugurated by the tsars. Islam, on the other hand, does not recognise a separation of the mosque and the state; it aims at encompassing the entire life of its adepts and wants to regulate all aspects of their individual existence and social endeavour. Islam wants to be present everywhere: from the planning office where economic projects are worked out, to a man's bedroom where he is alone with his wife.

Totally opposed in every aspect of doctrine and *Weltanschauung*, Islam and Bolshevism – in its pristine purity – resembled each other in one crucial respect: they both wanted to have exclusive domination over society. The Bolsheviks, at least in their early years, were convinced that Islam would disppear as a result of socio-economic reforms that deprived it of its material base. But this has not happened; on the contrary, it is Communism which has lost almost all of its original romantic vigour. Marx had promised a withering away of the state under Communism, but what is now happening in the USSR is a withering away of the Marxist–Leninist ideology. It is at a moment of grave self-doubts that Soviet Communism, a badly shaken church, faces what is routinely described in Moscow as 'the rise of Islamic fundamentalism'. Soviet thinkers do not hide their 'great concern' about what they see as 'a serious problem'.[2]

At a time when it is no longer possible for the Soviet regime to claim legitimacy solely on the basis of its ideological purity, the system as a whole is equally incapable of achieving new sources of legitimacy through, for example, offering the people a higher standard of living. As a result the Soviet state feels remarkably vulnerable to the challenge of rival ideologies such as militant Islam which are capable of dispelling doubts and mobilising the pent-up resentment of the people in the pursuit of radical changes.

Attempts made by official Islam to persuade the faithful that Islam and Communism have shared goals can no longer be taken seriously. The old Mufti Baba Khan of Tashkent had developed a theory according to which Communism was one method of achieving some of Islam's objectives in the field of social justice; this verbal gimmick was adopted by the Gorbachev leadership in the early stages of *glasnost* but was quickly abandoned after it inspired a cascade of anti-Communist jokes in Central Asia and Azarbaijan.[3]

Gorbachev has won much sympathy for his announced reforms by setting free large numbers of political prisoners, and Soviet officials claimed that no more than approximately 100 prisoners of conscience remained behind bars at the end of 1988.[4] But this did not cover scores of Muslim militants still held in Azarbaijan, Daghestan, Uzbekistan, Turkmenistan, Karakalpakia, Kazakhstan, Kirghizestan and Tajikestan. Political prisoners are usually held under articles 70 and 190 of the Constitution of the USSR which deal with 'opposition to the state'. But Muslim activists are almost always charged with common criminal offences such as 'illegal trade', 'black-marketeering' and 'hooliganism'. In other words, the Soviet authorities openly acknowledge that Muslim fundamentalists are political opponents but in practice treat them as common criminals.

Islamic revival in the USSR today cannot be described as a single movement with a coherent programme and a set of easily recognisable goals. It has many different sources of inspiration and represents a wide range of hopes, fears and aspirations. There is no doubt that it is strongly anti-colonial; the Soviet domination of the Muslim republics is certainly not a traditional colonial presence. But to most Muslims the USSR is no more than the successor of the Tsarist empire, a Russian state that had imposed its rule over Asia by the use of naked force. Right from the start of the Russian domination, many attempts were made to impress the Muslims with Russia's civilisation and grandeur, but these attempts only provoked resentment and anger. Muslims saw the Russians as a cold and sad people,[5] while Russia's claims to be the continuation of the Roman Empire were savagely ridiculed.[6]

The negative view of Russia's colonial mission was reinforced by early Bolshevik propaganda (1917–1924) and the tsars were described as 'bloodsucking hounds interested only in killing, maiming and plunder'.[7] Thus the Bolsheviks sought to dissociate themselves from the Russian past. But this policy was changed by Stalin, who emphasised the role of the Russian people in bringing civilisation to the backward peoples of the east (1924–41). Later, the role of the 'great Russian nation' was further emphasised in the context of the war against Nazi Germany (1941–1953). After Stalin the Muslim peoples were told by Khrushchev that those who had resisted the expansion of the Tsarist empire had been 'feudal lords', 'charlatan mullahs' and 'agents of western imperialism'. Imam Shamil, for example, was labelled 'a seasoned agent of British Intelligence services'. In other words, Khrushchev re-established the Russian character of the state by claiming the Tsarist past as part of a 'glorious history'. His anti-Islamic campaign helped to further antagonise the Muslims.

Few Muslims feel the Communist movement as part of their own heritage. Muslims were almost totally absent from the Bolshevik revolution and later joined Lenin's party either out of opportunism or in the hope of gaining some concessions for their peoples. Today less than

6 per cent of the CPSU members are of Muslim origin. But even those who are in the party have not necessarily abandoned their Islamic heritage. Gorbachev himself complained about those who describe themselves as Communists but continue to 'attend religious ceremonies and perform religious rites'.[7]

That Muslim Communists, even those with a background of activity in the atheist movement, are joining the search for God is illustrated by Chengiz Aitmatov, the best-selling Kirghiz novelist. A winner of the Lenin Prize and a member of the Supreme Soviet, Aitmatov provoked much furore among the Communists in 1986–87 by publishing *The Place of the Skull*, a novel which takes up the theme of 'searching for God'. He described his critics as 'immature'. 'They are afraid I might find God!'

The Aitmatov of *The First Master*, describing the early Bolshevik era in Central Asia, was already part of history. The writer knew that he was beginning to lose his Kirghiz audience by staying with old revolutionary themes which might have had some relevance in the 1950s but were totally out of place in the 1980s.

Aitmatov is not the only Muslim writer to 'stand back and take a look at our past'.[8] Old themes associated with the Islamic heritage have crept into the work of other famous Communist writers of Muslim origin such as Rasul Hamzatov, the doyen of the Daghestani literature, and Abdul-Jamil Nurbeysev, the old man of Leninist Muslims in Kazakhstan.

Between 1985 and 1989 the CPSU branches in all the Muslim republics were purged on a number of occasions. In virtually every case those purged were accused, among other 'crimes', of having manifested 'nationalistic sentiments', a code-word for loyalty to Islam. In his report to the Central Committee of the CPSU in January 1987, Gorbachev sounded distinctly pessimistic about finding an answer to what he described as 'the rise of nationalism'.[9]

The Soviet leadership routinely describes as 'the problem of nationalities' what is in fact a problem of fully-developed modern nations. The Kirghiz, for example, were not even a nationality in 1917 and lived as a tribal confederation. In the 1920s and 1930s they developed into a nationality, and today they are a nation. Karl Deutsch has argued that nationalism is an epiphenomenon in the process of modernisation. Thus modernisation could be expected to weaken nationalist sentiments. The experience of many 'modern' countries – the United States for example – shows this to be less than accurate. On the contrary it can be demonstrated that a degree of modernisation is necessary for the rise of nationalism. The tsars sought to prevent the rise of hostile nationalism among their subject peoples through policies of russification (*obrusenie*) but did not go far for lack of adequate means. Stalin revived part of the same policy and applied it in a more determined way. A russified elite was created in the 'peripheral republics', but the masses remained largely untouched. The russified elites learned about Western-style nationalism through their mentors and became carriers of nationalism amongst their own peoples, which was similar to the experience of Muslim elites in French North Africa. There, too, an assimilated elite took the idea of nationalism to the masses and subsequently led their anti-colonial revolt.

In French North Africa, Islam – because it cut across tribal and clannic divisions – quickly emerged as the mainstay of modern nationalism. A similar development has been taking place in the USSR's Muslim republics and regions. It is to Islam that many people now look as the most effective means of describing their identity. Here is how one intellectual puts the case:

> Soviet identity is too large; it is like saying one is an Asian. It is at the same time too narrow because it is limited to a specific type of socio-political organisation.... Soviet is how others see you, not how you feel yourself to be. Abroad many people even call you 'Russian'. Only the more knowledgeable call you 'Soviet'. But what is important is how you see yourself. I see myself as a Muslim. Even Uzbek is too restrictive. My mother is a Tajik, my father an Uzbek. So, who am I really? A Muslim. This is the only identity that is readily understood by everyone and provokes no 'ifs' and 'buts'. It describes your past as well as your present. It also indicates the type of future you like to build for yourself. There is a certain quality about it. It is authentic, not a label stuck on your chest by some authority that now happens to be in charge.... Personally I have no objection to being described as a Soviet Muslim or a Muslim citizen of the USSR. The 'Soviet' bit remains valid as long as I am associated with the Soviet state. What if I left the citizenship of the USSR? Would I suddenly evaporate? What if Uzbekistan left the USSR and chose another political system as it has the constitutional right, in theory at least? Would I cease to exist? What if Perestroika becomes a reality and the Soviet system itself is transformed into something else? Would I no longer be there? Whatever happens I will always be a Muslim; even if I became an atheist I would still be a Muslim atheist. Only the term 'Muslim' is large enough, accurate enough and, paradoxically, neutral enough to describe what we are in this corner of the world ...[10]

A number of developments since the 1940s helped focus the attention of the elites in the Muslim lands of the USSR on Islam's almost unique capacity for expressing the widest possible range of national grievances and aspirations. The long-promised Bolshevik revolutions in the Muslim east, especially Turkey and Iran, failed to materialise after the Second World War. The Soviet puppet republic of Tabriz in Iranian Azerbaijan collapsed like a pack of cards the day the Red Army withdrew behind the Aras river in 1946. The emergence of Pakistan in 1947 as a nation-state uniquely based on Islam reminded Soviet Muslims of the vitality of the faith of Muhammad. Islam was also recognised as a leading force in the decolonisation movement that led to the emergence of numerous new independent Muslim countries from Indonesia to Nigeria.[11] The oil nationalisation movement in Iran (1949–1953), the expulsion of the British from Egypt under Nasser (1952–1970) and the Arab–Israeli conflict also helped focus the attention of Soviet Muslims on what many of them saw as a series of confrontations between Islam and the west. The USSR's policy of support for the Palestinian cause – especially marked between 1967 and 1983 – was designed to create the impression that Moscow was on the side of the Muslims. This policy somehow 'legitimised' the expression of Islamic sentiments inside the USSR as long as these were directed against the West.

While playing the Islamic card for what it was worth, the Kremlin kept relations between Soviet Muslims and the rest of the Muslim world to a bare minimum. Soviet Muslims were allowed virtually no access to the literatures of Turkey, Iran, Egypt and other major Muslim countries. In 1989 the list of contemporary Muslim writers translated and published in the USSR included only 27 names compared with a similar list for French authors with no fewer than 108 names. This was despite the fact that there was 'a thirst' for Muslim literature and virtually no interest in European works in the Muslim regions. Even works by Lenin, Marx and other 'absolute musts' of official ideology 'evoked hardly any attention' in Uzbekistan, the largest of the Soviet Muslim republics in terms of population.

From the 1950s and until 1979 Soviet Muslims were told that Islam, although alive and combative elsewhere, was all but dead in the USSR. Islam was dissected, analysed and studied as a prehistoric fossil. 'All books about Islam in our country used the past tense,' complained Ershad Quli-Zadeh, a director of Baku television until his dismissal in 1989.[13] The task of studying this 'dead cold Islam' was mainly entrusted to Russian scholars who followed the tradition started by Barthold, Minorsky and Petroshevsky. Muslim scholars steered clear of Islamic studies for fear of being seen by party officials as nostalgics of the 'feudal era'.[14]

The Islamic revolution in Iran (1978–79), which led to the first major confrontation between a Muslim nation and the United States, was at first all but ignored by the Soviet media, which continued to support the Shah right to the end. The personal friendship forged between the Shah and President Brezhnev prevented Moscow from gauging the real mood in revolutionary Iran. The success of the Muslim revolt in bringing down what to many Soviet Muslims had looked like a strong and solidly-based state enhanced Islam's image as a living force. More importantly, Soviet Muslims saw that it was not Marxism–Leninism – whose imminent triumph in Iran had been forecast for more than half a century – which had brought down the Shah but a set of beliefs ridiculed as 'old women's tales' by many Soviet commentators.

The Islamic Revolution ended more than a decade of close and friendly ties between Iran and the USSR. One of the first steps taken by the new revolutionary regime in Tehran was to set up a special committee for 'reviving the message of Islam in the USSR'. This was headed by an ethnic Afghan Jalaleddin Farsi who fancied himself as the true successor of Sayyed Jamaleddin Afghani, the pan-Islamic firebrand in the nineteenth century.[15]

The new Islamic power in Iran began a major radio war against 'Soviet atheism' from the spring of 1979, when two new and powerful transmitters in northern Iran were used to beam Islamic programmes at Azarbaijan, Daghestan, Central Asia and Kazakhstan. Each week Iranian transmitters broadcast a total of 200 hours of programmes in Azari, Uzbek, Turkmen and Tajik (Dari) to the USSR. Iran's Islamic propaganda at first appeared too naïve to be considered a threat; it seemed unlikely that Soviet Muslim women would heed the advice to return to the purdah and accept an inferior social position. Nor were Soviet Muslims expected to be receptive to calls for the full implementation of the *shari'ah* (Islamic Law).

Nevertheless, the propaganda drive appeared to have had some effect and in 1980 and 1981 differences emerged between the leaders of the various Muslim republics of the USSR as how best to cope with the threat from Iran. The Soviet Azarbaijan leadership under Aliev, who saw himself as 'only slightly less important than God Himself',[16] supported a policy of help for the Iranian revolution in the hope of turning all of its energies against the West. Was this because Aliev underestimated the influence of shi'ism in his own native land? No one could tell for sure. What is certain is that the shi'ite hierarchy at Tabriz, Tehran, Qom and Najaf had succeeded in establishing 'satisfactory contacts throughout (Soviet) Azarbaijan'.[17] In 1978 'substantial amounts of money' were raised among shi'ites in Soviet Azarbaijan in the name of Grand Ayatollahs Kho'i and Shariatmadari.[18] Both ayatollahs, especially Shariatmadari, were bitterly attacked by Baku Radio on a number of occasions for their failure to devote enough attention to the struggle against 'American Imperialism'.[19]

Iranian radios devoted much time to the struggle of Muslims against Russian expansionism in the nineteenth century. Long-forgotten chapters in the histories of Daghestan, Azarbaijan and Central Asia were brought to the attention of vast audiences in the USSR, which made it difficult for Soviet propaganda to hit back: it was difficult to come out in defence of tsarist atrocities.

In Central Asia the local Communist leadership was hostile towards the Islamic Revolution of Iran right from the start. Mrs Nasruddinova published a number of articles on the theme of Islam's alleged discrimination against women; the then Uzbek party leader Nureddin Muhitudinov lashed out against the mullahs in speech after speech, which persuaded his audiences that the mullahs had truly emerged as a power to reckon with. The steady increase in the number of men who stopped shaving and of women who began to wear headscarves in many Central Asian cities showed that Islam was, if not rising as a political force, at least becoming fashionable even among the educated strata. An Islamic 'appearance' was seen as a statement against past humiliation by Russia and problems faced under the Soviet regime today. Concern about Islamic agitation, especially in Central Asia, began to be openly expressed in the official media.

It was this concern which helped to persuade the Soviet leadership that some flexing of the military muscle was necessary. An impressive military build-up completed on the borders between Iran and Soviet Azarbaijan and Armenia in the summer of 1979 provoked little reaction from the United States and, in turn, persuaded the Kremlin leaders that a military intervention in Afghanistan would also be quietly swallowed by the West. The Soviet invasion of Afghanistan in the last days of 1979 was at least in part motivated by fears that Kabul might fall into the hands of Khomeini-style Muslim militants who would then try to spread the message of revolutionary Islam into Central Asia and beyond. 'Yes. We had to secure our southern borders,' said one high-ranking Soviet official. 'We could not allow Afghanistan to catch fire.'[20]

Uzbek, Turkmen and Tajik Communist leaders tried to use the invasion of Afghanistan – which they had not advocated but did support when the decision was taken in Moscow – as an opportunity for restoring a sparkle of life to their corrupt and moribund movements. Detachments of 'volunteer' Uzbek, Turkmen and Tajik soldiers spearheaded the invasion, told that their mission was to help their 'Afghan Muslim brethren' preserve the independence of their country and the achievements of their revolution against 'Imperialist aggression'. Some Soviet Muslims might have genuinely believed the propaganda, but once inside Afghanistan they quickly found out that they had been duped into invading a country against the wishes of its people. Soviet Muslim soldiers began to defect to Afghan resistance or simply refused to fight. Some of them even participated in a quixotic attempt at invading the USSR itself.[21] The Afghan resistance demonstrated the vulnerability of Soviet Central Asian borders to guerrilla attacks on a number of other occasions. In 1987, for example, a detachment of Hezb-Islami (Islamic Party) commanded by Mir Muhammad attacked the Soviet frontier post of Moskovski in the district of Penj opposite the Afghan province of Tukhar. 'They attacked our frontier guards and made victims.'[22]

Disenchantment with the Afghan adventure was not long in coming and the Soviet media reported this in their own style. One Kirghiz paper wrote: 'When our lads began to sacrifice their lives in Afghanistan, a veritable eruption of self-consciousness occurred.'[23] The net result of the disenchantment felt in Central Asia was the withdrawal of Muslim units from the Soviet side of the Afghan war. While the first Soviet soldiers who entered Afghanistan all had black eyes and tawny skins and were called Muhammad and Ali, the last ones to leave were named Vladimir and Boris and had white skin and blue eyes.

The long-term impact of the Soviet decision to withdraw from Afghanistan in 1988[24] might take many years to be fully measured in the Muslim parts of the USSR, but most Muslims did not hesitate to see this as a defeat for Russia and a triumph for Islam. It was the first time since 1552 that Russians had been forced to abandon a conquered Muslim land. The process of Russian expansion at the expense of Muslim peoples came to a halt in the Hindukush, which to some Muslims looked like a historic turning point. Could Russia be rolled back into its own natural, historical habitat and out of Muslim Central Asia and Azarbaijan? Openly discussed in many Muslim capitals, the question could only be pondered privately in the USSR itself. Muslim intellectuals in Central Asia saw the Soviet retreat as 'proof that Russians are not ten-feet tall and that Islam is not an affair of vagabond mullahs only'. They dismissed suggestions that the Afghan 'victory' had been achieved at least partly thanks to massive financial and logistical support from the United States and that no one could be sure what kind of Afghanistan might emerge from the bloody war. What was important to many Muslim intellectuals who agreed to discuss the issue was that 'Russia had failed to re-draw the map of Asia yet again.'[25]

The Afghan war further strengthened traditional anti-Russian feelings among many Muslims. It is not so much Communism as such which is the object of hate amongst Muslims but a sense of continued domination by the Russians. In fact, Communism is disliked as part of the Russian policy of expansion and hegemony over weaker nations and it is partly for this reason that the official Soviet media constantly try to portray the 'building of socialism' as an international enterprise. The Muslim peoples of the union are reminded of the progress achieved 'under socialism' and not under Russian rule, though some Muslim intellectuals see even this constant reference to 'socialist achievements' as an indirect way of inviting them to show gratitude to Russian masters.

'All the time we are told that if we are where we are in terms of education, industry and health it is because of Socialism,' says one Tajik researcher. 'This means that we, as peoples, had little or no role to play. It is forgotten that socialism has produced different results elsewhere, in Vietnam and South Yemen, for example, not to mention Cambodia.'[26]

Glasnost has enabled the Soviet media to acknowledge that the USSR is faced with an Islamic revival. There is, however, no serious attempt inside the Soviet Union itself to study the organisational structures and the political and cultural demands of the *nahdhah*.[27] This has enabled a number of anti-Soviet writers in the West to portray the Islamic revival as a veritable revolt against the Kremlin with the specific aim of breaking up the Soviet 'empire'.

The Islamic revival in the Soviet Union, however, is not a monolithic movement with a set of clearly stated political objectives. It has no central organisation or even a set of organisations capable of using it as a political weapon or as a means of exerting pressure on Moscow. Russian Communism destroyed all the various political movements, largely of Western inspiration, which existed among the Muslims of the Tsarist empire until the 1920s, but it failed to fill the whole of the void thus created. Today Soviet Muslims, denied access to other political ideologies at a time when Communism is passing through a serious crisis of its own, are returning to Islam – the only natural fall-back position they have after seventy years of Soviet rule.

Communism, although it captured the whole of the public space in the lives of the Muslim republics, never quite succeeded in dominating the private space. The vast majority of people never stopped feeling they were Muslims when they were in the company of family and friends or alone with their consciences. The 1980s witnessed a slow but steady re-conquest of the public space by Islam, a process which assumed many different forms. The number of Muslim children taking part in the Red Octoberist and Pioneer Communist movements[28] has been on the decline for more than a decade. Fewer and fewer Muslims seek admission in the Komsomol, and Muslim membership of the CPSU is comparatively lower today than at any time since the 1920s. Many Muslim families have also withdrawn their children from Russian or multi-national schools, especially in Kazakhstan. Instead the number of exclusively Muslim kindergartens and schools has multiplied. In a number of universities in Azarbaijan, Central Asia and Kazakhstan, official curricula have been revised and remodelled to allow an Islamic vision of existence to be presented side by side with the Marxist–Leninist one. In these republics the university has become a veritable battleground between the 'natives' and the 'internationalists'. Although there are frequent purges aimed against the 'natives', the struggle is far from over.

One important arena for the struggle between the natives and the internationalists is history. Muslims no longer accept the traditional Communist view of the Islamic past as a period of chaos and brutal ignorance. In Uzbekistan Iman Momenov's books on the Teymurid era – ignored at the time of their publication in the 1960s – now have a growing audience. Momenov discards 'historical materialism' and relies heavily on methods of analysis developed by Muslim historians of the classical school. The historic epics of the poet Muhammad Rasuli, who idolises the Islamic past as 'the golden age', are put to music and have gained a popularity not dreamed of by their author.

The Uzbeks have developed a passion for historical novels with their Islamic past as the central theme. Primqora Qadirova has chosen Sultan Hossein Bayqara as the hero of her popular novels, and Aziz Qayyumov has come under attack for having supposedly idolised Babur, the Mongol conqueror of India. Muhammad-Ali Mahmudov's novel *The Eternal Heights*, published in 1981, has become a best-seller despite accusations by the local party leaders that it promotes 'aggressive nationalism'.

Calls by local party intellectuals for a ban on 'these ugly pulsations of the past'[29] have produced little result. One official commentator lamented, 'tyrants like Teymur are idolised in novels, films and plays'.[30]

Even the more recent past has not been ignored. Several novels and plays have chosen as their theme the anti-Russian uprising of Andijan, known as the Madali Ishan revolt, despite the fact that the movement is seen by Communist historians as 'retrograde, feudal and medieval'. Madali Ishan is now seen by the Uzbeks as a symbol of resistance against colonialism.

The Soviet Uzbek *Encyclopaedia* itself has come under official attack for having allowed 'infiltration by nationalists'.[31] The party's chief local mandarin bitterly complained about the fact that 'some of our writers praise rulers who made towers of the severed heads of their opponents'.[32] There is no word from him though about the hundreds of thousands of Muslims who were wiped out under Stalin.

Yet another battle-ground is that section of the press which has a better chance of escaping tight party control. In Azarbaijan, Kazakhstan and the Central Asian republics, many weeklies and periodicals dealing with literature, arts, sciences, the environment and other not directly 'political' areas have over the past decade developed into lively forums for unofficial views of life. They represent yet another part of the public space that is being wrested away from Communist control. Magazines such as *Sharq Yulduzi* (*Eastern Star*) in Uzbekistan and *Turkmenistan Adabiyat va San'at Gazetsi* (*Turkmenistan's Journal of Literature and Art*) allow some scope for an Islamic view of existence to be expressed. In Kirghizestan Murad Aliev's novel *The Cuckoo in the Month of May* is a veritable hymn to the Islamic past of the Kirghiz people. Persistent attempts at getting the novel banned, however, produced no results.

Poems and short stories related to the anti-Communist Basmachi movement of the 1920s and 1930s are also immensely popular in Kirghizestan. The poems of Qazibek Mambetiminov, himself a Basmachi killed by the Bolsheviks, now haunt the Frunze Communist establishment after a lapse of fifty years. The party organ bitterly noted that 'poems and songs of this traitor are being spread among the population half a century later'.[33] Worse still, a number of 'party cadres' organised the publication of the anti-Soviet poems in samizdat form. The party paper named two such culprits as 'comrade Bazarba'ev and comrade Isabekov'.

Also in Kirghizestan, the writings of Mulla Qelich Shemir-Khanov and Qassim Tunistanov – long banned because if their allegedly 'reactionary and anti-proletarian nature' – are widely distributed and read with growing interest.

One intellectual who is specially attacked for his 'nationalist' view is Professor Ata Kurov of the department of archaeology and ethnography at Frunze University. Kurov explains his method as one 'aimed at studying the past from different angles', but he was attacked for having 'criticised the Russian people and even calling them a tribe'.

In Kazakhstan even Alim Jaqshibayev, secretary of the official Writers' Union, has been accused of nationalist tendencies. Oljas Soleimanov, the president of the union, singles out 'Islamism' for attack and openly calls for a return to 'internationalist discipline'. In 1989 he appeared to be very much a lone voice among Kazakh intellectuals with only formal attachment to the party. Even *Zhulduzh* (*The Star*), the union's organ, could no longer be described as part of the exclusively Communist space of Kazakh life.

The purge of the universities in 1987 ended or interrupted the official careers of some Muslim scholars in Kazakhstan. Teymur Khajeh'ev, dean of the faculty of journalism in Alma-Ata, was sacked because he had included a study of nineteenth-century pan-Islamic movements in the curriculum. Sa'id Demirbekov, head of the education and science section of the Central Committee of the Kazakh branch of the CPSU, was dismissed for 'failure to stop nationalist influence at schools'. Abdullah Amirov, head of the languages department, was retired because he had initiated studies in religious texts in Arabic, while Abdullah Imanov, dean of the faculty of economics, had to leave because he had agreed to a study of Islamic taxation systems.

The official press in other Muslim republics offers frequent reports and still more frequent attacks on what is described as 'reactionary ideologies of the past'. The struggle over the public space of life is likely to remain intense for a long time. Everywhere traditional Communism, thrown into disarray by Gorbachev's unorthodox ideas as well as the blows struck against Mafias installed under Brezhnev, seemed to be losing its self-confidence against its 'nationalist' adversaries. It was difficult for Muslim Communists to try to be more royalist than the king, as it were, and to mount a spirited defence of a system and an ideology which Gorbachev himself no longer wished to defend.

The purge of the party and government structures under Gorbachev has nowhere been as wide-ranging as in Soviet Azarbaijan. There virtually all leading figures of the party were either dismissed from their posts or moved into less conspicuous positions. In one phase of the purge in 1988, more than 2,000 party cadres were 'disciplined' and 600 others expelled. Among those expelled were 19 'high-ranking party leaders'.[35] More than 200 top government officials were also sacked.[36] The dismissal of Hassan Sa'idov as prime minister was at least in part a direct result of his refusal in November 1988 to impose a ban on shi'ite mourning ceremonies in Baku and other Azarbaijani cities. Ayyaz Mutallebov, the man who succeeded Sa'idov, made it clear that he would not allow any such demonstrations in future.

The possibility that the Communist Party itself might one day be infiltrated by Islamic sentiments has been discussed by Western sovietologists for more than two decades.[37] In the late 1980s there were signs that this might well have started in many parts of Kazakhstan, Central Asia and Azarbaijan.

In Kazakhstan Sa'id Aqa-Zia'ev, head of the Jamboul section of the party, was expelled in 1987 because of his 'public show of respect for religious rituals'. Orhan Rajujanov, also excluded from the party in 1987, was accused of having diverted public funds for the construction of an illegal mosque. In Kirghizestan, the leader of the important party section at Osh, Ilhan Tajiba'ev, was attacked for having personally participated in Muslim pilgrimage rites led by unofficial mullahs. This does not mean that there are secret Islamic organisations capable of using permeation as a political weapon against Communism. What is happening is an unplanned and certainly uncoordinated spread of Islamic sentiments among party members. This is neither exceptional nor surprising. *Glasnost* has allowed many members of the CPSU in the Baltic states to bring their deep-felt Christian sentiments into the open. It is not possible for individuals to live a life that runs entirely counter to prevailing popular beliefs and traditions.

Yet another area where Islam is trying to regain territory lost first to Russia and then to the Bolshevik state is that of language. All Muslim languages of the USSR have been under heavy pressure aimed at russification for more than a century. In the 1980s, however, many Muslim writers and scholars upheld the cause of linguistic purity. Tugrulbey Sediqbekov of the Kirghiz Writers' Union has become an advocate of what he describes as 'each river in its own natural course', and has urged the revival of old Turkic, Arabic and Persian words or the coining of new words to replace those borrowed from European languages via Russian. Many writers, however, do not wish to turn this into a political issue and prefer to achieve the same objective by making their own prose or poetry as 'pure' as possible.

Another indication of this new taste for 'purity' is the renewed popularity of many Turco-Islamic names which had become old-fashioned because of their association with the supposedly 'feudal' past. It is no longer unusual to find young Uzbeks who are called Muhammad, Ali, Hossein, Osman and Abdullah. In most rural parts of Central Asia, Daghestan and Azarbaijan, exclusively Muslim names are used by almost all Muslim families. Sometimes this is given an additional pan-Turc or pan-Iran twist through the use of ancient Turkic or mythological Iranic names.

The slow but steady move away from russification is also reflected in the growing influence of Turkish, Arabic and Persian contemporary literature on the literatures of the Muslim peoples of the USSR. Despite difficulty of access, many Soviet Muslim writers and poets have opened windows towards the kindred literatures of other Muslim nations. In Tajikestan the modern style of Persian poetry, begun by Nima Yushij in the 1920s, is now the dominant influence in Tajik poetry. In Uzbek-istan the romantic realism of such Turkish writers as Yashar Kemal finds many echoes. In Azarbaijan the novel remains under Russian influence, but poetry is very much a preserve of Persian traditions and modes.[38]

Attempts at wresting the public space away from the exclusive control of Communists is also reflected in the decline in the number of enter-prises, kolkhozes, streets, monuments and other buildings named after figures from the Bolshevik mythology. In Azarbaijan, for example, the names of Muslim poets, philosophers and even old rulers are being increasingly used instead of those of Lenin and Kirov.[39]

Although more of a spontaneous movement rather than a planned project in the USSR, the Islamic revival is nevertheless in the process of developing its own distinct organisational structures. Leaving aside 'official' Islam which represents only the tip of the iceberg, so to speak, four separate forms of organisation could be distinguished in Soviet Islam today. None of these is new, but all of them are beginning to probe into new methods of thought and action against a background of uncertainty and hope in the Soviet society.

Probably the vast majority of practising Muslims, mostly in the rural areas, are covered by a network of unofficial mullahs, dervishes, aq-saqals, ishans, preachers, qaris (those who recite the Qur'an) and other servants of the faith. The Soviet media is full of references to them and their activities which range from officiating at wedding ceremonies and burials to leading pilgrimages at the numerous shrines of Daghestan, Azarbaijan, Central Asia and Kazakhstan. These 'servants of the faith'[40] can be found everywhere, including in or around the main Islamic monuments of Bokhara, Samarkand and Marv. They represent a very mixed bag. Some are true men of God in the noble and beautiful tradition of the *qalandars* of medieval Islam; content with the barest of necessities, they live a selfless life of devotion and service in the hope of gaining entry into paradise. They are men of few words and to communicate with them one must mostly depend on vibrations, to use a modern expression. Most discerning visitors will sooner or later encounter one of these *ahle-kholus* (the pure people), in Central Asia, Daghestan, Kazakhstan and Azarbaijan. Alongside them one would also encounter adventurers, fortune-tellers and other charlatans who often exploit genuine religious sentiments for the purpose of personal profit. There are indeed some ishans who charge up to 3,000 rubles (about £2,500) for a burial ceremony plus a prayer rug with the ka'aba as its main motif.[41] But even these profiteers play a role in preserving some Islamic traditions.

How many of these mullahs are there in the USSR today? Official media has on a number of occasions spoken of 'thousands' engaged in promoting religous sentiments in the rural areas.[42] What is certain is that the vast majority of Soviet Muslims, including members of the Communist Party, require the services of these mullahs for circumcision, wedding, burial and other traditional ceremonies. Each year millions of Soviet Muslims also go on pilgrimage on more than one occasion – and each pilgrimage is led by a mullah. The figure of at least 50,000 Muslim 'servants of the faith' need not appear as an exaggeration when we are told that it includes many part-time mullahs.[43] The number of mullahs is the highest in Daghestan, Turkmenistan, Tajikestan and Azarbaijan. It is relatively low in Kazakhstan and the Tatar and Bashkir autonomous republics. This network of rural mullahs is entirely financed through individual donations, although there are many instances of 'servants of the faith' receiving stipends or occasional payments in cash or kind from the kolkhozes and the state farms. Some mullahs actually live within the kolkhozes but are tacitly exempted from farming work. An increasing number of kolkhozes now include special prayer halls, or use common rooms as mosques on religious occasions.

The vast majority of the rural mullahs have only a very basic knowledge of Islamic theology and law. A number of unofficial seminaries have sprung up since 1985, especially in southern Kazakhstan, the Ferghana Valley and Tajikestan. At least five such schools existed in Doshanbeh in 1989. In Turkmenistan a number of sayyed[44] families consider it a duty to have at least one of their male offspring trained as an

Islamic scholar. In Azerbaijan, an unofficial shi'ite seminary – financed through donations by followers of Ayatollah Kho'i – has been in existence since 1973, with brief intervals during which it was forced to cease activities in 1978 and 1979.[45]

The education of unofficial mullahs received a boost in the 1980s thanks to the widespread introduction of short-wave radios and tape-recorders. A steady supply of these highly-desired goods reached the Muslim republics through Afghanistan. The radio sets enabled many would-be mullahs to follow special courses of Islamic theology offered by no fewer than thirty-eight radio stations situated in Turkey, Iran, Egypt, Jordan, Saudi Arabia, Kuwait, Abu Dhabi and Qatar and beaming to the Soviet Caucasus and Central Asia. Riyadh Radio began a series of broadcasts especially designed for the Soviet 'servants of the faith' in 1980. Tehran and Tabriz radio stations offered a university-of-the-air-type course leading to 'proficiency in the basic laws of Islam' throughout the 1980s. Radio Qur'an, operating from Arabia, offers courses in the study of the Holy Book.

Tape-recorders sold and bought on the black market are used for taping various courses broadcast by Islamic radios[46] or following Quranic lessons already taped in Iran, Egypt, Turkey and Saudi Arabia. In 1986–87 alone Iran invested a total of £5 million on producing special material, including audio and video-tapes for use by Soviet Muslims in Azerbaijan. Two Turkish firms based in Istanbul carried out the project.[47] Audio-tapes of the holy Qur'an were also smuggled into Azerbaijan thanks to the efforts of an otherwise unlikely ally: an informal group of US Republican Party supporters financed the distribution of 'an appreciable number' of Quranic tapes in Soviet Azerbaijan.[48] Thanks to all these efforts, the quality of the service offered by unofficial mullahs showed a steady improvement in the 1980s.

A desperate shortage of books, especially copies of the Qur'an, nevertheless remained a major handicap. The Russian poet Yevegeni Yevtushenko has complained that while the Bible is 'impossible to find' in the USSR, the Qur'an is freely available.[49] But this is just another example of Russian misconceptions about the reality of life in the Muslim republics. Even 'official' mullahs in Tashkent and elsewhere complain of difficulties in getting hold of an adequate number of Islamic books, especially the Qur'an. A copy of the Qur'an in Arabic fetched up to £1,500 in the Moscow black market in the winter of 1988–89. Microfilms of various psalms of the Qur'an are smuggled into the USSR where they are printed in the form of postcards and studied by Muslims.[50]

A much tighter organisational structure for Soviet Muslims is offered by the sufi *tariqats* which recruit their members mostly in urban areas and principally among the educated professional classes, including army and police officers.[51] Thanks to their deep historical roots and the wealth of literature inherited from more than eight centuries of tradition, the *tariqats* – especially the Naqshbandi – occupy a special place in Soviet Islam. The number of active *murids* has been estimated by one expert at between 300,000 and 500,000,[52] but this appears to be an exaggeration. The *tariqats* operate like highly exclusive clubs where gaining membership is no easy task. The figures cited might appear realistic if one also included the many thousands of non-initiates who attend special gatherings organised by the sufis without becoming full members of the *wirds*.

The Naqshbandis in the USSR never really lost contact with other branches of the same order in Turkey, Iran, Iraq and the Indian subcontinent. But contact which was hazardous and sporadic until the 1970s has since become regular and better organised. Financial and intellectual support for the Naqshbandis in the USSR came from a number of centres abroad. In Houston, Texas, a special committee was formed in 1983 to support members of the order in the USSR. Another group of Naqshbandis created a similar committee in Los Angeles, California, in 1983. Other such groups existed in Istanbul, Ankara and the emirate of Kuwait.[53]

The sufis in the USSR have adopted a basically defensive posture and appear to have somehow fallen behind the real pace of events in Soviet society. Their aim remained the preservation of 'the inner history of Islam' in the hope of making the promise of the Qur'an come true on a longer time-scale. They seemed determined to seek the fulfilment of Allah's will (*rida*) chiefly through self-preservation and 'the voyage within' and not by seeking changes in the political structures of society. In this way they were closer to the medieval sufis than to the warrior-dervishes of Daghestan in the nineteenth and early twentieth centuries. In the nineteenth century, the Tsarist state needed 25 years and an army of half a million to defeat the warrior-dervishes in a series of *ghazavats* (holy wars). Today, however, the sufi orders in the USSR do not appear to even think of launching a holy war against the atheist state in the near future.[54]

While the sufi movement remains strong and buoyant it by no means represents the whole of 'parallel' or 'underground' Islam in the USSR. A number of other smaller but more militant movements have been active in the Soviet Union since the 1930s. The Muslim Brotherhood (Ikhwan al-Moslemeen) had succeeded in creating a number of secret cells in Daghestan in the late 1920s.[55] The Wahhabi movement had also established a presence, especially in Turkmenistan, in the 1930s. Wahhabism was brought to Central Asia in 1912 by Sayyed Sharie Muhammad, a native of Medina in Arabia. He created many circles some of which remain active. An important circle in Tashkent is named after Bahauddin Vaisov, a Wahhabi teacher who died under torture in a Moscow mental hospital in the early 1950s. It is unlikely that the Brotherhood was able to survive the period of Stalinist terror in the mid-1930s, but judging by attacks made on it in the Soviet media during the 1970s and 1980s, the movement has almost certainly managed to retain some influence.

After Iran's Islamic Revolution, however, still more militant Muslim groups began to appear on the Soviet scene. Islamic samizdat, generally known as 'Islamizdat' and started from 1982 onwards, was part of the initiatives taken by these new groups of Muslim radicals. Judging by their literature, the groups are patterned after the Fedayeen of Islam and the Egyptian Takfir wal-Higrah (Anathema and Withdrawal) movements. They are committed to the eventual overthrow of the Soviet system which they describe in their literature as *shaytani* (satanic) and *taghuti* (in revolt against God). Because they operate in small, secret cells often with little or no formal organisational contact with one another, the new radical groups cannot be described as a single movement. Nor can their exact numerical strength be ascertained. But through the attacks made on them by official media and a survey of Islamizdat available, we know that such groups are active in Kazakhstan, Central Asia, Daghestan and Azarbaijan.

The new radical groups seem to be especially strong in Tajikestan, where over fifty Muslim militants were reportedly in prison in 1989. Those arrested belonged to five different cells dedicated to the propagation of a militant and combative version of Islam. Unlike 'official' Islam which attracts the older generation and the *tariqats* which have a special place among middle-aged professionals, the new radical groups appeal to the young and the less fortunate. The leader of one group, Asghar-Shah Jaberov, arrested in a raid on his home in 1986, was born in 1958. A native of Kulyab, he had turned his modest house into a meeting place for fellow Muslims. Another member of the same group, also arrested in Kulyab, is Ne'matallah Inayatov, a mullah born in 1950.

A second group of Tajik militants, dismantled in the Leningradsky district, was also led by a young mullah Abdul-Rahim Karimov. This group included three university students and operated a clandestine printing press.

A third group discovered in the Vakhsh district of Tajikestan consisted of the close supporters of Mullah Abdallah Ibn Nureddin Sa'idov, who has emerged as a charismatic figure in the region. Born in 1947, Sa'aidov spent many spells in Soviet prisons in the 1980s. Yet another young mullah Rajab-Ali Sha'yev (born in 1955) was arrested in Doshanbeh as the head of a group of Muslim militants.

A fifth group headed by Imaduddin Ahmadjanov, a young engineer (born in 1962), was dismantled in Doshanbeh in 1982. Ahmadjanov was sentenced to nine years' imprisonment, including three years in a labour camp.

Between 1982 and 1989 eight Muslim militant groups were broken up in Uzbekistan. One group, led by Sayyed Karim Khaj'ev, was active in Tashkent and had produced the samizdat booklet *Truth About Islam* in 1982. Khaj'ev was in contact with another group of militants led by Piyar Jaafarov, active also in Tashkent; Jaafarov was arrested in the summer of 1982. A third Islamic militant group functioned under the leadership of Sayyed Karim Azymov in Tashkent, where it operated a clandestine Quranic school.

A fourth group had at its head Mardan Puladov, a merchant who was arrested with his daughter Jamilah Qambrova in 1985. They operated an Islamizdat centre in the city of Samarkand, Abu-Zakar Rahimov, who led another radical group in Tashkent, was arrested in 1982 and sentenced to seven years' detention in a labour camp. In August 1985, another group was discovered in Bokhara, and its leader, Sayyed Ghafur Usulev, was sentenced to four years' hard labour. Two more groups were broken up by the police in Urgench and Khiva and their leaders, Abel-Qassem Yadagarov and Ashraf Bassirev, were arrested.

In Turkmenistan two clandestine cells were uncovered in Ashk-Abad and Charju in the winter of 1987. Their leaders, Arslan Salur-bayev and Akbar Khaqaov, were sentenced to three years' hard labour each.

In Kazakhstan a group of militants led by Kelim Qurbanov was broken up by the authorities in Jambul and its clandestine printing press seized in March 1988. This group was also accused of having organised 'an illegal school'.

In northern Caucasus two cells which acted as part of the so-called 'Islamic Opposition Group' (ISG) were broken up by police in the Komi autonomous republic in 1987 and 1988. The ISG was founded by Azmeddin Ibn Hamid Sahatov in 1986 in Daghestan. Released in 1988 after having served a 12-year sentence in a labour camp, Sahatov was rearrested in February 1989 after he had made it plain that he had no intention of giving up his struggle for an Islamic Daghestan.

Another veteran of radical Islam imprisoned in Daghestan in 1985 is Ghafur Soleimanov, who operated an illegal printing shop and taught at a secret Quranic school in the small town of Khasq-Yurt.

Muslim radical groups have also been active in Azarbaijan and suffered from repression throughout the 1980s. A group led by Ali-Reza Khalqin was uncovered in Baku in 1984. In the raid organised by the militia on Khalqin's home, large quantities of 'Islamic literature' were seized; some of them had been printed in Turkey and dealt with the history of Islamic radicalism. Khalqin was sentenced to seven years' hard labour in February 1985.

Also uncovered in Baku was a group led by Zayn-Ali Murad-Aliev, a chemist, who was arrested in 1988. The cell he led specialised in the dissemination of tape-recorded lectures on various aspects of Islamic history. One tape series dealt with a survey of writings by Muslim fundamentalist thinkers like Shaikh Hassan al-Banna and Sayyed Muhammad Qutb.

Ali Khaliqov, another Muslim radical arrested in Baku in 1984, led a cell that printed and distributed Islamic books and pamphlets. Arrested in Baku at virtually the same time was Mussa Ma'aliev, a native of Sheki who led an illegal 'Quranic discussion group'. Ma'aliev's arrest led to the uncovering of another cell which provided the discussion group with 'illegal literature'. The leader of this cell, Farid Aq-Babayev, was sentenced to five years' imprisonment in 1988.

Abdul-Rahim Mutzolghov, a native of Daghestan, was arrested in Baku in 1985 and sentenced to five years' imprisonment. Released in December 1988, he was rearrested in Daghestan in March 1989.

The Soviet authorities have invoked a variety of laws in their campaign against Islamic radicals. Some militants have been charged for anti-state activities and thus recognised as political prisoners. A majority, however, were tried and sentenced under criminal law and treated as ordinary felons.

While parts of Islamic radical literature could certainly be construed as an incitement to violence, none of the people arrested could seriously be charged with having posed a threat to public order. Soviet Muslim radicalism in its current phase is still a long way from preaching terrorism as a means of achieving its secular goals. Throughout the 1980s it tried to find its way to achieve a better understanding of the experience of other Muslim countries, especially Iran and Egypt, and to create the minimum of native literature needed for the future growth of the radical Islamic movement in the USSR. In other words, the best part of the energy of the clandestine groups was spent on theoretical work and education. At no point did they try to take on the Soviet authorities in a direct confrontation, and were content to allow official Islam and Muslim intellectuals associated with the Communist Party to fight to recapture from the Soviets as much of the public space as possible. At best the radicals acted as a pressure group militating for more decisive action by official Islam, student organisations, intellectual associations and even sections of local party structures. The tactic of 'leading from behind' – successfully tested by Muslim radicals in Egypt, Algeria, Turkey, Iran and Pakistan – seemed to have been copied by many members of the radical Islamic movement in the USSR. The radicals were able to apply a certain degree of pressure – during the Kazakhstan riots or throughout the demonstrations leading to the resignation of Mufti Shamsuddin Baba Khan – without exposing themselves to the danger of being arrested.

It is difficult to gauge the exact effect of the anti-radical crackdown in the 1980s. However, judging from the fact that Islamizdat continued to thrive and expand, and that the number of Quranic schools did not diminish, it was possible to suggest that radical Islam had by no means been rooted out from the Soviet Union.

The presence of quiet pressure from the radicals is felt almost everywhere in the Muslim republics. This is described by the man-in-the-bazaar in a number of ways. One is told that 'people are becoming more religious' or that 'people will no longer tolerate acts of sacrilege'. In some parts of Central Asia, an increasingly popular centre of tourism, foreign visitors feel an unusual degree of hostility from some locals. Muslim visitors from abroad, however, are treated with extra hospitality and questioned about life and thought in other Islamic countries.

The importance of setting an example is emphasised in several Islamizdat pamphlets. In one, entitled *Farayez va A'daab* (*Duties and Rites*) (probably produced in Samarkand), the faithful are told that they should 'live the life that God expects you to live under all circumstances'. 'Be present and active in the community,' writes the anonymous writer. 'Show your faith by your acts and not only by words. Men of faith need not speak much. It is enough that people watch their acts. . . . Every act is counted [by Allah?] and makes a mark on society. . . . Contrast your pure, devout and selfless life to the life of those who reek of alcohol and who revel in sin and rebellion against the Almighty . . .'

The attitude of the radicals towards the Slavs could be described as 'cold hostility'. One Islamizdat pamphlet is devoted to the alleged 'Slav colonisation of Islamic lands'. It does not urge preparation for holy war to liberate the Dar al-Islam (The House of Islam) from alien rule, as is required by the Qur'an, but invites the faithful to 'separate ways' wherever and whenever they come into contact with 'those who have no right to be in a land that is not theirs by any right'. In other words, some form of anti-Slav apartheid could act as a substitute for *jihad*, for the time being at least.

This relatively moderate response to large-scale Slav presence in Dar al-Islam could be partly explained by the self-confidence felt by most Muslims in Kazakhstan, Central Asia and Azarbaijan where high Muslim birth rates are cited as 'our secret weapon' against European domination. Muslims, including Communists, seem to have no doubt that the European settlers would be in a minority even in such cities as

Frunze and Alma-Ata before the end of the century. In some cities Muslims show their hostility towards Slavs by refusing to learn and to speak Russian. This makes life difficult for the settlers who are generally ignorant of 'native' languages. In many areas, Slavs have begun to leave Muslim lands and return to European USSR in increasingly large numbers. In the Chechen country, for example, the number of Slav settlers fell by sixty per cent between 1968 and 1988.

In cities where Muslims cannot have such faith in the effectiveness of the demographic weapon, relations with Europeans could easily deteriorate into physical violence. Fights between bands of Muslim and European youths in Ufa and Orenburg were described as regular occurrences in 1989. In Kazan the situation was even worse. The Tatar capital was divided by various Muslim and European gangs into 'reserved territories'. A Soviet newspaper estimated the number of these gangs at 150 and reported that no fewer than fifteen teenagers had been killed in gang warfare between 1985 and 1987.[56] The paper added: 'Nearly all the city youngsters – and some adults – are now under the control of the gangs in one way or another.'[57] The sociologist Xeniya Myalo identified the city's poor districts where the majority of Muslims live in ghetto-like cantonments as the real source of the trouble: 'Teen-agers from poor and culturally-backward sections of the population, denied access to shops and services reserved for the privileged, feel an urge for social revenge.'[58]

The emergence of a Muslim middle class that enjoyed a prosperous life by Soviet standards was considered at the end of the 1970s as a development likely to diminish the influence of Islam in Central Asia, Kazakhstan and Azerbaijan. This assumption was inspired by the experience of the older Tatar middle classes of the nineteenth century which have distanced themselves from Islam in favour of Western-style nationalism and pan-Turkism. In the 1980s, however, even the Tatar middle classes seemed to be affected by the crisis of Western ideologies and showed greater interest in their own Islamic roots. Even highly Westernised Tatar intellectuals admitted in conversation that their nation could never hope to play a prominent role in shaping history outside the Islamic context. They also felt that the Tatar nation risked being left on the wayside as Russia moved closer to Europe while the Muslim republics of the USSR forged a new Islamic identity.

The new middle classes of Kazakhstan, Central Asia and Azerbaijan did not seek to replace the traditional middle classes based on the bazaars and supported by the mosque. The bazaars of the Muslim republics are mere shadows of their past and enjoy less than a fraction of the economic power they had before the Bolshevik revolution. Rem-nants of such wealthy bazaari clans as the Mansurovs, Arabovs and

Khajeh'evs are still present in Uzbekistan and Tajikestan. Some have prospered through the so-called 'parallel economy' which came into being under Khrushchev but achieved real strength in the Brezhnev era. Under Gorbachev, the parallel economy is officially looked upon as the locomotive likely to set the Soviet economic train in motion.

Everywhere the economic power of the bazaars is on the increase. This is especially the case in Uzbekistan and Azarbaijan, where business acumen and the passion for trade and enterprise are deeply rooted in the psychology of the people. It was no surprise that the first private advertising agency in the USSR was created by Osman Ashirov, an Uzbek, and that the number of private cooperatives has nowhere grown faster than in Uzbekistan and Azarbaijan.

The bazaars are using part of their new-found wealth and economic power for the purpose of fostering Islamic traditions. In Azarbaijan and Uzbekistan a number of bazaar-based private charities came into being between 1986 and 1989. Also in 1989, the first private agencies offering interest-free loans began to operate in Bokhara, Baku and Sheki. *Perestroika* appeared to have restored to Soviet Islam important resources which had been taken away from it under Stalin and Khrushchev.

12

Perestroika: The Limits of Hope

Two catch-words dominated Soviet political thought through the latter part of the 1980s. One was *glasnost* (transparence), borrowed from Lenin, and promised to lift the veil of secrecy and open the party and the state to public scrutiny. The second catch-word, this time borrowed from Stalin, was *perestroika* (restructuring) which designated a desire to break the social, economic and psychological moulds which have shaped Soviet life since 1917.

Of the two, *glasnost* was the easier concept to grasp and could also be more easily realised – at least in part. The Soviet official media, at first unable to break out of their cynical lethargy, ended up as enthusiastic supporters of *glasnost*. The new 'transparence' allowed them to restore to words some of the meaning they had lost during some seventy years of 'living a life of lies'.[1] During those years, even words had become secret agents in the service of a totalitarian state which based its legitimacy on a falsification of the past, a distortion of the present and a totally unreal vision of the future:

> We were not ruled by a khan,
> a sultan, a khaqan or another tyrant.
> We were not even ruled by Stalin –
> the man of nightmares cast in steel.
> All the time on the throne of Moscow
> – wearing the mask of the Great Idea –
> sat our Supreme Ruler: the Lie![2]

Glasnost has opened up what is probably history's biggest Pandora's box. That part of past horrors already revealed with regard to the 1930s makes Ivan the Terrible appear more like a choir-boy in comparison with Josef Stalin. What more might come to light in the years to come is anyone's guess. What does seem certain is that the Soviet past has seen some of the masks with which it had been adorned torn asunder. And the process will continue.

Where *glasnost* remained less convincing was in matters of here and now. The Soviet media hardly ever discuss current issues and policies in a critical style. For one thing they still lacked the information necessary in a society where the omnipresent state, because it takes most of the decisions, remained the single most important source of news. By 1989 many banned authors – notably Anna Akhmatova[3] and Vladimir Nabokov – were published in the USSR. But many living 'anti-Soviet' authors, some in exile, continued to be banned – among them Aleksandr Solzhenitsyn, Joseph Brodsky, Vladimir Bukowsky and many others.[4]

It was not difficult for outside observers to gain the impression that *glasnost* had given the media a chance to criticise and, at times, even vilify the past, so that the present and the future could remain the preserves of the party and the state. 'Yes,' said a Soviet journalist, 'Stalin might look like a bone thrown to hungry dogs to keep them busy.'[5] According to another Moscow journalist it was not difficult to support *glasnost* and *perestroika* because both were official policies. 'The question is: can these concepts be defended if and when they cease to be supported by the party and the state?'[6]

Perestroika, the second of the two catch-words given currency by Mikhail Gorbachev, proved far more difficult to gauge and translate into concrete action. To some Soviet leaders it was 'a process of becoming, not a state of being'.[7] Others described it as 'a new revolution aimed at changing the mentality of the people'.[8] A more limited vision of *perestroika* was represented by other high-ranking leaders to whom it was a means of mobilising 'the colossal potential of developing socialism'.[9] This was to be achieved through a reform not of the basic structure of the society but of the organisational and managerial methods in use. Everyone agreed that *perestroika* must succeed in improving the people's standard of living if it was to have a real chance of success. 'If the shops continue to remain empty,' a member of the Supreme Soviet noted, 'then people will begin to have doubts about *perestroika*.'[10]

Gorbachev's hope was to modernise the Soviet economy and society without abandoning the basic structures of the Soviet state. There was to be no multi-party pluralism, although the formation of a wide variety of cultural, social and professional groups was allowed. In 1989 these new groups numbered more than 50,000 throughout the union. In the March 1989 general election for a new and more representative 'parliament', the CPSU did not field candidates for all seats and allowed the independent groups and other officially recognised associations to compete for votes. Nevertheless, there was no question of the CPSU giving up its monopoly on both political and economic power.

A number of steps was taken towards less rigid control of the economy. From January 1989, some 400 large industrial enterprises were given full autonomy and ordered to plan and manage their own business without reference to the state bureaucracy. This meant that they could produce what they could sell at a profit. Rules regarding the creation of economic cooperatives were also relaxed and tens of thousands of new private businesses, mostly in the service sector, came into being. Through the cooperatives, the thriving black market which has been the most dynamic part of the Soviet economy since the 1960s took a step closer to achieving an official status.

In 1989 the Soviet Gross National Product (GNP) was estimated at more than four trillion roubles (about the same in sterling), a figure which made the USSR the world's third major economic power after the United States and Japan. The average Soviet family reportedly had more cash at its disposal than its counterpart in any other industrial country. The trouble was that the cash available could not be spent on desired goods and services as the Soviet economy produced goods and services that Soviet consumers did not want. At least 20 per cent of the GNP was still devoted to defence in 1989.

The most serious stumbling block on the way to achieving economic development was the backward state of Soviet agriculture which employed nearly 12 per cent of the labour force but failed to produce enough to feed the country. More than 30 per cent of all farm production was wasted each year due to negligence and a lack of adequate storage and marketing capacities. The average Soviet farmer was not interested in growing more and better crops; there was nothing in it for him.

Gorbachev tried to correct this by offering a number of new incentives. Farmers were told to form cooperatives, for example, and to become leaseholders of the land they worked. But a number of experimental projects carried out, especially in the Ukraine, proved unsuccessful. Stalin seemed to have achieved at least one durable success: he had destroyed the farmers as a class and created a rural proletariat which treated agriculture not as a vocation – a condition essential for its success under any sky – but as just another source of employment. Today millions of Soviet farm workers live in concrete blocks of flats in suburban areas and commute to and from their places of work in buses or trucks provided by the kolkhozes and the state farms. They do not have the intimate, almost loving relationship that even the poorest of traditional peasants have with their soil in other parts of the world. In other words, Gorbachev must invent a new peasant class and then try to give it the economic incentives needed for a successful agricultural sector. Chief among these incentives is of course the private ownership of rural land. In 1989 almost everyone in Moscow agreed that collective agriculture had proved to be a failure during more than half a century; but few seemed fully prepared to go all the way and advocate privatisation.

Russia, Ukraine and Belorussia proved particularly unreceptive to the idea of agricultural reform. The Slav farm workers had lost their ancestral rural culture and did not welcome the idea of shouldering more responsibility and taking personal risks in the hope of greater rewards. Gorbachev could not hope to wipe out the experience of more than half a century at a stroke. His rural reform projects seemed to have a greater chance of success in Georgia, the Baltic states and the Muslim republics, where the spirit of enterprise was still alive in the countryside and a peasant culture could still be found and built upon as the basis for a system of private farming. The Soviet leadership, however, appeared to be unwilling to take such a major risk in the 'peripheral republics' where its moral and political authority could at any time be challenged by religion and/or nationalism.

It would hardly be an exaggeration to suggest that political freedom cannot be achieved within a system of the state ownership and control of the means of production, distribution and exchange. At the heart of all this is the crucial issue of the private ownership of agricultural land. Once that is established, other forms of private ownership will almost inevitably follow. Private ownership would render impossible a system of command economy in which party and bureaucratic organisations which have no direct role in the economic process take all the major decisions. Concentration of economic power inevitably leads to the concentration of political power and the establishment of a totalitarian state.

It is possible to argue that Russia failed to develop democratic traditions of its own because it never knew a system of private land-ownership. Under *Tatarchina* the entire country belonged to the khan and after liberation the tsars continued the Mongol system with only slight modifications. The abolition of serfdom produced some of the conditions required for the development of private enterprise in rural areas, but that development was interrupted by the 1917 revolution which restored collective ownership in the name of the proletariat. Russia's situation was no better in the industrial sector prior to the revolution; most educated and wealthy Russians preferred either to live the lives of the idle rich or to become revolutionaries. A good number of industrial entrepreneurs in Tsarist Russia were West Europeans, principally Germans. The 1917 revolution ended all chances of a Russian industrial entrepreneurial class ever emerging to run the economy on the basis of private ownership.

The entrepreneurial culture has deep roots in the Baltic states, Georgia,

Armenia and the Muslim republics. But with the exception of the Baltic states which have a highly developed industrial base, the other 'peripheral republics' still lack much of the infrastructure required for economic development. Paradoxically, these republics have a short- to medium-term interest in the continuation of the system of command economy and central planning, which system would enable them to benefit from the massive infrastructural investments needed for the modernisation of their economies. In a free-for-all capitalist system the Muslim republics, as well as Georgia and Armenia, would be at a comparative disadvantage vis-à-vis the more industrially advanced European regions of the union.

In other words, where potential entrepreneurs could be found the scope for economic enterprise is relatively limited due to the insufficient development of the infrastructure. And where the infrastructure does exist, the entrepreneurial culture is largely absent. One solution would be to persuade large numbers of Asians, both entrepreneurs and workers, to move into the European parts of the union as well as Siberia, although this could lead to racial tensions of the kind already experienced in Kazan, Ufa and Orenburg.

Gorbachev's ambitious hopes for the transformation of the Soviet society – he describes his project as 'our second revolution' – have raised more questions than they have provided answers. Lengthy discussions with Soviet leaders in 1989 showed that they did not have a clear idea of where they were going.

Political projects which seek radical changes in the existing order quickly run into trouble with one invisible adversary: time. If pushed through hastily, they instantly become adventures. If on the other hand they try to keep pace with time, the stern teacher of patience, they fade into the status of religions. Only religious faith could sustain a constant postponement of paradise. Lenin had an ambitious project, but was a man in a great hurry. 'We have everything except time,' he liked to say. For him what mattered most was to race ahead; one could always return in good time and correct one's mistakes.

Stalin gave Lenin's haste a certain structure through the five-year plans. At the end of each plan, one could celebrate a fresh victory over time. The process of history was thus reversed. Ordinary men write their histories after they have lived them. The new Soviet man, however, could write his history first and live it afterwards.

Khrushchev, who had his own catch-words[11] and his own ambitious project, faced the problem of time in his own typical way. In 1960 he fixed 1980 as the date at which the building of socialism would be completed and the era of Communism – 'from each according to his abilities, to each according to his needs' – ushered in. He thought that he had conquered two full decades in which he, and not time, would set the pace of events.

Brezhnev, who ousted Khrushchev long before the two magical decades had been completed, found his own way of coping with time; he simply announced 'real Socialism' to be already installed. Thus time could take the course and the rhythm it wanted; the Soviet state no longer had anything to prove in its race against time.

The successive Soviet leaders, each in his own idiosyncratic way, fell victims to the illusion of *volontarisme*, the belief that it is enough to want something for it to come to pass. The very idea that a group of powerful and well-intentioned men could alter the course of society – which is determined by complex undercurrents that develop over a very long time – is open to doubt. The temptation to do so, however, is always there. It is not only in totalitarian states that such ambitions are nurtured. Even in western democracies where the existence of numerous forms of decision-making – not least of all the way each individual orders his own life – makes the pursuit of 'revolutions from above' an uncertain enterprise, the temptation to make history and create a 'new society' is never fully absent from political discourse. But the damage that could be done by 'revolutions from above' is certainly greater in totalitarian states where the central political power is neither checked nor balanced.

In its early stages, *perestroika* seemed very much an adventure. It pretended to reshape life with a few large strokes of the reform brush. Gorbachev sincerely felt that since he was a good man and wanted nothing but good for his people, there was no reason why his sensible and generous efforts to modernise Soviet society should not succeed. One constant theme of all his speeches at the time was that he had not entered politics to become powerful or popular, but to serve the people and help them to have a better life. He did not realise that this apparent humility indicated a much greater conceit.

By 1989, however, *perestroika* seemed to be in danger of developing from an adventure into a religion, thus repeating the established pattern of Soviet political experience during the past seven decades. Praised in official incantations as 'our new way of life', *perestroika* was invoked in all domains. The season's melons from Georgia were sweeter than ever thanks to *perestroika*, which had also helped industrial output rise by 1.8 per cent. Even the mildness of winter in 1989 was attributed by some Moscow wisecracks to 'the magic of *perestroika*'.

Some Soviets realised the ultimate contradictions inherent in a project which hoped to use a system of controls based on command economy for the purpose of encouraging free enterprise. 'It is no use to try and hide behind such labels as "social market" or "market socialism",' said one Soviet student of *perestroika*. 'The real issue is the balance of economic forces. If the state abandons its hold over the productive forces it would weaken its own position at a time it needs all its strength to push through *perestroika*. If, on the other hand the state does not give up its economic power, there would never be a real *perestroika*.'[12] This was a Catch-22 situation: *perestroika* could become a reality only if it were abandoned as a project. That meant an end to the one-party system and the adoption of a basically capitalist economic system geared to production for profit.

Not surprisingly, opposition to *perestroika* mostly came from 'real socialists', veterans of Brezhnev-style populism who preach egalitarianism and play on the people's desire for security and fear of change. Millions of Soviets have learned to live with low wages in exchange for job security. People might have to wait up to seven years to secure a flat, but once they have moved in they pay incredibly low rents.[13] If economic reform projects discussed in 1989 were to be fully implemented, more than 50 million Soviet workers would have to change jobs within the next five years. No fewer than 10 million of them might end up unemployed in a society pledged to full employment at virtually any cost. Inflation is a part of Soviet life and threatens the already low living standards of millions of people. When Gorbachev promised the Soviets more freedom in exchange for less security, once again he faced a difficult question: could one be free without being secure and vice versa?

The populists were strongly present in the CPSU itself and insisted on the value of equality, even though this would be achieved at a relatively lower material base. Hatred of the rich remained a strong part of the CPSU psyche despite the fact that a good many of its upper cadres formed the backbone of the notorious *Nomenklatura*. The CPSU remained a party of industrial workers, not of managers and entrepreneurs. And support for *perestroika* was, by all accounts, lowest amongst urban workers and highest among intellectuals.

The tentative nature of Gorbachev's reforms was recognised by many Soviets, who could not be sure whether the new freedoms extended by the state were for keeps or only 'loaned' to the people. 'He who gives can also take back,' admit many Soviet intellectuals. 'We can support *glasnost* and *perestroika* as long as they remain official policies. But what if Gorbachev is pushed out or forced to change his policy?'

In its early stages *perestroika* all but ignored the problem of nationalities and future relations between Moscow and the union republics. In his book *Perestroika* Gorbachev devoted no more than 600 words to an issue the gravity of which he did not seem to appreciate. The Armenian–

Azari flare-up over Nagorno-Karabakh, coming after the Alma-Ata riots, meant that the problem could no longer be ignored or the dangers inherent in it underestimated. The Central Committee and the Politburo accordingly devoted a number of sessions to the topic. Vague ideas about progress towards a 'federal system' were discussed, partly in public. But the emphasis remained on economic rather than political reform.

One major weakness of the Soviet system in dealing with the problems of a multinational state is the uniformity of structures and policies it offers. The fact that different union republics live different lives – and, indeed, at different stages of socioeconomic development – did not receive the attention it merited from Soviet leaders. It was automatically assumed that the mere membership of the USSR meant that all the republics faced the same challenges and fostered the same hopes. To cite one example, it was forgotten how little Kazakhstan had in common with Estonia when it came to shared political experience and a vision of the future. The USSR's different republics were not divided only by the different time zones where they were situated but also by different historical time-scales. Being contemporaries on the Soviet calendar did not mean that they lived and, perhaps more importantly, felt that they all belonged to the same epoch. This does not mean that some were more advanced and others backward in the sense usually intended by 'growth' economists. In the absence of a single, universally accepted set of values, it would be difficult to divide the world into 'advanced' and 'backward' nations without denying the nations' sacrosanct, and systematically violated, right to self-determination.

The Baltic states focused their hopes in the era of *perestroika* on plans to revive their 'bourgeois' democratic system and protect their cultures and languages against the dangers of russification. They looked to Scandinavia and western Europe in search of political and economic models. Pluralism, human rights and private property were concepts that were readily understood and highly appreciated by most Balts. Religion, although popular especially in Estonia, was not an issue, since the Soviet state was no longer adamant in its attempts at limiting the scope of religious education and practice.

In the Muslim republics, on the other hand, religion was the central issue. It represented a good part of national identity and was intimately woven into the very fabric of culture, literature, language and tradition. To most people in the Muslim republics, the prospect of greater religious freedom seemed more important than promises of pluralism and even a multiparty system which they had never known in their history.

Officially the USSR is an atheist and not merely secular state in which all religions, including Islam, must eventually be destroyed. Yet this is at the same time a theocratic state with Marxism–Leninism as its official religion. Thus theocratic thinking is prevalent among the ruling elites whose political vocabulary is richly adorned with basically religious phrases and expressions.

During the past seven decades, and more especially since the mid-1960s, the Soviet state has steadily grown more tolerant of various religions, but the Communist Party has not. The Soviet state tends to feel a secret sympathy for the Russian Orthodox Church and other Christian churches are also tolerated. Islam, however, is rigorously dealt with, especially in official propaganda. This is not solely due to historical and possibly even racial prejudices against Islam; the CPSU recognises the fact that Islam, like itself, would ultimately not settle for any form of sharing political power and ideological domination of society.

It would be difficult to compile a complete list of demands made by Soviet Muslims who want to give *perestroika* a chance. Different republics have different priorities. Nevertheless, it is possible to identify the most important demands they all have in common.

By all accounts, greater freedom for religious practice and education tops every list. Islam is seen as the surest defence these societies have against loss of identity. Islam as a faith and a way of life has survived more than seven decades of often brutal repression and systematic propaganda attack. But Islam as a practice has had to beat the retreat. Numerous laws, at both union and republic levels, make its practice and its propagation a crime at times even punishable by death. 'It is important to realise that you may be executed in this country simply by trying to share your faith in God with others,' said one Muslim poet.[14]

The cessation of atheistic propaganda against Islam and the disbanding of the so-called 'Houses of Atheism' are demands that thanks to *glasnost* began to be openly expressed in the Muslim republics. Also demanded is the abolition or toning down of some of the harshest laws against religious education and proselytisation. Muslim intellectuals point out that no society could live without a system of ethics and, in its current crisis, that Soviet Communism cannot even pretend to offer society such a system. Islam, however, could assume that responsibility and prevent at least a part of Soviet society from degenerating into moral corruption and ethical drift.

Soviet Muslims also demand the restoration of Islamic shrines and monuments to acceptable Islamic authorities. In this context many Muslims seemed prepared to accept the 'official' structure of Islam as a legitimate custodian of this part of the Islamic heritage. An inventory of 3,416 Islamic monuments that have been 'diverted from their original purpose' and used for political, social and commercial purposes was prepared by two Muslim researchers in 1987. This list covered Muslim monuments and shrines in Soviet Azarbaijan and Soviet Armenia only,[15] but similar lists could be compiled in Daghestan, Kazakhstan, Uzbekistan, Tajikestan, Kirghizestan and Turkmenistan. Moscow's decision to let the Estonian church regain control over the numerous religious edifices in that republic in 1989 was cited by Muslims as a concrete example of double standards in Moscow's policy towards various religions.

The granting of official recognition to hundreds if not thousands of 'illegally-built and operated' mosques and prayer halls was also demanded by many Soviet Muslims. Soviet 'official' Islam had by 1989 recognised many of these places of worship as legitimate and even helped to staff some of them with servants of the faith.

Soviet Muslims also demanded recognition for those Quranic schools that could prove their bona fides as centres of religious instruction. A similar concession was granted to the Russian Orthodox Church in 1987. Since then other Christian churches have also been able to set up or expand theological seminaries.

The inclusion of a study of Islamic history, culture and art in the school syllabuses was also a demand advanced by many Muslims. Once again this was not a case for special favours. The Orthodox Church has already won a pledge that its 'true historical role' will be recognised in the new textbooks scheduled to be introduced in 1990. But in 1989 there was no official indication that the new textbooks would no longer portray Islam as 'a relic of feudalism' and Islamic history as a long night of tyranny and terror.

Muslim scholars also hoped that the lifting of official bans on so many Russian and other European poets, writers and philosophers might be extended to blacklisted Muslims also. Sultan Galiev, the father of 'Muslim Communism', remained one of only two prominent early Bolshevik leaders still considered as 'non-persons' in 1989. The other was Leon Trotsky. But Galiev was not the only banned Muslim writer. Thousands of poets, writers, philosophers and historians could not be published in 1989, four years after *glasnost* was announced. Soviet Muslims are denied access to the greatest part of their own classical literature and thought.

The issue of using native languages as the principal instrument of instruction at universities and institutes of higher education was also greatly emphasised by many Muslim intellectuals. Under the Soviet system many important subjects, especially in scientific fields, are taught only in Russian throughout the Muslim republics. This policy has at least two important effects, both of which are deeply resented by Muslims. First it helps perpetuate the fiction that Muslims could not have gained access to modern science and technology without Russian help and, by extension, that Muslim languages – being 'feudal tongues' – do not offer scope for scientific thought. Young Muslims looking for a career in modern scientific and technological domains were forced to accept a certain degree of russification.

It would simply do no good to tell a Kirghiz that his language was practically invented by Russian linguists and that more than seventy per cent of its vocabulary consisted of loan words from other languages. Kirghiz is now a national language and dearly loved by the Kirghiz people. They did not pretend that Kirghiz could compete with Russian in all scientific domains; but many wanted Kirghiz at least to be given a chance to try.

The domination by Russians of universities in Kazakhstan, Central Asia, Daghestan and Azarbaijan was unavoidable in the 1920s and 1930s when the Muslims simply lacked an educated elite capable of sustaining a system of higher education. But this was no longer the case in the late 1980s. All Muslim republics had the human, linguistic and scientific resources needed for a credible network of universities and technical colleges. The central authorities themselves recognised this fact by gradually dismantling the system of 'positive discrimination' in favour of Muslims who sought a higher education.

The language issue assumed a distinctly political character when Azarbaijanis and Tajiks staged a number of demonstrations in 1989 to demand that their native tongues be recognised as the sole official languages of their respective republics. This meant the elimination of Russian, which is widely used as the official language in many domains. Russian remained the sole language of the armed forces, the foreign services (including international trade), the KGB and a number of scientific fields. Part of this monopoly was pushed aside in favour of the Balt languages when Estonia, Latvia and Lithuania were allowed to use their native tongues in foreign trade relations in 1989. No similar concessions were granted to the Muslim republics however. Making the native tongues 'sole official language' in the different Muslim republics would certainly accelerate the decline of Russian in Kazakhstan, Central Asia and Azarbaijan.

The position of Russian in Tatarstan, Bashkiria and Daghestan, however, seemed secure as more than 60 per cent of the natives were fluent in Russian. But Russian is not the only language that would be affected by Tajik and Azari demands.

The imposition of a single official language could also threaten the position of other Muslim languages within each republic. The Azaris, for example, have pursued a systematic policy aimed at the elimination of Persian, Taleshi, Tati and Yammut in their republic for the past sixty years. The Tajiks pursue a similar goal and have tried to assimilate the

Uzbek, Turcoman, Uighur and Pamiri minorities in their republic. That the language issue has been capable of generating so much passion throughout the peripheral republics is partly due to the fact that many of the natives see a reduction in the role Russian plays in their lives as the first step towards persuading the Slav settlers to return to their own lands. Since few Slav settlers bother to learn the native languages of the peripheries, a decline in the position of Russian as a lingua franca will hit them most of all.

Combined with the reversal of demographic trends in favour of non-European nations of the union, the language issue has dramatically increased the value of a close alliance between the Russians on the one hand and their kindred Ukrainians and Belorussians on the other. Ukraine and Belorussia are of crucial importance if Russia is to avoid becoming a minority nation in the USSR within the next few decades. This fact is underlined by the special advantages that Belorussia and Ukraine enjoy within the union. Both have direct separate representation at the United Nations and many other international organisations. They are also heavily represented in the Politburo, the Central Committee and throughout the central apparatus of the state. What is seen as a pan-Slav axis remains a source of many suspicions and much resentment for non-Slav nations of the USSR.

The Muslim republics also resented the fact that none of the Islamic states were allowed by Moscow to establish cultural centres in Azarbaijan, Daghestan, Central Asia, the Volga region and Kazakhstan. European cultural centres, however, existed in the Baltic states and the RSFSR itself. Until 1978 Iran was the only Muslim country to have a cultural centre in Baku; the centre was shut in 1979 and did not reopen. One popular demand in the Muslim republics of the USSR is for greater cultural contact and exchanges with the Islamic world and this issue was raised by several Muslim heads of state who visited Moscow in the late 1980s. But the situation remained unchanged.

The issue of freedom for Muslims to perform the *Haj* pilgrimage has been a source of much tension between Islam and the Russian authorities for more than a century. The Soviet Union has effectively forced its Muslim subjects to forgo the performance of *Haj*, which is one of the principal duties of every believer. In the late 1980s there were hopes that *perestroika* might lead to a relaxation of the rules regarding applications for travel to Mecca. Some Soviet leaders seemed to imply that the issue was linked to negotiations aimed at restoring diplomatic ties with Saudi Arabia.[16] The Saudis, however, made it abundantly clear that no Soviet Muslim wishing to perform the *Haj* rites would be denied a visa.

One issue that few Muslims were prepared to discuss openly but almost all felt to be important related to the many Muslim prisoners of conscience still held by Soviet authorities. Muslims could not fail to notice that *perestroika* had brought them Soviet tanks in Baku and the killing of demonstrators by the militia in the streets of Sumgait. Military force was also used to crush riots in Kazakhstan and disturbances in Tajikestan. While in the Baltic republics, the RSFSR and the Ukraine, political prisoners and priests held in labour camps were being set free in the late 1980s, the number of Muslims (including mullahs) who were imprisoned continued to increase.

'Do we live in the same country or not?' demanded one Muslim intellectual. 'One can be arrested in Azarbaijan for saying things that are said on television in Vilnius and Talinn.'[17] Television stations in the Baltic states began to offer religious programmes and documentaries on various aspects of the Christian heritage from 1988 onwards. In Azarbaijan, however, a TV director was sacked because he had ordered a newsreel to be prepared about the Ashura ceremonies. Some apologists of *perestroika* have tried to explain the double standards applied to the Baltic states and the Muslim republics by pointing out the supposed danger of 'Khomeini-style fundamentalism'. Issa Qalandarov, head of the Tajikestan Radio and Television authorities, singled out 'reactionary Islam' as 'the most determined enemy of our people'.[18] And Tajikestan's foreign affairs minister Osmanov claimed that the Islamic revival movement was 'a tool of imperialism and colonialism'.[19]

People like Qalandarov and Osmanov did not wish to know that just as one could not identify Christianity as a whole with the Inquisition, so it would be wrong to see Islam as nothing but another name for Khomeinism. Forcing women back into the purdah, stoning adulteresses to death and hanging homosexuals in public are not the only items in the *shari'ah*. It is worth recalling that none of these excessive measures was applied anywhere in the Muslim world between the ninth century and the imposition of the Khomeinist regime on Iran in 1979.

In any case, what is at issue is not the so-called 'threat of Islamic fundamentalism' but equal treatment for all the members of the union. It was simply unfair to allow part of the USSR to enjoy freedoms denied to other parts. And greater freedom for Islamic practice and education remained an eminently legitimate demand.

Soviet officials speak with pride about more than half a century of industrialisation in the Muslim republics. The record is impressive indeed. Uzbekistan alone produces five times as much steel as the rest of the Muslim world combined. The Kazakhs have proportionally more scientists than Turkey or Iran, two of Islam's most advanced countries. Daghestan, one of the most backward parts of the world until the 1930s, today includes a number of modern industrial centres. For all this, Soviet Muslims do not share all of the pride expressed by Moscow public relations experts. To many Muslims, industrialisation has emerged as part of a broader scheme leading to Russian domination. The republics have had little or no say in shaping the industrialisation plans worked out by Moscow. Most industries are geared to the needs of European USSR and thus serve as an additional means of making the peripheries dependent on the centre. The best jobs created by industrialisation, and certainly most of the managerial positions, are occupied by Europeans who as a result also enjoy higher wages.

'Our industries do not cater for the real needs of our consumers,' said one Muslim economist. 'Often they produce parts and goods that are never seen here by people who produce them. We feed a larger, abstract machine, at the centre of which stands a veritable gargantua: the Soviet armed forces.'[20] Many of the industries in the peripheries seemed to have as their net effect the growing alienation of the natives. In recent years a growing awareness of the dangers caused by hasty and exclusively result-oriented industrial planning to the environment has added to Muslim misgivings about the 'economic miracle' of the Stalin and Brezhnev eras.

At times the factories that belch their poisonous fumes into the clear skies of Uzbekistan or Turkmenistan could remind visitors of the industrial death traps set up by Western capitalism in so many Third World countries. The more modern industrial units are reserved for Europe and Siberia. Pollution, a source of much political discontent in the Ukraine and the Baltic states, is much more intense in some areas of Central Asia and the Caucasus. The damage done to Amu-Darya, Syr-Darya, Zarafshan and hundreds of other Central Asian rivers by mismanagement and the dumping of domestic and industrial waste is only part of the problem. Many natural beauty spots have disappeared as a result of poor planning and indifferent management of resources.

The fear of a nuclear disaster, further emphasised by the Chernobyl accident, was strongly felt in the Muslim republics. Rich in oil, gas, coal and hydroelectric resources, these regions did not appreciate the logic of developing a nuclear industry as advocated by Moscow planners. Professor Ghias Omarov of the Uzbek Academy of Sciences rejected arguments in favour of 'going nuclear' in a number of learned papers. He showed that Central Asia could even develop the world's largest solar energy industry provided part of the investments reserved for nuclear power plants were diverted to this new type of energy. Moscow's decision to close down the Armenian nuclear power plant in the 1990s gave Omarov and his supporters the hope that their 'clean energy' campaign might now be more favourably received at the Politburo. The closure of the nuclear power station at Krasnodovsk on the Caspian was demanded more vigorously by the Muslims after the Armenian earthquake in 1988.

The nuclear issue was only part of the debate on greater regional autonomy in resource development and economic planning. Many Muslim economists supported new policies directly aimed at improving the living conditions of their peoples rather than 'creating abstract strength for a superpower machine'.[21] Poverty was still a live social issue in parts of Central Asia, Daghestan and Azarbaijan. Living standards in some Tajik villages were no higher than those in neighbouring Afghanistan before the Soviet invasion. The Soviet 'sun-belt' was a land of contrasts in the 1980s, where the ostentatious lifestyle of a few did not hide the abject poverty of many sections of the society. This contrast was nowhere more dramatic than in some of the Central Asian cities, notably Tashkent, where Muslim families lived in squalid conditions only a few miles from the European quarters with their wide boulevards and concrete blocks of flats and offices.

One issue that most Muslims considered as a symbol of their humiliation and the injustice they have suffered, especially during the past seventy years, was that of their Crimean brethren's quest to regain their homeland. The Crimean Tatars, who numbered nearly a million in 1989, demanded the reinstatement of their autonomous republic in the Crimean Peninsula. In 1989 Crimea itself did not host more than 1,200 Tatar families, a total of less than 6,000 people. Once a major part of the Muslim world, Crimea was totally colonised by Ukrainian and Cossack settlers and all but lost its Tatar personality. Soviet leaders, at times with less than complete sincerity, suggested that the Tatar diaspora could return to Crimea whenever it wished. But the Kremlin adamantly refused to repair the damage done by Stalin and order the reinstatement of the Crimean Tatar Autonomous Republic which had been abolished in 1944. Under Brezhnev the Crimean Tatars were fully exonerated from all charges of collaboration with the Nazis and promised full justice. And in 1988 Gorbachev created a special committee chaired by the then Soviet head of state Andrei Gromyko to devise a solution acceptable to the Tatars. The committee did not go beyond an unrealistic suggestion that the Tatars could return to their homeland as individuals or families and try to rebuild their lives as best they could, but that meant they could only hope to become marginal foreigners in their own ancestral land. The Soviet system would not give the Tatars even the chance to buy back their farms and houses which, confiscated by Stalin, were handed over to European settlers.

A few Tatar intellectuals drew a parallel between the aspirations of their people and the struggle of the Palestinians for a homeland. They expressed grief at what they saw as Moscow's double standards in supporting the Palestinian movement while rejecting the legitimate demands of the Crimean Tatars.

The Crimean Tatars began their campaign shortly after Stalin's death in 1953 and in 1989 they saw themselves as the last victims of Stalinism still to suffer from the ruinous rule of the *Vozhd*. They saw Moscow's refusal to allow the reinstatement of the Crimean Tatar autonomous republic as the continuation of a Russian policy inaugurated by Ivan the Terrible. That policy was clearly aimed at driving the Tatars out of Europe and dispersing them as a nation likely to challenge the rising might of the Slavs under Russian leadership. What was begun by Ivan the Terrible was faithfully continued by all Russian rulers and continued under Lenin and Stalin. The great Tatar nation – the dream of Galiev and many others – died a brutal death after the October Revolution. The Tatars were pushed into numerical weakness as a result of massacres, mass expulsions and enforced assimilation. In 1989 there were more Tatars outside the USSR than inside. This Tatar diaspora was unlikely ever to return to its original homeland in the Volga region, Astrakhan and the Crimean Peninsula; but it supported the Crimean campaign as a symbol of hope, as a means of keeping the dream alive.

The tragedy of the Crimean Tatars, although a clear case of brutal injustice against a Muslim people, remained largely unknown in most Muslim countries. This was partly because the Soviet system made all meaningful contact between the Tatars and their Muslim brethren in other countries extremely difficult. A more important factor in Islam's apparent indifference towards the Crimean Tatars was the desire of many Arab states not to antagonise the USSR which offered strong support to the Palestinian cause.

One of the few attempts at drawing greater Muslim attention to the plight of the Crimean Tatars came in 1989. In a long letter addressed to the Islamic Conference in Jeddah, Saudi Arabia, the Tatar Committee demanded 'energetic diplomatic and political action' aimed at persuading Moscow to allow the Crimeans to revive 'our rightful state'.[22] Nevertheless the issue was not put on the agenda of the March 1989 meeting of Muslim foreign ministers. *Glasnost* and *perestroika* meant that the Tatars could seek greater international support for their cause. But this did not lead to any positive change in Moscow's policy. Soviet leaders argued that allowing the Tatars to regain their homes and farms would require the dispossession and expulsion of the European, mostly Ukrainian, settlers. At a time when the Ukraine itself was threatened by nationalist fervour, it was difficult for Moscow to grant the wishes of the Tatars without provoking an explosion in the second most populous republic of the union. 'We cannot remedy one injustice by committing one that would be even larger,' stated one Soviet leader. 'The Tatars must be prepared to learn that elementary lesson.'[23]

In 1989 the consensus among Soviet leaders in Moscow seemed to be directed against any interpretation of *perestroika* as a prelude to the dismantlement of the one-party system and the emergence of other institutions more likely to represent the immense diversity of interests and aspirations inevitably existing in a complex multi-national society. Nevertheless, political organisations that looked very much like political parties had already began to operate in some of the European republics. In the Muslim republics the Communist Party, suffering from purges and a crisis of identity caused by *perestroika*, was totally on the defensive. It neither reflected public opinion inside the republics nor was strong enough to be used as a means of defending and implementing the policies of the centre. This in turn meant that the Muslim republics were faced with a veritable political vacuum at a time when they needed all their energies in order to make the most of *perestroika* before it came to an end or was interrupted by a palace coup d'état in Moscow.

Unlike the Baltic states, which quickly revived some of their pre-1940 political parties and associations, the Muslim republics seemed unable to create new political formations based on pre-Revolution experiments. In Azarbaijan some vague memories of such bourgeois parties as Mussavat (Equality) Himmat (Effort) and Adalat (Justice) were evoked by some intellectuals. And in Central Asia fresh interest was expressed in the attempts by the Muslim reformists of the pre-Bolshevik era to produce a synthesis of Islamic political doctrines and western statecraft. But the Muslim republics were still a long way from being able to organise their own political parties and help create the diversity of views that is the very foundation of meaningful pluralism. One fact had been made abundantly clear by *perestroika*: the CPSU had failed to strike genuine roots in the Muslim republics and remained politically isolated and generally regarded with mistrust by the masses. It was seen as an instrument of power and not as a popular forum for discussion and participation in the process of decision-making. It was this fact more than any other which kept the impact of *perestroika* severely limited in the Muslim republics. In some of the European republics Gorbachev had succeeded in by-passing the CPSU in the pursuit of *perestroika*. In the Muslim republics that was virtually impossible; Gorbachev needed the party which, at the same time, made *perestroika* meaningless because of its very opposition to it. The absence of new political formations capable of organising the masses in the Muslim republics led to a potentially dangerous situation in which an isolated and unsure Communist Party opposed to *perestroika* by instinct might clash with a series of Muslim organisations that rejected the entire Soviet system as a foreign imposition.

Conclusion

The Soviet Union, so often described as an empire on the verge of imminent dismemberment, faced the 1990s in a buoyant mood that surprised some of its friends and dismayed many of its enemies. Theories according to which no totalitarian state could seriously contemplate self-reform were subjected to much serious rethinking as a result of Mikhail Gorbachev's 'Revolution from Above'. Moscow in the late 1980s reminded many observers of Petrograd in the early phases of the 1917 revolution, when words had regained their beauty and combative spirit to create the impression that history could be made simply by *wanting* to make it. Even dissidents who had wondered whether the USSR could survive the 1980s agreed that the seemingly moribund monster had a great deal more life in it than they had suspected.

Gorbachev's 'revolution', however, was not confined to the realm of cosmetics and atmospherics. A number of major steps were taken. The constitution was reformed to allow for more decentralisation, a more accountable executive power and a distancing of the Communist Party from the process of economic decision-making. A fairly honest – though by no means free and democratic – general election was held, in which popular participation was not confined to the mere ritual of voting. A new plan under which the republics would enjoy much greater autonomy within a growingly federal system of association was completed in 1989. Hundreds of enterprises were encouraged to employ new managerial techniques and to gear their production more to the real needs of the consumers. Thousands of cooperatives were allowed to form as part of a broader policy aimed at expanding the private sector of the economy.

More importantly, Gorbachev's policy of *glasnost* allowed the Soviet media a measure of freedom they had never known. This did not make them genuinely free vehicles of information and discussion by Western standards. But under Gorbachev the Soviet media was no longer the distorting mirror of life that it had been under Stalin and all of his successors until 1986.

The Gorbachev leadership also demonstrated an unprecedented

degree of willingness to help reduce international tension and the risk of thermonuclear war. The various disarmament negotiations, stalled since 1979, were revived and led to significant – though largely symbolic – cuts in the nuclear arsenals of the two superpowers. A number of regional conflicts were also settled, or set on the way to settlement, thanks to the positive attitude adopted by the USSR under Gorbachev. Soviet troops were fully withdrawn from Afghanistan in 1989 after nine years of bitter warfare. Moscow also played a key role in helping end the Iran-Iraq war and in shaping agreements aimed at leading Namibia to independence and Cambodia to peace under a national government.

The leadership provided by Gorbachev and the small group of dedicated men and women around him was not always as imaginative, as bold and as coherent as the Soviet Union's many deep-rooted problems required, but there was no doubt that it was both serious and sincere. Gorbachev did not release all political prisoners, but under him the USSR had fewer such prisoners than ever before in its history. He did not take his own economic policy to its logical conclusion by allowing the private ownership of land and the emergence of privately owned industrial companies and banks capable of challenging state monopoly; nor did he dismantle the one-party system. But he did at least raise the possibility and the hope of such radical reforms.

One major area in which Gorbachev's leadership appeared hesitant, inconsistent, and at times even open to charges of 'Russocentrism', concerned the future role of the so-called 'peripheral republics' in deciding their own way of life. The constitutional provisions under which all the constituent republics of the USSR could exercise their right of secession were maintained and emphasised in public discourse, but the concrete steps needed to enable them to be as autonomous as possible without necessarily breaking away from the union were not taken. In fact, it was possible to argue that the peripheral republics were placed in an artificial situation in which they had to choose between a very real control by the centre and a purely theoretical right to demand independence. Stalin's cynical remark that the peripherals had the right to ask for independence, while Moscow had the right to reject that demand, continued to provide the basis of official Soviet thinking on the subject.

The problem of nationalities was eventually recognised by Gorbachev as probably the most potentially dangerous for the future of the USSR; yet it was precisely here that the performance of the new leadership remained especially open to criticism. Prepared to abandon all talk of consensus and autonomy when it sent troops into Alma-Ata and tanks into Azerbaijan and Georgia in 1986, 1988 and 1989, the leadership baulked at the prospect of the risks involved in allowing the Communist Parties in the peripheral republics to gradually fade away, and tried to put them back at the centre of political life through a number of massive purges.

While the Soviet and Western media paid special attention to developments in the Baltic states where 'bourgeois' democracy seemed to be very much alive and well and ready to dominate national life, it was in the underdeveloped Muslim republics that most clouds appeared on the Soviet horizon. The Muslims saw in Gorbachev a Western-oriented leader determined to make Russia once more part of Europe. They did not see themselves as part of the 'common European home' of which Gorbachev liked to talk on almost every occasion. For Muslims in the USSR, the late 1980s appeared as a period of soul-searching and uncertainty. Many Muslim intellectuals agreed that the existing system was no longer viable and might simply break under the growing weight of economic, social and political problems aggravated by the rising appeal of fundamentalism. But few could come up with clear ideas as how to reorganise the lives of the Muslim republics without creating new and even bigger problems. The only point of consensus was that things could not simply go on as before. It was a sign of the times that some Muslim intellectuals were prepared to discuss all options without the fear of provoking the anger of the KGB.

The Muslim peoples of the USSR, remarkable in their ethnic and linguistic diversity, are even more remarkable in their similarities as far as economic development and political aspirations are concerned. They all have a strong sense of attachment to Islam's history and culture, and are marked by a steadily growing interest in the affairs of other Muslim countries. The Islamic revolution in Iran and the war in Afghanistan helped to shock many Soviet Muslims into self-recognition. They also stirred unreasonable hopes in the hearts of many, but equally raised numerous illogical fears in the hearts of countless others. The vitriolic attacks made against Islam in the Muslim republics in the 1980s simply underlined the return of religious faith to the centre of political life in the Asian parts of the USSR. The power of fundamentalism to provoke scenes of ugly violence was demonstrated in 1989, when hundreds of fanatics – all wearing white shrouds as a sign of their readiness to die – rioted at Kurgan-Tapeh in Tajikestan and tried to seize an arms depot. Islamic explosions in neighbouring Afghanistan and Iran might at any time overspill into the USSR.

At least four scenarios regarding the future of Islam in the USSR were contemplated and discussed in Moscow and the capitals of the Muslim republics. All were founded on two basic assumptions: first, that Islam is likely to emerge as a major influence in Central Asia, Kazakhstan, Daghestan and Azarbaijan and, to a lesser extent, in Tatarstan and Bashkiria; second, that the existing structures were no longer capable of responding to the needs of the present and the challenges of tomorrow.

The first scenario envisaged a movement towards full independence for the Muslim republics, which could be achieved in a period of ten to twenty years. In 1989 full independence seemed to have few open advocates outside fundamentalist circles, especially in Azarbaijan and Tajikestan. There were a number of arguments in favour of independence. It would put an end to a whole period of colonial life in different forms. The Muslim republics today each had their national elites and were fully capable of joining international life on their own; with independence they would be able to have their own legal system, their own mode of life and formulate their own view of their past and future. They would be able to shake off the domination of their language and literature by Russia and develop cultural ties with the Muslim world. The four republics of Central Asia plus Kazakhstan would have little difficulty in forming a single state on the lines determined shortly after the fall of the Tsarist empire in 1917. At that time the state of Turkestan was put on the map before being wiped out by Stalin.

A new Turkestan would have a population of some 40 million and a GNP of over £120,000 million, which is equal to the combined GNPs of Indonesia and Bangladesh, the first and second most populous nations of Islam. Such a development, however, would mean nothing less than the redrawing of the entire political map of Asia and of Europe. Soviet Muslim republics cannot break loose without provoking a similar movement in European USSR; the Ukraine and the Baltic states would certainly not be prepared to settle for anything less. The effect could be even more dramatic in eastern Europe, where Soviet domination is both less formal and increasingly less effective. In central Europe, it would be hard to prevent the re-emergence of a unified German state. The consequences of such dramatic developments are too complex to ponder in the sole context of the politics of the Muslim republics of the USSR.

The present Soviet leadership is resolutely opposed to any changes in the status quo that might lead to a redrawing of the political map. Moreover the Soviet state, no matter how 'liberal' it might become in future or, indeed, how weak and irresolute, would be unlikely to allow regions that contain so much of the USSR's natural resources simply to break away. A regime which accepted such an eventuality would instantly lose a good part of its legitimacy in the eyes of the Russian people, and thus would be in danger of being overthrown even in its own homeland. What is at stake is no classical process of decolonisation of the type experienced by western European colonial powers between the 1950s and 1970s. Even the Algerian drama which brought France to the verge of civil war in the late 1950s and 1960s might appear as a minor historical incident compared with what the loss of Central Asia could provoke in Russia.

The independence scenario, although supported by some sections of the intelligentsia and a number of fundamentalist groups as a deeply-felt desire, was cited by few sizeable forces in the republics as a serious option – at least in the foreseeable future. In Azarbaijan the National Front (Milli Jibhassi) announced its formation in February 1989 and called for reunification with Iranian Azarbaijan. But other groups, including the Popular Front (Khalqi Jibhasi) and Yurt (Home) led by Anvar Aliev contented themselves with calls for a greater role for the Azari language and the control of the economy from within the republic. That Anvar Aliev was arrested by the KGB showed that Moscow was worried that the more moderate groups might be no more than covers for secessionist elements.

What was openly demanded was greater autonomy. The Muslim republics would remain part of the USSR and coordinate their foreign and defence policies within the federation. Beyond that, however, every republic would be totally free to organise its own national life. That would imply a measure of freedom in economic decision-making, in educational and cultural policies and in the development of a new legal system hitherto unheard of in the USSR. The Prophet Muhammad, himself a merchant, described businessmen as 'friends of God' and respect for free enterprise and private ownership remain major values in Islamic ethics. Given greater autonomy, the Muslim republics would be able to experience rapid economic development based largely on a new and dynamic private sector. The centuries-old traditions of the Tatars and the Azaris, born merchants and entrepreneurs, could provide a strong base for the creation of a new class of modern businessmen.

Many Soviet Muslims recall with pride the days when their lands played a crucial role in world trade, especially through the Silk Route which connected Europe with China via western and central Asia. The economies of Kazakhstan, Central Asia and Azarbaijan could develop closer ties with China, India, Pakistan, Afghanistan, Iran, the Gulf states, Turkey and Egypt. It is only by reintegrating these economies into their natural habitat that future crises caused by overpopulation, lack of investment in resource development and the absence of adequate markets could be intelligently addressed. Central Asia cannot be kept as a Soviet backyard at a time when the European republics of the USSR are knocking on the doors of Europe in the hope of improving their own economic prospects.

The application of the new policy of 'federalism' under which the republics will in effect be governed by elected national assemblies, might lead to a long period of tension between the centre and the peripheries.

Soviet leaders seemed little concerned about the possibility of the new promised federal system leading the USSR into a Yugoslav-style crisis. Lenin had resolutely opposed federalism as a system most likely to encourage nationalist and centrifugal tendencies. Gorbachev, however, regarded a federal system as the best means of isolating those forces which might seek total independence from the USSR. The main loser in a truly federal framework might well be the Communist Party, which would find it hard to obtain a working majority in the directly elected national assemblies. In the Muslim republics, especially in Daghestan, Tajikestan and Azarbaijan, Islamic groups, including the fundamentalists, might have a good chance of winning control of the national assemblies. That would almost certainly lead to tension between each republic and Moscow, since it would be difficult to reconcile widely divergent views of society and its proper functions and institutions.

In the March 1989 election to the new Soviet 'parliament', the task of mobilising the Muslim vote was left to the muftiates which fielded a number of candidates. The election showed that a potentially strong Muslim constituency does indeed exist in the USSR. It became equally clear that in the long run the muftiates would not be able to claim full representation on behalf of all elements in that constituency. The presence of substantial non-Muslim minorities within most of the Muslim republics could create a situation in which the local branches of the Communist Party are supported only by the European elements and forced to be content with the position of a minority within the national assemblies. The federal scenario strongly favoured by Gorbachev and his closest associates seemed fraught with many imponderables and likely to produce the worst of all worlds.

A fourth scenario, supported by the more traditionalist elements in the CPSU, was based on a new and massive campaign aimed at the drawing together of the peoples within the USSR. The main ingredients of this scenario were often presented as purely economic measures aimed at greater growth and development, especially in the national republics. Supporters of this scenario, heavily represented within the Gosplan (central planning) and allied organs of the central state, envisaged a massive population transfer that would see between ten and fifteen million Muslims abandon their native republics in order to settle in the European republics and Siberia within the next two to three decades. This would not be a straight loss of population as large numbers of better educated and more highly skilled Europeans, especially Slavs, would in turn be transferred to the Muslim republics to help with industrial and agricultural development that had lagged behind in the 1980s.

The population transfer plans were partly intended to deprive the

Muslim republics of what some Soviet observers saw as a demographic weapon; the USSR could not feel safe and secure if it were ringed by a number of republics with large non-Slav populations. The dramatic increase in the population of the Muslim republics – both in absolute terms and relative to the Slav nations – was recognised by some Soviet leaders and experts as a potential threat not only to the aim of sovietisation, which remained sacrosanct, but also to the very stability of the USSR as a multinational state. Thanks to their rapidly growing numbers, Muslims were likely to gain a greater voice in the new-style parliament in Moscow while other traditionally influential nations – notably the Ukrainians and the Belorussians – were certain to see their influence much diminished.

It was not at all certain that the transfer plans would not provoke much resistance among the inhabitants of Siberia as well as the European republics. Between 1970 and 1985, the Far East and Siberia were especially favoured for development within a system of organisation that divided the USSR into 18 economic regions. Attempts at persuading Europeans to settle in those regions for both economic and military reasons produced little result and by 1989 the regions had suffered a net outflow of population. The failure of that relatively modest attempt at the drawing together of nations through population transfers underlined the immense difficulties involved in plans to neutralise the demographic advantage of the Muslim nations through purely economic and administrative measures.

Confronted by the complexity of the problems faced by this most complex of state structures, many Soviet intellectuals expressed their faith in the promised democratisation which they believed would in time produce the needed solutions. However, it was not at all clear what exactly was meant by democracy, and whether a genuine and substantial constituency for meaningful democratisation did indeed exist outside the small but influential intellectual elites in the European republics. Gorbachev seemed to be more of a reflection of the new situation in the USSR than its initiator. He certainly appeared fully prepared to go a long way towards tackling some of the difficult problems which have remained unaddressed for more than a generation, but it was not at all certain that he would not at some stage baulk at the grave decisions that have to be taken. His decision to use force in Azarbaijan and the iron fist he employed against Armenian nationalists at the end of 1988 and Georgian nationalists in April 1989 were only a few instances of the new leadership's tendency to fall back on old policies whenever the risks that have to be taken appear simply too great.

As the 1980s drew to a close there were two USSRs living side by side: one was young, dynamic, warm, optimistic and Muslim; the other was ageing, grey, cold and uncertain of its ideological beliefs. In the Caucasus and Central Asia rising population, an appetite for enterprise and a growing attachment to the cultural roots of Islam were everywhere in evidence. In Russia, the Ukraine and Belorussia, on the other hand, a falling birth rate, the fear of taking personal and social risks and uncertainty about the future were features of life against a background of decaying industrial cities and virtually bankrupt collective farms. The USSR as a whole needed to mobilise more young Muslim workers to finance the retirement of a growing number of European old-age pensioners. It was difficult to see what could provide the basis for this new type of relationship between two parts of the same empire.

Some Soviet intellectuals expressed doubts regarding the irreversibility of the reforms introduced by Gorbachev. Supporters of the reforms, however, sought to counterbalance pessimistic views by invoking Marx himself, according to which reasoning the Soviet system was blocked: it was caught in one of those moments in history when the 'infra-structure' is hampered in its natural development by constraints imposed by the 'superstructure'. At all such moments the 'superstructure' – so Marx consistently promised – would be burst asunder to allow the living forces of society to create new realities out of the old.

Supporters of Gorbachev claimed that his reforms had changed the USSR to such a degree that Stalin himself, were he to return to life, would not recognise the empire he shaped out of the debris of the tsarist state. Gorbachev's critics responded to this assertion by claiming that the reforms were causing so much dislocation that very soon the president himself would not recognise the USSR either.

Three factors were seen as potential threats to the reform policy of the 1980s. The first was the persistent failure of the economy to respond to the new measures introduced. 'We must fill the shops if the people are to trust us,' said many Gorbachev supporters in Moscow and elsewhere. The second factor was the possibility of setbacks in the détente with the West which could provoke a new arms race. The USSR's military establishment remained strong and influential despite many political setbacks in the late 1980s. The decision to withdraw from Afghanistan and the cuts ordered by Gorbachev in Soviet military strength in Europe and the Far East did not go down well with the Soviet top brass and its supporters amongst the middle-ranking officers. Some of Gorbachev's opponents – including a few who masqueraded as his friends in the hope of a return to the old style of rule – secretly hoped that the United States would be tempted to push the USSR into even greater difficulties by slowing down the pace of disarmament or even provoking a new arms race.

The third and by far the most serious potential threat to the future of Gorbachev's reforms, as well as to his own political prospects, came from the so-called 'nationalities' problem.

All these three factors were directly related to developments in the Muslim republics. The USSR could not 'fill the shops' without launching a new and massive economic development programme in Central Asia, Kazakhstan and Azarbaijan, regions with still untapped natural resources and an abundant source of inexpensive labour. Such a programme's success, however, depended on a degree of political stability that could no longer be assured by virtually isolated Communist Parties and their conservative and unpopular *apparachiks*. Instability in the Muslim republics could endanger the security of the USSR as a whole and pave the way for a return of the military to political pre-eminence – which, in turn, could trigger a new arms race against both the United States and China. Finally, the problem of nationalities could not be solved by offering major concessions to the Baltic states and virtually nothing to the Muslim republics.

The problem of nationalities has not spared any part of the union. In tiny Moldavia, the ethnic Rumanian majority has become increasingly restless. In the Baltic states the revival of 'bourgeois democracy' has been put forward as a mainstream political programme. In the Ukraine, the nationalist discourse has widened its appeal. Even featureless Belorussia, the most russified of the union republics, has shown signs of nationalistic and anti-Russian fermentation. But it is only in the Asian republics – Georgia, Armenia, Azarbaijan, Kazakhstan, Uzbekistan, Tajikestan, Kirghizestan and Turkmenistan – that nationalist agitation has led to physical violence and claimed hundreds of lives. A *samizdat* leaflet distributed in Frunze in March 1989 recalled the assassination of the Kirghiz prime minister in 1972 as an 'example of what could be the fate of those who collaborate with Russian colonialists'. The violent tone of the leaflet did not reflect mainstream sentiments among Soviet Muslims, but it certainly indicated the immense potential for violence that is building up.

Why has the problem of nationalities assumed so much intensity at this precise moment? At least four reasons could be cited. First, Gorbachev has provoked deep doubts regarding the legitimacy of the Soviet system. He has removed the focus of loyalty that existed; the regime's moral authority is questioned by almost all sections of society. With the Communist experience portrayed as seventy years of tyranny, mass murder and corruption people are almost invited to look for alternatives to fill the ideological void thus created. Because other contemporary ideologies are unknown in the USSR it is either nationalism or religious faith – often a mixture of both – which appeal to the intellectuals throughout the union, including Russia itself.

The second reason for the seemingly sudden explosion of the problem is that *glasnost* has enabled people to air their genuine grievances and indicate their deeply-felt sentiments with greater freedom. Thirdly, *perestroika* has threatened both the broader interests of some republics and the narrower interests of some influential groups within each republic. It is hoped that nationalism will reduce Moscow's powers and thus cancel or postpone the more painful aspects of Gorbachev's reform programme, especially in economic domains.

Finally, the USSR is passing through a deep and potentially dangerous economic crisis which has provoked many fears and illusions. One illusion is that the republics would be better able to cope with the crisis if they were allowed to run their own economies independently of Moscow.

It is no accident that in many republics the new nationalist movements have assumed an ecological, environmentalist identity. Ecology is used to build up national pride and attachment to the motherland. By loving rivers, forests, mountains, villages, beauty spots and historical monuments, all parts of a vaster whole, one would end up by feeling attached to a certain geographical entity. Villages and towns have a history; they were inhabited by distinct peoples with their own specific way of life. In the mountains and forests roamed mythological heroes, ancestors who built the glorious past. Ecologism also rejects central planning: no one in Moscow could know 'our land' and 'our needs' better than ourselves. To sacrifice all to industrialisation and often useless and/or dangerous production is morally and economically wrong. Ecologism emphasises the importance of the nation independently from the union.

In the USSR even official Islam has adopted ecology as a channel through which it could communicate with the nationalist forces in the Muslim republics. The Qur'an and the Prophet are amply quoted to support typical environmentalist policies and principles.

The March–April 1989 general election for a new Congress of People's Deputies confirmed the immense popularity of environmentalist themes. The election was far from free in the Muslim republics, where non-Communist candidates were often forced to withdraw before polling day. Nevertheless, the Communist Party was fully exposed as an isolated and largely unpopular set-up in Kazakhstan, Central Asia and the Caucasus. The party has had two sources of strength before Gorbachev. First, it had maintained a certain appeal as the repository of the mystique of revolution, especially among some sections of the intelligentsia. At the same time it had acted as an instrument for favour distribution and connection (*blat*). Exposed as an instrument of terror and torture, the party has lost much of its appeal; and Gorbachev's reforms, aimed against the Nomenklatura, have deprived the party of much of its strength as a source of social and economic advantages. One Azari intellectual sums up the situation in this way: 'Gorbachev has destroyed all arguments for joining the Communist Party.' It is in the 'empty space' thus created that new political parties and associations are bound to step in during the next decade.

Gorbachev's evident charm and eloquence have helped to partly hide the tremendous problems faced by his regime. Some of these he has been able to formulate with eloquence. Gorbachev is, in fact, the first truly articulate Soviet leader. Lenin was handicapped by his stammering and was, in any case, more comfortable when he wrote down his thoughts. Stalin, a Georgian, never fully mastered the intricacies of the Russian language and had a heavy accent which at times rendered him unintelligible. Malenkov's high-pitched voice and Khrushchev's difficulties with the Russian grammar prevented them from ever appearing quite serious enough to many Russians. Brezhnev was often as silent as the Sphinx and when he spoke was badly served by his choked voice, deformed by alcohol and smoke. Andropov was only half-alive when he assumed the leadership and spent a good part of his tenure in a hospital bed and connected to a kidney machine. As for Chernenko, even in his best days he seemed as if he had been born half-dead.

Gorbachev's eloquence, however, might prove a disadvantage at this time of crisis; he focuses public attention on problems for which he has no visible solution. The first lawyer since Lenin to assume supreme leadership in the USSR, Gorbachev speaks of creating a 'state of law'. He has pinned many of his hopes on law reform; has also tried to steer Soviet politics away from problem solving through the use of force to a system of compromise; and has promised decentralisation and more autonomy for the republics. But the net effect of the constitutional and other legal reforms he has proposed and put into effect might well be a strengthening of the central authorities.

The new Congress of People's Deputies which, with 2,250 members, will act as a parliament, is likely to have greater authority than its predecessor the Supreme Soviet, which was little more than a rubber stamp for decisions taken by the Politburo. A union parliament with greater authority and legitimacy will inevitably weaken the national assemblies of the republics. How could the Tajik parliament, for example, overrule a decision of a body which represents the entire union?

Another step towards strengthening the centre will be the election in the autumn of 1989 of a new President of the USSR, who will head the executive branch and will enjoy far greater powers than any Soviet head of state since 1917. Gorbachev is expected to be the only candidate for the post. A president capable of claiming legitimacy as the representative of popular will throughout the union will almost certainly reinforce the powers of the centre at the expense of the republics. Some of Gorbachev's advisers speak of Switzerland or West Germany as models for the federal state envisaged by the reforms, but in neither Switzerland nor West Germany does the head of state enjoy anything more than ceremonial powers.

Gorbachev had at first considered the idea of seeking the presidency by taking up the challenge of a direct election in which all Soviet citizens aged 18 or over would choose the future head of state. However, he abandoned the scheme after he realised that it contained a number of major risks. He might have failed to attract a majority of votes in many peripheral republics, and would almost certainly have failed to win more than a quarter of the votes in Armenia, Azarbaijan, Uzbekistan, Turkmenistan, Tajikestan and probably Moldavia.

Some of Gorbachev's promised law reforms should be welcomed. The abolition of the notorious article 70 of the USSR constitution regarding anti-Soviet activities would be a major step towards democratisation. Hundreds of thousands of people have been sent to labour camps and prisons under that article. Thousands have been executed. Scores still remain in jail. Also welcome is the abolition of a law which prevented teenagers from attending religious ceremonies or receiving religious education. The abolition of another law which forbids religious education for children is demanded by almost all groups supporting *perestroika*. Another welcome law, enacted in 1988, provides for the formation of companies and associations for the construction or repair of churches and mosques.

The Soviet society in which legal culture remains underdeveloped, however, is not yet fully prepared for the acceptance of the rule of law. During the past seventy years laws were often enacted only to be brazenly broken by the party and the state. Gorbachev's excessive trust in the efficacy of law reform as an instrument of political change might distance him from reality at a time when policy implementation singularly lags behind policy formulation. Legally constituted bodies do not automatically become powerful because the law says so. The best example of this is provided by the soviets themselves; they were not created by Lenin, as is often assumed, but were a product of the 1905 revolution. In 1917 Lenin simply 'adopted' them and launched his famous slogan: 'All power to the soviets.' He even described the state he created as soviet, but in reality he emptied the soviets of their content; they had every legal power in the book but virtually no political power.

One major reform which Gorbachev will have to contemplate within the next two years concerns the legal status of the USSR as an atheistic state dedicated to the destruction of all religions. The issue is hotly debated in Moscow and no consensus was apparent in the spring of 1989. Many people wanted the USSR to become a secular state – that is to say, a state which has no religion of its own but treats all religions with equal respect and allows every one of them ample scope for self-expression. A number of powerful figures within the CPSU, however, strongly opposed the change from atheism to secularism. To them atheism was virtually the only aspect of Communist ideology which still had some relevance.

The fact that the USSR was officially an atheist state meant that many Soviet universities had chairs in 'scientific atheism' but none offered courses in Islamic or Christian culture and doctrine. Yet numerous official studies showed that less than five per cent of the USSR's population were prepared to describe themselves as atheists.

The Bolsheviks were true heirs to the narodniks of the nineteenth century who based their system of ethics on a denial of absolute truths and values. Indeed, they sought a foundation outside morality, beyond ethics, and thought they found it in the concept of the 'people' (*narod*). The victory of the October revolution was more of a triumph for the *narodnichestvo* than for Marxism. The concept of *narod* was replaced by that of 'the proletariat' and the tradition of revolutionary hubris, symbolised by Stalin, led to the great terror. Today's *narodnichestvo* – barricaded inside the CPSU – are as unable to see reality independently of their perceived idea of the real as were their intellectual forebears in the nineteenth century, which is why Gorbachev has been trying to find a new power base for himself outside and beyond the CPSU. The shedding of the atheist mission of the Soviet state would be one sure way of loosening the CPSU's hold over the machinery of government. A secular soviet state will have a better chance of managing the crisis ahead, a crisis in which religion will almost certainly play a central role.

Gorbachev has in fact launched an attack by the real society on the official society at the centre of which stands the Communist Party. He is trying to conquer not the space of the party and government machines, but that of the people throughout the union. He will not be able to succeed unless he forces the party and the government to relinquish much more of their powers and privileges than they have done in the past four years. As far as the Muslim republics are concerned, the CPSU machine is more of a hindrance than a help to Gorbachev's reform project.

The CPSU with a full-time cadre of around two million paid officials is a relatively small force in Soviet society today. It is not even sure of being able to mobilise its 19 million members. The CPSU machine is still more isolated in the Muslim republics. With a full-time cadre of just over 80,000 paid officials in Kazakhstan, Central Asia and Azarbaijan, the CPSU could quickly find itself irrelevant to broader developments in the Muslim communities. Its power and prestige directly stems from Soviet military might and Moscow's control of the main levers of the economy.

The general assumption in the West that Gorbachev's success will lead to the emergence of a more accommodating and less aggressive USSR may or may not be borne out by future developments. What is certain, however, is that Gorbachev's failure might well lead to a prolonged crisis in the USSR that could affect Central and Eastern Europe as well as China and the Middle East. In other words, virtually the whole of Europe and Asia could be affected by violent 'explosions' in the Soviet Union. The role that Islam is likely to play in either the success or the failure of Gorbachev has hitherto been largely underestimated in the West. The Muslim rejection of the Soviet system, first demonstrated by revolts between the 1920s and the late 1940s, was echoed in literature and art during the 1960s and 1970s. In the 1980s it came into the open, in the bazaars and streets, and led to violence and bloodshed.

There was little evidence in 1989 that Gorbachev and his close advisers fully grasped the crucial role Islam was bound to play in shaping the future of the USSR. More than seven decades of Communist propaganda against Islam made it difficult for many Soviet officials to recognise Islam not necessarily as a subversive force in Soviet society but as the undeniable and legitimate culture of a substantial section of the population of the USSR. Gorbachev and his friends recognised the strong appeal that Western ideas and the Christian heritage had for many Soviet citizens in the European republics; there were even signs that he was determined to use that fact as part of his own campaign against the conservative-populists within the CPSU. In the Baltic states, the Ukraine, Belorussia and the RSFSR itself, Gorbachev and his team were very much swimming with the tide. In the Muslim republics, however, they remained at the edge of the water and continued to curse the tide as it continued to rise.

Chronology

Russia

6th century: Slavs, migrating from Central Europe, begin to settle in the Russian forest.

7th century: Khazars conquer Black Sea steppe and create a khaqanate.

8th century: Khazars convert to Judaism and force Slavs to pay tribute. Viking clans begin to settle in Russia.

9th century: Norsemen extend their settlements to along the Volga and the Dnieper, and stage a raid against Constantinople. Novogrod and Kiev are united into one state under Prince Oleg (881).

10th century: Russians destroy the Khazar Khaqanate and conquer Bulgaria. Prince Vladimir converts to Christianity. Pechenegs raid

Central Asia and the Caucasus

The Sassanid Empire dominates the Caucasus while Byzantium has influence in Georgia and Armenia. In Central Asia, warlike Turkic tribes nibble at the frontiers of the Sassanids.

Islam, born in the Arabian Peninsula, conquers Iran and spreads into Central Asia. Marv is taken in 651.

Samarkand and Bokhara fall to Muslims (710). The Chinese are driven out of Central Asia by the Muslims after the battle of Talas (751).

Turkic settlement in Central Asia is speeded up and begins to alter the region's ethnic composition. Many Turkic tribes serve as mercenaries for the Caliph or local Persian dynasties. First Turkic clans begin to settle in the Caucasus.

The caliphate in Baghdad loses its hold on Central Asia and the Caucasus. Local Persian and Turkic dynasties assert their

Black Sea steppe. Norman domination of Russia completed.

11th century: Norman rule, based on Kiev, begins to decline after Great Prince Yaroslav divides his realm among his five sons.

12th century: Prince Andrei Bogoliuskii of Suzdal captures Kiev. Local councils (*veche*) are elected as the power of the Normans declines. Internecine feuds continue among the princes.

13th century: Polvotsy Turks seize control of the Kiev-Constantinople trade route. Crusaders capture Constantinople (1204). Mongols, under Batu, attack and conquer Russia and turn it into a tributary of their Golden Horde based on Sarai. A number of revolts by Russians are crushed. Vladimir gains importance under Aleksandr Nevski (1252–63).

14th century: Seat of the Orthodox Church transferred to Moscow which gains ascendancy under Dimitrii (1359–89). Dimitrii defeats a Mongol army (1380). Mongols return to sack Moscow in 1382. Moscow annexes Nizhni Novgorod.

authority and help spread Islam into China and the northern shores of the Caspian Sea. Mass conversion of Turks to Islam.

Persian is revived as literary language. Central Asia emerges as Islam's most dynamic centre. Turkic dynasties create vast empires and conquer India. Seljuk Turks capture Baghdad.

The Crusades draw the Seljuks into a prolonged confrontation between Islam and Christianity. The Kharazm-Shahs dominate Central Asia from their capital of Urgensh.

Mongols led by Chengiz Khan conquer the whole of Central Asia and parts of present-day Iran (1218–21). After Chengiz's death (1227), Mongols begin to convert to Islam. A Mongol army conquers the Caucasus.

Mongol power collapses in Iran (c. 1350) and in China (1368). Tamerlane (Teymur) invades Central Asia and Iran and then sacks Sarai (1395). Samarkand and Bokhara grow into major centres of Islamic culture and science. The Caucasus and parts of Anatolia are annexed to the Teymurid Empire.

15th century: Muscovites organise massacres in Novgorod and annex Tver and Viatka. Russian princes interfere in quarrels among the three Mongol khanates. Russia stops payment of tribute to Mongols. Ivan III declares himself Tsar, chooses the two-headed eagle as his emblem (1480).

The Golden Horde falls apart and is replaced by the khanates of Astrakhan, the Crimea and Kazan. Turks capture Constantinople. Christians capture Grenada and force the Muslims out of Andalusia. Muslim missionaries work in northern Caucasus.

16th century: Ivan IV (The Terrible) is crowned Tsar (1547). Ivan captures and annexes the khanate of Kazan (1552) and the khanate of Astrakhan (1556). Novgorod is razed to the ground and its inhabitants massacred (1570). Russian colonisation of the steppe (1551–61). Oprichnina terror leads to large-scale massacres and mass deportations (1564–72). The Muslim population of the khanates is persecuted and forced to convert to Christianity. The kingdom of Sibir destroyed (1598).

The Safavids rule in Iran and most of the Caucasus. Uzbeks emerge as the dominant ethnic group in Central Asia and set up the Shaybani dynasty based on Bokhara and Samarkand (1500–1599). Frequent wars between the Safavids and the Shaybanis. Wars between the Safavids and the Ottomans prevent them from sending help to Tatar Muslims now under Russian rule.

17th century: Siberia is conquered (1581–1639). Romanov dynasty is established (1613–1917). War with the Ottoman Empire (1676–81). War with the Crimean khanate (1687–89). Peter the Great crowned Tsar (1689). Peter's trip to western Europe (1697–8).

Kirghiz tribes begin to convert to Islam. Shaybani state is broken up into various khanates. Turcoman tribes raid cities and organise a slave trade. The Caucasus is divided into a number of small Muslim and Christian principalities.

18th century: Construction of St Petersburg (1709–11). Russia's capital transferred there (1712). Turks defeat Russians in the battle of Prut River (1711). Peter's reforms including establishment of a salaried civil service, creation

Astrakhanids overthrown by Mangitids, who retain Bokhara as capital (1753). Kazakh tribes convert to Islam. The khanate of Khojand and the emirate of Bokhara wage perpetual war against one another. Iran is also of Academy of Sciences, publication of first Russian newspaper (*Vedomosti*). Orthodox Patriarchate abolished and replaced by Holy Synod (1721). The fortress town of Orenburg built to stop Kazakh raids into the southern steppes. University of Moscow founded. War with the Ottoman Empire (1787–91). Catherine II (the Great) decrees religious freedom for her Muslim subjects. Her armies push into the Caucasus and annex Daghestan and Georgia (1762–96). Russia emerges as one of Europe's foremost military powers. Crimea annexed (1783).

gripped by civil war. The Caucasus is the scene of almost constant feuds among tribes and small city states. Scientific subjects dropped from the curriculum of schools in Bokhara and Samarkand. Irrigation networks suffer destruction for lack of repair in Central Asia, where many oases disappear.

19th century: Alexander I (1801–25). Napoleonic wars (1811–12). The whole of the Caucasus annexed (1809–1857). Russia begins to interfere in the affairs of Iran and the Ottoman Empire. Russia gains full control of navigation in the Caspian Sea. The Crimean War (1853–6). Emancipation of the serfs (1861). Alexander II assassinated (1881). Law allows peasants to buy their land allotments (1885). Rules regarding forced labour relaxed (1886). The military and secret police strengthened (1874–93). Mountain rebellion in the Caucasus (1856–1887). More than a million Muslims leave the Caucasus to settle in Turkey and Iran (1857–1890).

Tribal revolts by Kirghiz and Kazakhs (1820). Revolt of Qita-Qypchaks against Bokhara (1825). Capture of Khojand by Kazakhs who massacre the population (1858). Tashkent annexed by Russia (1865). Kokand sacked by Russians (1866). Holy War declared against Russia by Bokhara (1867). Samarkand sacked by Russians (1868). Bokhara becomes a Russian protectorate. Khanate of Khiva is conquered by Russia (1873). Khojand is annexed by Russia (1876). Turkmens defeat Russians at Geok-Tepeh (1879). Russians conquer Turkmenistan (1881). Russians annex Marv (1884).

20th century: Russian defeat in war against Japan (1904). First

Jadid reform ideas, developed by Tatar Muslims in the Crimea and

Russian Revolution (1905). Fundamental Law (Constitution) and the election of the first parliament (Duma) (1906). Russia enters First World War (1914). Tsar Nicholas II abdicates and provisional government led by Kerensky takes over (2 March 1917). Bolsheviks stage coup d'état in Petrograd and seize power (November 1917). Cheka is created.

Kazan, spread into Central Asia and the Caucasus. Newspapers in Persian and Turkic appear in Baku, Bokhara and Tashkent and propagate reform. Mullahs decree anathema against reformist intellectuals (1905–1917). Massive Russian colonisation of Central Asia and Kazakhstan (1890–1917). Support in the Caucasus and Central Asia for Iran's Constitutional Revolution (1906–11). Council of Muslim Peoples declares autonomy in Turkestan (1917).

After the October Revolution:

1918: Brest-Litovsk peace treaty with Germany takes Russia out of the war. Civil war begins. War Communism is announced and 'Red Terror' begins. Trotsky organises the Red Army. Stalin appointed People's Commissar for Nationalities. An attempt is made on Lenin's life. A Bolshevik decree dissolves all Muslim organisations throughout Russia.

Tsarist empire disintegrates. Central Asia rejects Soviet power. Armenians, Georgians and Azaris achieve self-rule in the Caucasus. Kokand burned and pillaged by Bolsheviks. Tatar government in Crimea destroyed by Bolsheviks. Stalin sets up the Central Muslim Commissariat under Sultan Galiev. Bolsheviks massacre 3,000 Muslims and seize control of Baku. National Council of Azarbaijan created in Ganjeh. Muslim revolt begins in the Caucasus mountains. Britain and Turkey send troops to the Caucasus.

1919: The Third International (Communist) is founded. Red Army is victorious on all fronts.

British troops withdrawn from the Caucasus. Azarbaijan national republic established in Baku. Bashkirs and Kazakhs leave the Whites and join the Reds. Basmachi revolt spreads in Central Asia.

238

1920: Civil war ends with Bolshevik victory. Britain signs trade treaty with the Bolsheviks.

Frunze conquers Bokhara and Khiva and ends Muslim rule. Muslim reformists cooperate with the Bolsheviks. Baku falls to the Bolsheviks. Congress of the Peoples of the East in Baku declares Holy War against Britain.

1921: Red Army annexes Georgia. The Tenth Party Congress adopts the New Economic Policy (NEP).

Kazakhstan and Central Asia hit by famine. Muslim leaders persecuted in the Caucasus. Thousands flee into Turkey and Iran.

1922: Stalin elected Secretary-General of Central Committee of Russian Communist Party. The foundation of the USSR is formally announced

Purge of non-Communist Muslim intellectuals begins in Kazakhstan and Central Asia.

1923: The Constitution of the USSR is promulgated. Lenin suffers a stroke and is effectively removed from government.

Muslim reformists eliminated from all government posts in Kazakhstan and Central Asia. The Soviet Socialist Republics of Bokhara and Khorezm are set up under exclusive Bolshevik control. Sultan Galiev arrested.

1924: Lenin dies. A triumvirate – Stalin, Zinoviev, Kamenev – takes over. The new constitution comes into effect.

Autonomous Kazakh republic set up. Forced settlement of steppe tribes claims thousands of lives. Uzbek and Turkmen republics declared.

1925: Triumvirate split on the continuation of NEP. Trotsky criticises Stalin.

Mass arrests among Muslim clergy. Many are shot, thousands flee into Afghanistan, Iran and Turkey.

1926: Zinoviev, Trotsky and Kamenev removed from the Politburo. Stalin begins his one-man rule. New secret police GPU

Central Asia and Azerbaijan exempted from new 'family code' which provokes riots in several cities.

is given additional powers.

1927: Peasant protests throughout Russia and Ukraine. Trotsky and Zinoviev expelled from the party.

Abolition of the veil in Muslim regions of the USSR. Arabic script replaced by Latin alphabet for 'Islamic' languages.

1928: Red Army intervenes to force peasants to sell grain to the state.

Polygamy, purchase of wives and other local practices declared illegal in Muslim regions.

1929: The first Five-Year Plan is launched and NEP comes to an end. Trotsky is expelled from the USSR. Stalin given the title of *Vozhd* (Supreme Leader), announces war on rich peasants (kulaks).

Tajik republic set up (detached from the Uzbek republic). The 'de-kulakisation' project is put into effect in Central Asia and provokes new Basmachi revolts.

1930: Trials of officials and engineers accused of creating famine. Dozens are sentenced to death. Mass collectivisation of farms.

Islamic courts of law deprived of legal status. More than 1.5 million people killed in de-kulakisation drive in Central Asia.

1931: Mass executions and deportation of peasants as collectivisation reaches 60 per cent of all farms. Mensheviks put on trial.

Islamic schools closed. Many Quranic teachers arrested or deported.

1932: All cultural and artistic organisations dissolved by decree. A five-year 'Plan to Eliminate Religious Belief' is launched. Churches, mosques and synagogues are shut or destroyed in many parts of the country. An internal passport is introduced ending freedom of travel.

Union of the Godless seizes control of mosques and Islamic seminaries. Many mosques are converted into social centres or clubs.

1933: Nationwide festivities mark the early completion of the first

Zakat (Islamic tax) abolished. Islamic endowments seized. Ban

Five-Year Plan. More 'enemies of the people' are put on trial.

1934: Seventeenth congress of the party firmly establishes Stalin's personality cult. Kirov is assassinated in Leningrad.

1935: Massive purge of the party. Ranks restored in the armed forces. Seventh Congress of the Communist International reverses previous policy and calls for the formation of 'popular fronts' against Nazism.

1936: Kamenev and Zinoviev sentenced to death, together with 14 other party officials at the Moscow trials. A new constitution is promulgated.

1937: Numerous army officers, including Marshal Tukhachevsky, are shot. Purge of the party continues and 13 top leaders, including Radek, are executed. First election to the Supreme Soviet approves Stalin's list by 99 per cent.

1938: Moscow trials continue. Bukharin and 18 other party leaders sentenced to death. Beria becomes chief of the secret police (NKVD). Russian declared a compulsory subject at all schools in the union.

1939: Soviet-German pact including a partition of Poland. Germans invade Poland (start of

imposed on Soviet Muslims wishing to perform the Haj rites in Mecca.

Printing, publication and possession of the holy Qur'an banned. Many Islamic books burned in public in Orenburg.

Grand Mufti of Ufa arrested and accused of being a German and Japanese agent. Arrests also made among mullahs in Tajikestan and Daghestan.

Kazakhstan is detached from the RSFSR and declared a Soviet Socialist Republic with Alma-Ata as capital. The Kirghiz SSR is declared with Frunze as capital.

Major railway and road-building projects completed in Central Asia, bringing the region under tighter control and speeding up its economic development.

Most leaders of the Azarbaijan Communist Party executed after being accused of nationalist and pan-Islamist tendencies. Veteran Bolshevik leaders also purged and shot in Kazakhstan.

Massive anti-nationalist campaign in all Muslim regions. Russian alphabet imposed in Central Asia

Second World War) as Soviets move in from the east. Soviet-Finnish war.

1940: Soviet-Finnish peace treaty signed. Bessarabia, northern Bukovina, Lithuania, Latvia and Estonia annexed by the USSR.

1941: Germany invades USSR. Stalin becomes Chairman of the Council of People's Commissars (prime minister) and assumes full command. USSR concludes an alliance with Britain. Soviet and British troops invade and conquer Iran. United States enters war on British-Soviet side.

1942: Germans continue siege of Leningrad and advance towards Moscow. German troops reach Greater Caucasus range and advance in the Volga region. Soviets achieve victory at Stalingrad.

1943: German forces at Stalingrad surrender. Stalin meets Churchill and Roosevelt at Tehran Conference.

1944: Soviet forces advance throughout eastern Europe. USSR annexes Tuva. More than 250,000 Ukrainians and Belorussians deported from their homes.

1945: Stalin receives Roosevelt and

and Azarbaijan. The Ferghana Canal completed in Central Asia.

Massive conscription efforts in Central Asia meet local resistance, especially in the Karakalpak autonomous republic in Uzbekistan.

Union of the Godless ordered to stop anti-religious campaign. Pressure reduced on Islamic clergy. Some mosques re-open. Spiritual Directions constituted.

Pan-Islamic conference held in Ufa calls on Muslims throughout the world to help USSR win war against Nazi Germany. Some Muslim elements collaborate with Nazi forces in Crimea and Caucasus.

Karachai and Kalmyk autonomous republics abolished by decree; peoples of the two republics deported to the east.

Chechen-Ingush autonomous republic and Crimean Tatar autonomous republic abolished; their peoples deported to Asia. The Kabard-Balkar autonomous republic becomes the Kabard autonomous republic. Balkars are deported to Asia.

Ban on haj pilgrimage for Soviet

Churchill at Yalta. Nazi Germany surrenders as Soviet troops enter Berlin. Stalin meets Churchill and Truman at Potsdam. USSR declares war on Japan. United States drops atom bombs on Japan, which surrenders. Second World War ends. USSR becomes founding member of United Nations.

Muslims lifted, but only a handful allowed to travel to Mecca.

1946: Cold War begins with speeches by Stalin and Churchill. First nuclear reactor completed in the USSR.

Soviet-sponsored republic in Iranian Azarbaijan collapses and its leaders flee to Baku.

1947: Anti-Western cultural campaign launched. Cominform created to replace Comintern.

Central Asia and Caucasus hit by massive food shortages that lead to local riots.

1948: First Soviet guided ballistic missile launched.

New wave of immigration from European republics of USSR begins towards Central Asia and the Caucasus.

1949: First Soviet atom bomb successfully tested. USSR consolidates its hold on eastern Europe through a number of economic and trade measures.

Muslim clerics ordered to register at official centres of the cult and obtain licences to practise.

1950: Revolt by prisoners in Gulag camps. Thousands executed without trial.

A handful of theological students from Central Asia are allowed to enrol at the al-Azhar university in Cairo.

1951: Summit of European Communist leaders meets under Stalin in Moscow and discusses seizure of power of western Europe within four years.

'Ashura mourning ceremonies resume in Soviet Azarbaijan despite a formal ban. The Azari shi'ites also organise 'Ashura rites in various Central Asian cities.

1952: Stalin addresses Nineteenth

Mir-Arab theological school

Party Congress and forecasts seizure of power in western Europe within reach.

1953: Stalin dies. A new triumvirate – Malenkov, Molotov, Beria – emerges. Soviet troops break workers' revolt in Berlin. First criticisms aired about Stalin. Khrushchev rises to power and becomes First Secretary of the Party after Beria is executed. First Soviet hydrogen bomb successfully tested. Measures to reduce peasants' taxes announced.

1954: Rehabilitation of some victims of the 'Personality Cult' begins. World's first nuclear power station inaugurated in the USSR.

1955: Malenkov sacked. Bulganin becomes prime minister. Warsaw Pact is created. USSR resumes ties with Yugoslavia and establishes relations with West Germany.

1956: Khrushchev addresses Twentieth Party Congress. Denounces Stalin's crimes. Soviet troops crush the Hungarian revolt.

1957: Several top party leaders, including Malenkov, Molotov and Marshal Zhukov are purged from party and government. The USSR launches the first space satellite (Sputnik).

1958: Khrushchev becomes prime minister. Education reform aimed

reopens in Bokhara after a lapse of 25 years.

Azarbaijan Communist Party purged with some of its leaders, notably Baqerov, accused of anti-Soviet activities.

Virgin Lands programme launched and leads to the settlement of nearly a million Russian and Ukrainian farmers in Kazakhstan.

New campaign against wearing of the veil by Muslim women launched in Central Asia, Kazakhstan, Daghestan and Azarbaijan. Komsomol (young Communist) militants move from village to village to organise veil-burning ceremonies. Azarbaijan Communist leader Baqerov is executed.

An Arabic edition of the Quran is published in Tashkent with official support.

Khrushchev launches massive anti-religion campaign. Union of at speedier russification of minorities is launched. Union of Godless revived and given new powers and means to fight religion.

1959: Hundreds of people arrested in Ukraine and the Baltic states and accused of anti-state activities.

1960: Soviet-Chinese ideological feud comes into the open. Mao Tse-tung denounces 'revisionism'. Soviet experts leave China.

1961: USSR tests first manned space craft (Vostok) with Gargarin aboard. Summit meeting between Khrushchev and Kennedy. Twenty-Second Party Conference. Stalin's body removed from the Lenin mausoleum.

1962: Cuban missile crisis ends with backdown by Khrushchev. Trial of anti-state elements in the Baltic states.

1963: Workers' strikes hit more than a dozen Soviet cities. USSR signs nuclear test ban treaty with Britain and the United States.

1964: Khrushchev removed from all his positions and forced to retire. Leonid Brezhnev becomes first secretary of the Party Central Committee.

1965: Decree of the Presidium of the Supreme Soviet exonerates

the Godless reactivated and many Muslim monuments and shrines closed or destroyed in Central Asia and Daghestan.

End of the veil (*paranja*) officially announced in Uzbekistan; the last veil publicly burned in Bokhara.

Results of 1959 census show the presence of 39 nations, nationalities and ethnic groups with a Muslim background.

Anti-Islam campaign intensified, with special radio programmes and propaganda caravans touring Central Asia and Kazakhstan to attack Muslim beliefs.

Anti-Soviet riots take place in Karakalpakia, followed by miners' strike in Kara-Khandaq (Karaganda) coalfields in Kazakhstan.

Muslims and Armenians clash in a number of Azarbaijani cities. Kazakhs riot against 'Virgin Lands' project, clash with European settlers.

New programme for restoration of some Islamic monuments launched, with the aim of repairing damage done under Khrushchev.

Russian racists attack Chechen and Ingus deportees in Grozny

Germans of the Volga of charges of treason during the war, but does not provide for their return from Kazakhstan where they had been exiled by Stalin.

1966: Party structure reorganised after the Twenty-third Congress. Brezhnev assumes the title of Secretary-General.

1967: Soviet military build-up speeded up by increases in defence budget. Brezhnev friends occupy crucial posts in the party and the republics.

1968: Soviet and other Warsaw Pact forces invade Czechoslovakia and end 'Prague Spring'. More than 100 people put on trial in Moscow on charges of anti-state activity. New Family Law promulgated.

1969: Border clashes between Soviet and Chinese forces. Brezhnev begins to build up own personality cult.

1970: Leading dissident Solzhenitsyn awarded Nobel Prize for Literature. First hijacking of a civilian aircraft in the USSR. Détente with the United States.

1971: Death of Khruschev. New measures taken to rehabilitate part of Stalin's legacy.

1972: President Nixon visits

and provoke bloody clashes. Committee set up to organise return of deported Meskhetians (Georgian Muslims) to their native land.

Tashkent is partly destroyed by earthquake. Several thousands reported dead.

Decrees of the Presidium of the Supreme Soviet exonerate Crimean Tatars, Turks, Kurds and Khemshins (Armenian Muslims) of treason during the war.

Crimean Tatars demonstrate in Chirchik (Uzbekistan) and clash with police. Demand right to return to their native home. Magazine *Muslims of the Soviet East* begins publication in five languages.

Crimean Tatars demonstrate in Moscow. A dozen Soviet theological students allowed to attend Islamic seminaries in Egypt and Syria.

International Islamic conference held in Tashkent, declares war on Zionism and 'US imperialism'.

Kazakhstan and Uzbekistan emerge as strongest bases of support for Brezhnev.

Official Islam made to play an

246

Moscow. First Strategic Arms Limitation (SALT) talks lead to treaty between USSR and United States.

1973: USSR nuclear forces put on alert during Arab-Israeli war. Moscow and Washington conclude agreement on prevention of thermonuclear war.

1974: New measures against dissidents. Solzhenitsyn expelled from USSR.

1975: USSR signs Helsinki accords aimed at respect for human rights. Campaign against dissidents intensified.

1976: USSR signs more than 50 accords with newly-established Communist regime in Afghanistan. Dissidents rounded up in six Soviet cities.

1977: Brezhnev becomes head of state while holding post of Secretary-General and takes own personality cult to new heights. Political prisoners organise mass hunger strike at a Siberian camp. New Constitution of USSR formally adopted.

1978: Trial of dissidents in Moscow. Brezhnev doctrine of military support for east European states extended to Soviet allies in Asia and Africa.

active role in Soviet diplomacy in Middle East with grand muftis multiplying visits to Arab countries.

Pro-Soviet forces stage *coup d'état* that ends monarchy in Afghanistan. Prince Daoud takes over and allows massive infiltration of Afghanistan by Soviet agents from Central Asia.

Four new Islamic seminaries open in Central Asia.

Muslim cadres, encouraged by Brezhnev, increase their representatives in party and government in Central Asia and Kazakhstan.

Iranian, Iraqi and Syrian Communist parties adopt policy of alliance with Islamic elements, reflecting new Soviet policy.

Soviet muftis attend a number of Islamic conferences as observers. Kazakh students riot at Alma-Ata university, stab four Slav undergraduates to death.

Soviet forces strengthened on Iranian and Turkish borders as Iran is hit by revolution. Number of units stationed in Azarbaijan nearly doubled.

1979: Soviet troops invade Afghanistan.

Prayer gatherings organised in Bokhara to mark Islamic Revolution in Iran.

1980: End of détente with United States. Poland shaken by workers' strikes.

Muslim units of Soviet army in Afghanistan withdrawn and replaced by Europeans.

1981: Brezhnev personality cult at peak. Twenty-sixth Party Congress adopts new 'peace programme'.

Kazakh, Uzbek and Tajik Communist leaders launch strong attack on 'Khomeinism'.

1982: Ten-year Plan to make USSR self-sufficient in basic food adopted. Death of Brezhnev. Andropov takes over as Secretary-General and head of state.

Clandestine Quranic school discovered in Tashkent and its teachers arrested.

1983: Soviet forces suffer major reverses in Afghan war. Labour laws amended to tighten control over workers' organisations throughout USSR.

Copies of book *About Islamic Truth* seized and burned in Bokhara. Several Muslim militants arrested.

1984: Death of Andropov. Chernenko becomes Party Secretary-General. CPSU Central Committee adopts project to divert some Siberian rivers to Kazakhstan and Central Asia.

Clandestine publishing centre for Islamic literature discovered in Baku. Tajiks clash with Soviet forces during a religious ceremony in Kurgan-Tapeh.

1985: Death of Chernenko. Mikhail Gorbachev becomes Party Secretary-General. Gromyko takes over as head of state.

Clandestine centre for printing Islamic literature seized in Samarkand.

1986: Gorbachev launches his ideas of *glasnost* (transparence) and *perestroika* (restructuring). New de-Stalinisation campaign begins. Brezhnev supporters

Alma-Ata hit by Kazakh riots protesting nomination of an ethnic Russian as local party chief. Thirty die in riots that spread to other cities in republic.

purged from key positions.
Chernobyl nuclear disaster.

1987: Gorbachev announces
Soviets want to withdraw from
Afghanistan. Gorbachev position
strengthened after CPSU Central
Committee Plenum adopts his
programme of reforms.
Censorship relaxed. Indirect
criticism of Lenin in public
allowed for first time in USSR.
New East-West détente begins.

Ethnic Armenians clash with
Azari authorities in Nagorno-
Karabagh. Anti-Armenian riots in
Sumgait. Anti-Azari
demonstrations in Yerevan. Soviet
tanks move into Baku as hundreds
of Azari dissidents are arrested.

1988: Gorbachev becomes head of
state while remaining Secretary-
General of the Party. Party
conference approves new
elections. Gorbachev visits United
Nations and announces major
reductions in Soviet military
presence in Europe. Soviet
Armenia devastated by
earthquake. Brezhnev associates
publicly tried for corruption and
given heavy sentences.

Plan for diversion of Siberian
rivers cancelled. Troops sent to
Baku and Yerevan which are put
under curfew. Thousands of
refugees leave Armenia and
Azarbaijan after bloody clashes.
Tajiks demonstrate in Samarkand
and Bokhara and demand
attachment of the two cities to
Tajikestan.

1989: Soviet troops withdraw
from Afghanistan. First phase of
economic *perestroika*
(restructuring) enters
implementation stage with some
400 industrial units given full
autonomy. New Congress of
People's Deputies elected, and
new constitutional draft prepared.

Clashes between Armenians and
Azaris continue in the Caucasus.
New plan to offer the republics
more autonomy coolly received in
Muslim regions. Top party
leadership echelons purged in
Soviet Azarbaijan, Uzbekistan and
Kazakhstan.

Glossary

'Adat: Common law (as distinct from Islamic Law: *shari'ah*).

Agitprop: Soviet office of agitation and propaganda, and persons engaged in the same.

Ahly Kitab: The People of the Book; i.e. Muslims, Christians, Jews and Zoroastrians.

Akhund: Abbreviation of Aqa-Khandeh, title given to Muslim clerics and seminarists in Azarbaijan.

'Al'em: Expert in theology.

Aq-saqal: 'White Beard', elders, village and clan notables.

'Ashiq: Bard, storyteller (Akin in Central Asia).

Aul: Village, hamlet.

Basmachi: (fake merchants); label given to counter-revolutionaries in Central Asia.

Batraq: Landless peasants.

Beig: Landlord.

Bek: Servant of the emir or khan.

Dehqan: Poor peasant (in Central Asia).

Fitwa: Religious edict on a specific issue.

Gorkom: (*Gorodskoi Komitet*); city committee of the Communist Party of the USSR.

Hadith: The sayings of the Prophet Muhammad as reported by tradition.

Haji: A person who has accomplished pilgrimage rites to Mecca during the *Haj* season.

Imam: Prayer-leader, also religious and political head of the community of the faithful.

Imam-Khatib: Head of a mosque, in charge of Friday sermons.

Ishan: Spiritual guide (not necessarily a cleric) in Central Asia, Tataria and Bashkiria.

Islah: Reform, restructuring (Russian equivalent: *perestroika*).

Ispolkom: (*Ispolnitel'nyi Komitet*) Executive Committee of the Soviets.

Jadid: Supporters of the *jadi* movement for Islamic renovation and reform.

Jema'at: Village or borough assembly, any structured gathering of the believers.

Jihad: Holy war, also known as *ghazvah* in Central Asia and Kazakhstan.

Kalym: Payment made by a man to the family of his bride-to-be. Bride money.

Khal'at: Kind of overcoat, often made of silk.

Khalfah: Senior students at Islamic madrassehs.

Khan: Prince, ruler, chief.

Khanehqah: Gathering place of members of sufi fraternities.

Krai: Territorial unit of the USSR composed of one or more autonomous regions or districts. (*Kraikom*: CPSU's territorial committee in a *Krai*.)

Madrasseh: Superior theological school.

Maktab: Primary and secondary Quranic school.

Manap: Clan chief in Kazakhstan.

Mazar: Holy shrine, place of pilgrimage.

Millat: Nation. Also describes the entire Muslim community (*Millat al-Islam*).

Mirath: Islamic heritage.

Mu'allem: Teacher at *maktab* level.

Mudarres: Teacher at *madrasseh* level.

Mufti: High-ranking Islamic jurist authorised to issue *fitwas*. Title of the heads of the four official sections of Islam in the USSR.

Mullah: Islamic preacher. Learned man.

Murad: Allah as reflected in the leader of a sufi fraternity.

Murid: He who has a *murad*. Member of a sufi fraternity.

Mursh'ed: Guide, head of a sufi fraternity. Also known as *Pir*, *Shaikh* and *Ishan*.

Namaz: The five daily prayers of Islam.

Oblast: Region, district (equivalent of a county). (*Obkom*: *Oblast* unit of CPSU.)

Okrug: Territorial division of the USSR, a district.

Qadim: Traditionalist movement (as opposed to *Jadid*).

Paranja: Long black cover-all for women, like the Iranian chador. In Central Asia completed with *chashvan* (veil made of horse-hair, for women).

Raion: District, subdivision of *oblast*. (*Raikom*: *Raion* division of the CPSU.)

Saddaqeh: Financial contribution by the faithful to *madrassehs*, mosques and mullahs.

Sha'gerd: Student at *maktab*.

Shari'at: Islamic law.

Suluk: Becoming part of a sufi fraternity through initiation.

Talqin: Initiatic knowledge transferred to a *murid* by a *mursh'ed*.

Tariqat: The path, a sufi fraternity.

Ta'yefeh: Clan, subdivision of a tribe.

Tubeteiqa: Uzbek and Kazakh cap for men, often made of velvet with embroidery.

Ulema: Plural of *Al'em*. Islamic theological experts, Muslim clergy.

Umma: Nation, community of the faithful.

Vakil: Assistant, deputy or representative of a *mursh'ed*.

Verd: Ritual chant. Also subsection of a sufi fraternity (in Daghestan).

Waqf: Islamic endowments. (Plural: *aquaf*.)

Ziarat: Pilgrimage. Also a holy shrine or tomb of a saint.

Zikr: Collective prayers, often invocation of ritual principles by members of a sufi fraternity.

Notes

CHAPTER ONE: A Russian Nightmare

1. The museum is named after Kamaleddin Behzad, the Persian miniature artist of the seventeenth century.
2. The discourse is not confined to Tajikestan, but is generally used by officials in Central Asia and Soviet Azarbaijan.
3. Samarkand, an ancient Persian word, means 'Famed Abode'.
4. Tashkent is the russified version of Taj-Kand, a Persian-Turkic word that means 'The Abode of the Crown'. Its original name was Shash.
5. During the Islamic period, the name of the city was corrupted to Eshq-Abad (The City of Love).
6. Nomadic tribes, probably originating in Asia, settled in the steppe and expanded into Europe from the sixth century BC.
7. Now renamed Lenin-Abad (City of Lenin) in Tajikestan.
8. Marv was known as Alexandria for a while.
9. The branch that invaded Asia was known as 'White Huns' or Hepthalites (*Hay-ataleh* in Arabic). The 'Black Hun' branch invaded Europe.
10. Ferdowsi, in his *Shahnameh* (Book of Kings), presents Turan as the eternal rival and enemy of Iran.
11. Not to be confused with the inhabitants of present-day Turkey who are for the most part of non-Turkic stock but whose culture and language is Turkic.
12. Means 'Heavens' in most Turkic languages. Tengri was the 'supreme God' of the early Mongols.
13. Christianity was brought to Armenia by Saint Gregory in the first century. Three centuries later, Saint Nino converted Georgia to Christianity.
14. Abu-Rayhan Biruni, the Muslim historian and scientist, although no Arabophile, distinguishes between the early excesses of the conquest and Islam's generally tolerant attitude towards conquered peoples.
15. cf O. Pritsak: 'The Origin of the Name Rus' in *Turco-Tatar Past, Soviet Present*, vol. IV, Paris 1986. p. 45.
16. The Soviet invasion of Afghanistan (1979–89), although ending in the withdrawal of the Red Army, was an almost 'natural' continuation of Russia's southwards and eastwards expansion.
17. Cf R. Pipes, *Russia Under the Old Regime* and G. B. Smith, *Soviet Politics: Continuity and Contradiction.*
18. Not to be confused with present-day Bulgarians who are of Slav extraction. The Bolghars were a Turkic people who converted to Islam in the ninth century. Prince

Sviatoslav conquered the Bolghar state in 971, four years after he had defeated the Khazars.

19. The Polvotsy had seized control of the Kiev-Constantinople route in 1201.

20. Constantinople was captured by Sultan Muhammad V, who immediately assumed the title of *Fat'eh* (The Conqueror).

21. Ancient Sakistan, literally: the land of the Scythians. It is likely that a branch of the Scythian tribes was forcibly settled there during the Achaemenid era.

22. Part of the wall still remains and is known as *Kampir Divar* (The Old Woman's Wall).

23. According to the Persian historian Estakhri who visited Bokhara in the eleventh century.

24. The other poet, Abuhofz Soghdi, was also a Central Asian from Sogdiana. He is reputed to have written the very first poem ever composed in Persian as spoken today in Tajikestan, Afghanistan and Iran.

25. Avicenna died in Hamadan, west of Tehran, and is buried there.

26. Of the volumes still extant, 140 are in Arabic and 21 in Persian. Avicenna wrote all of his poems in Persian.

27. Pope Clement V issued a Bull in 1309 authorising the study of Avicenna's work at the faculty of medicine at Montpellier.

28. The dynasty had other capital cities in different periods, including Urgensh and Otrar.

29. Hallaj's defiant cry of '*An al-haq*' (I am God) has provoked controversies in Islam for more than a thousand years.

30. The book is also used by some shi'ite masters at seminaries. The late Grand Ayatollah Borujerdi, for example, included Bokhari's work in his list of essential books at his Qom seminary until the early 1950s.

31. The Central Asian river's name in Greek. Its Persian name was Amu-Darya and is still in use in the USSR. The Arabs called it Jayhun.

32. Situated in present-day Turkmenistan.

33. The Seljuk sultans employed Iranian Grand Viziers, including the famed Nizam al-Molk whose treatise on politics, *Siasat-Nameh* (*Discourse on Politics*) is a classic of Islamic scholarship.

CHAPTER TWO: A Storm Strikes From the East

1. R. Pipes, *Russia Under the Old Regime*, p. 55.

2. The word horde came from the Turkic *ordu* meaning an encampment. The khanate was also known as the Qypchaqi state, after the main Tatar confederation of clans that inhabited the lower Volga.

3. *Sarai*, a Persian word, means mansion.

4. He also calculated the exact length of the solar year at 365 days, six hours, 10 minutes and 8 seconds. Twentieth-century research showed that Ulugh Beig was only a few seconds off.

5. Pierre Simon Laplace (1749–1827) quoted by H. Allen, *Etoile Rouge et Croissant Vert*, p. 248.

6. The remains of both Teymur and Ulugh Beig were discovered and identified by Soviet experts in 1941.

7. Emir al-Momen'een in Arabic.

8. Ganjeh was renamed Elizavetstpol under the tsars. Under Stalin it changed name

again and is now called Kirov-Abad (The City of Kirov).

9. For more on Nava'i, see A. Mombaci's *Histoire de la Literature Turque*, Paris, 1968.

10. J. Martin's 'The Tiumen Khanate's Encounters with Muscovy' in *Passé Turco-Tatare, Present Soviétique*, vol. VI, p. 79. Paris, 1986.

11. Two years after Kulikovo the Tatars captured Moscow and set it on fire.

12. Muhammad-Hossein Shahryar, the Iranian poet, in his ode 'Hail to Haydar Baba', first published in Azari in Tehran in 1954.

13. The exact date at which the payment of tribute was stopped is not known, but it was certainly after 1480.

14. Like the Black-Sheep clans, the White-Sheep tribes had been sheep-breeders in eastern Caucasus before devoting themselves to a basically military career.

15. The tradition was continued up to the eighteenth century even in Iran. Agha Muhammad Khan, the founder of the Qajar dynasty, described himself as 'the grandson of the Great Chengiz Khan' although there was no shred of evidence to support such a claim.

CHAPTER THREE: The Cross and the Crescent

1. Cited in S. A. Zenkovsky's (ed.) *Medieval Russia's Epics, Chronicles and Tales*, (New York, 1963) (Primary Chronicle).

2. A better translation of Ivan IV's nickname would be 'awe-inspiring'. The Russian word *grozniy* means someone or something that provoked awe or terror.

3. H. Troyat in *Ivan le Terrible*, p. 69.

4. Ibid, p. 73.

5. It is not clear whether or not the Tatar chief truly converted to Christianity. He might have practised the tradition of *taqiah* (dissimulation).

6. The church was at first named after Virgin Mary. It is built on the site of a graveyard where Saint Basil was buried, hence the name. According to some accounts, the architect of the church was put to death so that he could not attempt to build a similar edifice elsewhere.

7. H. Troyat, op. loc. cit., p. 96.

8. The title of the Ottoman Sultan, in Arabic *Bab al-A'li*.

9. The so-called 'testament' of Peter makes much of Russia's need to accede to warm waters. The 'testament' was almost certainly not written by Peter himself, but nevertheless reflected Russian views in the eighteenth century.

10. Kazakh means 'landless' in the Chagtha'i Turkic language. The Kazakhs were originally known as Qara-Kirghiz (Black Kirghizes).

11. The overwhelming majority of those who left the Crimean Peninsula were Muslims. But some Jews, Catholics and Karamites also emigrated to escape Russian rule.

12. The Druzes form an esoteric sect whose beliefs include Mazdeen, Hindu and Islamic elements.

13. Darband, a Persian word, means 'The Gate' or the barrier that seals the mountain.

14. Cf. H. Troyat's *Catherine la Grande*, Paris, 1972.

15. Ararat, geographically part of the Caucasus, is now within the territory of the Turkish Republic and marks the frontiers of Turkey, Iran and Soviet Armenia.

16. Kavkaz, in Russian.

17. Christianity was brought to Armenia by Saint Gregory, who is supposed to have constructed the very first Christian church in the first century AD.

18. Daghestan is a Turco-Persian word. *Dagh* means mountain in Turkic and *Estan* signifies province in Persian.
19. J. Chardin, vol. II, p. 89.
20. The word means 'young Nakh' or 'new Nakh'. Nakh is one of the appellations of the Chechen in northern Caucaus. According to some accounts, Nakh-Javan was constructed in early Safavid times and mainly populated with Chechen tribesmen brought from the north. Later the city was gradually taken over by Armenians.
21. The scene is described in I. Tinyanov's *Mort du Vazir-Moukhtar* and Emineh Pakravan's *Agha Muhammad Khan*. See bibliography.
22. A. Benningsen and Ch. Lemercier-Quelquejay, *Le Soufi et le Commissaire*, p. 76.
23. The Naqshbandi order is further discussed in Chapter 4.

CHAPTER FOUR: A Mountain of Blood

1. Quoted by P. B. Henze in *Turco-Tatar Past, Soviet Present*, vol. VI, p. 243.
2. He was beheaded by a fanatical mob that attacked and burned down the Russian legation building in Tehran in 1834.
3. Baku's original name is Baadkubeh, a Persian word meaning 'Windbeaten'. The city is notorious for its seasonal winds.
4. Today known as Nagorno-Karabagh. The Turkish word *Qara-bagh* means 'Black Garden'.
5. *Turco-Tatar Past, Soviet Present*, vol. VI, p. 255.
6. Ibid, p. 257.
7. Ibid, p. 261.
8. Means 'The Faithful' in Russian. Founded in the 1860s, it is now called Alma-Ata (Father of Apples) and is the capital of the Soviet republic of Kazakhstan.
9. Not to be confused with the geographical term Turkestan, which applied to virtually the whole of Central Asia until the 1920s.
10. N. A. Khalin in *Politika Rossii v Srednezh Azii* (*Russian Policy in Central Asia*), p. 57, Moscow, 1960.
11. It later developed into the port-city of Novo-Alexandrovsk.

CHAPTER FIVE: The Imperial Prison

1. In Russian: *tyur'ma narodov*.
2. A tsarist survey in 1897 listed 33 ethnic groups as 'of Islamic faith'.
3. This included the Qara-Qalpaq (Black Bonnet) tribes, who were developed into a distinct ethnic group or 'nationality' after the October Revolution.
4. R. Portal, *Les Nationalités Slaves de 1871 à 1939*, Centre de documentation universitaire, Paris (nd), p. 109.
5. V. Monteil, *Les Mussulmans Soviétiques*, p. 21.
6. Ibid, p. 31.
7. Franz von Schwarz, quoted by V. Monteil, p. 27.
8. Bahauddin corresponded with Tolstoy but failed to secure the eminent Russian writer's support for the cause of Islamic self-determination in the Volga.
9. The phrase is that of Shaikh Hassan Ruhi as applied to Muslim relations with Russia and the West in general.

10. Al-Afghani was one of the founders of the masonic movement in the Muslim east.
11. Many of these publications were produced by exiled Muslim communities in Paris, London and various Indian cities.
12. According to Muslims only Islam, Christianity, Judaism and Zoroastrianism are veritable religions. Thus the Japanese could not be considered to have any religion at all!
13. Talebov, who wrote in Persian, became the founder of the Persian novel by writing his famous picaresque *Ahmad* in the 1890s.
14. Cf N. Berdiaev's *Khomiakov* (see bibliography).
15. Quoted by H. Kohn, *Le Panslavisme*, p. 113.
16. This is the central theme of B. Pilnyk's novel *The Naked Year*, published in Moscow in 1922.
17. V. V. Barthold, quoted in A. Bennigsen and Ch. Lemercier-Quelquejay in *L'Islam en Union Soviétique*, p. 32.
18. In Turkish *Uch terz i siyasset*. Ibid, p. 41.
19. Ibid, pp. 41–42.
20. Hussein-Zadeh, a shi'ite from Shiravan (Azarbaijan) was, of course, himself a Turkicised Iranian.
21. They have four distinct dialects plus Bashkir which has developed into a separate Turkic language during the past seventy years.
22. In Turkish: *Dilde, fikirde, ishta, birlik*.
23. A pan-Turkist pamphlet still popular in Turkey is called *White Lilies* and describes Finland as the illustration of the ideal pan-Turk society!
24. Mehmed Fatih al-Karimi in 'Yovrupa siyahatnamesi' ('European Travelogue'), quoted in *Turco-Tatar Past, Soviet Present*, vol. VI, p. 407.
25. Ibid.
26. Hakims were polyvalent scholars. Marjani was a theologian, an archaeologist, a mathematician, a historian and a political scientist all at once. He wrote several books on Tatar history, and is considered as a founding father of Tatar nationalism.
27. Was this an indication that he had fallen under the influence of Wahhabi ideas?
28. Nothing happened to either of them. Fakhreddinoghlu became the Mufti of Russia and Siberia under the Bolsheviks in 1922 and remained in that post until his death. Jarallah Beygi, however, found life under the Bolsheviks unbearable and fled to Finland where he spent the rest of his life.
29. In Turkish: *Russiyah mussulmanlarinin ittifaqi*. Cf H. Carrere d'Encausse, *Reforme et Revolution chez les Mussulamns de l'empire Russe*. (See bibliography).
30. Tupchibashi was elected a member of the Duma and later led the Azari delegation at the Versailles Peace Conference in 1919. Aftet the Bolshevik occupation of Baku, he went into exile and died in Paris.
31. Cf H. Carrere d'Encausse as cited in 29, above.
32. Persian was the city's lingua-franca and was spoken not only by peoples of Iranic origin but also by a sizeable Jewish community, as well as Hazara Mongols.
33. The emir himself was a sunni Uzbek.
34. The charge of heresy was lifted only in 1947 when shi'ites and sunnis signed a *taqreeb* (convergence) accord in Cairo.
35. Among Fetrat's best-known works are *Rahbar Nejat* (*Guide to Salvation*) *Munazereh* (*Debate*) and *Shayheh* (*The Cry*).
36. Mirza Ali-Muhammad (1819–1850) was a Shirazi mullah who received the title of 'Bab' (The Gate) from his followers. He claimed that he was the promised Mahdi of the shi'ites and attracted the anger of the Shah. He was hanged in Tabriz.
37. The supplement was called 'Turan' (Land of the Tur), the counterpart of 'Iran'.

CHAPTER SIX: Red Star Over the East

1. The party had split into Bolsheviks (majority) and Mensheviks (minority), the latter led by Plekhanov, Martov and Trotsky in 1903.
2. Rasul-Zadeh became the first President of the independent Republic of Azerbaijan in 1919 until 1920.
3. He later changed his name to Narimanov and became Secretary-General of the Azarbaijan Communist Party. He died in 1932 but was 'purged' from the party after his death on Stalin's orders.
4. He became a member of the Baku Commune and was shot by the British in 1918.
5. Alash is considered by the Kirghiz-Kazakhs as their mythological ancestor.
6. Cf A. Nurpeissov's novel *Childhood*, Moscow, 1967.
7. A leading writer and poet, he later became President of the Soviet Republic of Tajikestan.
8. The revolution took place on 7 November, which corresponded with 23 October of the old calendar discarded by the new regime.
9. V. I. Lenin, *Collected Works*, vol. VI, p. 213, Moscow, 1962.
10. Lenin, vol. V, p. 337.
11. Ibid.
12. Lenin, vol. XVI, p. 618.
13. J. V. Stalin, Collected Works, vol. II, p. 296, Moscow, 1946 (reprinted in Tirana 1961).
14. The department was abolished in 1924.
15. This was how Trotsky liked to describe Stalin.
16. In the second congress of the Muslim Communist Party, the word 'Muslim' was replaced by 'Oriental'.
17. Quoted in A. Benningsen and Ch. Lemercier-Quelquejay's *Sultan Galiev*, p. 154.
18. Ibid, p. 213.
19. Ibid.
20. The Emir, 'Alim Khan, fled to Afghanistan where he made some attempts at raising an army and staging a comeback. He died in exile.
21. The Bund (League) was a Jewish organisation within the Russian Social Democratic Party. Its abolition was a primary objective of Lenin, who opposed the idea of a federal structure for the party.
22. Mikhail V. Frunze (1885–1925), from a Moldavian family, joined the Bolshevik party in 1903. During the civil war he commanded the Fourth Army Corps that defeated the White General Wrangel in the Crimean and became the architect of the Red Army's victory in the east against Kolchak. Frunze died under mysterious circumstances while undergoing a simple operation in a hospital in Moscow. B. Pilniak, in a short story called *The Tale of the Unextinguishable Moon*, published a year after Frunze's death, more than hinted that the Bolshevik hero had been murdered on Stalin's orders. Today the capital of the Soviet republic of Kirghizestan is named after him.
23. He later joined the Bolshevik Party.
24. The most prominent of Basmachi leaders had more than 20,000 men under his command when he captured practically the whole of present-day Tajikestan in 1921. Defeated by the Red Army in 1928, he crossed into Afghanistan where he tried to create an Uzbek emirate. His forces, however, were ousted by the Afghan King Nader at the battle of Panj River in 1931. He was handed back to the Soviets, who executed him in Doshanbeh in 1933.

25. He died alongside Enver Pasha in 1922 after having assumed the title of Minister of War in Enver's 'government'.
26. Also known as Zeki Velidi Toghan (1890–1970) was a Bashkir teacher who became a member of the Russian Duma in 1916. One of the founders of the short-lived Republic of Bashkiria in 1917, he also created a Bashkir army which fought the White armies. At the end of the civil war he collaborated with the Bolsheviks for 15 months before joining the Basmachi movement in Central Asia. In 1922 he escaped to Afghanistan and thence to Turkey, where he became a university professor and an advocate of pan-Turk ideas.
27. He was the emir's chief of police.
28. He abandoned the rebellion early and stayed in the USSR until his arrest and execution on a charge of 'nationalism' in 1937.
29. Enver Pasha (1881–1922) was a brother-in-law of the last Ottoman Sultan. One of the founders of the Unity and Progress (*Ittihad ve Tarraqi*) movement he became an opponent of Kemal Pasha (Ataturk) and attended the Bolshevik-organised Baku Conference in 1920.
30. Qurban Muhammad (1860–1938) assumed the aristocratic title of Junaid Khan and, although the son of a peasant, claimed that he was a descendant of Prophet Muhammad. He began his career as inspector for water distribution and, despite the fact that he could neither read nor write, rose to become a *qadhi* (Islamic judge).
31. Under the leadership of the so-called Union of the Militant Godless. In Muslim regions it assumed a number of different titles: *Allah-syzlars* (without-Allah), *Din-syzlar* (without religion), *Khoda-syzlar* (without God) and *Bi-Kohdayan* (the Godless ones).
32. The famous adage is that of Heinrich Heine, the German poet whom Marx merely quoted.
33. For example an Armenian, Ardashes Ovanessian, was chosen by the Comintern as contact-man with the Iranian Tudeh (Communist) Party.
34. Official Soviet figures quoted by R. Conquest in *The Harvest of Sorrow*, p. 190.
35. Ibid, p. 191.

CHAPTER SEVEN: Parallel Lives

1. Lahuti wrote long odes in praise of Lenin, Stalin and even the Cheka, the Bolshevik political police!
2. One of Satan's titles in the Qur'an, meaning 'the rebel'.
3. Kubra died in 1221, probably killed by the invading Mongols in Urgensh. His tomb at Urgensh is one of the holiest sites of Muslim Central Asia.
4. Shaikh Gilani died in 1166.
5. Shaikh Yassawi died in 1167. His tomb in the city of Turkestan in the south of Kazakhstan is a major centre of pilgrimage.
6. Literally: 'the carefree one'.
7. In Turkic: Shashtun Ishandar.
8. Shaikh Bahaeddin died in 1388. His tomb at Bokhara is an important Muslim shrine.
9. Named after Shaikh Muhammad Bamat Giray Mita'ev who founded the group. He died in a Russian prison in deportation.

10. Named after Batal Haji Belhoroy who died in deportation.
11. The *murshid* of the group, Pir-e-Maragheh, was forced into exile by Ayatollah Khomeini in 1979.
12. In the 1950s yet another group, known as the White Bonnets (Aq-Kalpaks) was founded among the deported Chechens in Kazakhstan by Vis Haji Zaghiev.
13. Ali-Mardan Muhajeri lists a total of 179 top officials in Soviet Azerbaijan alone as members of the Naqshbandiyah in the 1940s. (In 'Tasawwuf dar Kafkaz' (Sufism in the Caucasus), unpublished paper, Tehran 1973.)
14. Dairush Pirnia in 'Our Way', an essay on sufism, typeset paper in English, Washington DC, 1986.
15. It marks the choice of Muhammad as prophet by Allah.
16. It marks the choice of Ali Ibn Abitalib by Muhammad as his successor. (According to shi'ite traditions, disputed by sunnis.)
17. Nowruz is an ancient Persian tradition that predates Islam by more than 1,000 years. Nevertheless, it has become an integral part of the Islamic cultures of the peoples of Iran, Afghanistan, Central Asia and Soviet Azerbaijan.
18. Term used by A. Bennigsen and Ch. Lemercier-Quelquejay in *Le Soufi et le Commissaire*.
19. Ibid.
20. Shaikh Osman Serrajeddin Naqshbandi in interview granted to the author in Paris, November 1983.
21. Ibid.
22. State Committee for Security. In Russian: *Kumityet Gosudarstvyenny Byezopasnosti*.
23. Azarbaijani linguist Ifran Hadarov in conversation with the author in Baku in August 1988.
24. Lavrenti Pavlovich Beria (1899–1953) began his career with Cheka in his native Georgia and rose to become Minister of Interior and Police chief (1942–46). Promoted to the rank of Marshal of the Soviet Union in 1945, he became Vice-President of the Council of Ministers in 1946. He was executed in 1953.
25. A. Bennigsen and Ch. Lemercier-Quelquejay, *L'Islam en Union Soviétique*, p. 133.
26. Ibid.
27. Stalin (born Josef Vissarionovich Jugashvili) was a native Georgian, but quickly developed into what Lenin called 'a Great-Russian chauvinist'.
28. A Mongol people converted to shi'ite Islam and speaking Persian.
29. Ethnic Chinese converted to Islam. They were later dotted with a language of their own.
30. A mixture of Kazakhs and Uzbeks speaking a dialect of their own.
31. The Ingush, which was given an alphabet in 1923, and the Chechen which became a written language after 1925.
32. Balkar and Kabard became written languages in 1924.
33. In Ossetia, Soviet linguists tried to establish three languages: the Ossetian, the Iron (a form of Persian) and the Digor. Only the Ossetian survived beyond 1940.
34. Cherkess, Abaza and Karachai.
35. A. Bennigsen and Ch. Lemercier-Quelquejay, *L'Islam en Union Soviétique*, p. 135.
36. Ibid. The languages are: 1. Slavic family: Russian; 2. Turkic family: Azari, Kuryk, Noghay; 3. Ibero-Caucasian: Avar, Dargin, Lak, Lezgi, Tabasaran, Chechen; 4. Iranic family: Tat.
37. Nikolai Efimov, deputy director of the CPSU's Department of Ideology, in conversation with the author in Moscow, February 1989.
38. Ibid.

39. H. Ghafuri in 'Islam va Hokumat Shuravi' ('Islam and the Soviet State'), study paper published by National Defence College, Tehran, 1970.

40. Soviet Azari, for example, now includes Russian loan words which make up more than 35 per cent of its vocabulary, while Iranian Azari has retained its traditional vocabulary which is more than 60 per cent Persian and Arabic.

41. For more on this, see A. Taheri's *Nest of Spies: America's Journey to Disaster in Iran,* Hutchinson, London, 1988.

42. H. Alleg in *Etoile Rouge et Croissant Vert* makes much of this, as if colonialism was only about who serves at whose dinner table.

43. Poets such as Abdul-Rahman Jami, Athireddin Akhsikati, Suzani-Samarkandi, Kamal Khojandi and Menjik Termezi provide only some examples in this respect.

44. Especially Urdu, which became the official language of Pakistan after the partition of India. One major Indian language shared between Muslims and Hindus, Bengali, however, retained its own ancient script.

45. *Bultan Mahramaneh (Confidential Bulletin),* published by the Ministry of Information, Tehran, Iran, vol. XXII, 1974, for example, reported a raid by Iranian Turcomans on a Soviet Turcoman settlement. The raiders returned with two would-be brides and over 300 sheep.

46. In 1989 the number of people of Tatar origin in Turkey was estimated at over 6.5 million.

47. Both Communist states deny the existence of Tatars and pursue aggressive policies aimed at effacing Islamic and Turkic aspects of life among their respective Tatar minorities.

48. Most Kirghiz pronounce it *Plodsu*.

49. The tsars had renamed the city Elizavetspol.

50. In 1989 Kazakhs were estimated to form just over 41 per cent of the total population compared with 40 per cent Russians.

51. Ghafuri, cited in 39, above.

52. Mufti Baba Khan in conversation with the author in Tashkent, August 1973.

53. The languages are English, French, Persian and Arabic. An edition in Uzbek was authorised from 1977 onwards.

CHAPTER EIGHT: Islam: Faith, Culture and Identity

1. Nikolai Efimov, deputy director of the Ideological Department of the CPSU, in conversation with the author in February 1989, Moscow.

2. In conversation with the author in Tehran, 1969.

3. Ibid.

4. This includes more than one million Karakalpaks.

5. Udmurts, Maris, Chuvashs.

6. Projection based on results of the 1979 census of the USSR.

7. Ibid.

8. He succeeded Shaikh Shamsuddin Babakhanov in January 1989 after the latter was forced to resign.

9. The figures include a large number of historical ruins which have received little or no attention during the past 70 years of Communist rule.

10. The relic was originally guarded at the Petrograd museum. It was presented to the Muslims by the Bolsheviks in 1918 and, after a brief spell in Kazan, ended up in Tashkent.

11. The total circulation of all the editions did not exceed 100,000, in a country where some novels are distributed in more than five million copies!
12. In 1988 there were 732 candidates for admission at Mir-Arab, according to sources in Bokhara.
13. In Arabic *Ilm al-Rijal,* it deals with the works and lives of prominent figures of Muslim history and theology.
14. Mufti Taj-eddin was born in Kazan in 1949.
15. In conversation with the author, August 1988.
16. Ibid.
17. *Literaturnaya Gazeta,* 20 May 1987.
18. Ibid.
19. Head of the propaganda section of the Azarbaijan Communist Party.
20. In *Nauka i Religia (Knowledge and Religion),* vol. XII, December 1986.
21. Ibid.
22. *Literaturnaya Gazeta,* 13 May 1987.
23. *The Muslims of the Soviet East,* vol. III (79), 1988.
24. Reliable sources in Moscow, in conversation with the author in February 1989.
25. A. Benningsen in interview with *Le Point* (Paris), 26 January 1987.
26. Zbigniew Bzrezinski, National Security Adviser to US President Jimmy Carter, 1977–1980.
27. *Literaturnaya Gazeta,* 20 May 1987.
28. Ibid.
29. Vadim Zagladin of the Supreme Soviet in conversation with the author in Moscow, February 1989.
30. Nureddin Muhitudinov, who served as ambassador to Damascus, was the author of *The Koran, its Doctrine and Philosophy,* a vicious anti-Islamic tract published in English and Arabic in 1973. Rafiq-Muhammad Rahmatov, who became ambassador to Mauritania (a West African Muslim state) in 1974 was the author of *Peut-on Croire au Coran?' (Can one Believe in the Quran?).* Muslim reaction to these pamphets was so strong that Moscow had to stop their publication and even blamed their production on the CIA!
31. *Sotsialistik Kazakhstan,* 26 December 1986.
32. Muhammad Develatov, Professor of Marxist-Leninist philosophy at the Tajik National University, in *Agitator Tadzhikistana,* vol. XXIII, December 1986.
33. Ibid.
34. *Sovetskaya Kirgizia,* 19 February 1987.
35. *Sovetskaya Etnografia,* No. II, 1986.
36. Ibid.
37. Cf. M. Heller and A. Nekrich in *Utopia in Power.*
38. H. Alleg in *Etoile Rouge et Croissant Vert,* p. 231.
39. 'European' undergraduates were excluded from the survey.
40. *Literaturnaya Gazeta,* 20 May 1986.
41. *Sovetskaya Etnografia,* Vol. V, 1984.
42. *Parvada Vostoks,* 22 February 1987.
43. *Sovetskaya Etnografia,* Vo. VI, 1986.
44. Estimate based on projections from the 1979 census.
45. There are an estimated 1.2 million Germans in the region, mostly Protestant Christians.

CHAPTER NINE: The Mafia of 'Real Socialism'

1. In a speech at the Baku conference of the peoples of the East.
2. They produced an average of 22 million tonnes each year between 1971 and 1988.
3. Situated near Karsakpay in the desert of Kazakhstan between Karaganda and the Aral Sea.
4. M. Volsensky in *Les Maîtres de la Nomenklatura*, p. 246.
5. Kazakh party member Velikhan Ihsanev in conversation with the author in Alma-Ata, September 1988.
6. Kuna'ev rose to become member of the Politburo of the CPSU's Central Committee, the union's highest political organ, until his dismissal in 1986.
7. Ihsanev, see note 5 above.
8. *Izvestia*, 20 November 1988.
9. In a speech quoted by *Pravda Vostoka*, 11 August 1984.
10. Ognyok, No. 26, 1988.
11. Radio Baku commentary, 11 February 1980.
12. *Pravda*, 2 February 1986.
13. *Literaturnaya Gazeta*, 20 January 1988.
14. Ibid.
15. In conversation with the author in Moscow, August 1988.
16. *Sovetskaya Tajika*, 2 March 1989.
17. TASS report from Doshanbeh, 1 March 1989.
18. *Sovetskaya Kirghizia*, 27 February 1988.
19. Ivan Buynin, university teacher at Tashkent, in conversation with the author in August 1988.
20. Official Soviet sources speak of nine deaths only. The total of thirty is based on accounts given by unofficial sources.
21. In conversation with the author in Alma-Ata, August 1988.
22. *Kazakhstanskaia Pravda*, 14 January 1987.
23. *Sotsialistik Kazakhstan*, 26 December 1986.
24. Her name was Meliga Allaverdyeva.
25. *Literaturnaya Gazeta*, 1 January 1987.
26. *Sotsialistik Kazakhstan*, 26 December 1986.
27. Ibid.
28. Alma-Ata Radio broadcast 8 January 1987.
29. *Kazakhstanskaya Pravda*, 7 January 1987.
30. *Kommunistik Zhol*, Mangyshlak, 9 April 1987.
31. Untitled leaflet published in Jambul, dated 30 May 1987.
32. Ibid.
33. *Pravda*, 11 February 1987.
34. Ibid.
35. Ibid.
36. *Kazakh Adebiyati*, 12 December 1986.
37. *Bilim Janeh Enbek*, December issue, 1986.
38. The same theme was taken up by the Kazakh party press in numerous articles throughout 1987 and 1988.
39. *Sovetskaya Kirghiziia*, 24 February 1987.
40. Ibid.
41. *Sovetskaya Kirghiziia*, 19 February 1987.
42. Frunze had been an important centre for training Muslim students from friendly countries since the 1950s. President Hosni Mubarak of Egypt and President Hafez

al-Assad of Syria were among those Arab students who studied at Frunze in the 1950s.

43. *Sovetskaya Kirghiziia*, 19 February 1987.
44. *Pravda Vostoka*, 25 November 1986.
45. Ibid.
46. The mausoleum is situated near the town of Khalq-Abad in the autonomous republic of Karakalpakistan.
47. Account given to the author by Muslim militants, September 1988.
48. Situated near the town of 'Ayni in the district of Lenin-Abad.
49. Eyewitness account by Muslim militants, September 1988.
50. Ibid.
51. This mausoleum is supposed to contain the tomb of Ali Ibn Abi-Taleb, the fourth Caliph of Islam and the first Imam of shi'ism. But this is historically incorrect. Ali is buried at Najaf, in Mesopotamia, and the Uzbek mausoleum is most probably related to other saints or even pre-Islamic figures.
52. Account given to the author by Muslim militants in September 1988.
53. In interview with *Literaturnaya Gazeta*, 14 January 1987.
54. Ibid.
55. Press conference in Alma-Ata, 18 February 1987.
56. Ibid.
57. Speech at Central Committee meeting in Alma-Ata, 29 December 1986.

CHAPTER TEN: Explosion in the 'Black Garden'

1. The Russian language lacks the sounds of 'q' and 'gh' which exist in Persian, Arabic and Turkic languages. Thus 'k' replaces 'q' and 'kh' is substituted for 'gh'. The imposition of the Russian alphabet on Muslim languages has led to numerous cases of confusion and great difficulties in transliterating Turkic, Arabic and Persian words.
2. There are still Armenians who are called Assadollah (Lion of Allah) or even Abdullah (Slave of Allah).
3. Mirza Ibrahimov in *Sovetskaya Kultura*, February 1989 issue.
4. Ibid.
5. Arsalan Demirbey quoted by M. A. Alavi in *Tarikhe-Aqwam Tork* (*History of the Turkic Peoples*), monograph, Tehran 1973, p. 46.
6. Seyyed Amanallah Nateq in *The Idea of Muslim Unity from the Early Days to the 1950s*, Karachi, 1962, p. 12.
7. The population of Soviet Armenia was estimated at under four million in March 1989. Of this, 89 per cent were Armenians.
8. Most of the Kurds in Armenia belong to the Yazidi sect of Zarathustrians who traditionally described themselves as Muslims in order to escape persecution. A small number belong to the Ali-Allahi sect of pseudo-Muslims who believe that Ali, the fourth Caliph, represented a physical vision of God on earth.
9. Garry Kasparov, the Soviet Armenian grand master of chess, writes: 'My roots are in Baku. The knowledge gives me strength when I go off to conquer other worlds and gives me solace when I return.' In *Child of Change*, London, 1987, p. 11.
10. Echmiadzin literally means 'The Son of God Come to Earth', and has been a centre of Christian worship since the first century.
11. Mikoyan was President of the Presidium of the Supreme Soviet in 1964–65. He was purged by Brezhnev and died in 1978.

12. The Dashnak Party continued to operate in Iran, Syria and Lebanon, but was banned and persecuted in the USSR after 1925. A nationalist party of the traditional type in the 1930s and 1940s, it developed strong Fascist tendencies.

13. Los Angeles, California, has an Armenian colony estimated at 200,000. George Deukmejian, an ethnic Armenian, was Governor of California in 1989. According to 1989 estimates Tehran, the Iranian capital, hosted more than 100,000 Armenians.

14. Mirza Ibrahimov in *Sovetskaya Kultura,* February 1989.

15. At press conference in Yerevan, 12 November 1988, reported by TASS.

16. The term has been used by the Soviet leadership, including Gorbachev, and Soviet media on a number of occasions.

17. *Pravda,* 13 December 1988.

18. Russian spelling of his name makes him: Geidar Aliyev.

19. During Yuri Andropov's tenure as CPSU general secretary and USSR head of state (1983–1984).

20. *Literaturnaya Gazeta,* 21 September 1988.

21. *Pravda,* 13 December 1988.

22. TASS, 11 December 1988.

23. *Pravda,* 13 December 1988.

24. Yerevan Radio broadcast 8 December 1988.

25. Hussein fell on Ashura, the tenth day of Muharram and the peak of mourning ceremonies by shi'ites.

26. Considered as the 'Aalam al-Ulema (The Most Knowledgeable of the Ulema), he is number one in the shi'ite hierarchy of grand ayatollahs. Kho'i lives in Najaf Iraq.

27. The lion is a symbol of Imam Ali, whose title is Assad-Allah (The Lion of Allah). The sun is an ancient Iranic symbol associated with Mithra.

28. *Financial Times,* 28 November 1988.

29. Takiyehs are places of shi'ite assembly, especially during the months of Muharram and Safar.

30. Tehran Radio news bulletin, 30 November 1988.

31. The term 'state of siege' was not used by Soviet official media. They described it as 'a special state'. (Cf TASS report on Nagorno-Karabakh 22 September 1988.)

32. According to Armenian and Azari spokesmen, in conversation with the author in Moscow, March 1989.

33. G. B. Smith, *Soviet Politics,* p. 121.

34. Ibid.

35. Term used by engineers interviewed in Tashkent in September 1988.

36. A summary of A. Kuna'ev's statement was supplied to the author in Tashkent in September 1988.

37. Only twice a week in 1989.

38. The quota was decided during the Islamic Conference in Jordan in 1988.

39. Gorbachev tried to correct the lapsus by saying that Russia was synonymous with the Soviet Union! Even the Ukrainians felt concerned.

40. Mikhail Sergeyvich Gorbachev was born on 2 March 1931 in the village of Privol-noie, almost at the same time as Stalin's collectivisation drive was hitting the Soviet countryside.

41. A survey of 'Pamiat' literature was presented to the author by A. G. Mametbayev, Tatar journalist, in Moscow in March 1989.

CHAPTER ELEVEN: Godless in Search of God

1. Vladimir Efimov, CPSU's deputy head of ideology, in conversation with the author in Moscow, February 1989.
2. Leonid Vladimirov in interview with BBC Radio 4, 30 October 1988.
3. One joke is: 'What is the difference between Islam and Communism? Islam asks a man to give part of his own wealth to the poor but Communism takes away all of a man's wealth to give it to the Nomenklatura.' Another joke is related to the sumptuous palace built for the party in Bokhara: 'Communism has marble mosques but no one to pray in them, Islam has the prayers but no mosques!' Yet another version of the same refers to the multi-million palace constructed for Brezhnev in Baku. 'The dead idol has a palace, the living God is in the peasant's hut!'
4. USSR Foreign Ministry spokesman Gennadi Gerassimov at press conference in Moscow, 28 October 1988.
5. Ahmad Makhdum Danesh, the great Uzbek writer of the nineteenth century, described a ball at the tsars' palace in St Petersburg in 1828 as a miniature representation of all Russian life. He wrote: 'A violet haze of sadness enveloped the entire Imperial Ballroom ... Everyone present appeared to have a mask of death. ... The same sadness, the same atmosphere of mourning was present throughout Petersburg. In all those boulevards no one seemed happy and content. Envy ruled everywhere.' In *Navadar al-Waqa'ye* (*The Rarest of Events*), quoted in Sadruddin Ayni's *Khaterat* (*Memoirs*), Tehran 1984.
6. This is how one Muslim writer sees Russia: 'Russia was in the past the abode of savage and lawless peoples who lacked unity and lived through razzias against their neighbours. With the passage of time these peoples managed to create a central government and a country which, bearing the name of the largest tribe among them, they called Russia. From then on banditry and plunder were transformed into policies of a state. Now it was a powerful state based on a populous country that practised expansionism. In other words banditry and plunder became organised and thus could be carried out on a much larger scale.' Ahmad Bashiri in *Kitab Naranji* (*Orange Book*), Tehran 1988, p. 2.
7. In address to the Uzbek Communist Party's central committee, 28 November 1986 in Tashkent.
8. The phrase belongs to Ilham Ne'matov, an Uzbek poet.
9. *Pravda*, 28 January 1987.
10. In *Niqab ve Iqab* (*The Mask and the Consequences*), samizdat leaflet dated 12/3/1988 and signed 'Makhdum', published in Tashkent and Bokhara.
11. Nigeria is routinely included in the list of Muslim nations despite the fact that at least 40 per cent of its population consists of Christians and Animists.
12. *Pravda Vostoka*, 4 December 1986.
13. His dismissal was announced by Soviet Foreign Ministry spokesman Vadim Perfiliev in Moscow in January 1989.
14. There were some notable exceptions to this rule, for example Professor Rustam Aliev who is recognised as a major figure in Islamic studies. But he too concentrated on Iran and not on his native Central Asia.
15. Afghani (Assad-Abadi) was an Iranian but described himself as an Afghan. Farsi is an Afghan who calls himself a 'Persian'; in 1989 he was special adviser to Ayatollah Ruhollah Khomeini for pan-Islamic movements, notably dealing with Palestine, Lebanon and the USSR.
16. *Literaturnaya Gazeta*, 21 September 1988.

17. Ayatollah Muhammad Qazi-Tabataba'i in conversation with the author, Tabriz, December 1978.
18. Ibid. The money collected was *sahm-e-Imam* (the share of the Imam) which shi'ites ought to pay to an ayatollah of their choice. Ayatollah Qazi-Tabataba'i explained that the money collected 'reached its proper destination' thanks to the black market of roubles that operated in Tehran until 1981.
19. E.g. Baku Radio commentary entitled 'Progressive Islam, Reactionary Islam', 15 June 1979.
20. Five Afghan resistants were killed by Soviet border guards on 30 July 1980 in the Termez region. According to Afghan resistance sources, the five were accompanied by two defecting Uzbek soldiers who were captured by the Soviets.
22. *Literaturnaya Gazeta,* 20 May 1987.
23. *Sovetskaya Kirghiziia,* 19 February 1987.
24. The withdrawal was completed on 15 February 1989.
25. No names could be given for security reasons.
26. Kushan Ahmad-Zadeh in conversation with the author in Doshanbeh, August 1988.
27. The term means 'resurgence' and is used in virtually all Muslim languages.
28. They cover respectively children of up to primary school age and adolescents before they qualify for joining the Komsomol.
29. *Pravda Vostoka,* 4 December 1986.
30. Ibid.
31. The warning comes from Muhammad Vahabov, the Uzbek party's principal anti-Muslim spokesman.
32. Ibid.
33. *Sovetskaya Kirghiziia,* 24 February 1987.
34. Ibid.
35. *Pravda,* 21 January 1989.
36. Ibid.
37. E.g. H. Carrere d'Encausse in *L'Empire Eclaté.*
38. The language is a branch of Turkic, but the literature belongs to the Persian sphere.
39. Kirov's name caused intense embarrassment in Azerbaijan where the word *kir* denotes the male organ. As a way round this, the party decided to replace the 'k' in Kirov by other sounds. The 'q' would have done the job, but it did not exist in the Russian alphabet imposed on Azari. The next nearest sound would have been 'gh', but this too did not exist in Cyrillic script. Hence a 'g' was tried and Kirov became 'Girov'. This led to another problem, as the word *gir* means 'black tar' in Azari. So Stalin's close associate is known as 'the son of the black tar' in Azarbaijan.
40. In Arabic *kuddam,* the term used especially in Central Asia.
41. *Agitator Tajikestana,* 15 December 1986.
42. *Nauka i Religiia (Knowledge and Religion),* vol. XXI, Baku 1988.
43. This figure was suggested to the author by a number of Muslims in Central Asia in August 1988.
44. Sayyeds claim descent from the Prophet Muhammad.
45. Mahmud Kho'i, the grand ayatollah's son, in conversation with the author in Frankfurt, December 1988.
46. Most broadcasts are in Arabic, Turkish and Persian, but special programmes are also offered in the native languages of the Soviet Muslim republics.
47. Necati Velioghlu, director of one of the two firms involved, in conversation with the author in Istanbul, May 1988.
48. Miachel Ledeen, former consultant with the National Security Committee in Washington DC, in conversation with the author in Chamonix, September 1988.

49. *Soviet Anti-religious Campaigns and Persecutions,* vol. II, p. 189, London, 1988.
50. The author was shown one of the films in Moscow in March 1989.
51. Cf. A. Bennigsen and Ch. Lemercier-Quelquejay, *Le Soufi et le Commissaire.*
52. A. Bennigsen in interview with *Le Point*, Paris, 26 January 1987.
53. Shaikh Osman Ziaeddin Naqshbandi, leader of the *tariqat,* in conversation with the author in Paris, November 1983.
54. For more on the *tariqats* see Chapter 7.
55. For more on the Muslim Brotherhood see A. Teheri's *Holy Terror: The Inside Story of Islamic Terrorism*, London 1987.
56. *Moscow News*, September 1988.
57. Ibid.
58. Ibid.

CHAPTER TWELVE: *Perestroika:* The Limits of Hope

1. Aleksandr Pumpiansky, associate editor of *New Times* magazine, in conversation with the author in Moscow, February 1989.
2. Part of a poem by Kemal Mirquoliev, Tajik poet.
3. The ban on Akhmatova had been partly lifted under Khrushchev in the 1960s.
4. Some works of these authors are published but all have major writings that remain banned.
5. A journalist on the *Moscow News*. He did not wish to be identified.
6. Vladimir Kulistikov, managing editor of *New Times,* in conversation with the author in Moscow, February 1989.
7. Valentin Falin, member of the CPSU's Central Committee, at briefing given in Moscow, February 1989.
8. Vladimir Efimov, deputy head of the department of ideology of the CPSU, at briefing in Moscow, February 1989.
9. Politburo member Nikolai Slyunkov in *Restructuring the Economy is the Paramount Political Task*, Novosty Press, Moscow 1989.
10. Vadim Zagladin in conversation with the author in Moscow, February 1989.
11. Such as 'de-Stalinisation' and 'the thaw' (Ottopel).
12. He requested anonymity.
13. Rents on the average represent between 1.5 and 3 per cent of a family's income in most republics.
14. K. Mirqoliev in conversation with the author, September 1988.
15. The list was shown to the author by Fathi Mirzayev in Moscow, March 1989.
16. Vadim Zagladin in conversation with the author in Moscow, February 1989.
17. Azari intellectual in conversation with the author. He asked not to be named.
18. Radio Doshanbeh commentary, 13 November 1988.
19. Ibid.

Bibliography

AGANBEGYAN, A., *The Economic Challenge of Perestroïka*, Bloomington, Indiana, 1988.

AGHABEKOV, G., *OGPU: The Russian Secret Terror*, New York, 1931.

ALBRECHT, M., *L'Asie Centrale Russe*, Hamburg, 1896.

ALEXEYEVA, G. L., *Soviet Dissent*, Middletown, Connecticut, 1985.

ALIOSHIN, D., *Asian Odyssey*, London, 1941.

ALLEG, H., *Etoile Rouge et Croissant Vert*, Paris, 1983.

ALLEN, W. E. D. and HURATOFF, P., *Caucasian Battlefields*, Cambridge, 1953.

ALLWORTH, E., *Central Asia: a Century of Russian Rule*, New York, 1967.

————, *Ethnic Russia in the USSR*, New York, 1980.

————, (ed.) *Nationality Group Survival in Multi-ethnic States*, New York, 1977.

AMALRIK, A., *Will the Soviet Union Survive Until 1984?*, New York, 1970.

AMBOLT, N., *Karavan, Travels in Eastern Turkestan*, London, 1939.

ANDERSON, M. S., *The Eastern Question 1774–1923, a Story in International Relations*, New York, 1966.

ANWEILER, O., *Les Soviets en Russie – 1905–1921*, Paris, 1972.

ARENDT, H., *The Origins of Totalitarianism*, London, 1973.

ARMSTRONG, J. A., *The Politics of Totalitarianism*, New York, 1961.

ARNOLD, T. W., *The Caliphate*, London, 1965.

AZIZ, Ph., *Les Sectes Secrètes de l'Islam*, Paris, 1983.

AZRAEL, J. (ed.), *Soviet Nationality Policies and Practices*, New York, 1978.

BACON, E. E., *Central Asia under Russian Rule*, New York, 1946.

BAILEY, Col. F. M., *Mission to Tashkent*, London, 1946.

BARMINE, A., *One Who Survived*, New York, 1945.

BARTHOLD, W., *Turkestan Down to the Mongol Invasion*, London, 1928.

BATSELL, W. R., *Soviet Rule in Russia*, New York, 1929.

BAUER, R. A. et al., *How the Soviet System Works*, Cambridge, 1956.

BAWDEN, C. R., *The Modern History of Mongolia*, London, 1968.

BAYNAC, J., *La Revolution Gorbachevienne*, Paris, 1988.

BECKER, S., *Russia's Protectorates in Central Asia: Bukhara and Khiva – 1865–1924*, Cambridge, Massachusetts, 1968.

BELENITSKY, A., *Asie Centrale*, Paris, 1968.

BENNIGSEN, A. and WIMBUCH, S. E., *Muslim National Communism in the Soviet Union. A Strategy for the Colonial World*, Chicago and London, 1979.

BENNIGSEN, A. and BROXUP, M., *The Islamic Threat to the Soviet State*, London, 1983.

BENNIGSEN, A. and LEMERCIER-QUELQUEJAY, Ch., *L'Islam en Union Soviétique*, Paris, 1968.

––––––, *La Presse et le Mouvement National chez les Musulmans de Russie avant 1920*, Paris, 1984.

––––––, *Le Soufi et le Commissaire. Les Confréries Musulmanes en URSS*, Paris, 1986.

––––––, *Sultan Galiev, le Père de la Révolution Tiers-mondiste*, Paris, 1980.

––––––, (eds.) *Turco-Tatar Past, Soviet Present*, Paris, 1986.

BERDIAEV, Nicolas, *The Origins of Russian Communism*, Ann Arbor, 1960.

–––––– *Khomiakov*, Paris, 1988.

BERGSON, A. (ed.), *Studies in the Modern World System*, New York, 1980.

BERGSON, A. and LEVINE, H. S. (eds.), *The Soviet Economy Towards the Year 2000*, London, 1983.

BERQUE, J. et al., *Normes et Valeurs dans l'Islam Contemporain*, Paris, 1966.

BIALER, S., *Stalin's Successors, Leadership, Stability and Change in the Soviet Union*, Cambridge, 1980.

––––––, *The Soviet Paradox: External Expansion, Internal Decline*, New York, 1986.

BLACK, C., *Rewriting Russian History*, New York, 1962.

BLACKER, L. V. S., *On Secret Patrol in High Asia*, London, 1922.

BLACKWELL, W. L. (ed.), *Russian Economic Development from Peter the Great to Stalin*, New York, 1974.

BORNSTEIN, M. (ed.), *The Soviet Economy: Continuity and Change*, Boulder, Colorado, 1981.

BRADSHER, H. S., *Afghanistan and the Soviet Union*, Durham, North Carolina, 1981.

BROCKELMAN, C., *Histoire des Peuples et des Etats Islamiques depuis les Origines jusqu'a Nos Jours*, Paris, 1949.

BROOK-SHEPHERD, G., *The Storm Petrels*, London, 1977.

BRUN, Cap. A., *Troubled Times: Experiences in Bolshevik Russia and Turkestan*, New York, 1931.

BRUNNER, E. Jr., *Soviet Demographic Trends and the Ethnic Composition of Draft Age Males 1980–1995*, Santa Monica, California, 1981.

BUTSON, Th. G., *Gorbachev: A Biography*, New York, 1985.

CAHEN, C., *L'Islam des Origines au Début de l'Empire Ottoman*, Paris, 1970.

CALVOCORESSI, P., *World Politics Since 1945*, London, 1987.

CAROE, O., *Soviet Empire. The Turks of Central Asia and Stalinism*, London, 1983.

CARR, E.H., *The Bolshevik Revolution 1917–1923* (3 volumes), London, 1950–53.

———, *The Russian Revolution, from Lenin to Stalin, 1917–1929*, London, 1986.

H. CARRERE d'ENCAUSSE, *Réforme et Révolution chez les Musulmans de l'Empire Russe*, Paris, 1960.

———, *L'Empire éclaté*, Paris, 1978.

———, *Le Grand Frère*, Paris, 1983.

———, *Le Grand Défi*, Paris, 1987.

———, *Ni Paix, ni Guerre*, Paris, 1987.

———, *Le Malheur Russe*, Paris, 1988.

CASSEN, R. (ed.), *Soviet Interests in the Third World*, London, 1985.

CASTAGNE, J., *Les Basmatchis: le Mouvement National des Indigènes d'Asie Centrale depuis la Révolution d'Octobre 1917 jusqu'en Octobre 1924*, Paris, 1925.

———, *Le Turkestan depuis la Révolution Russe*, Paris, 1922.

CHALIDZE, V., *To Defend These Rights: Human Rights and the Soviet Union*, New York, 1974.

CHAMBERLIN, W.H., *The Russian Revolution 1917–1923* (2 volumes), London, 1965.

CHARDIN, J., *Voyage de Paris à Ispahan* (2 volumes), Paris, 1983.

CHARLES, R., *L'Etoile Rouge contre le Croissant*, Paris, 1962.

CILIGA, A., *The Russian Enigma*, London, 1979.

COATS, K.W.P., *The Soviets in Central Asia*, New York, 1951.

CONNOR, W., *The National Question in Marxist-Leninist Theory and Strategy*, Princeton, New Jersey, 1984.

CONQUEST, R., *The Harvest of Sorrow*, London, 1986.

———, *Religion in the USSR*, London, 1968.

DALLIN, D., *The Rise of Russia in Asia*, London, 1950.

DANIEL, N., *Islam and the West: the Making of an Image*, Edinburgh, 1960.

DANIELS, R., *The Conscience of the Revolution: Communist Opposition in Soviet Russia*, Cambridge, 1960.

DANILOV, V., *Rural Russia under the new Regime*, Bloomington, Indiana, 1986.

DAVIDSON, B., *Turkestan Alive*, London, 1957.

DAVIES, R. W., *The Socialist Offensive, the Collectivisation of Soviet Agriculture, 1920–1930*, Cambridge, Massachusetts, 1980.

DENRO, G. J., *The Russian Colonization of Kazakhstan 1896–1916*, The Hague, Netherlands, 1968.

DEUTSCHER, I., *Stalin: a Political Biography*, London, 1949.

DIAITH, H., *L'Europe et l'Islam*, Paris, 1978.

DMYTRYSSHYN, B., *USSR, a Concise History*, London, 1978.

DOLOT, M., *Execution by Hunger*, New York, 1985.

DORNBERG, J., *Brezhnev: the Masks of Power*, London, 1974.

DUNN, D. J., *Religion and Modernization in the Soviet Union*, Boulder, Colorado, 1984.

DUPREE, L., *Afghanistan*, New Jersey, 1973.

DZUYBA, I., *Internationalism or Russification? A Study in Soviet Nationalities Problems*, London, 1968.

EGRETAUD, M., *L'Orient Soviétique*, Paris, 1959.

ELLIS, C. H., *The Transcaucasian Episode 1918–1919*, London, 1963.

ESSAID, M. B., *Allah est grand! Décadence et Résurrection du Monde Islamique*, Paris, 1937.

ETHERTON, Lt Col. P., *In the Heart of Asia*, Boston, Massachusetts, 1926.

EUDIN, X. J. and NORTH, R. C., *Soviet Russia and the East, 1920–1927*, Stanford, California, 1957.

IBN-FADLAN, *Voyage chez les Bulgares de la Volga*, Paris, 1983.

FAINSOD, M., *How Russia is Ruled*, London, 1963.

FERRO, M., *La Révolution de 1917*, Paris, 1967.

FISCHER, L., *Life of Lenin*, New York, 1964.

———, *Russia's Road from Peace to War*, New York, 1969.

FLEMING, P., *News from Tartary*, London, 1936.

FLETCHER, A., *Afghanistan: Highway of Conquest*, New York, 1966.

FLORINSKY, M. T., *The End of the Russian Empire*, London, 1961.

FRASER-TYLER, W. K., *Afghanistan*, London, 1950.

FRITERS, G. M., *Outer Mongolia*, London, 1951.

GAFOURAV, B., *Les Nations en URSS*, Paris, 1962.

GARDET, L., *Connaître l'Islam*, Paris, 1958.

———, *L'Islam, Religion et Communauté*, Paris, 1967.

GIBB, H. A. R., *Studies in the Civilization of Islam*, Boston, Mass., 1962.

GOLDHAGEN, E. (ed.), *Ethnic Minorities in the Soviet Union*, New York, 1968.

GORBACHEV, M., *Perestroïka*, London, 1987.

GOSSET, P. and R., *Les Russiatiques,* Paris, 1963.

GRENVILLE, J. A. S., *A World History of the Twentieth Century* (2 volumes), London, 1980.

GROSSIR, C., *L'Islam des Romantiques*, Paris, 1984.

GROUSSET, R., *L'Empire des Steppes,* Paris, 1965.

HAMBIS, L., *La Haute Asie,* Paris, 1968.

HAMM, M. (ed.), *The City in Late Imperial Russia,* Bloomington, Indiana, USA, 1986.

HARDING, N. (ed.), *The State in Socialist Society,* London, 1984.

HECHTER, M., Internal Colonialism, Berkeley, California, USA, 1975.

HELLER, M. and NEKRICH, A., *Utopia in Power, a History of the USSR from 1917 to the Present,* London, 1986.

————, *70 ans qui ébranlèrent le Monde, Histoire Politique de l'Union Soviétique,* Paris, 1988.

HOANG, M., *Gengis Khan,* Paris, 1988.

HODNETT, G., *Leadership in the Soviet National Republics,* Oarville, USA, 1978.

HOLMES, L. (ed.), *The Withering Away of the State,* London, 1981.

HOPKIRK, P., *Setting the East Ablaze,* London, 1984.

HOSTLER, C. W., *Turkish and the Soviets: the Turks of the World and their Political Objectives,* London, 1975.

HUNKE, S., *Le Soleil d'Allah brille sur l'Occident,* Paris, 1963.

INKELES, A. and BAUER, R. A., *The Soviet Citizen, Daily Life in a Totalitarian Society,* Cambridge, Massachusetts, 1959.

INOYATOV, Kh., *Central Asia and Kazakhstan Before and After the October Revolution,* Moscow, 1966.

————, *Towards Freedom and Progress (The Triumph of Soviet Power in Central Asia),* Moscow, 1970.

JACOBS, E. M. (ed.), *Soviet Local Government and Politics,* London, 1983.

JONES, E., *Red Army and Society,* Boston, Massachusetts, 1985.

KAPUR, H., *Soviet Russia and Asia 1917–1927,* Geneva, Switzerland, 1986.

KARKLINS, R., *Ethnic Relations in the USSR,* Boston, Mass., 1986.

KATZ, Z. et al. (eds.), *Handbook of Major Soviet Nationalities,* New York, 1975.

KEDOURIE, E., *Nationalism in Asia and Africa,* New York, 1970.

KENNEDY, P., *The Rise and Fall of the Great Powers,* London, 1988.

KESTON COLLEGE, *Religious Prisoners in the USSR,* Keston, Kent, 1987.

KHAN, H., *Nationalism in the Soviet Union,* New York, 1953.

————, *Islam and Muslims in Red Regimes,* Lahore, Pakistan, 1970.

KHRUSCHEV, N. S., *Khruschev Remembers,* Boston, Mass., 1970.

————, *Khruschev Remembers: the Last Testament,* Boston, Mass., 1970.

KOCHAN, L., *Russia in Revolution,* London, 1970.

KOHN, H., *Panslavism,* New York, 1960.

KOLARZ, W., *Russia and her Colonies,* London, 1953.

KOZLOV, V., *The Peoples of the Soviet Union,* London, 1988.

KRADER, L., *Peoples of Central Asia,* Indianapolis, Indiana, 1962.

KRIST, C., *Alone Through the Forbidden Land,* London, 1939.

LANE, Ch., *The Rites of Rulers: Rituals in Industrial Society – The Soviet Case,* London, 1981.

LAMOUCHE, L., *Histoire de la Turquie depuis les Origines jusqu'à Nos Jours,* Paris, 1953.

LATIMORE, O., *Pivot of Asia,* Boston, Massachusetts, 1950.

LEWIN, M., *The Gorbachev Phenomenon: A Historical Interpretation,* New York, 1988.

LEWIS, E. G., *Multilingualism in the Soviet Union,* New York, 1972.

LEWIS, R. A. et al., *Nationality and Population Change in Russia and the USSR,* New York, 1976.

LOWENTHAL, R., *World Communism: the Disintegration of a Secular Faith,* New York, 1964.

LUBIN, N., *Labour and Nationality in Soviet Central Asia,* London, 1984.

MACE, J. E., *Communism and the Dilemma of National Liberation,* Cambridge, Massachusetts, 1983.

McCAULEY, M. (ed.), *The Soviet Union Under Gorbachev,* London, 1987.

MACLEAN, E., *Portrait of the Soviet Union,* London, 1988.

MAILLART, E., *Des Monts Celestes aux Sables Rouges,* Lausanne, Switzerland, 1986.

MANDEL, W. M., *Soviet but not Russian: the 'Other People' of the Soviet Union,* Alberta, Canada, 1984.

MARABINI, J., *Cavaliers Rouges et Dragon d'Acier,* Paris, 1969.

MARWAT, F. A. K., *The Basmachi Movement in Soviet Central Asia,* Peshawar, Pakistan, 1985.

MEDVEDEV, R., *Khrushchev,* Oxford, 1982.

————, *All Stalin's Men,* Oxford, 1983.

————, *Gorbachev,* Oxford, 1986.

MELVILLE-HOWE, G., *The Soviet Union, a Geographical Study,* London, 1986.

MILIBAND, R., *Marxism and Politics,* Oxford, 1977.

MILLAR, J.R. (ed.), *Politics, Work and Daily Life in the USSR*, Cambridge, 1987.

MONTEIL, V., *Les Musulmans Soviétiques*, Paris, 1982.

MORE, Ch., *Les Kurdes Aujourd'hui: Mouvement National et Partis Politiques*, Paris, 1984.

MURARKA, D., *The Soviet Union*, London, 1971.

———, *Gorbachev, the Limits of Power*, London, 1988.

NETTL, J.P., *The Soviet Achievements*, London, 1969.

NICHOLSON, R.A., *Studies in Islamic Mysticism*, Cambridge, 1921.

ORDOUBADI, G.H., *La Tradition des Ashighs du Caucase, du XVIe Siècle jusqu'à Nos Jours*, Tehran, Iran, 1970.

ORLOV, A., *The Secret History of Stalin's Crimes*, New York, 1953.

PAQUIER, J.P., *L'Asie Centrale à Vol d'Oiseau*, Paris, 1981.

PARK, A.G., *Bolshevism in Turkestan, 1917–1927*, New York, 1957.

PARKER, W.H., *An Historical Geography of Russia*, London, 1968.

PIPES, R., *The Formation of the Soviet Union (Communism and Nationalism 1918–1923)*, Cambridge, Mass., 1954.

———, *Russia Under the Old Regime*, London, 1977.

POLIAKOV, L., *De Moscou à Beyrouth, Essai sur la Désinformation*, Paris, 1983.

———, *Les Totalitarismes du XXe Siècle*, Paris, 1987.

POPOVIC, A. and VEINSTEIN, G. (eds.), *Les Ordres Mystiques dans l'Islam*, Paris, 1986.

POSPIELOVSKY, D.V., *Soviet Anti-religious Campaigns and Persecutions* (2 volumes), London, 1988.

POTOCKI, J., *Voyages au Caucase et en Chine*, Paris, 1980.

POWELL, D.E., *Anti-religious Propaganda in the Soviet Union: a Study of Mass Persecution*, Cambridge, Massachusetts, 1975.

QUATREMERE, E.R., *Histoire des Mongols de la Perse*, Amsterdam, Holland, 1968.

QUCHBEGUI, M.A., *Une Étude Descriptive de la Littérature Tadjik Contemporaine*, Tehran, Iran, 1975.

RADKEY, O.H., *The Unknown Civil War in Soviet Russia*, Stanford, California, 1976.

RIASANOVSICH, N.B., *A History of Russia*, New York, 1984.

ROI, Y., *The USSR and the Muslim World*, London, 1984.

ROLLIN, H., *La Revolution Russe*, Paris, 1931.

ROUX, J.P., *L'Islam en Asie*, Paris, 1958.

———, *La Religion des Turcs et des Mongols*, Paris, 1984.

RYWKIN, M., *Russia in Central Asia*, New York, 1963.

SAINT-QUENTIN, S. de, *Histoire des Tatares*, Paris, 1965.

SAUVAGET, J., *Introduction à l'Histoire de l'Orient Musulman*, Paris, 1946.

SCHAPIRO, L., *The Communist Party of the Soviet Union*, New York, 1960.

———, *The Government and Politics of the Soviet Union*, New York, 1965.

———, *Russian Studies*, London, 1986.

SCHMIDT-HAUER, Ch., *Gorbachev, the Path to Power*, London, 1986.

SCHOLL-LATOUR, P., *Les Guerriers d'Allah*, Paris, 1986.

SHAMS UD DIN, *Secularisation in the USSR*, New Delhi, 1982.

SETON-WATSON, H., *From Lenin to Khruschev*, New York, 1960.

SMITH, G. B., *Soviet Politics, Continuity and Contradiction*, London, 1988.

SMITH, W. C., *Islam in Modern History*, Princeton, New Jersey, 1957.

SOURDEL, D., *L'Islam*, Paris, 1975.

SOUVARINE, B., *Stalin, a Critical Survey of Bolshevism*, New York, 1939.

SOUVAROV, V., *The Liberators*, London, 1981.

SPENCER TRIMININGHAM, J., *The Sufi Orders in Islam*, London, 1971.

STALIN, J. V., *Marxism and the National and Colonial Question*, London, 1942.

STEBER, Ch., *L'Asie Centrale Soviétique et le Kazakhstan*, Paris, 1939.

STEELE, J., *The Limits of Soviet Power: The Kremlin's Foreign Policy – Brezhnev to Chernenko*, London, 1985.

STEIN, M. A., *Innermost Asia* (2 volumes), London, 1928.

STRONG, J. W. (ed.), *The Soviet Union Under Brezhnev and Kosygin*, New York, 1971.

STUERS, J. de, *La Route de Byzance*, Geneva, Switzerland, 1950.

SZAMUELY, T., *La Tradition Russe*, Paris, 1976.

TATU, M., *Power in the Kremlin*, London, 1969.

TAUBMAN, W., *Governing Soviet Cities: Bureaucratic Politics and Urban Development in the USSR*, New York, 1973.

TEICHMAN, Sir E., *Journey to Turkistan*, London, 1937.

TROTSKY, L., *The History of the Russian Revolution*, New York, 1932.

TROYAT, H., *Ivan le Terrible*, Paris, 1982.

———, *Catherine la Grande*, Paris, 1976.

TSAMERYAN, J. P., *Equality of Rights between Races and Nationalities in the USSR*, Unesco, Paris, 1962.

TUCKER, R. C. (ed.), *The Soviet Political Mind*, New York, 1963.

———, *Stalinism, Essays in Historical Interpretation*, New York, 1977.

TUZMUHAMEDOV, R., *How the National Question was Solved in Soviet Central Asia*, Moscow, 1973.

TYNIANOV, I., *La Mort du Vazir-Moukhtar*, Paris, 1969.

TYTLER, F. W., *Afghanistan: a Study of Political Developments in Central and Southern Asia*, London, 1967.

ULAM, A. B., *The New Face of Soviet Totalitarianism*, Cambridge, 1963.

———, *Expansion and Coexistence: the History of Soviet Foreign Policy 1917–1973*, New York, 1974.

———, *Dangerous Relations: the Soviet Union in World Politics 1970–1982*, New York, 1983.

VADNEY, T. E., *The World Since 1945*, London, 1987.

VAMBERY, H., *Travels in Central Asia*, New York, 1965.

VENTURI, F., *Roots of Revolution: a History of the Populist and Socialist Movements in Nineteenth-Century Russia*, New York, 1966.

VERNADSKY, G. and KARPOVICH, M., *A History of Russia*, New Haven, 1953.

VERNANDSKY, G., *The Mongols and Russia*, London, 1953.

VON GRUNEBAUM, G. E., *L'Identité Culturelle de l'Islam*, Paris, 1973.

VOSLENSKY, M., *Les Maîtres de la Nomenklatura*, Paris, 1989.

WALKER, M., *The Walking Giant, the Soviet Union under Gorbachev*, London, 1986.

WALTER, G., *Lenine*, Paris, 1950.

WARDENBURG, J. D. J., *L'Islam dans le Miroir de l'Occident*, Paris, 1961.

WESTWOOD, J. N., *Endurance and Endeavour, Russian History 1812–1917*, Oxford, 1973.

WHEELER, G., *The Modern History of Soviet Central Asia*, London, 1964.

WIMBUSH, G. S. and ALEXIEV, A., *Racial Problems in Soviet Muslim Asia*, London, 1960.

———, *The Peoples of Central Asia*, London, 1966.

———, *The Ethnic Factor in the Soviet Armed Forces*, Santa Monica, California Rand Corp., 1982.

WIMBUSH, W. E. (ed.), *Soviet Nationalities in Strategic Perspective*, New York, 1985.

WITTFOGEL, K. A., *Oriental Despotism*, New Haven, Connecticut, 1953.

WOLFE, B. D., *Three Men Who Made a Revolution: Lenin, Trotsky, Stalin*, New York, 1948.

WOLFG, T., *Soviet Power and Europe, 1945–1970*, Baltimore, Maryland, 1970.

WU, A. K., *Turkestan Tumult*, London, 1940.

YANON, A., *The Drama of the Soviet 1960s: a Lost Reform*, Berkeley, California, 1984.

ZASLAVSKY, V., *The Neo-Stalinist State: Class, Ethnicity and Consensus in Soviet Society*, New York, 1982.

ZENKOVSKY, S. A., *Pan-Turkism and Islam in Russia*, Cambridge, Massachusetts, 1960.

ZENUSHKINA, I., *Soviet Nationalities Policy and Bourgeois Historians*, Moscow, 1975.

ZEYONS, S., *La Revolution des Femmes au Cœur de l'Asie Soviétique*, Paris, 1971.

ZIEGLER, Ch., *Ivan IV, dit le Terrible*, Paris, 1957.

ZWICK, P., *National Communism*, Boulder, Colorado, 1982.

Index

Compiled by Gordon Robinson